ek

before the last

Development Law and
International Finance

International Economic Development Law

VOLUME 10

Series Editor

J.J. Norton

Centre for Commercial Law Studies
University of London
London Institute of International Banking
Finance and Development Law
SMU Institute of International Banking and
Finance, Dallas, Texas
Asian Institute of International Financial Law
University of Hong Kong

Executive Editor

Rosa M. Lastra

Centre for Commercial Law Studies
University of London

The titles published in this series are listed at the end of this volume.

SMU Institute of International
Banking and Finance
Dallas, Texas

Centre for Commercial Law Studies
University of London

Institute of International
Banking, Finance and
Development Law, London

Asian Institute of
International Financial Law,
University of Hong Kong

Development Law and International Finance

by

Rumu Sarkar

Office of the General Counsel,
US Agency for International Development (USAID)
Adjunct Law Professor, Georgetown University Law Center

KLUWER LAW
INTERNATIONAL

THE HAGUE – LONDON – BOSTON

Published by
Kluwer Law International Ltd
Sterling House
66 Wilton Road
London SW1V 1DE
United Kingdom

Sold and distributed in
the USA and Canada by
Kluwer Law International
675 Massachusetts Avenue
Cambridge MA 02139
USA

Kluwer Law International incorporates
the publishing programmes of
Graham & Trotman Ltd,
Kluwer Law & Taxation Publishers
and Martinus Nijhoff Publishers

In all other countries, sold and distributed by
Kluwer Law International
PO Box 322
3300 AH Dordrecht
The Netherlands

ISBN 90-411-9715-X (hardback)
ISBN 90-411-9743-5 (paperback)
CIP 99-11059
© Kluwer Law International 1999
First published 1999

British Library Cataloguing in Publication Data is available

Library of Congress Cataloging-in-Publication Data
Sarkar, Rumu
   Development law and international finance/by Rumu Sarkar.
     p. cm. — (international economic development law: v. 10)
   Includes index
   ISBN 90-411-9715-X
   1. Law and economic development. 2. International finance—Law and legislation.
I. Southern Methodist University. School of Law. II. Queen Mary and Westfield College
(University of London). Centre for Commercial Law Studies. III. Title. IV. Series.
   K3820.S22   1999
   341.7'51—dc21

Typeset in Palatino 10/11 pt by EXPO Holdings, Malaysia
Printed and bound in Great Britain by Athenaeum Press Ltd., Gateshead, Tyne and Wear.

Foreword

I am pleased to have been invited to contribute this Foreword to a work which represents an important attempt to map the contours of the subject of development law by someone who combines the discipline of an academic with the insight of a practitioner actively engaged in the field. Although there is much in this area which is controversial, Rumu Sarkar's work manages to avoid the pitfalls of ideology which seem so often to beset writings on this subject.

The work begins with what the author has termed a *'fin de siècle* analysis' of trends affecting the milieu of development and the evolution of legal principles involved in this movement. Indeed, this stock-taking element is a constant feature of the book, being further represented by the author's notion of the 'Janus Law Principle', emphasizing 'the importance of looking backwards into the past of the developing country as well as ahead into the future, like the Roman god, Janus'. While, however, this is a work that sees the past—and *context* more generally: economicl, sociological, philosophical—as an important foundation of the law relating to development, the work recommends itself principally as a forward-looking attempt to examine the framework within which this law is evolving.

A key feature of this analysis is the link identified from the outset, and reflected in the title of the work, namely, the connection between the law relating to development and that pertaining to international finance. It is in this context, in particular, that Ms Sarkar addresses the issues in Part II of the monograph under the general heading of 'Structural Legal Reform'— namely international borrowing and the problems of the debt crisis, the trends and implications of privatization as a development strategy and the importance of emerging capital markets, both as concept and practical reality. This is where the meat of the subject lies.

Inevitably, in a work of this nature, which attempts to present a holistic view of a subject in a state of flux, there will be elements of the analysis that will occasion debate and dispute, both for what is said and for what is not. That is a good thing. The particular merit of the work lies in its view of the horizon and its ability to identify concrete landmarks thereon. There is bound to be debate about such matters as the New International Economic Order, the status of the 'right' to development, the meaning of the notion that there is 'an inchoate right to become a stakeholder in the development process', as well as many other significant concepts. This work will set the debates in context, particularly in view of the clarity of exposition that

v

comes from the fact that the author is writing about what she is engaged in on a day-to-day basis. The book is a valuable and welcome contribution to the scholarly literature in an increasingly important area of international, and transnational, law.

Professor Sir Elihu Lauterpacht CBE, QC
Cambridge
February 1999

Table of Contents

Sponsoring Organisations

Centre for Commercial Law Studies
The Centre was established in 1980 as a distinct department within the Faculty of Laws of Queen Mary and Westfield College, University of London. The primary objectives of the Centre are to promote the systematic study and research of national and international commercial law and its social and economic implications and to develop a body of knowledge, information and skills that can be placed at the service of government, public bodies, overseas institutions, the legal profession, industry and commerce.

SMU Institute of International Banking and Finance
Established within Southern Methodist University, Dallas, Texas in 1982, the Institute serves as an interdisciplinary forum for research, publications, conferences and research seminars in the international finance area, with input from SMU's Law School, Political Science and Economic Departments, and the Edwin L. Cox School of Business. The Institute conducts several major international conferences and is actively involved in economic law reform projects in relation to emerging economies. Finally, the Institute regularly produces books and other scholarly articles and papers.

Asian Institute of International Financial Law
An Institute of the University of Hong Kong Law Faculty, in cooperation with UHK's School of Business and Management and Department of Economics, that is committed to postgraduate programmes, research, publications, conferences, short courses and seminars in the international financial law area, with emphasis on the East Asian and Greater China Areas.

London Institute of International Banking, Finance and Development Law
The London Institute is a privately incorporated, educational institution. Among other functions, the Institute assists the International Financial and Tax Law Unit at the Centre for Commercial Law Studies at Queen Mary and Westfield College, University of London, in directing research seminars, professional conferences, executive training sessions, law reform and consulting projects, and major journals and book series. This legal think-tank is also responsible for conducting research and publishing articles and essays on an array of important legal issues concerning banking, finance and development, of which a series of Essays in International Financial and Economic Law and the *Yearbook* serve as examples.

To my grandfather,

Rabindra Mohan Biswas, M.A. (Econ.), LL.B. (Calcutta)

Preface

The study of development law is a personal journey for me since it combines the disciplines of law and political science, the two subjects of inquiry that fascinate me the most. Having been privileged to teach the 'Law and Development' course at the Georgetown University Law Center for several years, certain overarching themes have become increasingly clear to me. I realized that these issues deserve a fairly comprehensive treatment, which lay outside the confines of the course offering. Writing a book, although a serious undertaking, seemed to be the only logical step in the direction of fully exploring my current thoughts on the subject.

What exactly is the subject of *Development Law and International Finance*? For most legal practitioners, the subject of development law is neither well understood nor clearly defined. In fact, since it is generally not taught in law schools, nor is it the subject of continuing legal education courses, exposure to the subject-matter for most legal practitioners tends to be rather limited. Further, there appear to be no agreed notions of what the subject is or should be comprised of. Development law, at least to most observers and commentators, seems to be a multidisciplinary mixture of certain technical aspects of international corporate practice overlaid with economics, political science, history, and sociology.

To begin with, 'development' seems to be a choice to view certain issues from the perspective of encouraging the economic, political, legal (and even cultural) development of Asia, Africa, Latin America and the Caribbean, and now Central and Eastern Europe along with Central Asia (i.e., the former Soviet Bloc). For most practitioners and theorists, however, the overall objective of alleviating poverty and human suffering, and of improving the human condition more generally, is the desired end product of the development process.

It is highly unlikely that a final and binding definition of development law will ever be agreed upon by its practitioners or theorists, but suffice to say that development law is designed to address complex issues of human endeavour and change and, even more broadly speaking, issues concerning the context for global change. In particular, development law is concerned with analysing, implementing and evaluating global *legal* change.

The subject of *Development Law and International Finance* has a new relevancy for both common law and civil law legal practitioners, who are struggling to understand and compete in an increasingly globalized economy. The legal practice of most international law practitioners has been profoundly affected by these changes. Not only has the potential geographic reach of common-law based legal practitioners exploded, but the complexity of the legal questions has increased exponentially as well. Whereas in the past, international law practice was usually confined to transactional work and related international litigation in Europe, Latin America and certain parts of the Far East, this is no longer the case. Countries in previously unknown or inaccessible parts of the world, from Kazakhstan to Mongolia to Vietnam, have suddenly burst on the scene, offering potential legal markets where none existed before.

Relations between developing countries or transitional economies (i.e. the countries of Eastern Europe and the former Soviet Union), on the one hand, and Western Europe and North America, on the other, have assumed a legal dimension which affects the international or general legal practitioner with an immediacy that did not exist before. And perhaps for the first time, international lawyers must grapple with the questions and challenges that are raised by the subject area of *Development Law and International Finance*. The new legal markets which are opening up in developing countries do not, generally speaking, share compatible legal infrastructures, and international legal practitioners are now being confronted with societies with radically different legal histories, institutions and cultures. In addition, these societies are, in most cases, undergoing tremendous transformations, both socially and economically.

Although the scope and practice of *Development Law and International Finance* may not yet be well-defined, it has increased in importance and relevance for the international law practitioner. In recognition of this change, the following text offers a perspective on some of the legal issues and practice-oriented questions that are raised by a new and unprecedented global interdependence. This discussion is designed to give private international law practitioners in particular, and public international law specialists in general, an overview of development law and, in particular, some insight into certain current trends and worldwide developments which have an important impact on international legal practice.

The introduction which follows gives some background on the theoretical underpinnings of *Development Law and International Finance*. A grounding in the theoretical background of the subject is quite important, particularly since the impact of certain philosophies and assumptions are clearly felt in the policy framework and the development strategies pursued by both developed and developing societies.

The main discussion treats three separate, but related, aspects of *Development Law and International Finance*. First, the text examines development law, particularly in the context of the policy framework of Rule of Law (ROL) programmes. ROL programmes can be catalysts for legal change which may be systematized to create fundamental, structural legal changes. Such programmes often address (and challenge) the most basic legal concepts and institutions within a developing society, and provide a window of insight into the types of legal changes being contemplated (and actually instituted) by developing countries. In addition, the text will outline the contours of a new, emerging body of development law:

constitutional principles, certain substantive principles of law, and the institutional framework in which development law is unfolding.

Secondly, *Development Law and International Finance* will examine private international transactions which may act as a catalyst for initiating structural legal reform in the financial sector, and which have many downstream implications. Specifically, the role of the state in financing development through international borrowing from private commercial and public multilateral banking sources will be examined. Sovereign borrowing practices of the past failed to yield tangible development results, and contributed to the enormous debt crisis of the early and mid-1980s, ultimately leading to the imposition of strict structural adjustment policies by the International Monetary Fund and the International Bank for Reconstruction and Development. The gradual withdrawal of the state from productive sectors of the economy through privatization mechanisms will be critically examined, and the implications of this recent evolution in the role of the state will also be discussed.

These two factors: the severe economic repercussions caused by an over-reliance on short-term sovereign borrowing, and the privatization of public sector enterprises, have resulted in a critical reconfiguration of the state's role in the development process. Indeed, developing states are relying increasingly on private equity markets to finance their development needs. The implications of this development, including the impact this may have on developed countries, will be explored later in the text. And finally, the public international legal aspect of development law in determining whether there is a human right to development will also be addressed.

Since the subject poses some far-reaching queries, it would be remiss on my part not to advise the reader of the limitations of this text. This book will examine the relationship of certain legal, historical and economic ideas to one another. It is not intended to be used as a primer for international business transactions; nor is it intended to be a restatement of blackletter law on subjects such as bankruptcy law, secured transactions or intellectual property law, as such subjects may affect relations between the developed and the developing world. This discussion is meant to put into perspective the dramatic legal changes that have taken place over the past decade, and to explore the relationships between these changes and examine their significance for the future.

With regard to the methodology employed here, the subject-matter of *Development Law and International Finance* is still at a formative stage and comprises a rather unorthodox legal study. In fact, the normal channels of discourse (e.g., case law which distils principles of law from court cases) are not readily available to apply to this type of analysis. *Development Law and International Finance* also intersects other disciplines, including economics and political theory, which makes legal analysis of the topic somewhat unwieldy in this respect. Empirical case studies have been used illustratively to show certain trends, and help draw certain conclusions; thus, much of this material is anecdotal in nature. Any shortcomings or inaccuracies in the analysis presented are the full responsibility of the author.

Acknowledgements

To Professor Sir Eli Lauterpacht, Q.C., my sincere thanks for setting me on the right course so long ago when I was a law student at Newnham College, Cambridge University, and for your kind words concerning this effort. I also owe my sincere gratitude to Professor Don Wallace, Jr., Georgetown University Law Center, for his insightful comments on earlier drafts of this text.

To my two law assistants, Jonathan Evans and especially Maura Griffin, I owe my thanks for their patience, diligence and creativity in working with me on the research and editing required by this undertaking. Further, I wish to express my appreciation for the support and assistance in researching this work which I have received from so many of my friends and colleagues at USAID, the World Bank and the IMF. Their field experiences and observations added invaluably to my own. And my heartfelt gratitude also goes to Major Zachary Kinney, US Air Force, for his faith in me and this project.

The views expressed in this book are the author's personal views, and do not necessarily reflect the policies or views of USAID, the US government, or Georgetown University Law Center.

List of Abbreviations

ACP	African-Caribbean-Pacific
ACT	Agreement on Textiles and Clothing
ADB	Asian Development Bank
ADR	Alternate Dispute Resolution
ADR	American Depository Receipts
AFP	Administradoras de Fondos de Pensiones
AMEX	American Stock Exchange
BIS	Bank for International Settlements
CERDS	Charter of Economic Rights and Duties of States
CLS	Critical Legal Studies
CTAB	Capital Transfer Appellate Board
DSB	Dispute Settlement Body
DSU	Understanding on Rules and Procedures Governing the Settlement of Disputes
EAI	Enterprise for the Americas Initiative
EBRD	European Bank for Reconstruction and Development
EC	European Community
EEC	European Economic Community
EFM	Emergency Financing Mechanism
ESAF	Enhanced Structural Adjustment Facility
ESOP	Employee Stock Ownership Plans
EximBank	US Export-Import Bank
FDI	Foreign Direct Investment
FPI	Foreign Portfolio Investment
G-7	Group of 7
G-8	Group of 8
GATT	General Agreement on Tariffs and Trade
GDR	Global Depository Receipts
GNMA	Government National Mortgage Association (Ginnie Mae)
HIPC	Heavily Indebted Poor Countries
IBRD	International Bank for Reconstruction and Development (World Bank)
ICCPR	International Covenant on Civil and Political Rights
ICESCR	International Covenant on Economic, Social and Cultural Rights
IDA	International Development Association
IDB	Inter-American Development Bank

IMF	International Monetary Fund
IPO	Initial Public Offering
JEXIM	Japanese Export-Import Bank
LDC	Lesser Developed Countries
LIBOR	London Interbank Offered Rate
LOI	Letter of Intent
M/EBO	Management/employee Buy-Out
MFN	Most-Favored Nation
NAFTA	North American Free Trade Agreement
NASDAQ	National Association of Securities Dealers Automated Quotation System
NCB	National Commercial Bank
NEP	New Economic Policy
NGO	Non-Governmental Organization(s)
NIE	Newly Industrializing Economies
NIEO	New International Economic Order
OAU	Organization of African Unity
ODA	Office of Development Assistance (UK Development Aid Agency)
ODA	Official Development Assistance
OECD	Organization Economic Cooperation and Development
OPIC	Overseas Private Investment Corporation
OTC	Over-the-counter
PEMEX	Petroleos Mexicanos
PTF	Zambian Privatization Trust Fund
ROL	Rule of Law
SDR	Special Drawing Rights
SEC	US Securities and Exchange Commission
SFA	Special Facility for Africa
SIBOR	Singapore Interbank Offered Rate
SOE	State-Owned Enterprise
SPA	Special Programme of Assistance
SPA	Hungarian State Property Agency
SRO	Self-regulatory organizations
TRIMS	Agreement on Trade-Related Investment Measures
TRIPS	Agreement on Trade-Related Aspects of Intellectual Property Rights
UCC	Uniform Commercial Code
UDHR	Universal Declaration of Human Rights
UN	United Nations
UNCTAD	UN Conference on Trade and Development
UNDP	UN Development Programme
UNDRD	UN Declaration on the Right to Development
UNESCO	UN Education, Scientific, Cultural Organization
UNICEF	UN Children's Fund
UNICTRAL	UN Commission on International Trade Law
USAID	US Agency for International Development
WTO	World Trade Organization
ZPA	Zambia Privitization Agency

Introduction

1. *FIN DE SIÈCLE* ANALYSIS

There are certain historical trends which form a backdrop to the overall discussion which follows, and which merit some discussion. This section is termed a *'fin de siècle* analysis' because it is appropriate at the end of a century—which, incidentally, is also at the end of a millennium—to revisit and assess the historical and other implications of this eventful and stressful century, and explore the lessons it may hold for the future.

First, certain definitional changes that have taken place over the past decade may be somewhat confusing and misleading. For example, most readers will be familiar with the phrase 'Third World', with reference to the developing world. The phrase was coined from the term *tiers état* in an article published by Alfred Sauvy in *L'Observateur* on 14 August 1952, referring to the marginalized poor in France prior to the French Revolution of 1789.[1] Objective criteria by which to define the Third World are a problem. For instance, both gross domestic product (GDP) and per capita income can be misleading indicators. Certain Arab countries, for example, have extremely high GDP levels and per capita figures which disguise significant levels of poverty and deprivation for large segments of their populations. Moreover, Third World countries generally lack a set of unifying characteristics or a common history. Macedonia, Mali and Mongolia, for example, can all be considered to be 'developing' states, but they share no common bonds of history, geography or ethnicity.

The idea of 'development' is itself problematic in this context, since the designation of 'less-developed' and 'lesser-developed' countries (LDCs) implies that these nations are mired in a process of 'becoming', and therefore have a somewhat impaired international status, an implication that is both patronizing and condescending.

Another term that is applied to the developing world is the Group of 77, which was formed in 1964. However, this also is a misleading term, as out of the roughly 180 states of the world, almost 120 can be considered to be 'developing'. It could also be argued that China, India, Mexico, Brazil, South Korea and Taiwan should be elevated from 'developing' status, on

---

[1] T. Lewellen, *Dependency and Development: An Introduction to the Third World* (1995), p. 3.

the basis of their large and expanding industrial bases.[2] Thus, the membership of the Group of 77 is always in a state of flux.

The First World is comprised of a fairly homogeneous group of European and North American nations, together with Japan, Israel, Australia, New Zealand and South Africa. The G-7, composed of the United States, the United Kingdom, France, Germany, Italy, Canada and Japan, is often used as shorthand to refer to advanced, industrialized nations which have market-based, democratic societies.[3]

The now-defunct 'Second World' consisted of the former Soviet Union, Eastern Europe and Central Asia, or in other words, the 'transitional economies' of the former Soviet Bloc. The Second World also included other socialist nations such as China, Cuba, Vietnam, and North Korea. Most of its members are now striving to join the First World; for some countries, such as the Czech Republic and East Germany, this transition is more or less complete. For others, such as Kazahkstan and Albania, the transition will be more painful, and the danger of slipping instead into the Third World is a real possibility.[4] The transition of the Second World countries into the First World has important implications, which will be explored later in this text. As the Second World no longer exists, the terminology of the First, Second and Third Worlds has now been largely discredited.

Geography is sometimes introduced into the picture, so that development is judged by the parameters of 'East–West/North–South'. The East–West dichotomy tends to reflect the cultural divide between the industrialized 'West' and the non-industrialized, non-Western economies. However, since 'East' encompasses more than just Asia and must, by definition, include Africa and Latin America (in the Western Hemisphere), the use of this terminology can be somewhat misleading. Moreover, this division has other obvious flaws, since Japan, a country in the Far East geographically, is a fully Western-styled, democratic, market economy, both politically and economically.

Similarly, Australia and South Africa are in the 'South' geographically, but are recognized members of the 'North', economically speaking. The neo-Marxist overtones of the 'North–South' dichotomy, the legitimacy of which has waned in recent years, is fairly obvious.

To add a further layer of complexity, Australia now wishes to be considered part of the Pacific Rim, and politically now tends to identify more with its Asian neighbours than its European antecedents. Australia's actions make it clear that it is trying to join the group of East Asian 'Tiger economies' led by Japan. This configuration of Far Eastern states has also been referred to as the 'flying geese' formation, with Japan in the lead and the newly industrialized nations (NICs) in tow: Hong Kong, Taiwan,

---

[2] See Note, 'The New International Economic Order and General Assembly Resolutions: The Debate over the Legal Effects of General Assembly Resolutions Revisited', (1985) 15 *Cal. W. Int'l L. J.* 647, n.1.

[3] *Ibid.* at p. 648, n. 7.

[4] The term 'Fourth World' also exists, and has been applied to nations that are deeply mired in poverty such as Bangladesh or, alternatively, has been applied to indigenous populations.

Singapore, Thailand, South Korea, Indonesia, Malaysia, and China, with Vietnam, Laos and Cambodia struggling to keep up. If Australia is trying to join this flock then, truly, politics can make strange bedfellows.

Perhaps the most important point regarding the geography of development is the apparently haphazard way in which certain countries have been favoured over others. For example, sub-Saharan Africa's growth has been well below that of East Asia. Poor natural resources, bad government, poor infrastructure and short life expectancy due to tropical diseases all contributed to the shortfall in sub-Saharan growth.[5]

The Asian Development Bank, based on analysis done by Jeffrey Sachs at the Harvard Institute for International Development, has determined that simply following neo-classical prescriptions for capitalist health may not be enough, citing Bolivia's case.[6] For sub-Saharan Africa and other parts of the world that have been left out of the development equation, geographical hindrances must be overcome by developing a solid export-oriented manufacturing base. This means, in effect, that industrialized economies must open their markets to basic manufactured goods such as shoes and toys from these disadvantaged countries, if broad-based, global development is to be achieved.[7]

Neo-Marxist dependency theorist, Immanuel Wallerstein, devised a concept of a world capitalist system in which an international division of labour separated the world into three parts: the core, the periphery, and the semiperiphery.[8] The core represents all fully industrialized nations, the periphery refers to undercapitalized societies mainly involved in agricultural production and processing, and the semiperiphery, which has characteristics of both, would include countries such as Mexico, Argentina, and Taiwan. However, with the decline of this type of economic analysis, this terminology has been all but abandoned.

For the purposes of this text, the terms 'developed' and 'developing' will be used to indicate (however imperfectly and condescendingly) the problems and issues confronting various nations at differing stages of economic prosperity. The transitional economies of the former Soviet bloc will be referred to as such, particularly with regard to the unique problems involved in overhauling their macro-legal frameworks. In addition, the directional terms of East–West and North–South may also be used (despite the polemical overtones) to indicate the clash of ideas and cultures, within the framework of *Development Law and International Finance*. It is my hope that the continuing dialogue between the 'developed' and the 'developing' nations of the world will eventually bring about a more value-neutral terminology that will clearly and fairly express the differences that are the subject of this discussion.

---

[5] P. Passell, 'Economic Scene: Capitalism Doesn't Always Take. Location, it Seems is Destiny', *New York Times*, 12 June, 1997, p. D2.
[6] *Ibid.*
[7] *Ibid.*
[8] See T. Lewellen, *supra*, n. 1, p. 65.

2.   SIGNIFICANT HISTORICAL TRENDS

The far-reaching implications of having entered a post-Cold War era have yet to be fully appreciated. However, before we reach any conclusions concerning the Brave New World that we have been ushered into, perhaps a brief examination of what has transpired historically may be useful.

First, it should be noted that the development of colonialism, spanning the fifteenth to the twentieth centuries, set the stage for mercantile capitalism and later, the more mature stages of capitalism. The economic and political relations that this historical process established between the colonizers and the colonized had profound implications for 'development' in the twentieth century. The historical, economic, military, cultural, sociological, psychological and linguistic implications of colonialism have been the subjects of a rich body of scholarly and artistic works, to which I have only the following footnote to offer.

The historical process of establishing colonies overseas was episodic and haphazard. For example, was there some reason why Belgians, rather than the Portuguese, colonized the Congo? Why did the British establish themselves in India, but refrain from colonizing Argentina? Why did the French colonize Indochina/Vietnam rather than South Africa? And why did the Spanish dominate the Philippines, but fail to intervene in Australia?

There was nothing intrinsic to Indian society, for example, that pre-ordained a match with the British, or vice versa. Nor was there something intrinsic to the Ethiopian character that drew Italian colonial ambition. Even the choice of cash crops that fuelled colonial trade relations may have been haphazard, such as rubber (rather than jute) from Indonesia and tea (rather than coffee) from India. My point here is simply to state that much colonial domination (and the subsequent preferential trade relations it fostered in favour of the colonizing power) may properly be viewed as accidents of history, rather than as inevitable historical events.

The Second World War and its aftermath marked the beginning of a new political era when Latin American, Caribbean, African and Asian colonies became independent nation-states. However, the Cold War which followed on the heels of the end of the Second World War created a world stage for ongoing international conflict which was fuelled, in part, by the conflict in ideology. The ending of the Cold War, in 1989, has meant that past political relations organized around two competing camps are now defunct.

Over the past decade, we have witnessed another profound transformation: the dismantling of preferential trade relations fostered in the post-colonial era. Preferential trade relations of the past have become archaic and outmoded. And now, perhaps for the first time in world history, there has been an emphatic levelling of the playing field where any commodity, product or service may be obtained from anywhere by anyone, regardless of the past historical relations of the parties, or the lack thereof. Whether we consider trade in goods, technology or capital, the marketplace has become truly global.

Thus, trade relations and capital investments are being 'rationalized' in a new international economic order that no longer conforms to the outlines of the post-colonial relations of the past. Perhaps most importantly, the resources of the developed world are now accessible to the developing world on an unprecedented scale. This is dramatically illustrated by the rise of the Internet, a concept almost unthinkable just a few years ago, but which has now become an indispensable way of life for many people across the world, including those living in the developing nations. The old extractive and exploitative relations between the developed and the developing worlds have been transformed in a critical reconfiguration of relationships.

We can now see that the tidal wave of investment from the developed world is a critical (and, in some cases, catalytic) ingredient in transforming developing countries into more fully capitalistic societies. The developing world now has unprecedented access to the investment capability of the developed world. Thus, trade and investment relations between the developed and the developing worlds have become much more of a two-way street. This clearly has important implications for political relations between the two as well.

Institutional or portfolio investors in the developed world, as well as in the developing world, now have a real choice in whether to invest domestically or internationally. In fact, it could be argued that every individual is now a potential investor (and a stakeholder) in development, which is a truly revolutionary change from the past. The means by which development takes place can become accessible to almost everyone, and the peoples of the developing world have the potential for moving away from a passive role to a more proactive one in determining their choices for development within their society.

Although arguably, peoples of developing countries may now have an economic stake in the development process by exercising the option of participating in emerging capital markets as entrepreneurs and/or investors, this is highly problematic. First and foremost, this potential is more theoretical than real. Obviously, not every individual is empowered to participate in the international capital markets; the restraints of poverty, lack of education and gender, for example, are important impediments to equitable participation in the development process.

Secondly, if the emerging capital markets in the developing world are to succeed, they must meet the expectations of the Western investor. In practical terms, this means that market performance will be judged closely, if not strictly, on the basis of whether a developing country has the ability to generate expatriable profits. Portfolio investments in emerging capital markets—as elsewhere—tend to be performance-based, and only the short-term profitability of the enterprise will be rewarded by future investments. But more importantly, while the dependency relations of the past may be replaced by the global interdependency of the present and future, there is an implicit risk involved. This risk may be more insidious because it either is not perceived or is simply ignored.

In the past, culture determined the market. For example, the outstanding seafaring capabilities of the Phoenicians, Greeks, and Arabs made them superb traders, which had important ramifications in their respective cultures, and in the ways in which they were perceived by other cultures. Now, it is the market which determines culture. For example, whether you drink Coke and wear Levi jeans in Boise, Idaho or in a remote village in Papua New Guinea, the cultural imprint is still distinctly American.

Moreover, a globalized economy has the potential to give a new sovereignty to the will of the individual. In other words, the individual has a new and untrammelled freedom to exercise his or her freedom of choice. The realm of choice may vary from culture to culture but, essentially, consumerism gives individuals the exclusive right to make independent decisions on how to appease their senses. By this, I mean that whether the sensations of seeing, hearing, feeling, tasting or smelling are being considered, the film, music, fashion, restaurant and perfume industries have a wealth of choices to offer. The universe of choices is practically unlimited, since international trade, travel and global satellite communications makes the appeasement of the senses obtainable, affordable and, in the case of telecommunications, practically instantaneous. Thus, an individual's 'pursuit of happiness' can now truly take place on a global scale.

Science and technology are creating almost unlimited access to international markets, eliminating the traditional barriers or impediments of time, space, language, religion, physical disabilities, age and gender. Alvin and Heidi Toffler comment that:

The emergent Third Wave economy,[9] based on knowledge-intensive manufacture and services, increasingly ignores existing national boundaries. As we already know, large companies form cross-border alliances. Markets, capital flows, research, manufacture—all are reaching out beyond national limits ... New technologies are simultaneously driving down the cost of certain products and services to the point at which they no longer need national markets to sustain them.[10]

However, eliminating national boundaries also means that the cultures and cultural taboos contained within them are being left behind. While some may feel that this is an intensely liberating phenomenon, it is important to recognize that the realms of ethics, morality, law and justice, religion, symbols and iconography, language, history, mythology, art and culture are also being left behind. The aesthetic and cultural dimensions of human life are ill-equipped to deal with the magnitude and the speed of the changes that science and technology are bringing about. Once cultural parameters are lost, the loss of respect for the culture and the violation of

---

9 See A. and H. Toffler, *War and Anti-War: Survival at the Dawn of the 21st Century* (Little, Brown & Co., 1993), pp. 248–249 reproduced by kind permission of the publishers. The authors set out a new paradigm whereby the world is divided (yet again) into three parts. The 'First Wave' economies are composed of natural resources-based rural economies which rely principally on agricultural commodities for their livelihood. These economies also tend to lack industries as well as 'exportable knowledge-based services' (*ibid.*, p. 248).
 'Second Wave' economies rely heavily on manual labour and mass manufacture. They rely heavily on imports of raw materials and need export markets for their mass-manufactured goods, and tend to be more urbanized. In contrast, 'Third Wave' economies are 'post-nations' which are neither agrarian nor industrial economies, but constitute the 'newest tier of the global system', with access to knowledge that is convertible to wealth. *Ibid.*
10 *Ibid.*, p. 206.

cultural taboos are the next, very predictable steps. The potential for progressive degradation and trivialization of the human element in this context is deeply disturbing.

If, on the other hand, we opt for a pluralistic, relativistic world in which cultural traditions and religions are preserved, this may be viewed in some quarters as 'anti-progressive' and reactionary. Societies that are protectionist in nature (whether in terms of trade, religion, or culture) are often viewed in this light. For example, the trade protectionist practices of Mexico and China are deeply frowned upon by other states and by bodies such as the International Monetary Fund (IMF). Not only do such policies impede the unrestricted flow of international commerce, but history has proven in case after case that protectionist policies are often self-defeating as well.

Nevertheless, the price of development may be exceptionally high. A world without borders profoundly changes the terms of reference. Culture, and the uniqueness and specificity implicit therein, is becoming marginalized and may gradually become irrelevant. Over time, we may be headed in the direction of greater technological complexity, but cultural oversimplification. In other words, the depth, passion, particularity and contradictions of all cultures (and especially those of developing countries) may soon be lost to us. Thus, the risk inherent in the post-Cold War era of development is that of losing the sacred meaning of culture, religion, language, symbols and history. In the final analysis, the *quid pro quo* of development may be the loss of culture; that would, indeed, be a high price to pay.

How is tradition to be reconciled with the unrelenting pace of technology? Consumerism has an overwhelming tendency to destroy cultures by creating a single global market which, in turn, tends to create an increasingly universalist culture. Will Western 'universalism' triumph over non-Western 'multiculturalism' through the force of the international market alone? The 'end of history' has been a much touted idea over the past decade, but a post-Cold War hegemony of Western economic, political and legal ideals implicitly raises the question of whether multicultural diversity will be lost in the process.

Viewed in terms of social Darwinism, the lack of diversity means the beginning of extinction. In a strictly biological sense, the lack of genealogical diversity is a fatal flaw, leading to an increased probability of congenital defects, and ultimately, extinction. Although the 'end of history' is a superficially appealing idea in its orderliness, finality, and sense of inevitability, this 'twilight of the gods' may prove to be a highly problematic proposition.

The principal differences between the developed and the developing worlds are most often viewed in economic terms (the 'haves' and the 'have-nots'). The salient difference between the two groups is seen in terms of their relative economic power to pursue their individual happiness. However, there is at least another difference which may be more significant, ultimately, in terms of the subject-matter of *Development Law and International Finance.* That difference lies in the absolutist objectivity of the developed world versus the relativist subjectivity of the developing word. Developed societies have the capacity to create, grasp, and rely on a belief system of abstract ideals (e.g., equal justice for all, equal application of the law, due process, democratic representation and governance). In developing societies, the subjective, personal element, where loyalties are given not to abstract concepts but to families, patrons, rulers, ethnic or religious identities or leaders, tends to be much more prevalent.

For example, in a Middle Eastern country such as Jordan, if someone is a corporate insider with access to confidential information concerning, say, a stock offering, their failure to release this information to their family and friends would probably be regarded as a betrayal. Indeed it may be seen as the duty of such a person to provide their family and associates with the information and the means by which to enrich themselves. After all, such gains may fund a son's tuition to college. In this cultural context, adhering to a legal regime where insider trading is deemed a criminal offence may be seen as incomprehensible, alien and bizarre, and in conflict with the mores and expectations within Jordanian society.

It would be a pat assumption on the part of Western experts and consultants that such leaps of faith are a logical, necessary and inevitable part of the development process. It might be more helpful, for instance, to establish a dialogue on the rationale for criminalizing insider trading and to come to terms with the underlying cultural values that are affected (or offended) by this proposed new legal practice. If Western consultants merely assume that the criminal nature of insider trading is 'self-evident', then the interests of their mission to bring legal change, as well as the broader interests of the Jordanians, are not well-served.

The struggle between the developed and the developing worlds is not only one of economic accumulation, but is also a struggle of ideas around which societies are organized. It is this struggle that is taking place, in part, on the battlefield of law which is the subject-matter of this discussion.

3.   THE FAILURES OF THE STATE

In engaging in our *fin de siècle* analysis, let us first examine what has failed. Two noteworthy historical failures are, first, certain failures of the nation-state, and secondly, the failure of ideology. The new global interdependence that has become an undeniable fact of life is weakening structures such as the nation-state. At one extreme, we can consider the implications of the Maastricht Treaty and the ongoing unification of Europe into a regional trade, political and finance centre. A unified Europe could, therefore, be seen as the first example of discrete nation-states evolving into a new federation which can legitimately be considered to have a 'post-nation-state' status. At the other extreme of this spectrum, we have witnessed the collapse into near-anarchy of states such as the Sudan, Somalia, Afghanistan, Rwanda and Burundi. The state is capable of imploding altogether, leaving chaos and political and economic uncertainty in its wake.

In certain important respects, the nation-state is becoming less powerful as an international actor. State sovereignty has been eroded, and in the transitional economies of Eastern Europe and Central Asia, the previously authoritarian complexion of the state has been rejected wholesale. Other examples, such as the ousting of the autocratic ruler Mobutu Sese Seko in the Congo (formerly Zaire), indicate that authoritarian regimes in developing countries, too, are gradually being dismantled, notwithstanding exceptions such as Iraq and Cuba, of course, which remain problematic. The rejection of authoritarian rule (most evident in the transitional economies of the former Soviet bloc) has been part of a great democratic experiment in many of these nations. Thus, the nature of governance by the state in many developing countries is changing in response to demands for more transparent and more representative forms of government.

The retreat of the state from entrepreneurial functions has also been significant in this context. (Indeed, in the United States, this process has gone so far that initiatives to privatize schools and other traditional government functions are being experimented with, although the final results are unclear.) In the developing world, too, the private sector is assuming greater importance, and is the increasing focus of attention of both domestic and foreign investors. After the Second World War, in the newly independent former colonies, the state was usually the only creditworthy corporate entity capable of assuming the necessary entrepreneurial role in society to provide for the basic economic needs of its citizens. The nationalization of enterprises and industries not only echoed national sentiment in protecting the patrimony of the developing country, but may have been the only viable option where the private sector was weak or non-existent. However, these nationalizations generally resulted in huge, inefficient and unprofitable state-owned enterprises (SOEs), which are now being privatized. In these countries the state is beginning to relinquish its role in the productive sectors of economies, delegating that function to the private sector.

In most developing countries, the state relied heavily on international borrowing from both commercial and multilateral sources to finance development projects. This strategy proved to be both short-sighted and ineffectual. The failure of state policies regarding international borrowing strategies in order to finance development, and the crushing debt burden that was created by such borrowing practices, further impeded the development process. As developing nations became more indebted to foreign banks and institutions, development floundered.

The resulting failure of the development process created severe macro-economic imbalances, which led to IMF and World Bank intervention. This intervention usually took the form of structural adjustment programmes which addressed short-term balance-of-payments crises, but which also led to the imposition of harsh austerity measures, creating political as well as economic instability. This was particularly so in cases where there were inadequate social safety nets. Inability to manage the economic health of the nation further debilitated the entrepreneurial function of the state, and created a persistent crisis of confidence.

As a strategy for dealing with the huge government deficits created by sustaining inefficient and unprofitable SOEs, the IMF and other international advisors recommended that developing states privatize their SOEs. Privatization, in turn, is leading to the creation, deepening and strengthening of domestic capital markets. As the following discussion in this text will attempt to demonstrate, the creation of these so-called 'emerging capital markets' is an important part of the global development process. These emerging capital markets are the new (and internationally favoured) source of financing development.

Of course, the development and regulation of emerging capital markets is a complex process, of which privatization plays but a small, contributory part. However, during the past decade, these capital markets have literally exploded onto the worldwide financial scene. The implications of this development, not only in financial terms, but also in terms of revising the role of the state, will be explored in this text. Moreover, it should be noted that these emerging capital markets are also a critical factor in further dismantling the preferential and predetermined trade relations of the past between the developed and the developing worlds. Opportunities to invest capital now exist practically worldwide; and this has far-reaching implications.

4.   THE FAILURE OF IDEOLOGY

The second important failure that we have witnessed over the past several decades has been the failure of ideology. In the Second World War the British Empire and its allies fought against, and triumphed over, fascism. The end of the Cold War marks the demise of Stalinism and Soviet-style communism in the so-called Second World. Even the more derivative forms of Soviet-backed socialism, prevalent in certain African and Asian countries, have faltered and failed. Since the fall of the Berlin Wall in 1989, and the subsequent collapse of the Soviet Union ushering in a post-Cold War era, it has become increasingly apparent that the old policies— 'containment', supporting proxy wars, traditional nuclear disarmament strategies, and seeking to enlarge political spheres of influence—are now defunct.

With the ending of the Cold War, the lid has been lifted off a Pandora's Box, so to speak. Ethnic and religious conflicts in the developing world have erupted with unexpected force. For so long, historical and personal enmities between peoples had been overlooked, ignored or manipulated to further other political objectives in proxy conflicts. These ethnic conflicts are not based on ideological differences, but represent very old wounds that are now reopening. For example, in Burundi the massacre of thousands of Hutu in 1972–73 is now being revisited upon the sons and daughters of the Tutsi, a generation later.[11]

Unless there is an agreed consensual strategic response to humanitarian crises, we will remain vulnerable to such conflicts. Political destabilization will be caused not by superpower competition for supremacy, but by nuclear proliferation among secondary and tertiary powers such as

---

[11] U.O. Umozuike, 'The African Charter on Human and Peoples' Rights', (1983) 77 *Am. J. Int'l L.* 902 at 903.

Pakistan, Iraq and North Korea. Political conflict will no longer follow strict ideological lines, and further civil wars and the break-up of states will occur.

Samuel Huntington writes:

It is my hypothesis that the fundamental source of conflict in this new world will not be primarily ideological or economic. The great divisions among humankind and the dominating source of conflict will be cultural. Nation states will remain the most powerful actors in world affairs, but the principal conflicts of global politics will occur between nations and groups of different civilizations. The clash of civilizations will be the battle lines of the future.[12]

Huntington also argues that: 'cultural and civilizational diversity challenges the Western and particularly, American belief in the universal relevance of Western culture ... Normatively the Western universalist belief posits that people throughout the world should embrace Western values, institutions, and culture because they embody the highest, most enlightened, most liberal, most rational, most modern, and most civilized thinking of humankind'.[13]

However, he concludes: '[i]n the merging world of ethnic conflict and civilizational clash, Western belief in the universality of Western culture suffers three problems: it is false, it is immoral and it is dangerous.'[14] Thus, 'the requisites for cultural coexistence demand a search for what is common to most civilizations. In a multicivilizational world, the constructive course is to renounce universalism, accept diversity, and seek commonalities.'[15] Indeed, '[t]he security of the world requires acceptance of global multiculturality.'[16]

Not only does Huntington's thesis reveal the peculiar Western preoccupation with the idea of universalism (of Western ideals, that is), but it also reveals the deep-rooted distrust, fear and antipathy that most Western scholars feel towards the 'particularism' of other cultures. In other words, universalism is fine, as long as it is Western ideals that are being universalized.[17]

---

[12] S. Huntington, 'The Clash of Civilizations?', *Foreign Affairs*, Summer 1993, p. 22. Reprinted by permission of *Foreign Affairs*, Summer 1993, copyright (1993) by the Council on Foreign Relations , Inc.

[13] S. Huntington, *The Clash of Civilizations and the Remaking of World Order* (Simon and Schuster, 1996), p. 310.

[14] *Ibid.*

[15] *Ibid.*, p. 318.

[16] *Ibid.*

[17] The resistance to Western universalism—in particular, to American hegemony—was made rather pointedly clear at a 19-member conference held in Ottawa, Canada on 30 June 1998. Canadian officials organized the conference (to which US officials were not invited) in order to facilitate closer cooperation among the invitees to protect their respective cultures from the onslaught of the US entertainment industry. At the conference, the participants emphasized that culture was an important component of a nation's identity, and was not simply another commodity which should be made subject to treaties on international free trade, in particular, the OECD-sponsored Multilateral Agreement on Investment. See A. dePalma, '19 Nations See US as Threat to Cultures', *New York Times*, 1 July 1998, p. B1.

Although I agree with Huntington's conclusion, if not his means of reaching that conclusion,[18] as I indicated above, a fundamental and critical difference between Western and non-Western cultures is the ability to absorb abstract ideals. Ethnic and religious loyalties are felt at a deeply personal level by most individuals in non-Western societies. This particularism is abated only through exposure to (and schooling in) the Western ideals of humanism and secularism. These abstract concepts tend to elevate the ideal of the common good over individual gain or domination. Secularism, in particular, permits the individual to adopt a 'live and let live' approach to everyday life. This approach does not challenge or confront the differences implicit in other cultures or religious beliefs, and tends to smooth away potential areas of communal or sectarian conflict.

The Western ideals of humanism and secularism, in turn, ameliorate the strictly Hobbesian view of the individual person in relation to society where 'every man is Enemy to every man'[19]. In Thomas Hobbes's darkly apocalyptic vision, 'To this warre of every man against every man ... [t]he notions of Right and Wrong, Justice and Injustice have ... no place. Where there is no common Power, there is no Law: where no Law, no Injustice.'[20] Thus, Hobbes felt that the authoritarian state was the final solution to curb and control our destructive (and self-destructive) impulses.

Adam Smith and John Locke took a more positive view of human nature, and elevated the idea of personal acquisitiveness and our natural indifference towards the well-being of fellow human beings to the level of classical economics and liberal political theory. Charity and humanity became strictly optional. The welfare of the soul and of society were relegated as afterthoughts, vanquishing for ever the medieval preoccupation with such matters The sovereignty of individual will, the pursuit of happiness (and in the case of Locke, the pursuit of personal wealth and private property as well) became a sanctified ideal that remains untouched even today.

---

[18] For example, Huntington states that: 'Multiculturalism at home threatens the United States and the West; universalism abroad threatens the West and the world. Both deny the uniqueness of Western culture. The global monoculturalists want to make the world like America. The domestic multiculturalists want to make America like the world.
A multicultural America is impossible because a non-Western America is not American . . . The preservation of the United States and the West requires the renewal of Western identity.' See S. Huntingdon, *supra* n. 13, p. 318.
      The idea that only 'Western' cultural ideals can legitimately constitute what is 'American', simply cannot be supported. Indeed, this argument misses the point completely, since American 'Westernized' culture is able to incorporate and assimilate non-Western cultures with such shocking success. In fact, immigrant cultures in America clearly assimilate with the mass culture over time, perhaps observing a few holidays in the year to remind themselves of their distant origin. This incorporation is possible because the underlying theme is to succeed in a Western-based, capitalist world. 'Culture' in this context is immaterial. It is the ideals and cultural specificities of *other* cultures that are sacrificed in this process, not those of Western culture.
[19] T. Hobbes, *Leviathan* (Penguin Books, 1968), p. 186.
[19] *Ibid.*, p. 188.

This fairly simple idea would end up by revolutionizing the history of the world by elevating the baser instincts and natural proclivities of man to a classical ideal. It cleared the path from feudalism to mercantilism and finally, to capitalism. While the rest of the world remained rooted in feudal ideas of loyalties to clan, tribe, village chieftain, the Western world was busily forming modern nation-states and revolutionizing economic modes of production by incorporating new technologies and inventions. This frantic economic activity both created and fed the appetites of a growing mass consumer society, first nationally and then internationally.

The ideal of the pursuit of happiness through material acquisition may, indeed, be universal. This ideal may articulate the most fundamental and deepest human desires. The reductionist force and logic of the pursuit of happiness through material acquisition is irresistible, where success and happiness are measured by the single indicator of material wealth. The terrifying aspect of this 'classical' ideal lies precisely in its unifying force.

But perhaps the real difference between the Western 'classical' ideal and the non-Western view of it lies in the method of achieving this ideal. From a Western perspective, the ideal is grounded in individual liberties, and the protection by the state of an individual's right to private property. In contrast, non-Western societies, by and large, failed to form similar institutions which would protect individuals' freedom and property.

What is revolutionizing our world is not the adoption of a Western ideal by the developing world, but the adoption of the Western *methodology* for achieving the ideal of the pursuit of happiness. This ideal is achieved in the West by means of private property, democratic governance, and the rule of law. The rest is up to the individual: a very serious challenge, indeed. Non-Western societies are increasingly experimenting with, and relying on, this methodology in order to accomplish the same end. It is this fundamental shift in the underlying paradigm that is truly setting the course in the new millennium. Now that we have entered into a post-modern, post-Cold War, post-ideological era, we are witnessing a new era of global interdependence. This interdependence is being expressed in economic, legal as well as cultural spheres.

In light of what has failed, what has succeeded? Has the ideology, economics and consequently, the law of the West triumphed? What is falling into the gap? And what does all this mean from the standpoint of *Development Law and International Finance?* The discussion which follows is intended to shed some light on the possibilities. However, it is increasingly clear that the competition to succeed in this new world order is fierce, precisely because the stakes are so high.

Part I
The Rule of Law

1.   The Rule of Law: Theoretical Principles

The relationship between law and the process of development is highly problematic and has been the subject of intense controversy for several decades. This debate has been reinvigorated by the recent explosion of Rule of Law (ROL) programmes being implemented in transitional economies and most developing countries. This chapter will explore the theoretical foundations of development, and describe a possible reconciliation of opposing viewpoints and approaches to development, both in practice and in theory. This chapter will also set forth a new analytical framework for legal reform programmes in light of the ROL work that has been completed since 1989.

The definition of 'development' usually lies in the eye of the beholder. For a child nutritionist, for example, 'development' lies in birth weight, child survival rates and pre-natal care, while for an agronomist, it may lie in crop yields, access to export markets and agricultural supports. For legal practitioners, law is the key to 'development'. Development is too broad and complex a concept to be viewed exclusively (or even primarily) as a legal process; but it is the starting point for this discussion.

1.   THEORETICAL BACKGROUND

Development theory, a post-war phenomenon, has been grounded in two fundamental, yet opposing, viewpoints, as expressed by modernization theorists and dependency theorists. These two camps held widely differing views as to why and how development should be pursued by developing countries, and were also at great variance on what the final outcome of the development process should be.

The theoretical foundation for the modernization theory of development goes much further back, to the turn of the twentieth century. It evolved from the pivotal work of Max Weber, as described below.

1.1   Max Weber and the sociology of law

Under a 'liberal' theory of law, law expresses rational thought. Further, the existence of coherent, legally determined relationships between individuals in a well-ordered society provides a framework within which the individual may achieve the ideals of liberty, equality and the pursuit of happiness. This theoretical perspective on the function of law in modern society was greatly expanded by the work of Max Weber, who made two important linkages:

first, between the relationship of capitalism to Protestantism, and secondly, between law and capitalism.

Weber's *The Protestant Ethic and the Spirit of Capitalism,* first published in the form of two long essays in 1904–05,[1] linked Protestantism (particularly Calvinism) with modern capitalism. Although the connection between the European Reformation and the rise of capitalism may not have been new,[2] Weber cast it in a new light. Weber tied Protestantism inextricably to the ascendancy of modern capitalism. Modern capitalism rationalized the process of economic production by maximizing profit, and Weber argued that Protestantism harnessed this energy in a disciplined way, by imposing the obligation of work as a moral duty. The emergence of a new capitalist 'spirit' which infused the modern capitalist entrepreneurs is what, according to Weber, distinguished modern capitalism from other economic forms.[3]

Max Weber addressed two other important questions: first, how are Western legal systems different from those of other civilizations; and secondly, what is the relationship between the unique features of Western law and the rise and expansion of the Western capitalist system?[4] In his study, Weber identified several facets of Western law that were important to the supremacy of the capitalist system: (1) the contract; (2) uniformity in the rule of law and its application; and, (3) the growth of an autonomous legal profession.[5] Weber argued that the formal, rational and logical characteristics of the Western legal tradition provided the basis for creating a steady, predictable system which supported capitalism.[6] Thus, Weber's concept of formal, rational, modern law as instrumental to the growth and success of modern capitalism has shaped the legal analysis of development.

Weber's concepts are particularly relevant since much of the discourse on development centres around *economic* development, or raising the overall standard of living for the peoples of the developing world. With the collapse of Soviet-style command economies, capitalism has become, in effect, the sole viable economic mode of production.[7] Therefore, the linkage

---

[1] See A. Giddens, *Capitalism and Modern Social Theory: An Analysis of the Writings of Marx, Durkheim and Max Weber* (Cambridge University Press, 1971), p. 124.

[2] *Ibid.,* p. 125.

[3] It has also been argued that the Protestant work ethic is not the only 'spirit' which motivates capitalist production. Overseas Chinese communities have been singularly successful in generating economic wealth—relying not on rational laws, but rather on their traditional customs. Thus, informal relationships rather than formal laws prescribe successful capitalist behaviour for them. It follows that traditional customs need not be inimical to a Rule of Law framework, and may effectively control behaviour integral to the successful generation of capitalist wealth. J. Wu, 'Overseas Chinese Capitalism and the Marginalization of the Rule of Law: A Reassessment of the Relationship Between Law and Economic Development', available on Internet at http://www.aad.berk., pp. 3, 5.

[4] See M. Weber, *Economy and Society* (G. Ross and C. Wittich (eds.), 1978). (This three-volume work contains excerpts from Weber's *Sociology of Law*.)

[5] *Ibid.*

[6] *Ibid.*

[7] D. Kellner, 'Globalization and the Postmodern Turn', available on Internet at http://www.gseis.uc, pp. 7, 8 (last visited on 28 July 1998).

created by Weber between rational, modern law and capitalism establishes the theoretical foundation for an inquiry into the meaning of 'development' from a legal perspective.

Although the idea of 'development' is a post-war phenomenon, Weber has had a profound influence on the philosophical assumptions underlying most development efforts, particularly those sponsored by donor countries.[8] Most development efforts of the past several decades have been grounded in 'modernization' or 'neo-classical' economic theory.[9] Modernization theorists assumed that development follows a linear process whereby a free market economy, once created, provides for the economic prosperity and liberty of all.

This approach is predicated on the belief that a capitalist, free market system allocates resources through private ownership so as to maximize profits and minimize costs. Moreover, neo-classicists assume that the benefits of capitalist production will 'trickle down' to the masses. On an institutional level, this translates into a donor-prescribed plan of action for developing countries, to wit: balance-of-payments stability, a well-managed fiscal budget, a market economy with a highly developed private business sector, and a reasonably developed capital market.[10]

Further, neo-classical theorists assume that all nations and peoples are 'rational', and that a free market economy rewards competitive values. The nexus that Weber established between modern, rational law and the success of capitalism becomes key in the modernization context. Neo-classicists assume that every society is capable of 'modernization' or, in other words, is capable of gradually transforming itself into the established model of the Western-style modern capitalist state.[11] This progression is conceived of as being linear in nature, which may require replacing traditional values with

---

[8] See L. Cao, Review of *Law and Development: A New Beginning?* (1997) 32 *Tex. Int'l L. J.* 545 at 547–548.

[9] See, e.g., W.W. Rostow, *The Stages of Economic Growth* (Cambridge University Press, 1960). The modern-day descendant of this type of approach is generally referred to as the 'Washington consensus'. See D. Trubek, 'Law and Development: Then and Now', (1996) *Am. Soc. Int'l L. Proceedings,* 90th Ann. Mtg. at 223-224, who writes: 'The 'Washington consensus' is a term often used to refer to the dominant paradigm in development thinking among Bretton Woods institutions [i.e., the World Bank and the IMF]. This approach is radically different from development thinking in the 1960s when the Law and Development idea was first articulated. Then emphasis was placed on central planning, state enterprise and inwardly oriented import substitution industrialization. The Washington consensus, on the other hand, promotes markets as allocative institutions, favours privatization and promotes closer linkages to the global economy'. Reproduced with permission, copyright (1996), The American Society of International Law.

[10] See, e.g., IMF Home Page, 'What is the IMF?', available on Internet at http://www.imf.org., p. 4 (last visited on 13 August 1998).

[11] Rostow divides that linear process into several stages: (1) the traditional society; (2) the creation of the pre-conditions for capitalist development; (3) the mature capitalist state; and, (4) the final stage of mass consumption. Under modernization theory, the role of an entrepreneurial class which saves and invests wisely is critical to this linear progression. Creating a consumer-based society is the final dictate of capitalist success. See W. W. Rostow, *The Stages of Economic Growth* (Cambridge University Press, 1960). (See also W.W. Rostow, *The Stages of Economic Growth: A Non-Communist Manifesto*, 3rd edn. (1990), pp. 4–16.)

modern ones. But neo-classicists believe that this is a transformation that can, and should, be undertaken by all developing nations. Thus, 'development' can be seen as the creation of an industrialized society in the image of Western, democratic, market-based economies. This expectation has profoundly shaped the discourse on development.

1.2 Modernization theory v. dependency theory

1.2.1 Modernization theory

The 'modernization' theory of development, the predominant post-war school of thought, held to the belief that modernization was a progressive, evolutionary process that would result in the transformation of 'less developed' societies into Western political, social and legal institutions. According to modernization theory, four elements were critical in this transformative process: rationalization, nation building, democratization and participation.[12]

Further, it is apparent that modernization theory is predicated on the Western-styled modern state historically based on Christianity (and in particular, Protestantism), individualism, and the rule of law, to which the values of secularism and pluralism were later added. The modernization approach is also predicated on the belief that non-Western peoples should incorporate Western values, institutions and laws because such values are the most rational and the most civilized, and should be considered 'universal' in nature.[13] Thus, Western 'universalism'[14] identifies Western-based indicia of modern society, i.e., individualism, the rule of law, a free market economy, and democracy, as the foundation for development.

From a legal perspective, modernization theory spawned the 'law and development' movement in the mid-1960s which produced its most important legal scholarship from roughly 1965 to 1975.[15] The 'law and development' movement followed the basic tenets of modernization theory, espousing the belief that there is a natural, inevitable progression towards Western legal concepts, institutions and legal structures. Law was deemed essential to the formation of a fully functioning market system. Further, the

---

[12] R. Bilder and B. Tamanaha, Reviews of *Law and Development* (A. Carty (ed.), Dartmouth Publishing Co., 1992) and *Law and Crisis in the Third World* (S. Adelman and A. Paliwala (eds.), Hans Zell, 1993), in (1995) 89 *Am. J. Int'l L.* 470 at 471–472.

[13] See S. Huntington, *The Clash of Civilizations and the Remaking of World Order* (Simon and Schuster, 1996), p. 310.

[14] Within a human rights context, for example, universalists believe that all individuals are entitled to the same set of human rights by virtue of the fact that they are human beings. See E. Mountis, 'Cultural Relativity and Universalism: Reevaluating Gender Rights in a Multicultural Context', (1996) 15 *Dickinson J. Int'l L.* 113 at 113. The terms 'universalism' and 'cultural relativists' are used in this text in a broader development context.

[15] R. Bilder and B. Tamanaha, *supra* n. 12, pp. 472–473. See M. Galanter, 'The Modernization of Law', in *Modernization* (M. Weiner (ed.). 1966), p. 156. See also J. Merryman, 'Comparative Law and Social Change: On the Origins, Style, Decline and Revival of the Law and Development Movement', (1977) 24 *Am. J. Comp. L.* 457; E.M. Burg, 'Law and Development: A Review of the Literature and A Critique of "Scholars in Estrangement"', (1977) 25 *Am. J. Comp. L.* 492 at 496–498, nn. 17, 18, 22.

legal infrastructure of a society was seen as providing the basic foundation in support of a liberal, democratic, modern state.

Indeed, the lack of a Western-style legal infrastructure was often cited as an impediment to the legal and overall development within the society in question. Thus, the Law and Development movement (rather uniquely American in its adherents and its overall thrust) advocated the speedy adoption of Western legal infrastructure, with a corresponding adaptation of legal education and the legal professions within developing countries.[16]

Modernization theory and its practical approaches to development, however, were not universally accepted. Two basic (and related) critiques of modernization theory will be examined here: first, that offered by the leftist Critical Legal Studies movement of the 1970s,[17] and secondly, the scathing attack by the Marxist school of dependency theorists.

Modernization theory came under attack for being too Eurocentric (or ethnocentric), too conservative, and too naive.[18] The death knell to the Law and Development movement was sounded by David Trubek and Marc Galanter, two American legal commentators, who announced its premature death in 1974 in a law review article entitled 'Scholars in Self-Estrangement: Some Reflections on the Crisis of Law and Development Studies in the United States'.[19]

After less than 10 years of legal scholarship, the obituary of the Law and Development movement (and of the 'legal liberalism' that it espoused) had been duly filed.[20] The Law and Development movement, in effect, collapsed after this attack, and David Trubek subsequently became a central figure during the 1970s in a uniquely US-based legal movement known as Critical Legal Studies (CLS).[21] The CLS movement offered an 'eclectic critique' of the Rule of Law approach to development, and warned against the dangers of exporting Western laws and legal institutions to the developing world.[22]

Indeed, it may be argued that Max Weber established himself as a precursor of the CLS movement for, like Weber, CLS scholars were concerned about the legal consciousness of capitalist societies. Proponents of the CLS movement wanted to change that consciousness through social transformation or, perhaps more succinctly, through law as a form of social engineering. How is this related to law and the question of development? CLS scholars examined the relationship of law to capitalism, and questioned a fundamental presupposition of modernization theory:

---

[16] R. Bilder and B. Tamanaha, *supra* n. 12, p. 473.

[17] *Ibid.*, p. 474.

[18] *Ibid.*, p. 472.

[19] D. Trubek and M. Galanter, 'Scholars in Self-Estrangement: Some Reflections on the Crisis of Law and Development Studies in the United States', (1974) *Wisc. L. Rev.* 1062.

[20] *Ibid.*, p. 1071. See also D. Trubek, 'Toward a Social Theory of Law: An Essay on the Study of Law and Development', (1972) 82 *Yale L.J.* 1 at 16; D. Trubek, 'Back to the Future: The Short Happy Life of the Law and Society Movement', (1990) 18 *Fla. St. U. L. Rev.* 4 at 20–21.

[21] R. Bilder and B. Tamanaha, *supra* n. 12, p. 474.

[22] *Ibid.*, p. 475.

that the modern capitalist society is the desired end of all developing nations.

The now defunct CLS movement made several important contributions in this area, by: (1) questioning the centrality of the state in the development process; (2) questioning the Eurocentric nature of Law and Development; and (3) being aware of the potential use of law to perpetuate underdevelopment in developing societies.[23] Unfortunately, the CLS movement did not offer any alternative to the modernization approach to legal development.[24]

Indeed, it may be argued that the CLS critique was not altogether original, since its genesis was contained in the scholarship of the Law and Development movement. Not all modernization proponents believed that the US legal model could be easily exported to and transplanted in a developing country context. Americans rely heavily and rather uniquely on law and legal institutions, a practice that is not easily recreated in other societies.[25]

Moreover, the CLS movement failed to resolve the tension between legal universalists who believed that the Western mode for development was the most logical and, ultimately, the only acceptable mode for development, and cultural relativists who believed that '[i]mperialism is the necessary logical consequence of universalism'.[26] The proponents of cultural relativism believe that there is no universal norm for human development, and no fixed parameter for the end result of development. Indeed, cultural relativists argue that different cultures have differing views on what constitutes 'development'.[27] CLS scholars may have incorporated certain tenets of cultural relativism in making their critique of modernization approaches to legal development, but the underlying tension between the two viewpoints was not satisfactorily resolved. This schism represents the fault line between modernization and cultural relativism.

---

[23] *Ibid.*, pp. 474–475.

[24] *Ibid.*, p. 474.

[25] See, e.g., T.M. Franck, 'The New Development: Can American Law and Legal Institutions Help Developing Countries?' in A. Carty (ed.) *Law and Development* (1992) Vol. 3, pp. 18–24.

[26] See S. Huntington, *supra* n. 13, p. 310.

[27] Indeed, this may be a propitious time to renegotiate what constitute 'universal' or 'fundamental' rights—long considered 'self-evident' to Western scholars—which we are all entitled to by virtue of our humanity. If, however, this effort is to be undertaken seriously, non-Western societies may need to re-examine the principles of cultural relativism, which can all too easily be used to camouflage and perpetuate violations of basic human norms. Not all practices contained under the rubric of 'culture' are supportable. For example, many cultural forms which oppress women (e.g., dowry, female circumcision) should be critically re-examined to assess their value as a cultural 'norm'.

Despite the 'imperialist' pretensions of modernists, however, past experience clearly demonstrates that any real change to cultural norms must come from within a society—conformity to non-indigenous cultural norms cannot be imposed from outside. See E. Mountis, 'Cultural Relativity and Universalism: Reevaluating Gender Rights in a Multicultural Context', (1996) 15 *Dickinson J. Int'l L.* 113. (See the discussion on whether there is a human right to development in Chapter 6 of this text.)

1.2.2 Dependency theory

All of the foregoing discussion takes place against a backdrop of dependency theory, which offered a fundamental critique of modernization theory. Dependency theorists attempted to fill the vacuum that was left following the demise of the Law and Development movement in the mid-1970s, by offering their own Marxist brand of analysis.[28] Rather than ascribing a backward state of development to the lack of Western-based capitalism (and supporting laws and institutions), dependency theorists argued that 'underdevelopment' was caused by the system of world capitalism, which perpetuated extractive and exploitative relations with the developing world. Whereas modernization theorists tended to 'blame the victim' (i.e., the developing nation) for its lack of modern capitalism and a supportive ROL framework, dependency theorists tended to blame the system. In other words, modernists would urge developing countries to 'get with the programme', whereas dependency theorists would argue that the problem lay with 'the programme.'

Dependency theorists felt that the starting point for underdevelopment was colonialism, but even where harsh political repression had ended with the independence of former colonies, the exploitation of developing countries did not end. Economic, rather than political, domination continued by way of 'neo-colonial' relations between the former colonizer and the formerly colonized, perpetuating the economic dependence of the latter. Thus, dependency theory is deeply rooted in the specifics of colonial history, and its aftermath. Dependency theorists view 'development' as an intensely political process in which advanced industrial societies are pitted against developing nations.

On a practical level, dependency theorists advocated nationalization, import substitution and other forms of protectionism in support of nascent industries (discussed at length later in the text). As events over the past few decades have shown, these policies, while well-intentioned, led to uneven results and generally did not bring about the concrete development benefits which were originally hoped for. Ultimately, the neo-classical economic prescriptions advocated by the IMF were imposed on developing economies that were floundering under the weight of massive sovereign debt, crumbling infrastructures and crushing poverty.

Dependency theorists did not emphasize law, following Marx's prescription that law, as the 'superstructure' of the underlying economic structure of a society, was secondary in importance. Thus, economics rather than law was the focal point of their discussion and analysis. Regardless of law's reduced status, dependency theory nevertheless led to the creation of the 'international law of development'.[29] The international law of development became the driving force in the late 1970s advocating such changes as preferential trade relations with developing counties, preferred access to

---

[28] See e.g., D.F. Greenberg, 'Law and Development in Light of Dependency Theory', in A. Carty (ed.), *Law and Development* (New York University Press, 1992).
[29] R. Bilder and B. Tamanaha, *supra* n. 12, p. 479.

development assistance from industrialized countries, and the transfer of technology to developing nations. The international law of development also urged that a new 'human right to development' be created. This is addressed later in the text.

These principles were articulated in a series of UN resolutions, declarations, reports and other documents advocating the establishment of a 'New International Economic Order', or 'NIEO'. The NIEO was designed to 'level the playing field' between the developed and the developing worlds, redressing the imbalances created by colonization.[30]

Indeed, echoes of the NIEO may be detected reverberating in the Kyoto Protocol on Climate Change which was adopted by about 160 countries in December 1997 as parties to the UN Framework Convention on Climate Change. The Kyoto Protocol specifically required industrialized countries to use 1990 or 1995 as the base year upon which to reduce their levels of toxic emissions, while exempting developing countries from the same or similar requirement. Additionally, the Kyoto Protocol specifically required developed economies to promote, facilitate and finance the transfer of technology for mitigating climate change, a point that we will return to.

It is clear that both modernization and dependency theory are united in the fundamental importance of capitalism to the overall development of a society. The two theories tend to part company on where capitalism ends: with the good of the individual or the good of society. Modernization theory emphasizes the individual, and the greater good of the individual. The natural proclivity of the state to restrain an individual's freedom and interfere with his/her ownership of private property is held in check. Capitalism is integral to modernization as it provides the basis upon which to seek the individual pursuit of happiness. In contrast, dependency theory, in support of a socialist form of governance, elevates the good of society above that of the individual. It is the natural acquisitiveness of the individual that is restrained by abolishing private forms of ownership.

The end of the development process for modernization theorists rest with the triumph of individualism, whereas the final vision of neo-Marxist dependency theorists is of a classless state where the will of the individual is subordinate to that of the state. Now, this may be a distinction that no longer matters. With the demise of Soviet-style approaches to economics, politics and law, the firmest advocates of dependency theory have been overtaken by history.

It may be difficult to argue with the proposition that the legacy of colonialism caused a great deal of economic, political and power imbalances in the post-colonial world. However truthful or compelling this analysis may be, at best it provides an explanation of certain imbalances; it does not resolve them. Therefore, in a very real sense, dependency theory resulted in a dead-end.

---

[30] See L. Cao, *supra* n. 8, pp. 554–555.

Moreover, dependency theorists were wrong in a vital respect. Capitalism was viewed as a zero-sum game where the exploitation of the developing world was inextricably linked with the creation of capitalist wealth in advanced, industrial societies. This fundamentally misinterprets the nature of capital which can be produced, in theory, *ad infinitum* by any entrepreneur, regardless of his/her location in the developing world. Thus, dependency theorists seriously miscalculated the impact of creating capitalist market conditions in developing nations, the global repercussions of which are clearly being felt now.

Indeed, in a globalized society, the creation of wealth in East Asia not only enriches entrepreneurs in East Asian countries, but it also enriches investors in the West. Similarly, the impoverishment of East Asian economies may result in the unemployment of US factory workers who can no longer compete with the drastically reduced price of East-Asian manufactured goods. Dependency theorists correctly identified the fact that extractive and exploitative neo-colonial economic relations between the developed and the developing world lay behind the 'underdevelopment' of developing nations. It is less clear, however, that dependency theorists anticipated a global economy where developing countries are also able to profoundly affect the capital markets and labour conditions of the developed world. By dismissing the ability of developing nations to successfully stimulate capitalist economic growth, dependency theory has bankrupted itself, perhaps by revealing its paternalistic view of the potential of the developing world.

Whatever the shortcomings of both development approaches, there is a philosophical convergence with regard to the role of law in the development process under both modernization and dependency theory. Insofar as law may reflect the underlying economic 'structure' behind dependency theory, we may be witnessing an unprecedented globalization of commercial laws. As the world economy becomes more integrated, commercial laws are becoming harmonized on a global scale so that business may be conducted more smoothly and efficiently, without having to accommodate the 'unnecessary' complications of different legal cultures.

Dependency theorists may view this an inexorable progression whereby the legal superstructure has slowly begun to reflect the underlying unity of the economic structure. (Rather unfortunately for dependency theorists, the underlying economic structure remains capitalism, not socialism.) Modernization theorists would see this evolution as a linear progression towards a Rule of Law regime on a truly international scale. Thus, the rational order of law in support of world capitalism (whether viewed from the perspectives of Marx or Weber) can be seen as the wave of the future.

1.3 The globalization of laws

There is a curious synchronicity between neo-classical liberalism (modernization theory) and neo-Marxism (dependency theory), insofar as the end-result of both leads to a post-modern, homogenized global culture where cultural differences and potentially dangerous ethnic rivalries are levelled off. Nationalism, cultural particularism, and traditionalism will become relics of the past. For modernists, the creation of a global world culture, and for neo-Marxists, instilling a proletariat-dominated communist state are the respective end visions of the development process.[31] Indeed, Marx and Engels wrote that:

Modern industry has established the world market, for which the discovery of America paved the way... [the] need of a constantly expanding market for its products chases the bourgeoisie over the whole surface of the globe. It must nestle everywhere, settle everywhere, establish connections everywhere... The bourgeoisie, by the rapid improvement of all instruments of production, by immensely facilitated means of communication, draws all, even the most barbarian nations into civilization.... In a word, it creates a world after its own image.[32]

For both modernists and neo-Marxists, the ability of modern capitalism to capture and exploit technological innovations was key to the success of capitalism. The successful penetration of even the remotest 'markets' through technology is ultimately bringing about a global capitalist market. Technology has been catalytic in this regard since the territorial nature of economic production has been vitiated. Cross-border financing, corporate subsidiaries located across the globe, and a global web of decentralized economic 'centres' for the manufacture of tailored rather than mass-produced goods are all present realities. Indeed, states are less able to regulate or control such cross-border exchanges, especially as the measure of wealth moves from real property to virtual property in the form of patents, copyrights and other non-tangible assets.[33]

In fact, it may be argued that the globalization of economic production, the growth of technology and information-based societies, and cross-border financing has begun to level the playing field between developed and developing countries. Developing countries which have a base of well-educated but low-wage workers, capable of generating technology-added goods which are merchandised globally, may have a comparative advantage. The reaction to increased global interdependence has been a backlash of fear and protectionist sentiment from more advanced, industrialized nations.[34] These are precisely the preconditions that give rise to the need for a new reconfiguration of the relationship between the developed and the developing worlds.

If the globalization of the world economy is followed by the globalization of laws, this begs the question of whether the globalization of culture, too, is an inevitable sequence in this process. Although modernists tend to view 'law' as an abstraction, law is an expression of culture in much the same way as art, music or dance are. Law is a manifestation of the underlying mores and social norms by which a people or society live. While law may

---

[31] See D. Kellner, *supra* n. 8, p. 8.
[32] See K. Marx, *Capital: A Critique of Political Economy* (1883) pp. 823–826 (F. Engels (ed.), S. Moore and E. Aveling (trans.), Modern Library, 1936), as quoted in D. Kellner, *supra* n. 8, p. 5.
[33] See Lan Cao, *supra* n. 8, pp. 558–559.
[34] See *ibid.*, p. 559.

be an objective ideal, it has its genesis in the particularities of the culture from which it emerged. Thus, if laws are to be harmonized on a global scale, will the underlying elements of culture be harmonized also? It seems at least possible that this may be so.[35]

Yet, even within the mantle of commercial transactions, there is a core of culture. For example, is insider trading a corrupt practice, or should individuals with access to privileged information be allowed to profit from this as an expected business norm? Should women be allowed to vote at shareholder meetings in conservative Islamic countries? The downstream effects of creating international legal norms, especially as they may impact traditional cultural expectations, are as yet undetermined.

As might be expected, globalization has its opponents and proponents. Its opponents fear the destruction of traditional legal norms and customs, and their replacement with 'universal', rational and formal law. Locally based and politically determined legal solutions to local problems might also be lost.[36]

In more general terms, opponents fear that local culture and traditions will be usurped by universalist ideals and trends and, more importantly, that individualism will come before the larger interests of the community. An implicit fear is that emotions, intuition and non-rational thought will be overtaken by logical, formal and rational thought. This may have interesting implications for law, since non-Western legal systems may reflect (for lack of a better word) 'non-rational' thought, and this element may be lost to us in the globalization process.

Further, many fear that myths will be forgotten in light of science; that traditional remedies will be vanquished by post-modern technology; and that the wisdom of age will yield to the innovation of youth. The homogenization of specific cultures and everyday life is a threatening and

---

[35] If centrifugal force is applied to 'culture' in order to disaggregate it into its separate components, it would seem that certain elements of culture are 'heavier' than others. For example, different types of 'ethnic' food are almost universally appreciated. International cuisines can be seen as a lighter element of culture, one that can be universally shared without negative repercussions.

Literature, the cinema (especially if film subtitles are involved), music, dance and art are slightly 'denser' elements of culture. However, the globalization (and commercialization) of these elements have created common ground for their understanding, sharing and appreciation. It would not be considered uncommon in cosmopolitan circles for the same individual to appreciate Irish dance, Mexican art, Czech films, Japanese poetry (in translation, of course), and Caribbean music.

There are still heavier elements to culture that do not have as much transferability as others. Fashion, for example, can be somewhat problematic. Wearing saris or other 'ethnic' dress in many Western countries is still disapproved of. The preservation of language, while valued by the ethnic enclave for whom it is part of their heritage, can yet be seen as overtly or vaguely threatening by others outside that culture. Religion, the rights and status of women, morality and ethics are other subtle indicia of culture which do not always cross frontiers very well.

[36] For an excellent discussion of the dangers of globalized legal norms, see M.G. Gopal, 'Law and Development: Toward a Pluralist Vision', (1996) *Am. Soc. Int'l L. Proceedings*, 90th Ann. Mtg., pp. 231–237.

disagreeable prospect for neo-Marxists, traditionalists, multiculturists, and environmental protectionists alike.[37]

However, the relentless march towards post-modern globalization is not without some redeeming qualities. For example, it may also mean that the inexorable nature of one's birth, fate or caste can be mitigated by exercising independent choice. It also opens up the possibility that an individual may be recognized more on the basis of his or her individual merit and achievement. The exclusive domain of men may also be opened so that women are included in the development equation. Moreover, a certain intolerance implicit in ethnicity may be softened by a new focus on a common humanity, and a more cosmopolitan, secularized lifestyle.

Post-modernists may argue that the creation of a global culture is not a force of insipid homogenization and destruction, but a force which produces progress, heterogeneity and diversity.[38] This position is highly problematic since the creation of a global culture necessarily means that the specificity and richness of local traditions, myths, and cultures are sacrificed in the process. Although the modernist view of globalization espouses a pluralist vision, the superficiality of 'culture' within this context makes this vision more of a mirage than a plausible reality. Nevertheless, the post-modern globalization of culture (and laws as an expression of culture) need not be an oncoming juggernaut for developing societies. Developing countries can, and should, take a proactive stance in multiplying their development options, and take a more discriminating stance with regard to exercising these options.

2.   THE RULE OF LAW: AN ANALYTIC FRAMEWORK FOR LEGAL REFORM PROGRAMMES

In light of the above discussion concerning the theoretical foundations for dependency theory, it is clear that both the modernization and dependency approaches have limited application in the new global culture. The following discussion proposes a fresh approach to development that is more responsive to the changing global needs in legal systems development, coordination and integration.

In suggesting an analytic framework for developing an ROL regime, three basic divisions may be useful in this context: (1) creating a civil society, (2) instituting structural legal reform, and (3) improving the administration of justice.

First, in terms of creating the conditions for establishing a broad-based civil society, there is a growing movement away from more autocratic forms of government and towards a more open, participatory style of governance. A civil society is the foundation of a representational democracy—an idea that we will return to. In practical terms, this generally

---

[37] See D. Kellner, *supra* n. 8, p. 2.
[38] *Ibid.*, p. 3.

translates into curtailing the power of the executive branch (and possibly the military or paramilitary forces in the country), giving the judiciary more independence and autonomy, and instituting parliamentary reform. The aim of all of these reforms is to create a more open, democratic, and more participatory society with an appropriate emphasis on institution-building and strengthening. Integral to this process is encouraging the growth of non-government organizations (NGOs). NGOs, by representing the private, organized interests of society, help counterbalance the interests of business and government.

Structural legal reform, which will be dealt with at length in this text, principally involves the restructuring of existing laws, creating new regulatory frameworks to enforce and regulate sectors such as banking, securities markets, the environment, and other potentially new areas of the law for the host country. In addition, new government agencies may need to be created in order to implement new laws and regulations. This area generally requires the legislation of new laws and regulations, and institutionalizing the means for their enforcement by the host government.

Finally, the administration of justice involves court and judicial reform designed to make the criminal justice system more transparent, speedier, and more accessible to the lay person. This area of legal reform deals with basic 'law and order' issues, controlling corruption and strengthening the institutional capacity to carry out the administration of justice function. This area of law reform may also involve a renewed (or new) commitment to abstract ideals of equal justice, due process, and equality before the law. Although these may seem straightforward assumptions for highly developed Western, industrial societies, for certain developing societies such ideals may require a fundamental reorientation in the approach to justice. Indeed, certain Western-based concepts of due process and fundamental liberties of the individual guaranteed by the state may be deeply threatening to the established legal order. Effecting fundamental change to any legal order requires tremendous political will, as well as the requisite time.

2.1   The Janus Law Principle

The unipolar, post-Cold War world has given new legitimacy to Western universalists, especially with the former Soviet bloc now scrambling to adopt Western forms of governance, economics and popular culture. A full-fledged modernization approach, however, may not necessarily be the best way to encourage legal reform in support of development. The modernization approach to legal development may need to be tempered in order to more effectively bring about a Rule of Law regime. The following discussion proposes a rapprochement between the opposing principles of Western universalism and non-Western cultural relativism.

The modernization approach to instituting a Rule of Law regime in a developing society does not take into account any historical factors or cultural components. However, it is important to realize that legal reform cannot take place in a vacuum. Every society has indigenous legal traditions and, in the case of much of the developing world, a tradition of 'received' law from former colonizers. In addition, religious laws based on specific doctrines of the Christian, Muslim, Hindu and Buddhist faiths may also have played a significant role in the creation of legal norms. Further, in many societies, there exist quasi-institutional means for resolving disputes, as well as established traditions for arbitrating legal rights and entitlements. For example, the *panchayat* (village council) is an established means of resolving territorial, property and other types of disputes in rural India. A similar tradition is found in many parts of Africa.

Indeed, the overall legal picture is often quite complex, being the culmination of hundreds of years of legal history, concepts, institutions and legal codes. Apart from these historical factors, the legal picture in any country is constantly changing, based, at least in part, on the ongoing input from the legal profession and judiciary. Thus, in order to change the existing legal structures, institutions, or legal codes of a developing society, the legal history of that society must first be taken into account. Unless the historical foundation of legal reforms are clearly understood, attempts at legal reform will risk failure.

In proposing the Janus Law Principle, I wish to stress the importance of looking both backwards into the past as well as ahead into the future, like the Roman god, Janus. Legal reform rarely takes place in a vacuum. It is dangerous to look at ROL programmes as being imposed, *tabula rasa*, as if the host country had no pre-existing legal history or traditions. It is important to understand whether existing laws are being amended, modified, modernized, abolished or replaced with something different. In some cases, certain laws such as bankruptcy or uniform commercial codes may not exist in the first place, and may need to be legislated into law for the first time.

It is important to assess how legal reform measures will affect other areas of the law. How will a new bankruptcy code affect the securitization of bank loans? Will bankruptcy courts or administrative tribunals need to be created if the backlog of cases is too great? Is a bankruptcy code being adopted as part of a host government effort to privatize national industries? More generally, what regulatory regimes and institutions need to be created, or changed, in order to give new legal reforms true meaning and enforceability? Is institution-building and strengthening a vital component of these legal changes? Does it involve a re-education effort so that other government agencies, as well as the private sector, know how to utilize this new legal and institutional framework?

Having looked backwards into the host country's past, it is equally important to examine the development objectives in mapping out its future. What is the purpose of enacting these legal reforms? Is the country under pressure from the IMF or other international institutions to adopt an ROL regime as part of an overall modernization process? Is there pressure from international capital markets to institute structural legal reform of the country's capital markets and stock exchanges? In light of the availability of funds from bilateral and multilateral institutions to underwrite legal reforms, is the host country tempted to enact laws merely for the sake of impressing foreign institutions or potential foreign investors? What forces, from within and without, are compelling legal reform?

Perhaps most importantly, is it the right time for such reforms? Does the requisite political will and government leadership exist to make the proposed legal reforms successful? It is highly unlikely that the political will for effecting real legal change can be conjured up without the critical participation of relevant host government officials, the judiciary, and an educated legal profession. In the case of commercial legal reform, the participation of the business community in the legal reform process may also be a critical factor in ensuring its success.

If sources of critical support for law reform are not solicited, then laws that are enacted purely as 'window dressing' (usually in response to conditionality imposed by outside institutions) will remain unenforced, incompletely understood by the legal profession, and ignored. The final outcome will be frustration and confusion for all parties concerned. Thus, the objectives of legal reform must be clearly articulated, and be politically supported, if catalytic legal change is to occur.

Finally, it is also important to look inward into the society seeking legal transformation. Which segments of the population are urging legal reform? Which segments oppose such reform, and how are their vested interests affected by the proposed measures? Has there been adequate public notice and public debate surrounding the proposed measures? Is coalition and consensus-building part of the overall strategy in the legal reform process? At the same time, the host country may also need to look outward to assess the expectations of the international community with regard to legal reforms being considered by it. Do these measures help the host country integrate into the international community? Is that the objective? Or is the objective a narrow one of simply meeting conditionality in order to be eligible for the next tranche of a World Bank loan? Is the international community, including foreign investors, governments and multilateral financial institutions, involved in and supportive of this reform effort?

The Janus Law Principle is meant to underscore the multifaceted nature of legal reform. It acknowledges both the time and spacial dimensions implicit in legal reform. As far as a timeframe is concerned, its past legal history as well as its motivations for future change should be carefully weighed by the developing country in question. What are the motivations for instituting change, and what sequencing of these proposed changes is the host government considering? How much law needs to be created afresh, and how much needs to be modified from past laws and practices? Perhaps the laws on the books do not need significant revision, but their implementation needs to be overhauled. For example, if excessive or burdensome government permits are required, businesses will be inhibited from growing, and entrepreneurs may be forced to operate 'underground' in the informal sector.[39]

---

[39] See generally, H. de Soto, *The Other Path: The Invisible Revolution in the Third World* (Harper and Row, 1989), which discusses the success of the informal business sector in Peru in the face of abysmal government over-centralization and bureaucracy.

If incorporation is difficult, or the process is expensive, time-consuming or insufficiently transparent, then businesses will have no incentive to incorporate. As a consequence, the host government loses a taxable business entity, and a potential legal employer. Corporate tax income as well as employer/employee income taxes and pensions, the regulation of businesses and the protection of consumers, the environment and other interests are all lost opportunities for the government. In addition, foreign investment opportunities (e.g., joint ventures, equity ownership, or the transfer of technology) may also be lost, since there may be no local, legitimate, legal entity with which to do business.

Thus, the host government needs to determine whether its legal bureaucracy needs to be streamlined (e.g., eliminating excessive registration or other forms which create ripe rent-seeking opportunities). Eliminating excessive and ineffective government regulation may help liberalize the economy, and make the legal process more accessible to greater numbers of people—that is the hope behind most host government deregulation efforts.

Additionally, there is a spatial dimension involved in the Janus Law Principle, since the developing country must assess the domestic and international implications of legal reform measures. ROL reform is a complex domestic political process, so it is important to start off with a clear understanding of what the domestic expectations are for that process. What do individual constituencies, ruling political parties, or other stakeholders in the development process believe the end result of legal reform efforts should be? How are these concerns being articulated? Is there consensus or dissent on critical components of reform measures? Who is vested in reform, and why? Finally, what, if any, international expectations are at stake in the legal reform process? Is the developing country simply responding to international pressures, or is the will to reform an articulated political goal that has broad-based support?

In sum, the Janus Law Principle is meant to be a value-neutral approach by which the developing country comes to terms with its past legal history as well as the future for its legal development. The Janus Law Principle simply sets forth tools of analysis that are organized on a time-space axis to help participants in the development process articulate their needs for and interests in legal reform. The country in question should carefully examine and define its priorities and goals in dealing with both its past and its future, and its role at home and in the world.

There is a strong temptation to use the Hegelian framework of dialectical materialism to define modernization theory as the 'thesis', and dependency theory as the 'antithesis.' This, of course, begs the question of formulating a synthesis, the outlines of which have been sketched out above as the Janus Law Principle. Of course, as both modernization theory and dependency theory are fundamentally Western concepts, the resulting synthesis is not one between Western and non-Western approaches to 'development', but rather one between two distinctly Western modes of analysis. Thus, the Janus Law Principle may be a false or misleading 'synthesis' which merely reconciles two opposing poles of *Western* values.

The Janus Law Principle does not purport to reconcile the modernization approach with, say, Zulu law. Non-Western approaches to law and legal systems development were never truly present at the table for discussion. Thus, the implicit tension between the West and the East (or the North and the South) in terms of their differing approaches to law remains unresolved. Perhaps a real synthesis is no longer possible where post-feudal, non-Western styles of development have been lost to history. If this is the case, there may be no real way for addressing this question adequately. But it is my hope that any underlying tension between 'received law' and indigenous legal traditions can be dealt with openly in a disciplined manner by applying the tenets of the Janus Law Principle. The tools offered by the Janus Law Principle may help develop a fresh perspective on, for example, the implications of Zulu law on the development process in South Africa, and achieving a new, authentic synthesis.

In the final analysis, the Janus Law Principle simply posits the challenge of making deliberate development choices to developing countries. Not all Western norms are good, viable or even inevitable choices for all other non-Western societies. But equally, the deliberate protection of indigenous norms may result, in certain cases, in lost development opportunities, which may be too high a price for a developing country to pay. Development choices must be exercised in a disciplined fashion, and this is a difficult task for any society.

Instituting ROL legal reforms is a daunting task, and should not be lightly undertaken. Of course, Western legal forms, institutions, and laws provide important models and guidance, but it would be a mistake to incorporate such laws and legal approaches without careful consideration of the objectives in undertaking such an exercise. Crude replication, as if by rote, of another country's laws does a great injustice to the continuing and newly defined needs of the developing society, and perpetuates a very backward 'post-colonial' type of thinking. The implementation of such laws is also compromised if the various legal institutions required to support their enforcement do not exist. Western models may be an important starting point, but new definitions and objectives must be iterated, and agreed to in a consensual manner, by the developing country in question. This will take time, and both the host country and the international community must exercise some degree of patience, since achieving consensus is a complex and delicate political process.

If, for example, Romania, based on its civil law tradition, decides to adopt France's commercial law as a model for legal reform, certain important considerations immediately come to mind regarding the use of the French model. First and foremost, there are significant differences between the two countries' economic complexities, stages of economic development and future needs, their populations and their respective skills, the mix of natural and human resources, history and development objectives. Those subtleties may be expressed in the individual 'wrinkles' of the French civil code, which may need substantial modification before it can be considered appropriate in the Romanian context. The French model offers a starting point, not an end result.

Yet, I would even venture to say that adopting the Massachusetts commercial code in Zambia, for example, without changing a word, would be an acceptable approach—*provided* Zambian legislators had dedicated sufficient time and effort to understanding the legal principles and institutional support for the Massachusetts commercial code, and agreed that this approach would be optimal for Zambia. It is also important to note that the Massachusetts legislature fully vetted the commercial code before enacting it into law, and it is an organic document that may be amended, from time to time, in order to reflect the changing needs and priorities of the society that it is meant to serve.

Can traditional law survive in a global legal environment which has no place for alternative approaches to the Western legal model? Should traditional law coexist with Western legal forms, or is it being selected out in an evolutionary process? What other approaches, if any, are viable alternatives to the new hegemony of Western legal concepts and institutions? These, and other, questions are part of the ongoing development challenge for lawyers.

2.2   Interfacing structural legal reform with the financial sector

Rule of Law reform involves a three-step process which incorporates the following: (1) drafting and enacting laws; (2) implementing laws; and (3) enforcing newly enacted laws.

With regard to enacting new laws, draft model codes of other countries, or draft codes that have been developed by multilateral legal organizations or legal consultants, are a starting point. However, the process of drafting and enacting laws is a domestic legislative process for the host country. The success of this essentially political process is heavily dependent on building an internal consensus within the developing country dedicated to financial sector reform. Reforming the legal processes, bureaucracies and management of internal/external financial relations may be a painful and painstaking process, particularly since many vested interests in the host country may be opposed to any proposed change. For example, vested interests such as managers, owners, workers, and the government may now need to accommodate the new needs of private shareholders, minority shareholders, and foreign investors.

Secondly, the implementation of financial sector reform hinges on the delicate, difficult, complex and time-consuming aspects of building a political process which facilitates change. Change can be difficult to assimilate and accept in certain developing societies which may be much more bound to tradition and the *status quo*. The uncertainty introduced by legal changes may also produce confusion and anxiety. Often the implementation of financial sector reforms is predicated on the tension between financial market development and short-term macro-economic needs (e.g., foreign exchange crises, recession, fiscal and balance of payments crises, debt crises, etc.). The overall macro-economic picture may or may not support long-term financial sector reform, thereby creating an additional layer of complexity.

Thirdly, a key component to successful financial sector reform is putting effective and appropriate enforcement mechanisms in place. The promulgation of these regulations must be done openly and fairly, with sufficient access to the process by the interested public, not just by interested parties. In particular, the host government may need to issue and enforce regulations with regard to corporate governance issues. There may be a very imperfect understanding of the duties, responsibilities and liabilities of corporate officers and this may require significant re-education efforts if the reforms are to have any real impact on changing corporate behaviour.

In addition, if the legal rights, duties and responsibilities of the participants in the financial sector are enforced by courts, this poses another set of legal issues. The developing country may need to ensure the existence of an independent, well-informed judiciary that understands the financial system of that country as well as the legal rights and duties flowing therefrom. This may also mean that enforcement may be left to corporations, since private litigation may be prohibitively expensive for individual litigants. Further, there should be equal and fair access to the judicial enforcement of legal rights stemming from financial sector relations—the public should have faith in the legal system.

More generally, the analytical framework for ROL projects/activities should be problem-driven. In developing an ROL agenda, it may be important to design demand-driven reform measures which are responsive to short and long-term goals of the participants in the legal reform process (e.g., the host government, NGOs, and the existing legal profession in the host country). Further, continuing legal education may also be a key component in instituting permanent legal change. The participants, as they become more familiar with the changes introduced by legal reform measures, need to 'own' these new concepts and ways of doing legal business if such measures are to succeed over time. Legal education is a principal means for ensuring a fuller understanding and acceptance of legal reforms.

Upon completing the necessary diagnostic work, it is important to identify constraints to structural legal reform and ROL development. For example, how difficult will it be to remove these constraints? Does the requisite political support for legal change exist, or will it need to be created through coalition-building between various interests? How committed is the host country to implementing change and enforcing a new legal regime? Do the judiciary and the legal profession understand and support the contemplated legal changes? Or, is a serious re-education campaign necessary before such changes can be effectively implemented? These are all serious questions which must be addressed in the design and implementation of any ROL reform programme.

2.3   Good governance

A fundamental ideal of good governance that was established by nineteenth century European liberalism is the principle that the legitimacy of any government is conditioned on the consent of the governed. This principle still determines, in large part, the legitimacy of the power wielded by the modern state. The individual's natural rights and basic freedoms (e.g. of expression, religion and speech) were harnessed in relation to the state by means of a social contract. This relationship of trust between the individual and the state was, however, conditioned on the consent of the governed, rather than upon the absolute right of the sovereign state.

John Locke laid the foundation for our understanding of the liberal, democratic state and argued for the separation of powers between the executive and legislative powers of the state. Locke, and other Enlightenment thinkers, set in motion the powerful and far-reaching idea that the power of the state should be limited by the natural rights and liberties of the individual. (Of course, nineteenth-century political liberalism did not envision such rights for or the participation of women, minorities or even non-propertied classes in this political process.)

This liberal political tradition thus set the stage for an enduring confrontation between the rights of the individual and the arbitrary deprivation of these rights by the state. 'Good governance' was regarded in large part as restraint of the state's exercise of power. This, in turn, has had an enormous influence on the ideas, purposes and processes of 'good governance' in the current debate on democratization, the role of government and participatory development.

Why is development connected to the idea of good governance? More importantly, should it be? As discussed earlier, the view that a pluralistic, civil society is integral to development is part of the modernization approach to development. Nevertheless, integrating the idea of 'good governance' into the development process was not attempted in a systematic way until very recently. The World Bank, for example, did not deal with the issue of 'good governance' until 1989, when it released a report entitled *Sub-Saharan Africa: From Crisis to Sustainable Growth*, which identified the critical importance of governance as it relates to sustainable development.[40] With the fall of the Berlin Wall in 1989, and in the brief period since then there has been a sea-change in strategic thinking for development. Democratization and good governance are now inextricably linked to the Rule of Law regime.

Although the World Bank, under Art. I, §10 of its Articles of Agreement, is expressly prohibited from interfering with the 'political affairs of any member', this has been interpreted by the Bank's General Counsel to mean that, provided governance issues are linked to economic development, the Bank's intervention may be justified.[41] Since the pivotal events of 1989, the World Bank has identified non-economic constraints to development

---

[40] See generally World Bank, *Sub-Saharan Africa: From Crisis to Sustainable Development* (World Bank, 1989). See also *Governance* (World Bank, 1996), p. xiv. In addition, the United Nations Economic Commission for Africa released a report in 1989 entitled *African Alternative Framework for Structural Adjustment Programmes* ((1989) U.N. Doc. E/ECA/CM. 15/16 Rev. 3 at p. 17), which commented on World Bank and IMF structural adjustment programmes, and made the linkage between development and democratic, popular participation.

[41] See J. Cahn, 'Challenging the New Imperial Authority: The World Bank and the Democratization of Development', (1993) 6 *Harv. Hum. Rts. J.* 159 at 164.

stemming from public sector mismanagement, corruption, poor financial accountability and practices, poor environmental regulation, and a poor legal and regulatory framework.[42] By 1996, the World Bank's report entitled *Governance* identified the following four major components of governance: (1) public sector management, (2) accountability, (3) the legal framework for development and (4) transparency and information.[43]

'Good governance' involves measures to address corruption, transparency in the political process, accountability of public officials and standards of public sector management. The lack of good governance creates waste and corruption, and tends to compromise the entire development process. This can result in a crisis of confidence in both the developing country and in external institutions attempting to contribute to the development of the host country in question. Democratization is intended to encourage transparency and openness in the governance process, as well as better access to the means of governance by the general public, and greater accountability of elected representatives.

A democratic form of governance also provides a forum in which the individual may express his/her political will. Just as the individual may express his free will in the marketplace by choosing what to buy (or not to buy), this freedom is mirrored in the political world where the individual is given the means for making independent political choices. Thus, the individual has a greater stake in the governance process, and this in turn creates the potential for engaging in a more participatory development process.

---

[42] See *ibid.*, p. 164. Indeed, it may be argued that the World Bank has lagged behind the times, since this conclusion was reached in the 1970s by the US government, for example, which began funding programmes ('non-projectized assistance') in support of institutional and legal reforms aimed at overcoming non-economic, systemic problems. For example, poor administration of justice was regarded as a key impediment to the development process in Latin America and the Caribbean, resulting in the passage of section 534 of the Foreign Assistance Act of 1961, as amended (P.L. 87-195, 75 Stat. 424), as codified at 22 USC §2346c (1997).

[43] *Governance* (World Bank, 1996), p. xiii. Stung by criticism of its lending practices to members with abysmal human rights records, autocratic forms of government and rampant corruption, the World Bank re-examined the issue of good governance as a critical factor in the development process.

In 1991 the General Counsel to the World Bank, Mr Ibrahim Shihata, issued a legal memorandum to the Bank's Executive Directors which defined five areas falling outside the Bank's mandate as expressed in its Articles of Association: (1) the Bank cannot be influenced by the political character of its members; (2) it cannot interfere with the partisan politics of its members; (3) it cannot influence a member based on the desires of an industrialized member of the Bank; (4) it cannot be influenced by political factors which do not have a preponderant economic effect; and (5) its staff cannot be influenced by the possible political reaction of a Bank member. See 'Issues of "Governance" in Its Borrowing Members: The Extent of their Relevance Under the Bank's Articles of Agreement' (21 December 1991), cited in Ibrahim Shihata, *The World Bank in a Changing World* (World Bank) p. 54, note 4. A discussion paper followed the issuance of Mr Shihata's legal memorandum, 'Managing Development: The Governance Dimension' (26 June 1991), also cited in *ibid.*, p. 54, note 4.

Democracy, by providing the means for articulating diverse and, at times, conflicting views and interests in the governance process, tends to encourage political pluralism. Indeed, a democratic means of governance can give women, minorities, or disenfranchised elements of the population a chance to voice their views in the political process. Of course, a democracy provides an opportunity, not a guarantee, that such voices will be heard.

Participatory development—empowering the disenfranchised, disadvantaged or indigenous groups, women and minorities—is often cited as an essential part of creating a strong civil society. The equitable participation of all segments of a society has the potential to make everyone a stakeholder in the development process. Participatory development, as underscored by a strong democratic element, establishes a vital link to a Rule of Law regime.

Democratization, of course, posits the familiar debate of whether the state should wield its power in a mildly autocratic manner (with the good of its people in mind) in order to achieve economic prosperity quickly, or whether the equal participation of all segments of the population should be encouraged even at the cost of slowing the development process. Is true development the speedy economic improvement in the living conditions of as many people as possible, or is achieving a democratic society part of the journey towards development? Should development include more than economic prosperity by incorporating the political and social freedoms available to the individual as well? In other words, should democracy be viewed as the icing on the cake, or the cake itself?

Each society must make its own choice in this matter; there simply is no formulaic approach. Moreover, there is no predictable nexus between democratization and economic growth. The 'soft' authoritarian regimes of South-east Asia, for example, have achieved strong economic growth with a minimum of pluralistic democracy. China has clearly achieved fierce economic competitiveness in the world market without the benefit of Western-style democratic institutions, elections or ruling parties. In contrast, India's strong democratic tradition has not led to such overwhelming economic success.

Nevertheless, there is some evidence that economic prosperity may lead to more democratic forms of governance, as in Chile's case, where General Pinochet's military regime instituted critical financial sector reforms, and was ultimately replaced by a democratic form of government in 1980. Political liberalization does not necessarily follow economic liberalization, but an argument for this can be made based on the examples of Taiwan, South Korea and Argentina.[44]

2.4 The changing role of the state

An ROL agenda, as discussed above, is political in nature, and must be implemented, at least in large part, by the host government. Reforming the

---

[44] See L. Cao, *supra* n. 8, p. 558.

legal infrastructure of a country, however, implicitly requires a redefinition of the role of the state. This redefinition, whether slight or fundamental, may involve a painful readjustment. Four roles of the state are critically important in the context of an ROL reform programme: the state as provider, the state as entrepreneur, the state as regulator and the state as the administrator of justice.

First, the state is generally responsible for providing public services, redistributing wealth on some equitable basis, and establishing social safety nets in areas such as welfare, medical care and pensions. Most states world-wide have mechanisms for redistributing income among their citizens and residents in order to provide a minimum living standard for all (although clearly this is very problematic in highly impoverished developing nations, and is more true of highly industrialized states). Nevertheless, the state assumes a role in mitigating the harshness of capitalism in simple recognition of the fact that not everyone in a society is able to be a successful entrepreneur. Additional help in obtaining certain basic necessities in life (e.g., social welfare benefits, medical benefits, housing, pensions) is generally guaranteed by the state. The state plays a central role in deciding what type of social safety nets to provide.

Secondly, in many developing countries the state has often acted as the sole entrepreneur by nationalizing industries and taking responsibility for economic production in strategic sectors (e.g., transportation, telecommunications, heavy industry). The role of the state as entrepreneur will be discussed at length later in this text, but it is clear that the wave of whole-sale privatization occurring across the developing world, particularly in Latin America and Asia, is an indication that a serious transformation of this role is now underway. The state in much of the developing world is clearly moving out of economic production and into the role of regulating the economy.

Thirdly, many developing nations and transitional economies are rethinking their role in terms of regulating the economy rather than being the principal economic agent. The under-regulation of capital markets, in particular, has been a serious problem, and highlights the need for the state to be more proactive in managing and regulating the economy, along with other vital sectors such as the environment, food and drugs, and health.

Finally, with regard to the state as the administrator of justice, this role cannot, in practical terms, be delegated to the private sector. To do so would effectively involve 'justice' being bought from a private company. There are, however, serious problems with the administration of justice in many developing countries which are now taking the initiative in creating alternate dispute resolution mechanisms, and strengthening their judicial capacity so that the delivery of justice can be both speedy and effective. Many Latin American countries, for example, are taking measures to address the crisis of public confidence in their criminal justice systems. Renewed attention is being paid to the transparency of the justice system, its accessibility to the lay person, and the accountability of public officials who are responsible for delivering justice.

2.5 A template for ROL legal analysis

Table 1.1: ROL legal analysis template

	Good Governance	*State as Provider*	*State as Entrepreneur*	*State as Regulator*	*State as the Administrator of Justice*
Rule of Law (ROL) programmes — Building a civil society	Encouraging NGO development; parliamentary reform; controlling corruption; liberalized and modernized legal education; public–private partnerships				
Structural legal reform		Social safety issues (e.g., welfare, medical and pension benefits)	Privatization; strengthening the private sector	Drafting new laws and regulations; legislating new regulatory institutions;	
Administration of justice					New courts; greater transparency, accountability, accessibility; judicial reform; alternative dispute resolution

3. A SUMMATION

The matrix in Table 1.2 is designed to give a quick overview of the interface between a Rule of Law regime and good governance issues. In light of the above discussion, the matrix is divided into three components: (1) good governance (building a civil society and parliamentary reform); (2) structural legal reform (commercial law reform, privatization, capital market development, decentralization, and microfinance); and (3) the administration of justice (legislative drafting, legal education, improving court administration, criminal justice reform, and judicial capacity building). This matrix is, however, illustrative rather than exhaustive in nature.

Table 1.2: ROL matrix

Good Governance	*Structural Legal Reform*	*Administration of Justice*
A. Building a civil society	**A. Commercial law reform (revision and modernization)**	**A. Legislative drafting**

• NGO capacity building
 • NGO registration
 • NGO tax exemptions
	• contract/company law
	   • corporate governance
	   • ADR for commercial disputes
	   • joint venture laws
	 • property law
	   • land titling and registration
	   • restitution or compensation
	 • banking
	   • commercial and central bank reform
	   • prudential supervision
	   • audit/reports
	   • foreign exchange and currency controls
	 • securities exchange and commodities laws
	   • establish stock exchanges
	   • broker–dealer rules
	   • foreign investment
	 • bankruptcy code
	 • secured transactions
	 • antitrust
		• legislative drafting
		 • codification, promulgation, distribution of laws
		 • modernize law libraries
		 • computerize legal data bases
		 • publish and computerize judicial opinions for retrieval

Table 1.2:   (Cont'd)

Good Governance	Structural Legal Reform	Administration of Justice
	• public procurement • uniform commercial code • tax reform (corporate) • intellectual property rights • environment • regulatory framework for above legal reform measures	

• Labour organization
  • trade unions
  • worker cooperatives
  • collective bargaining training
• Media and journalism
• Free press
• Investigative journalism
• Watchdog function
	B. Privatization
	
	• pre-privatization work
	  • privatization scheme/sequencing
	  • valuation of SOEs
	  • legislative framework (e.g., transition of state from productive sectors to regulation of economy)
		B. Legal education
		
		• judicial training
		• training prosecutors, public defenders, criminal investigators, police
		• law school curricula reform (include new legal subjects)
		• bar associations (continuing legal education for practising lawyers)

• Human Rights monitoring and reporting • Local community development • Mediation training • Municipal development	**C. Capital market development** • removal of market entry barriers • savings mobilization • pension reform and privatization • create investment vehicles (e.g., mutual funds) • tax incentives to invest in capital market • encourage public-private partnerships • project finance for capital infrastructure growth	**C. Improve court administration** • computerize case docketing • provide legal advocacy and free legal representation • publish opinions • improve infrastructure (e.g., build new courthouses, improve jails)

Table 1.2:   (Cont'd)

Good Governance	Structural Legal Reform	Administration of Justice
B. Parliamentary reform • Electoral system reform	**D. Decentralization** • municipal finance • local governance • small business development	**D. Criminal justice reform** • ensure due process, equality before law, civil rights • legal access creation (legal clinics, legal NGOs, public defender services)
• Constitutional reform: separation of powers between executive and judicial branches	**E. Microfinance**	**E. Judicial capacity building**

• Voter registration
  • local election monitoring
  • voter education
  • computerization of voter rolls and votes
	• small business development
	• microenterprise for women
	• create credit unions, bank cooperatives
	• local institutional building
	• create special financial intermediaries (e.g., mutual funds, insurance companies, investment funds)
	• special government bond and credit guarantees
		• form anti-crime task forces
		• curb corruption
		• institute civil service reform
		• explore ADR, mediation and arbitration as legal recourse

• Education on free assembly and speech		
• Legislative research and computerization of draft legislation		
• Training legislators on parliamentary skills (especially women) • legislative drafting skills		

• Establish libraries
  • computerized data bases
  • Internet links		

• Campaign reform		
• Proportional representation • constituency building		

Most ROL programmes and initiatives are undertaken with the objective of changing the legal infrastructure to better support modern political and economic institutions. Encouraging a more pluralistic society, supporting NGO growth and registration, and giving a political voice to under-represented segments of the population are fundamental building blocks of creating a civil society that supports democratic institutions.

In terms of creating a broad base of support for a more open civil society, the involvement of the participants in the legal system is vitally important. This means a re-education of lawyers, judges, prosecutors, public defenders, criminal investigators, and the police. Reforming law school curricula to assimilate new areas of the law may also be an essential step in revitalizing the legal system.

In addition, the legal education effort should include business groups, professional associations and other civic groups so that broad-based changes to the legal system are understood and supported by interested policy-makers and legal system participants. The deregulation of the legal process through the involvement of such civic groups will help create the ground for forging new public-private partnerships. There may be many opportunities for such partnerships in the area of municipal governance programmes, NGO development in the legal arena, and establishing legal clinics to provide greater access to the legal system by the general public.

Structural legal reform is perhaps the most difficult and problematic, and requires the most focused attention by participants in the process (e.g., legislators, government officials, judges, local bar associations). Legal drafting and the implementation of new laws through regulatory schemes and institutions has been discussed above, and will not be reiterated here.

Finally, in terms of the administration of justice, many developing countries need to devote a great deal of work to reforming the judiciary. Substantial technical assistance, in the form of new courthouses, information database retrieval, computerized systems for case docketing and reporting, renovation and modernization of legal libraries, and legal information retrieval, may be required in this effort. Further, case management so that cases are speedily disposed of through formal or informal judicial procedures (e.g., alternative dispute resolution, mediation, and arbitration) are avenues which may need to be explored and institutionalized. Substantial financial outlays may be necessary for implementing these changes, which will require a great deal of political support.

Overall, the legal system may also need to deal with a public crisis of confidence in the ability of the legal system to deliver justice. Therefore, substantial work may be needed to control corruption and eliminate rent-seeking opportunities, and generally making the legal system more open, transparent and accountable for its actions. Meaningful ethics enforcement of government officials, for example, may also need to be initiated to create future confidence in the integrity of public officials.

Nearly all ROL programmes and good governance initiatives fit into this template. Individual case studies will provide the empirical base for deriving 'lessons learned' and 'best practices'. This empirical analysis of the avalanche of ROL programmes initiated since 1989 is the next wave of legal analysis.[45] Once completed, this analysis will reveal whether the principles of legal reform, as outlined above, are suppotted by real world experience.

---

[45] One type of approach to this analysis is to establish an empirical linkage between the laws and the financial markets. One such attempt was made by R. La Porta, F. Lopez De Silanes, A. Shleifer and R. Vishny, 'Legal Determinants of External Finance', (1997) 52 *J. Finance* 1131, which found that common law countries legally protect the rights of shareholders and creditors the most, French civil law countries protect them the least, and German/Scandinavian countries fell somewhere in the middle. *Ibid.*, p. 1132.

2. Development Law: Substantive Principles

The preceding chapter outlined the theoretical foundations and conflicts inherent in a discussion of development law. This chapter will outline the contours of development law as a new legal discipline. A transition to this new discipline, however, requires a movement away from the terminology of 'law and development'. As the scholarly literature on the subject definitively concludes, the Law and Development movement, its intellectual adherents, and its viability as a legal doctrine have long been defunct.[1]

It would be a critical error, both intellectually and pragmatically, to remain wedded to this terminology or the intellectual underpinnings of the Law and Development approach to legal systems development. Moreover, there is an implicit stigma attached to legal disciplines that are described in a conjunctive fashion such as 'law and development', 'law and literature' or 'law and the rights of women'. Development law has moved past the conjunctive stage, and has come of age.

Further, development law should also be distinguished from the tradition of the 'international law of development' popularized during the 1970s as part of the NIEO agenda. The international law of development approach advocated a constructive change in the relations between the developed and the developing worlds by attempting to establish, *inter alia*, a 'right to development' as a new human right.

In light of past inequities, the international law of development also attempted to radically restructure the relationship between the developed and developing worlds by supporting developing countries' preferred access to credit, development assistance, trade relations, and technology transfers. In so doing, the international law of development established differential legal norms which separated advanced industrial countries from developing nations.

---

[1] See L. Cao, Review of *Law and Economic Development: A New Beginning?* (1997) 32 *Tex. Int'l L.J.* 545 at 546; see also D. Trubek, 'Back to the Future: The Short, Happy Life of the Law and Society Movement', (1990) 18 *Fla. St. U. L. Rev.* 1; D. Trubek and M. Galanter, 'Scholars In Self-Estrangement: Some Reflections on the Crisis in Law and Development Studies in the United States', (1974) *Wis. L. Rev.* 1062.

A differential norm has been described as 'a norm that on its face provides different, presumably more advantageous, standards for one set of states than for another set.'[2] Not only is this type of legal distinction politically controversial and inherently unfair, but it also became untenable and, ultimately, failed to move the development agenda forward. Indeed, the international law of development stagnated over time, eventually becoming extinct. Development law must move beyond its related, historical antecedents into a new global age.

Development law is no longer a mere 'paradigm' with which to explain breathtaking new changes in global legal development. Jonathan Cahn writes:

The case studies suggest that we are not watching the emergence of a new legal field. A legal field typically is a classificatory designation, based on compartmentalizing groups of legal rules in terms of the categories of conduct intended to be directed: Corporations law, contract law, tort law, criminal law, constitutional law, and property law are all different fields in this sense. A more appropriate analogy is to a new mode of analysis or 'paradigm'. Thomas Kuhn in *The Structure of Scientific Revolutions* describes a scientific paradigm as the structure of fundamental assumptions within which scientists conduct their empirical research and organize and articulate their perceptions. It defines a scientific tradition by creating consensus about the appropriate 'methods' and the 'legitimate problems' within the 'research field'. Development, governance, transactions, and enabling environments represent a new empirical tradition in the law, defining a new array of 'legitimate problems' and appropriate 'methods'.[3]

This statement was published in 1993, and much has happened since then. Development law has moved beyond a shared set of assumptions about a field of legal inquiry. It is no longer merely an empirical exploration of legal questions within the development context. Professor Cao dryly observes that, '[r]ather than wallowing in self-criticism, law and development scholars should work to institute a legal regime that promotes the principled application of law in the developing world.'[4] Development law is, hopefully, the response to that challenge.

Development law has taken shape in the form of underlying constitutional principles and substantive legal principles which are still evolving. It does, however, need a better focused institutional framework within which to further define these principles and enforce the rights created thereunder. This is not to say that development law has taken its final, or even definitive, shape at this stage. Nevertheless it has emerged as a new legal discipline, although much work needs to be done before its acceptance is secured by the wider legal community.

---

[2] D.B. Magraw, 'Legal Treatment of Developing Countries: Differential, Contextual, and Absolute Norms', (1990) 1 *Colo. J. Int'l Envtl. L & Pol'y* 69 at 73.

[3] J. Cahn, 'Challenging the New Imperial Authority: The World Bank and the Democratization of Development', (1993) 6 *Harv. Hum. Rts. J.* 159 at 193, note 149, citing T.S. Kuhn, *The Structure of Scientific Revolutions*, 2nd edn. (1970), p. 10. Copyright (1993) by the President and Fellows of Harvard College.

[4] L. Cao, *supra* n. 1, p. 553.

Development law is a newcomer to the legal scene, and a certain amount of time will need to elapse before it will be regarded with the same legitimacy as other branches of international law, such as those relating to foreign investments or foreign exchange. However, it is important to remember that even these latter legal subjects were not rooted in ancient legal practices, but have very modern genealogies in legislation passed within the past 50 years or so.

This is not to say that legal reform initiatives did not exist before this time. Indeed, certain law reform efforts are heavily steeped in the history of the Romans, the Napoleonic conquests, the 'received law' traditions of the Russians and the British, and even in the legal modernization efforts of the Turks. Development law, however, differs significantly from these historical law reform movements insofar as it is not truly connected with formal, imperial or military conquests. Development law is a response to recent trends in globalization that is overwhelming both in terms of its volume and its overall significance. Thus, development law represents a change, in degree and in kind, in legal systems on a global scale.

The legitimacy of development law as a legal discipline should be judged not by its relative age, but by the legal principles that give it character, meaning and applicability to the dynamic and fast-changing world in which we live. Indeed, development law is meant to respond to the pressures being exerted by the entire globalization process, and the need to articulate, promulgate and implement organizing legal principles around those needs. Development law bridges the elusive gap between the laws of the developed and the developing worlds.

Indeed, development law builds a bridge between the respective bodies of law that affect development issues, including contract and company law, property, securities, commodities, banking, secured transactions, bankruptcy, intellectual property rights, antitrust, criminal law and international law, to name but a few. Development law does not provide new 'black-letter' law on these subjects, but sets up a new frame of reference in which to evaluate, assess and judge the impact of such national laws in a global economy. In other words, development law is a subset of the above-delineated topics of substantive legal inquiry, and specifically addresses the development-related impact of these, and other, legal subjects.

Development law also goes beyond the traditional confines of private and public dimensions of international law. In a global economy, for instance, it may not be sufficient to simply rely on choice of law provisions in contractual agreements between private parties. Such agreements may not exist. Development law, by applying legal principles in situations where there is an absence of an agreement, an absence of privity of contract, and, indeed, an absence of law, helps bridge this gap.

Finally, 'development' is not simply a process which takes place with sovereign states as the primary, if not exclusive, actors. Development is a complex process, with many stakeholders with diverse and conflicting interests. The development process should be as widely participatory as possible. It cannot be seen as the exclusive prerogative exercised by sovereign states, especially in light of the critical role of the private sector in creating sustainable development options. Moreover, many of the tenets of development law will emerge from, and as a result of, private transactional law practice. International transactions taking place in the private sector are fundamentally shaping both the substance and the form of development law.

The following discussion will (1) set forth the organizing, or 'constitutional', principles underlying development law, (2) explain the substantive content and application of development law principles and (3) discuss the institutional framework for enforcing the rights, duties and responsibilities created under this new legal discipline. Development law uses a problem-driven methodology so that the application of its rules and precepts helps resolve actual development problems. The ideas expressed herein provide a synthesis of what has been taking place over the past decade, which now requires a baptism by fire.

1. ESTABLISHING THE PARAMETERS OF DEVELOPMENT LAW

First, it is important to define a development law question, distinguishing it from other types of non-development-related legal questions. Not all legal issues are actually development law questions. Where does the distinction lie? If, for example, a private citizen files a tax return, and the national tax authority questions certain exemptions claimed therein, this poses a tax question under the law of that nation on whether a lawful tax exemption has been claimed.

If, however, this private national is working in Kazakhstan as an independent consultant, and files a UK tax return, and is also assessed local taxes, this may raise a question of public international law. This international tax question may depend, in part, on whether a mutual tax treaty exists between the United Kingdom and Kazakhstan, and what provision is made therein for the income tax treatment of foreign nationals who are not entitled to diplomatic privileges and immunities. In the event that Kazakhstan's tax regime does not address this matter adequately, or conflicts with the international tax regime in place to address such issues, this raises a development law question if it effectively impedes Kazakhstan from dealing with this legal issue in a coherent, predictable manner. In other words, Kazakhstan may need to pass new tax laws, revise existing ones, or enter into an appropriate international tax protocol to address the new reality of foreign consultants providing professional services in-country.

Distinguishing development law questions from private international law questions may not be easy, since implications of both may be present in any given fact scenario. The distinction between an international legal issue and a development law question may be drawn by asking the following question: does a domestic law question of a developing country have a foreseeable impact on the development of that country? For example, if the host country wishes to build a seaport in order to boost its overall economic development, this does not necessarily raise a specific development law question. If, however, the host country is building a seaport using project finance that involves joint ventures with foreign operators and requires that a new foreign investment regime be put in place, then development law questions do arise.

Similarly, the issue of whether women should have the right to the legal custody of their children following a separation from the marital domicile may pose a family law issue under domestic law, or an international human rights question, or, if legal reform of existing family law is contemplated in order to change the legal status of women, a development law question.

Alternatively, an international law question having a direct or indirect impact on the economic or social development of one party may also raise a development law question. For example, the extraterritorial application of US federal copyright laws to impose penalties for the unlawful duplication of CDs in Singapore may simply pose a question of private remedies under international law. If, however, there is an issue of whether a country will agree to comply with an international intellectual property rights regime which may actually affect its national output in a critical manufacturing sector, this may pose a development law question. With the increasing globalization of the world economy, the impact of development law questions may not solely affect developing countries. Repercussions are being felt in unexpected ways by advanced, industrial countries whose stake in 'development' is inching higher.

As development law covers such a vast array of legal questions, the scope of this examination of development law principles must necessarily be narrowed. As the engine of the global economy is fuelled by the exchange of capital, commodities and technology, for purposes of the discussion below, the examination of development law principles will be confined to three principal areas: cross-border financing, trade, and technology transfers. These exchanges have important Rule of Law implications which will be explored below.

It is important to set out the framework of development law by first, identifying the actors in and parties to the development process; secondly, defining the rights, privileges, duties and responsibilities of these actors; thirdly, defining the contours of the substantive legal principles of development law; and finally, describing the institutional framework in which these rights and responsibilities are implemented and enforced.

2.   PARTIES UNDER DEVELOPMENT LAW

The actors in the development process who are ultimately affected by the principles of development law fall into three categories: private, state and institutional. Private actors within the development law rubric are composed of individuals, local and international NGOs, and other private entities such as corporations, associations and cooperatives.

Secondly, there are state actors. Although it is customary under NIEO principles and related doctrines to divide sovereign actors into developed and developing countries, I argue that this distinction is misleading and anachronistic. As discussed earlier, global capitalism which we have seen develop over the past decade is creating a more level playing field between the advanced industrial states and the developing ones. The economic distinctions between these two categories of states are in constant flux, and do not represent a viable legal distinction for the purposes of development law. A further danger is posed by the perpetuation of legal distinctions in the rights and liabilities of state actors: this may create more inequities over time, thus impeding rather than furthering the development process.

The equal treatment of sovereign actors regardless of their respective economic status is more equitable, fair, and sustainable in the long run. This is especially so since many developing countries are 'graduating' from their 'developing country' status, so these distinctions tend to create a more confused picture over time. For example, the Czech Republic, now considered to be a 'transitional economy', may in five years' time be an industrialized state with 'First World' status. Therefore, to treat the Czech Republic differently because of its current status as a 'developing' country may be confusing and misleading.

The third set of actors are institutional players such as multilateral banks like the International Bank for Reconstruction and Development (i.e., the World Bank), and regional banks such as the European Bank for Reconstruction and Development, the Asian Development Bank and the Inter-American Development Bank. Also included in this category are other international organizations such as the United Nations Development Programme, and international financial institutions such as the International Monetary Fund and the International Finance Corporation.

Bilateral aid agencies such as ODA and USAID, and export finance agencies such as JEXIM, are generally considered to be state actors since such government agencies tend to implement their country's official aid policies and assistance to developing countries. However, these bilateral lending institutions share characteristics of multilateral lending institutions such as the World Bank. Depending on the context, bilateral institutions may be grouped under the second category of state actors as discussed above, or may fall into the third category of institutional actors.

In different ways, these three categories of actors are the 'stakeholders' in the development process. The rights and responsibilities of each are discussed below.

2.1   The rights and privileges of individual actors

The issue of whether there is an individual right to development is discussed at length in Chapter 6, and will not be reiterated here except to conclude that such a right will not be recognized on an international scale for a long time to come.[5] Although it may be concluded that there is no

---

[5] See L. Cao, *supra* n. 1, p. 556.

affirmative right to development, there is nevertheless an inchoate right to become a stakeholder in the development process.

This inchoate right can be analogized to the right to run for public office. This right is not constitutionally or legally guaranteed, but if this option is exercised, it cannot be arbitrarily withdrawn from a qualified individual. Similarly, a stakeholder in a development question has the right to actively participate in the development process. However, in order to make his or her grievances heard, or to seek redress, a stakeholder needs to establish a nexus to or an interest in the outcome of a development law question, akin to establishing his or her standing as a party in a legal action. Once this nexus is firmly established, then a stakeholder may bring complaints, grievances, seek redress, compensation, restitution, and other remedies.

In more general terms, a stakeholder (for instance, a farmer who is being displaced by a dam project) can seek to make the decision-makers in the dam project accountable for their actions. Such decision-makers may include local and national government officials, official lenders such as the World Bank and perhaps, ultimately, commercial banks and other private financiers. The means by which the rights of stakeholders in the development process may be pursued will be addressed later.

Finally, the issue of whether privileges should be accorded to certain private actors within the development law context is a tricky matter. There may be legal justification to establish special protectorates in order to preserve 'human habitats' to help certain indigenous peoples maintain their traditional lifestyles. If special privileges were accorded for this purpose, it would mean that such peoples would be entitled to certain legal exemptions and other entitlements not available to the general populace. The establishment of such protectorates, and the certification of 'indigenous peoples' for this and related purposes, if deemed necessary, can be done under the auspices of the United Nations.

Indeed, the UN's work on indigenous peoples has a long history. The UN Commission on Human Rights has received expressions of support for establishing a permanent UN forum for indigenous peoples, and for drafting a declaration of the rights of indigenous peoples, who are too often left out of the development debate.[6] The Commission's principal subsidiary, the Subcommission on Prevention of Discrimination and Protection of Minorities, established a Working Group on Indigenous Populations in 1982. The Working Group celebrated the twentieth anniversary of the First International Conference to Counter Discrimination Against Indigenous People on 25 July 1997, attracting more than 700 people from over 50 countries.[7]

This Working Group has already drafted a declaration on the rights of indigenous peoples which is now being reviewed by the Commission.[8] This draft, and related protocols, may be used to set forth 'privileges' to which

---

[6] See UN Press Release HR/CN/733, 12 April 1996.
[7] See UN Press Release HR/4332, 25 July 1997.
[8] See UN Press Release HR/CN/733, 12 April 1996.

indigenous peoples should be entitled under the principles of development law. The procedure for establishing such privileges must be carefully defined, vetted and consensually agreed to by the affected parties, however, before doctrinaire pronouncements can be offered on the subject.

2.2   The duties and responsibilities of sovereign actors

The development process must be open and transparent if it is to be regarded as legitimate. It must be accessible to the general public, and must allow for equitable participation in the development process. An essential ingredient in ensuring an open and transparent development process is that government officials, and other decision-makers, must be held accountable for their actions. This reduces the risk of arbitrary action in the development process.

Further, by increasing the accountability and predictability of the overall development process, the 'comfort level' of the participants is increased. Participants will feel vested in the process of development if they know that their contributions are valid, and may have a significant impact on the eventual outcome. This may ensure their continued future participation in the development process. The articulation of rights, interests and views within the development process does not dissipate the momentum of development, but rather gives it the potential for expressing the needs of the people truly affected by its eventual outcome. This, in turn, further ensures the legitimacy of the development process for all stakeholders.

The principles set forth above are the supporting pillars for the entire structure of development law. These constitutional principles define the framework of the development process: openness, transparency, accessibility and accountability. In other words, these are the 'constitutional rights' of the stakeholders in the development process. Stakeholders need not be individuals, since these constitutional rights are not 'human' rights as such. Stakeholders, whether they be individuals, private NGOs, corporate entities, sovereign states or public institutional actors, are entitled to certain minimum guarantees of transparency and legitimacy in the development process. Ensuring that these constitutional principles are adequately protected and upheld is, however, a duty which must be assumed by sovereign and institutional actors in the development process.

Of course, sovereign and institutional actors may argue that information concerning development choices is subject to 'executive-type' privileges protecting secret, sensitive and strategic national interests which may be adversely affected by the disclosure of such information.[9] States may further argue that releasing this type of non-public information will

---

[9] See e.g., Articles of Agreement of the International Monetary Fund, Art. IX, §. 3 which grants the IMF immunity from judicial process, unless the IMF waives this immunity, and §. 7 which provides the IMF with the right to assert a privilege for its communications. See also Articles of Agreement of the International Bank for Reconstruction and Development, Art. VII §§3–7, 60 Stat. 1440, 2 U.N.T.S. 134, Art. III, §§3–7.

mean relinquishing a sovereign right to protect their national security interests.

While the exercise of such privileges is integral to the smooth functioning of government, and governance by international organizations involved with development, such privileges should be exercised with discretion in appropriate situations.[10] It might well be counter-argued that development questions pose the most appropriate context for inviting public participation in an open debate concerning development options which can, and should, be exercised. Indeed, the role of sovereignty may need some rethinking in the development law context:

Sovereignty in international law indeed is no longer the descendant of the eighteenth-century divine right of kings. Sovereignty now is the power by which a nations defines itself and enables an entire body politic to exercise some control over its destiny, to promote the general welfare, and to determine the terms on which it will live with scarcity, address deprivation, and redress disparities and injustices. Sovereignty is subject to the right of each individual and of the body politic to give informed consent to governance.[11]

The use of sovereignty, or executive privileges, to block public participation impairs the legitimacy of the development process. The more inaccessible the decision-making process is, the less accountable the officials of governments and international organizations are. If development-related decisions are viewed as being made in 'Star Chamber' secrecy, there is no transparency, accessibility or accountability. Further, there is no way to predict the outcome of such deliberations, since there are no defining principles to govern the decision-making process. The constitutional backbone of the development process is thereby damaged.

For example, following the Mexican peso crisis of 1994–95, US Treasury Secretary Robert Rubin urged G-7 nations (now the G-8, with the inclusion of Russia) and the developing world to agree to more stringent disclosure standards for financial data.[12] Rubin argued that if international investors had known the extent to which Mexico's financial situation had been compromised, stricter fiscal discipline would have been

---

[10] Articles of Agreement of the International Bank for Reconstruction and Development, Art. V §2(f), provides that the Board of Executive Directors may adopt regulations, as necessary, to protect the confidentiality of the Bank's business.

Such internal regulations are given effect through the local law of the Bank's members. The United States, for example, under §. 11 of the Bretton Woods Agreements Act, as codified at 22 U.S.C. §286(h) (1988), specifies that the World Bank has the same rights to confidentiality under US law as are accorded under its Articles of Agreement. See also Exec. Order No. 12.356, 3 C.F.R. Sec. 166 (1982), reprinted in 50 U.S.C. §401 (1988). Although the necessity of protecting the confidentiality of the World Bank's operations may be necessary, at times, it should not be overused in a way that masks the accountability of its officials, or clouds the legitimacy of its policies and procedures.

[11] J. Cahn, *supra* n. 3, p. 187.

[12] D.E. Sanger, 'Rubin to Press Central Banks to Disclose Financial Data', *New York Times*, 19 September 1997, p. C5.

imposed on Mexico sooner, thereby avoiding a full-blown crisis. (Mexico's financial crisis is discussed in further detail in Chapter 3.)

The same issue was raised during the Asian currency crisis—the Thai government, for example, kept certain financial data secret.[13] Central banks do report the amounts of their foreign exchange reserves, but tend not to release information concerning their own intent to use those reserves to buy or sell currencies. This could be potentially misleading since the amount of actual reserves available may be overstated, as in Thailand's case.[14] Arguably, if this information had been revealed earlier, the financial crisis which took international investors by surprise might have been averted.

Secretary Rubin's proposal to adopt new disclosure rules through the IMF could, if implemented, exert pressure on non-disclosing countries to comply as well. Failure to disclose pertinent financial data under this proposal may result in non-complying countries being charged a 'risk premium',[15] thus significantly increasing their cost of obtaining loans. This proposal would also force commercial bankers to report their non-performing assets, which could help avert severe financial problems.

The failure to disclose such financial data in a timely manner can precipitate a deep financial crisis, as in Japan's case, where non-performing bank loans have been kept well hidden.[16] Thus, there is an argument to be made that withholding financial data which central banks, and even commercial banks, guard jealously does not necessarily facilitate the development process, and may even seriously compromise it. The need for secrecy and the need to protect sensitive financial information should be better balanced against the public need for disclosure in order to ensure the stability and transparency of financial markets.

2.3   Duty to cooperate

The international law of development of the 1970s failed to establish a viable 'human right to development', as mentioned above and discussed at length in Chapter 6. As there is no individual 'right to development', there is also no independent 'right to development' which may be exercised by developing states. Certainly, development options may be vigorously pursued by developing states, but no right to development as such exists as international normative law.

Although the NIEO agenda advocated the preferential treatment of developing nations, the attempt was not successful. This means, in effect, that developing countries have no right to borrow funds, no right to preferred access to credit (or concessional credit), no right of preferred access to technology transfers, no right to be granted preferential trade terms or most favoured nation status, no right to receive development

---

[13] *Ibid.*
[14] D.E. Sanger, *supra* n. 12, p. C5.
[15] *Ibid.*
[16] *Ibid.*

assistance, and no right to receive such assistance free of 'conditionality' imposed by the lender.

Developing countries are, thus, not granted a special or different legal status by virtue of their 'underdevelopment'. Development law makes no legal distinction between developed and developing countries, and by so doing helps establish the legal parity between both. By eliminating differential norms which prescribe unequal treatment among developing and developed countries, development law helps establish a more level playing field between the two.

While developing countries may not be entitled to preferential legal treatment or special status under the principles of development law, there is nevertheless a mutual duty to cooperate in the development process. The duty to cooperate should be imposed equally on industrialized and developing states alike. This simply means that both developed and developing nations should bargain with each other in good faith, and facilitate, where practicable, the development of other nations. More importantly, the act of cooperating with each other is more than joint or simultaneous action, it is the unity of action to a common end or common result.[17] The common end result is the development of all nations.

2.4 Procedural safeguards

In practical terms, developing states and institutional actors may need to establish the following: (1) certain procedural safeguards, such as public hearings for certain type of development projects while still in the design and early implementation phases; (2) public access to non-classified government or official documents which describe the decision-making process for development undertakings; and (3) institutional means and procedures for addressing grievances and complaints concerning the development process and individual projects.

The importance of establishing procedural safeguards which involve the public participation by development stakeholders was clearly demonstrated in the watershed case of the Sardar Sarovar projects on the Narmada River in western India. The Sardar Sarovar projects (roughly 30 in number) seek to provide irrigation water for drought-prone areas in the states of Gujarat and Rajasthan, at an estimated 1992 construction cost of $5.2 billion.[18] Under its current design, the project will submerge 245 villages, home to about 41,000 families.[19] The projects will affect land owned by an additional 68,000 families, and will inundate forest land, change the rate of sedimentation in the Narmada River, and adversely

---

[17] H.C. Black, *Black's Law Dictionary*, 6th edn. (1990), p. 334: 'Co-operate: To act jointly or concurrently toward a common end.' 'Co-operation: In patent law, unity of action to a common end or a common result, not merely joint or simultaneous action.'

[18] Operations Evaluation Department (OED) Précis No. 88, *Learning From Narmada*, (World Bank, May 1995), pp. 2, 12. Cite available on internet at http://www.worldbank.org/html/oed/pr088.htm (last visited on 13 August 1998).

[19] *Ibid.*, p. 12.

affect local fisheries.[20] Altogether, the livelihoods of over 140,000 people will be affected by the building of the Sardar Sarovar dam and its associated canals, both of which may have serious negative environmental impacts.[21]

The World Bank's involvement since 1985 with the Narmada project has caused a maelstrom of controversy. Environmentalists, local activists, local and international NGOs, the media and other interested parties have vigorously criticized the Narmada project, particularly since no satisfactory resettlement and rehabilitation in the Narmada Valley has taken place.

In response to such criticism, the World Bank commissioned an independent review which completed its evaluation in June 1992. A report was released which was heavily critical of the Bank for its failure to ensure the adequate resettlement of people affected by the project, and for failing to comply with its own resettlement and rehabilitation procedures in relation to indigenous peoples.[22] Further, the review found that the Narmada project disregarded the environmental regulations of both the Indian government and the Bank itself. In addition, as late as 1992, seven years following project approval, the legal conditions stipulated in underlying agreements between the parties had not been met.[23]

In response to the findings of the independent review, the World Bank laid down standards of performance for the Narmada project in September 1992. In addition, the Bank's Board of Executive Directors approved an action plan which was completed in consultation with Indian authorities. Nevertheless, in March 1993, the Indian government requested the World Bank to cancel the remaining undisbursed amount of the loan, having decided to complete the Narmada project using other sources of funds, and to proceed with adequate resettlement procedures for the people affected by the project.

The Narmada project has many far-reaching implications. First, the public participation and advocacy which took place once the adverse effects of the project were assessed by local populations and interested parties, shows the impact that a vigorous civil society can have in the development equation. Secondly, it forced the Indian government to realign its political priorities by requesting cancellation of the remaining, undisbursed balance of the World Bank. Thus, the mere offer of development assistance does not constitute a 'gift horse' that cannot be scrutinized.

The open, participatory process that the Narmada debacle gave rise to drew attention, for the first time on a scale of that magnitude, to the human impact that development projects have. The end-users of this project articulated their views in a politically effective manner, stopped further financing by the World Bank, and forced the Indian government to reaffirm its

---

[20] *Ibid.*

[21] *Ibid.*, p. 1.

[22] OED, *supra* n. 18, pp. 2, 3. See also Resources Futures International, *Sardar Sarovar: The Report of the Independent Review*, June 1992.

[23] OED, *supra* n. 18, p. 4.

commitment in January 1994 to coordinate dam construction with the resettlement process.[24] Thus, the people affected by the dam project created a vital link with responsible local officials, and made such officials responsive to their immediate as well as their long-term needs.

The impact of the Narmada project on the World Bank is incalculable.[25] It made Bank officials aware of how high the stakes are in the development process, and how important an open, participatory process can be in ensuring the ultimate success of such projects. As one of the factors identified by the independent review was the failure to adhere to World Bank policies and procedures, the Bank responded by creating an independent Inspection Panel.

The Inspection Panel began its operations in September 1994, with a mandate to ensure that Bank policies are being fully implemented. The Panel, in effect, permits the end-user of a World Bank project to begin a dialogue and create a nexus with the Bank itself.[26] The implications of this, and the initial work of the Inspection Panel, will be reviewed below.

2.5 Multilateral actors

Finally, multilateral actors such as the IMF and other international financial institutions, regional development banks and development institutions such as the UNDP, UN Environmental Programme, and others also play a critical role in facilitating the development process. The monetary stakes for both the multilateral institutions and the recipient countries are generally quite high. These institutions not only funnel enormous amounts of official assistance in furtherance of development purposes, but they are also intimately involved in the strategic planning, design and implementation of development projects. In addition, these institutions arrange for technical assistance in all stages, including project design, implementation, completion and evaluation. The importance and relevance of such institutions on a worldwide scale should not be underestimated in terms of the finance, resources and critical thinking devoted to the development process.

Multilateral actors are also vital stakeholders in the development process, since they facilitate development assistance policies. Their institutional viability may depend on the success of such policies to achieve institutional goals and objectives. Since these objectives may change constantly in reaction to varying political winds, multilateral actors are a dynamic component in the development process.

The rights of multilateral lending institutions (as well as bilateral lending institutions and development agencies) stem from their individual mandates which may be set out in their respective charters or authorizing national legislation. For instance, the World Bank was originally formed to assist in the reconstruction of post-war Europe and, in addition, to 'assist in

---

[24] See OED, *supra* n. 18, pp. 1, 7.

[25] See *ibid.*, p. 10.

[26] See *ibid.*, p. 11. See also I. Shihata, *The World Bank's Inspection Panel* (Oxford University Press, 1994).

the reconstruction and development of territories of members'.[27] This role, however, was vastly overshadowed by the US Marshall Plan which, in financial terms and political importance, had a far greater historical impact.[28]

Under its Articles of Agreement, the World Bank is not authorized to make loans to its members unless it is 'satisfied that in the prevailing market conditions the borrower would be unable otherwise to obtain the loan under conditions which in the opinion of the Bank are reasonable for the borrower'.[29] Although the World Bank made limited loans in support of development prior to the 1950s under the leadership of Bank President Robert McNamara, the World Bank had firmly entrenched itself as the lender of last resort for developing nations by the 1970s.

The IMF was established, *inter alia*, to promote international monetary cooperation and international exchange stability, and to make the general resources of the IMF available to its members under 'adequate safeguards'.[30] The IMF came into official existence on 27 December 1945, when 29 countries signed its Articles of Agreement. Actual operations of the IMF began on 1 March 1947.[31]

Most importantly, the World Bank and the IMF, along with bilateral donor agencies of OECD countries, are empowered to impose 'conditionality' on the recipient countries of their loans or technical assistance. Conditionality for loans and other grant-based assistance is generally stipulated in an implementing legal agreement which describes the terms and conditions under which such assistance is being furnished.[32] Such conditionality may, for example, require the aid-recipient country to make sectoral policy changes, macro-economic adjustments, or adopt austerity measures such as cutting back on government expenditures in order to balance fiscal deficits.

Most multilateral lending institutions such as the World Bank and bilateral institutions have specific remedies against defaulting borrowers. (The IMF's financing contributions are not considered to be loans as such, and will be discussed separately.) Remedies available to international financial

---

[27] Articles of Agreement of the International Bank for Reconstruction and Development, Art. I, §1. Both the World Bank and the IMF were established pursuant to the Bretton Woods conference held in New Hampshire from June 1–22, 1944, prior to the formation of the UN. The World Bank became a specialized organ of the UN through a Relationship Agreement. See Agreement Between the United Nations and the International Bank for Reconstruction and Development, 15 November, 1947, 16 U.N.T.S. 346. (See also E.S. Mason and R. Asher, *The World Bank Since Bretton Woods* (1973), pp. 54-59, for a fuller discussion of this special relationship.)

[28] E.S. Mason and R. Asher, *supra* n. 27, pp. 52–53, 60–61.

[29] Articles of Agreement of the International Bank for Reconstruction and Development, Art. III, §4(ii).

[30] IMF home page, *What is the IMF?*, available on http://www.imf.org., p. 4 (last visited on 13 August 1998).

[31] *Ibid.*

[32] See J. Cahn, *supra* n. 3, pp. 170–171, (citing E.S. Mason and R. Asher, *The World Bank Since Bretton Woods*, pp. 52, 420).

institutions are generally set out in the underlying loan, or other legal, agreement that the institution enters into with the borrower nation. These legal provisions give lending institutions the right to seek the following remedies if the borrower defaults on repayment, or otherwise violates the provisions of such an agreement: (1) to suspend undisbursed amounts of the loan; (2) to cancel undisbursed amounts of loan; or (3) to accelerate immediate repayment of the loan in full (an option which, incidentally, has never been exercised by the World Bank).[33]

Thus, if the 'conditionality' set forth in underlying loan or assistance agreements entered into by aid-recipient countries with such international

---

[33] World Bank loan agreements, for example, include detailed provisions for their cancellation, suspension, or acceleration. The World Bank's 'General Conditions Applicable to Loan and Guarantee Agreements' (third printing, March 1995), dated 1 January 1985, Art. VI, §. 6.02(k) provides, in relevant part:

The right of the Borrower to make withdrawals from the Loan Account shall continue to be suspended in whole or in part, as the case may be, until the event or events which gave rise to the suspension shall have ceased to exist, unless the Bank shall have notified the Borrower that the right to make withdrawals has been restored in whole or in part, as the case may be.

Moreover, §. 6.03 states:

If . . . the right of the Borrower to make withdrawals from the Loan Account shall have been suspended with respect to any amount of the Loan for a continuous period of thirty days, . . . the Bank may, by notice to the Borrower and the Guarantor, terminate the right of the Borrower to make withdrawals with respect to such amount. Upon the giving of such notice, such amount of the Loan shall be cancelled.

In addition, the Bank specifies in §. 7.01 that if certain events occur, and continue for specified amounts of time,

the Bank, at its option, may, by notice to the Borrower and the Guarantor, declare the principal of the Loan then outstanding to be due and payable immediately together with the interest and other charges thereon and upon any such declaration such principal, together with the interest and other charges thereon, shall become due and payable immediately.

For grant-based technical and other assistance, for instance, USAID has provisions under which such assistance may be suspended or terminated (USAID Automated Directives System (ADS), Chapter 350, §. M.1(a)):

Either party may terminate this Agreement in its entirety by giving the other Party 30 days written notice. USAID also may terminate this Agreement in part by giving the Grantee 30 days written notice, and suspend this Agreement in whole or in part upon giving the Grantee written notice. In addition, USAID may terminate this Agreement in whole or in part, upon giving the Grantee written notice, if (i) the Grantee fails to comply with any provision of this Agreement, (ii) an event occurs that USAID determines makes it improbable that the result or related objective of this Agreement or the assistance programme will be attained or that the Grantee will be able to perform its obligations under this Agreement, or (iii) any disbursement or use of funds in the manner herein contemplated would be in violation of the legislation governing USAID, whether now or hereafter in effect.

Further USAID may also request that grant funds be refunded by the Grantee, if for example,

the failure of [the] Grantee to comply with any of its obligations under this Agreement has the result that goods or services financed or supported under this Agreement are not used effectively in accordance with this Agreement, USAID may require the Grantee to refund all or any part of the amount of the disbursements under this Agreement for or in connection with such goods and services in U.S. dollars to USAID within sixty (60) days after receipt of a request therefor. (See ADS, Chapter 350, s. M.2(b))

financial institutions is not met or is violated, this may trigger the exercise of one or more remedies available to such institutional actors. Of course, exercising such remedies means that the underlying objective in rendering the development assistance has failed. This failure is generally attributed to both the aid-recipient country for not conforming to the agreed-upon conditionality, and to the lending institution for not successfully implementing a programme of assistance.

Nevertheless, the remedies which may be invoked by international lending institutions show that such institutional actors have certain clear, contractually based rights. Failure to comply with the terms and conditionality of such loan and assistance agreements may be met with a sharp revocation of such assistance. It should be noted that the aid-recipient country has the mutual right to cancel a loan, as in the Narmada case where the Indian government opted to cancel the World Bank loan. However, other remedies which may be exercised by lending institutions are not mutual in nature— that is to say, these are remedies which can only be exercised by the institutional actor, and are not available to the borrower.

If the rights of institutional actors are well-defined and protected, what rights do state borrowers or grant recipients have? What remedies do they have at their disposal?

With regard to sovereign members who are borrowing funds from international development institutions, there are three distinct levels of engagement. First, with regard to a failure to repay loans in a timely manner, borrowing countries may exercise a menu of options in order to reach a mutually acceptable debt work-out. Those options may include, but are not limited to: renegotiating the terms of repayment of the loan, rescheduling the debt, thereby extending the time in which to repay the loan, requesting debt forgiveness, or seeking access to international capital markets. (World Bank loans cannot, however, be rescheduled in the same manner as government-to-government debt which is rescheduled by the Paris Club, discussed in further detail in Chapter 3.) These are fairly complex financial issues which are addressed in Chapter 3 in relation to the Mexican financial bail-out of 1994–95.

It is important to note that this level of engagement with international financial actors (which may loosely be seen as the exercise of borrower 'remedies') is the most desirable position for a borrowing country to be in, particularly if this country has fairly easy access to world capital markets. The sovereign debtor may seek out creative financial solutions to its debt-related problems, such as issuing exit bonds. The borrowing country is thus able to seek tailor-made financial solutions that allows it to exercise its sovereign decision-making power in a fairly uncompromised manner. Moreover, the same menu of options may be exercised by the sovereign borrower with commercial lenders.

This type of debt work-out approach is limited to circumstances where there has been a simple failure to repay the loan in a timely fashion. Failure to meet the terms of the conditionality agreed to by the parties (e.g., structural adjustment terms for macro-economic reforms) leads to the second level of 'engagement'. This level of engagement results in economic and fiscal discipline being imposed on the borrower country.

The lending picture between sovereign borrowers and international financial institutions as described in relation to the first level of engagement is usually not so simple and indeed, rarely, if ever, is. This is because most international lending institutions do not act as commercial banks, which simply lend funds with the expectation of receiving repayment of the principal with interest. In contrast, institutional financial institutions engage in 'policy-based' lending which means that credit (i.e., loans) will be extended on the condition that the recipient government undertake certain policy reform measures.[34] These policy reforms are generally aimed at helping the sovereign borrower regain its balance-of-payments equilibrium by reforming its macro-economic policy framework. This may mean, for example, changing host government policies in certain sectors, such as eliminating agricultural subsidies, or enacting enabling legislation to privatize certain industrial sectors.

In fact, a principal function of the IMF is to assist its members to regain their external debt repayment ability, and resume their foreign exchange stability.[35] In furtherance of this goal, the IMF instils fiscal discipline in the borrower by imposing 'conditionality'.[36] This conditionality must be satisfied before further disbursements of IMF financing will be made available to the sovereign member seeking such financing. Moreover, compliance with a new policy framework, rather than simple repayment of the loan, is the real objective of policy-based lending.[37] At the end of the day, however, international financial borrowings often add up to a tremendous debt overhang which further impedes development for the debtor nation.

Sovereign borrowers usually only approach the IMF when a default on the debtor's international payment obligations is fairly imminent.[38] In this case, the terms of a 'structural adjustment' programme are negotiated with the IMF, the successful conclusion of which is a precondition to making an IMF 'stand-by facility' available to the sovereign debtor.[39] The facility may be used to draw down on an IMF line of credit to provide short-term financing, thus enabling the sovereign debtor to meet its immediate international payment needs. A stand-by arrangement is normally repayable within three to five years and, if extended, within five to ten years.

Further, an IMF structural adjustment programme must be agreed to in principle before any World Bank structural or sectoral adjustment loans

---

[34] J. Cahn, *supra* n. 3, p. 171.

[35] IMF Home Page, *supra* n. 30, p. 4.

[36] See J. Gold, *Conditionality* (IMF Pamphlet Series No. 31, 1979); M. Guitian, *Fund Conditionality: Evolution of Principles and Practices* (IMF Pamphlet Series No. 39, 1981).

[37] See J. Cahn, *supra* n. 3, pp. 170–171.

[38] Discussions with the IMF and a sovereign member may be initiated by the sovereign state based on its critical financing needs, or by IMF staff who are responsible for the general surveillance of the country's economic condition, and who may undertake a special mission to the country in question regarding a proposed use of Fund resources. See IMF, Articles of Agreement, Art. VI, §1.

[39] See J. Cahn, *supra* n. 3, p. 172.

will be made available to the sovereign debtor.[40] In addition, the sovereign debtor may not seek to have its bilateral official debt owed to donor countries rescheduled under the auspices of the Paris Club unless an IMF stand-by arrangement is in place.[41] Thus, Paris Club reschedulings which, in effect, consolidate official government-to-government debt are pre-conditioned on IMF Executive Board approval of an official stand-by (or extended) arrangement. To make matters worse, private commercial creditors (acting through the London Club or simply as an independent syndicate of lenders) may also require an IMF stand-by agreement to be entered into before making any 'new money' available to the sovereign debtor. (These matters are discussed in greater depth in Chapter 3.)

Korea provides a recent example. On 4 December 1997, the IMF's Executive Board approved Korea's request for a three-year stand-by credit equivalent to SDR 15.5 billion (or about $21 billion) in support of a structural adjustment programme.[42] The fast-disbursing loan was tranched in the following manner: SDR 4.1 billion (about $5.56 billion) was made available immediately; SDR 2.6 billion (about $3.58 billion) was made available on 18 December 1997, following a preliminary review of the programme; and, SDR 1.5 billion (about $2 billion) was made available on 8 January 1998, following a second review.[43] This loan represented almost 2000 per cent of Korea's quota in the IMF, amounting to about $1.09 billion.[44]

In arranging this stand-by credit, the IMF used the streamlined procedures set forth under its emergency financing mechanism (EFM) which was adopted on September 12, 1995, following the Mexican fiscal crisis.[45] In addition to the IMF's total financing of $21 billion, the World Bank will

---

[40] World Bank Structural Adjustment Loans (SALs), and Sectoral Adjustment Loans (SECALs) are medium-to-long term loans which may only be entered into if IMF approval for stand-by credit has already been obtained by the borrowing country. SALs are linked to key economic reforms, and SECALs emphasize reforms in certain 'sectors' such as trade, agriculture, industry, public finance, energy or education. The conditionality specified in these World Bank agreements often mirrors or supports that set forth in the underlying IMF financing arrangement.

[41] J. Sanford, 'Foreign Debts to the U.S. Government: Recent Reschedulings and Forgiveness', (1995) 28 *Geo. Wash. J. Int'l L. & Econ.* 345 at 359–360.

[42] IMF, 'IMF Approves SDR 15.5 Billion Stand-By Credit for Korea', Press Release No. 97/55, 4 December 1997, p. 1, available on internet at http://www.imf.org (last visited on 28 July 1997). See also IMF, 'Camdessus Welcomes Conclusion of Talks with Korea on IMF Program', News Brief No. 97/27, 3 December 1997; A. Spaeth, 'Biting the Bullet: With the IMF's Help, Battered South Korea is Bracing for a Painful Economic Recovery. If It Fails, the Whole World Could Suffer the Fallout', *Time*, Vol. 150 No. 24, 15 December 1997.

[43] IMF, *supra* n. 42, p. 1.

[44] *Ibid.* A member's quota in the IMF determines its share in allocations of Special Drawing Rights (SDRs), which are an artificial value represented by a basket of hard currencies, namely the US dollar, the pound sterling, the French franc, the German mark, and the Japanese yen. This allocation also determines the member's access to IMF financing and relative voting power in the IMF.

[45] For a discussion of the IMF's emergency financing mechanism, see 'Emergency Financing Mechanism', Summing up by the Chairman, Executive Board Meeting 95/85, 12 September 1995, reprinted in *Selected Decisions and Selected Documents of the International Monetary Fund*, Twenty-Second Issue (30 June 1997), pp. 156–160.

make up to $10 billion in structural adjustment loans available. The Asian Development Bank will also support this international bail-out effort by dedicating up to $4 billion in support of macro-economic reforms. Finally, up to $20 billion in additional bilateral financing, on an as-needed basis, is contemplated. The main contributors to Korea were expected to be Australia, Belgium, Canada, France, Germany, Italy, Japan, the Netherlands, Sweden, Switzerland, the United Kingdom and the United States.[46]

Of course, this financing package is 'conditioned' on an ambitious programme of macro-economic reforms that has been agreed to in principle by the government of Korea, consisting of, *inter alia*:

- a strong macro-economic framework to reduce Korea's external current account deficit, building up internal foreign exchange reserves and control inflation;
- restructuring, recapitalizing and reforming the financial sector, including financial audits of large firms which will also be required to incorporate new disclosure standards for financial data on non-performing loans and capitalization levels in conformity with international best practices; and the passage of domestic legislation to consolidate the financial sector supervisory functions into one government agency, thus encouraging the financial sector to become more open, transparent and sound;
- trade liberalization measures, including the elimination of trade-related subsidies and restrictive import licensing in accordance with a timetable coordinated with World Trade Organization commitments;
- capital account liberalization, eliminating restrictions on foreign access to money market accounts and corporate bond markets and simplifying foreign direct investment approval processes.[47]

Thus, Korea is expected to make complex and deep structural adjustments, and it is clear that the release of approved funding is explicitly conditioned upon making these policy changes.

The specific terms and the negotiations surrounding structural adjustment programmes often create an impenetrable wall of secrecy. A letter of intent (LOI) is normally submitted to the IMF by the sovereign member seeking IMF financing. This LOI is generally issued by the host country's minister of finance, central bank board of governors or other appropriate government official. The LOI describes the host government's commitment to overcome economic structural imbalances. This letter of intent is generally attached to an IMF staff report (i.e., a memorandum of economic policies) which discusses the nature of the structural imbalances in the borrowing country's economy.

The IMF staff report also generally describes the proposed stand–by (or extended) arrangement which states the terms and conditions of the

---

[46] IMF, *supra* n. 42, p. 4.
[47] IMF, *supra* n. 42, pp. 2–3.

loan, usually incorporating the LOI by reference, and sets forth the structural reform measures to be implemented by the sovereign borrower. The finalized LOI and staff report are approved by the Executive Board of the IMF, providing the basis for approving IMF financing for the country in question. The fact that such IMF staff reviews are often cloaked in secrecy and are not subject to public (or US Congressional) scrutiny has drawn sharp criticism from conservative members of the US Congress who urge that the concept of 'transparency' be applied to the IMF.[48]

The stand–by arrangement approves tranches of financing, generally to be disbursed within a period of one year. Periodic reviews of the programme, and post-programme monitoring may also be required. However, these tranches are not truly 'loans' as such, but instead permit the borrowing country to use its local currency to purchase hard currency from the IMF.[49] These hard currency purchases must be repaid to the IMF by the sovereign borrower. Further, this repayment must be made in the time specified and in the hard currency denominated by the IMF. For instance, Indonesia may use its local currency, the rupiah, to obtain German marks from the IMF. When Indonesia has sufficient reserves of foreign exchange earnings, it is responsible for converting its rupiahs to German marks (or to pound sterling, as required by the IMF), in order to repay its currency purchase from the IMF.

These understandings between the sovereign borrower and the IMF are not, however, considered to be international treaties, agreements or contracts. Indeed, the IMF's Executive Board has issued a decision which clearly states that, '[s]tand-by arrangements are not international agreements and therefore language having a contractual connotation will be avoided in stand-by arrangements and letters of intent'.[50]

The stand–by arrangement, thus, is simply treated as a unilateral declaration of intent to follow the prescriptions laid out therein. Contractual remedies found in other loan documentation of the World Bank and multilateral/ bilateral lending institutions are specifically avoided by the IMF. Indeed, it may be argued that no contractual 'meeting of minds', so to speak, is reflected by the Arrangement, which simply reduces to written form the unilateral undertakings of the sovereign borrower and the IMF.

---

[48] 'A Little Transparency at the IMF, Too', *Washington Times*, 8 July 1998, p. A18. In March 1998, the US Senate approved $18 billion in funding for the IMF, but this appropriation has been languishing in the House of Representatives where conservative Republican members have been clamouring for some transparency and accountability on the part of the IMF. Speaker Newt Gingrich and Majority Leader Dick Armey have urged President Clinton to seek the release of the IMF's secret operating budget and its closely-held staff policy reviews. Thus, these conservative critics have joined the ranks of other prominent critics of the IMF, including economists Jeffrey Sachs, Milton Friedman and Martin Feldstein as well as George Schultz, a former US Secretary of State and of the Treasury. *Ibid.*

[49] See, generally, Articles of Agreement of the International Monetary Fund, Art. V, §§3(b)–(e).

[50] IMF Executive Board Decision No. 6056-(79/38), §. 3, 'Guidelines On Conditionality, Use of Fund's General Resources and Stand-By Arrangements', 2 March 1979, reprinted in *Selected Decisions and Selected Documents of the International Monetary Fund*, Twenty-Second Issue, 30 June 1997, excerpt on file with author.

Further, since IMF stand–by arrangements do not have the legal status of being international agreements or accords, they do not require parliamentary approval by the host country. Thus, such arrangements are negotiated by the executive branch of the host government, and generally bypass any political oversight or approval process by the legislative branch of the host country. Although this adds to the speed in which such arrangements can be concluded with the IMF, a swiftness that may be mandated by the exigent circumstances faced by the host country, a certain level of public scrutiny of these arrangements is nevertheless absent.

The IMF's role has been likened to that of a trustee in bankruptcy, although it is duly noted that unlike the private trustee, who is appointed by, and held accountable to, a bankruptcy court, there is no equivalent accountability for the IMF.[51] The issue of whether there should be an institutional means for holding the IMF and other international financial institutions account-able for actions taken in relation to the imminent 'bankruptcies' of sovereign members is an important one, and is addressed later in this text.

Finally, the third level of 'engagement" consists the imposition of economic (including trade) sanctions on a developing country in order to punish unlawful or impolitic conduct. Such economic sanctions are imposed by governments, rather than international financial institutions, and are unlike the economic austerity measures imposed as fiscal discipline by the IMF (which may also be reflected in the conditionality required by the World Bank, the Paris Club, and private creditors).[52] This type of punitive action is not, however, designed principally to support development in the sanctioned state. As such, it lies outside the scope of this discussion.

Thus, there are three levels of engagement with the international financial community. The first, negotiating a debt work-out by developing a menu of options, is particularly effective where the host government has fairly easy access to international capital markets. The second level of engagement involves imposing fiscal discipline on a sovereign country by international and bilateral financial institutions as well as by private creditors. And finally, the third level is where bilateral governments impose economic sanctions for wrongful or politically offensive conduct; however, these sanctions fall outside the scope of this discussion. A summation is provided in the development law matrix in Table 2.1.

3. SUBSTANTIVE PRINCIPLES OF DEVELOPMENT LAW

The new, globalized, international community now has the opportunity to form a social contract for the common good, in the same fashion as Rousseau believed individuals formed a social pact in furtherance of their

---

[51] J. Cahn, *supra* n. 3, p. 172.
[52] See e.g., Foreign Operations, Export Financing, and Related Programs Appropriations Act, 1997, P.L. 104-208, 110 Stat. 3009, §570 (imposing US government sanctions against Burma) and §540 (imposing US government sanctions against Serbia and Montenegro).

Table 2.1:   Development law matrix

Stakeholder	Rights/Privileges	Duties/Responsibilities
Individual actors	Right to participatory development; right to seek redress	Exercise rights responsibly; abide by local/int'l laws
Sovereign actors	Right to mutuality; right to fair dealing	Duty to cooperate and ensure openness, transparency and accountability, and to abide by local/int'l Laws
Int'l financial institutions; bilateral lending institutions	Right to seek remedies; right to seek repayment of loans/financing; right to impose conditionality	Duty to cooperate and ensure mutuality, openness, transparency, accountability, and to abide by local/int'l laws

mutual interests.[53] The new millennium offers an opportunity to move away from the paradigms of the 'haves' and 'have-nots', of the privileged and the deprived, and the affluent and the impoverished. Rather than fixating on the static dynamic of the past in which two worlds are inextricably locked together, it is time to break free of that concept and create a new paradigm. A world divided in two has been replaced by a dynamic continuum, a spectrum that is in constant flux. Today's economic miracle may be tomorrow's financial disaster, when today's lost cause may come bouncing back to self-sufficiency and financial success.

New constructive rules of engagement must be devised for a newly globalized economy. The following discussion will explore the substantive principles of development law which focus on mutuality, equitable participation in development, and creating a new methodology for establishing new legal norms.

3.1   Mutuality

Mutuality must be established among all sovereign and institutional actors in the development scene. Development law offers the opportunity for a new kind of reciprocation or mutuality. A mutuality of obligation, for example, means that an 'obligation rests on each party to do or permit the doing of something in consideration of the other party's act or promise; neither party being bound unless both are bound'.[54]

---

[53] See J-J. Rousseau, *The Social Contract* (1762) (trans. H.J. Tozer) (Scribner, 1898), reprinted in *Classics of Western Thought III, The Modern World* (C. Hirschfeld, ed.) (Harcourt Brace Jovanovich, 1964), p. 173.

[54] H.C. Black, *Black's Law Dictionary* (revised 6th edn., 1990), p. 1021.

Indeed, the obligations created by the development process do not simply lie with the developing nation receiving assistance in some form, but rest with all of the actors in the development process. Everyone has an obligation to make disciplined and careful development choices. In order to give this obligation true meaning, however, developing nations alone cannot be expected to fulfil this obligation. An equivalent obligation must be imposed on industrialized states and international financial institutions insofar as they, too, have a duty to cooperate with developing states in seeking responsible, sustainable and equitable development solutions.

There has been an unequal bargaining relationship in the past between industrialized nations and international financial institutions on the one hand, and aid-recipient, 'developing' nations on the other. Indeed, most of the people actually affected by development problems, projects and failures have had little or no bargaining power. These two factors have led to an imbalance in the development equation, over time. This means that the inequities between developed and developing nations as well as the inequities between the impoverished of the world, and the representatives authorized to speak on their behalf, have been exacerbated.

Development law offers an equalizing force for both issues. By not imposing differential legal norms on developing countries, but by holding the entire international community to the same legal norms, development law helps establish a more level playing field. Rather than perpetuating legal distinctions that highlight the differences between the developed and developing worlds, development law offers parity and equitable treatment among sovereign and institutional actors.

3.2 Equitable participation in development

Secondly, participatory development establishes a nexus between the most impoverished or deprived, and the most lofty decision-maker in the development process. By creating a dialogue, a relationship is fostered between the two ends of the spectrum. This, over time, has the potential for supporting the creation of mutual insight, understanding and respect among the development decision-makers, and the people whom their decisions affect. It also gives more definition and clarity to development law questions as the affected parties may illuminate the potential human and societal impact of impersonal, bureaucratic decisions. This can only strengthen the development process, thus better serving those whom it is meant, at least in theory, to assist.

The equitable participation by persons and entities who are affected by the development equation need not be viewed as destructive, meddling interference. In fact, this type of open participation may actually make the development process more efficient and self-sustaining. Indeed, in furtherance of creating better opportunities for participatory development, the Executive Directors of the World Bank and the International Development Association (IDA), which is part of the World

Bank Group, adopted parallel resolutions in 1993[55] establishing an independent Inspection Panel.

The Inspection Panel provides an independent forum for private citizens[56] who believe that they have been, or could be, directly harmed by a project financed by the World Bank or the IDA. Such parties may request that the Panel conduct an inspection of their claims. The Inspection Panel consists of three members with staggered terms, first appointed by the Executive Board, and then elected by the Panel itself. The Panel assumed its responsibilities on 1 August 1994, and issues annual reports which are available as public documents from the World Bank.

The Inspection Panel creates a liaison between the end-users of the development process and the critical decision-makers in the World Bank (although not the IMF at this point). The mandate of the Inspection Panel is extremely limited insofar as it receives requests for investigations from private parties, and issues recommendations to the World Bank's Executive Board advising it on whether an investigation should be commenced.

In light of this recommendation, the World Bank may authorize the Panel to conduct an investigation, the findings of which are reported back to the Board for further action, as appropriate. Thus, the function of the Panel is simply to react to complaints filed by participants in the development process, investigate these claims, and issue findings and recommendations. Executive action is then taken by the Executive Board of the World Bank, as appropriate. Thus, the Executive Board, not the Inspection Panel, makes a final disposition of the claim.

A request for inspection, for example, was filed with the Inspection Panel by the Jamuna Char Integrated Development Project on 23 August 1996. The Project, a non–government organization representing people who live on islands (chars) in the project area, alleged that the World Bank's project harmed their interests, and that the Bank had failed to institute its own policies regarding involuntary resettlement, environmental assessments and NGO participation.

The Inspection Panel agreed in substance, finding that the project would result in the flooding or permanent destruction of the islands where the char people lived and that, further, 'the existence of the char people was not even acknowledged in the initial resettlement plan of the project, and that

---

[55] IBRD No. 93-10 and IDA 93-6, respectively, dated 22 September 1993, (hereinafter referred to as the Joint Resolution) reprinted in *The Inspection Panel: International Bank for Reconstruction and Development, International Development Association, Annual Report* (1 August 1996 to 31 July 1997), p. 23.

[56] A 'private citizen' cannot be an individual (unless acting as a representative), but must be an: 'affected party [who] must demonstrate that its rights or interests have been or are likely to be directly affected by an action or omission of the [World] Bank as a result of a failure of the Bank to follow its operational policies and procedures . . . (including situations where the Bank is alleged to have failed in its follow-up on the borrower's obligations under loan agreement with respect to such policies and procedures) provided in all cases that such a failure has had, or threatens to have material adverse effect'. See Joint Resolution, §12, p. 25.

they appeared to have been forgotten during the project design and appraisal, and in the implementation of the resettlement plan'.[57]

The Panel held that if adequate supervision and constant monitoring were instituted by World Bank management, an inspection would not be needed. World Bank management is expected to make a progress report on the implementation of the Project, and report back to the Panel.[58] Thus, it may be safe to conclude that without the ability of private citizens to seek redress for their grievances directly to the Inspection Panel, this oversight would not have been corrected, and irreparable harm would have resulted.

Another example of equitable participation strengthening the development process is the Yacyretá Hydroelectric Project. This project was financed by the World Bank, co-financed by the IDB, and jointly owned and developed by the governments of Paraguay and Argentina.[59] The affected party claimed that by filling the Yacyretá Reservoir, the World Bank had not only caused water pollution, affected sanitation systems, flooded farmlands and disrupted fish migration and wildlife, but had also violated ten of its own policies.

The 20-year Yacyretá Project, exceeding more than $8 billion in cost, was found by the Inspection Panel to have resulted in 'material adverse effects which may have resulted from policy violations of a serious nature'.[60] The Panel recommended that the matter be investigated, and the World Bank's Executive Board accepted the recommendation. The investigation carried out by the Panel revealed that certain aspects of the project's implementation could be regarded as new violations. These new violations were incorporated into an ongoing, parallel investigation being carried out by the Investigation Mechanism of the IDB. Both were expected to report to their respective Boards of Directors by August 1997.[61]

Another important illustration of participatory development arises from an IDA project in Bangladesh. On 13 November 1996, the Inspection Panel received a request for investigation filed by the Bangladeshi shareholders and CEOs of private jute mills, claiming that they had been adversely affected by the IDA's supervision of a sectoral adjustment programme.[62] The World Bank's management response to the Inspection Panel was that all relevant policies and procedures had been observed and that, further, acts related to adjustment credits (as opposed to loans) were outside the mandate of the Panel. Specifically, the Banks management asserted that, the 'implementation of adjustment credits—in contrast to investment credits—were the sole responsibility of the borrower', and therefore lay outside the Panel's mandate.[63]

---

[57] Inspection Panel, *Annual Report* (1 August 1996 to 31 July 1997), p. 10.
[58] *Ibid.*, p. 11.
[59] *Ibid.*, p. 11.
[60] *Ibid.*, p. 12.
[61] Inspection Panel, *supra* n. 57, pp. 12–13.
[62] *Ibid.*, p. 13.
[63] *Ibid.*

The Inspection Panel disagreed. It found that the complainants had suffered substantial damage as a result of the adjustment programme and, moreover, that the Panel did have jurisdiction over such claims.[64] As it was unclear that IDA would retain its presence in the jute sector in Bangladesh, the Panel felt that an investigation was not warranted. The Bank's Board of Executive Directors agreed with the Panel's recommendation at its April 4, 1997 meeting, and the loan was closed out in June 1997.

This Inspection Panel decision is significant for several reasons. First, it asserted its jurisdiction over structural adjustment credits which are loans conditioned on the borrowing country meeting specific macro-economic targets, a bone of controversy for many developing countries. The effect of the Panel's decision is that a stakeholder who is not a party to the adjustment credit agreement may, nevertheless, question the conditionality agreed to by a sovereign borrower. This has now become a legitimate ground for inspection and review by the Inspection Panel.

Secondly, the Panel rejected the management's claim that the World Bank had 'no responsibility for implementation of adjustment credits'.[65] The Panel's view was 'reinforced' by the legal opinion of the Bank's General Counsel, Ibrahim Shihata, 'who listed a range of remedies that would be available to the Bank in the case of non-compliance with covenants of adjustment credits'.[66] Since the World Bank has enforceable remedies for the borrower's non-compliance with the terms and conditions under which adjustment credits were being made available to it, the Panel held that the Bank could also be held accountable for its failure to perform its obligations under the credit programme. Thus, the Panel established that the World Bank as well as the borrower had mutually supporting obligations. This conclusion lays the foundation for a mutuality of obligations among actors in the development process.

Therefore, the World Bank itself is beginning to realize that there is a mutuality of obligation (as well as an obligation of fair dealing) which must be accepted by all development actors if sustainable development solutions are to be forged. In other words, the borrower, financier and end-user are now placed on a continuous spectrum where each, ultimately, owes certain duties to the other. These mutual obligations clearly go beyond the formal contractual remedies contained in financing agreements. Moreover, the scope of such obligations extend beyond the formal, contracting parties.

Indeed, the mutuality of obligation in the development process is key in ensuring the success of the development undertaking. Development can no longer be viewed as a linear, time-limited equation which only affects the developing nation in question. Development choices can no longer be viewed in isolation, as any single development equation may profoundly affect the globalized economy.

---

[64] *Ibid.*
[65] Inspection Panel, *supra* n. 57.
[66] *Ibid.*

3.3   Establishing legal norms

Finally, development law as a new legal discipline requires that new, substantive legal norms be established. This has been attempted before by the international law of development which was created in the 1970s as a legal dimension of NIEO principles. As discussed above, the NIEO agenda tried to establish differential legal norms whereby developing countries would be held to a different standard than developed nations. The NIEO agenda, *inter alia*, advocated that developing countries be given preferential access to credit, development assistance, and technology transfers, as discussed earlier.

The NIEO advocated a historical view of development, whereby reparations for past colonial wrongs would be made and enforced through a new legal regime. Past inequities were reinforced through the imposition of unequal legal treatment of the 'haves' and 'have-nots'. The disparate legal treatment of these two categories of sovereign states tended to perpetuate, rather than ameliorate, the inequities between them. In any case, differential legal norms were never fully accepted by the international community and have, by the operation of history, lost much of its relevance.

Dependency theorists were wedded to the historical context of 'underdevelopment' whereas modernization theorists ignored it. Indeed, modernization theorists took an 'ahistorical' view of the development process, and believed that the values espoused by 'modernization' were value-neutral.[67] The issue of whether such modernization values are, in fact, 'value-neutral', has been addressed in the discussion of the Janus Law Principle in Chapter 1. However, the ahistorical basis of the modernization approach to development may prove to be quite useful in a post-modern era. History now matters less where, for example, 'virtual laws' must be applied to regulate and control internet commerce and the virtual legal rights and properties created thereunder.

If, however, the application of differential legal norms is not feasible under development law, what norms do apply? Contextual legal norms have been described as

a norm which on its face provides identical treatment to all States affected by the norm but the application of which requires (or at least permits) consideration of characteristics that may vary from country to country. The application of a contextual norm thus typically involves balancing multiple interests and characteristics.[68]

---

[67] See M.G. Gopal, 'Law and Development: Toward a Pluralist Vision', (1996) *Am. Soc. Int'l L. Proceedings* 231 at 235: 'The law and development movement should recognize that laws are not socially, culturally and politically neutral. Consequently, it should reevaluate, analyze and demonstrate the underlying social, cultural and political assumptions of law that are considered for adoption by developing countries, so as to facilitate informed choice by the recipient state regarding the reception of laws. The law and development movement adopted a view that the law is a neutral instrument for the resolution of economic issues, independent of the social, cultural and religious foundations of the societies in which they develop. [Footnote omitted.] This view was also based in part on explanations provided by Max Weber. [Footnote omitted.]'. Reproduced with permission copyright, (1996), The American Society of International Law.

[68] D.B. Magraw, *supra*, n. 2, p. 74.

The Kyoto Conference on Climate Change, held in December 1997, for example, established differential norms, reminiscent of NIEO-type of legal norms. The Conference required developed nations to commit themselves to reducing their airborne emissions over the course of the next 15 years, whereas no similar commitment was required of 'developing' countries, a term which, incidentally, was given no concrete definition. By establishing a differential norm, the Conference, perhaps unwittingly, has lowered its chances of ratification by the respective parliaments of developed nations. A differential norm creates a facial inequity in its application based on a distinction tied to the relative economic status of the signatory countries. Not only can a country's economic status change in the short-run, but differential norms tend to create and perpetuate inherent inequalities between the parties in the long-run. This approach is simply unworkable.

More importantly, differential legal treatment is unnecessary. By establishing objective, value-free criteria that are equitably applied to all signatories, the chances of fostering international cooperation in reducing the adverse effects of global warming would be significantly increased. In other words, if the Kyoto Protocol simply called for the reduction of emissions into the air at a baseline level of X, each country would then be responsible for its implementation. So, for the United Kingdom, meeting this standard might mean a 7 per cent reduction in its air pollutants, whereas for Mali, it might mean a reduction of 2 per cent.

This is an example of a contextual norm where identical treatment is accorded to all participants, but its practical application may vary, depending on the circumstances of each country. This leaves no room to argue that differential treatment is being granted to a certain category of countries based on their membership in that group, or based on certain legal preferences. Equitable participation is encouraged by this type of approach, and the chances that the Kyoto Protocol will be ratified by individual governments may increase accordingly.

Thus, by eliminating differential bases for establishing new legal norms under development law, the possible stigma that is attached to being a developing country, or the additional burdens imposed on developed nations, are removed. In this way, development law can redress inequities in the law. It is still possible to take account of differences between countries, and their relative development needs, without establishing preferential legal categories in order to do so.

For example, the WTO Agreement on Trade Related Investment Measures (TRIMs)[69] recognizes that certain investment measures can restrict and distort trade. This Agreement requires that all such TRIMs be notified to the WTO. Further, these TRIMs must be eliminated within two years for developed countries, and within seven years by 'least-developed' countries. The WTO has established a Committee on TRIMs which monitors the implementation of commitments made by WTO members to eliminate

---

[69] The WTO Agreement on TRIMs is set forth in J.H. Jackson, W.J. Davey, A.O. Sykes, Jr., *Legal Problems of International Economic Relations* (1995 Documents Supplement), p. 170.

non-conforming TRIMs. Thus, this WTO Agreement establishes a single standard for all its members to meet, but provides a longer time frame within which developing countries must meet this standard.

Creating contextual norms is very important within the framework of development law, especially in light of the Janus Law Principle. In order to develop such contextual norms, it may be useful to develop a model law approach which incorporates a menu of options. For example, the UN Commission on International Trade Law (UNCITRAL) has developed a model procurement law[70] that can be used by countries to create their own procurement codes.[71] The UNCITRAL model is being used by over 20 countries, including Eastern European countries such as Poland and Bulgaria, to develop their own procurement codes.[72] The model code covers such topics as international bidding rules, promoting competition, and the fair and equal treatment of suppliers and contractors.[73]

The model law adopts a 'menu of options' approach to procurement law providing different options tailored to fit specific procurement needs.

---

[70] See generally D. Wallace, Jr., 'The Changing World of National Procurement Systems: Global Reformation', (1995) 4 *Public Procurement L. Rev.* 576.

[71] See generally United Nations Commission on International Trade Law, 'Model Law on Procurement of Goods and Construction', reprinted in 33 *I.L.M.* 445 (16 July 1993). At its 26th session, held in Vienna in 1993, UNCITRAL adopted this model law. The text of the model law, which was adopted (without a vote by the UN General Assembly) by UNGA Resolution 48/33 on December 9, 1993 was annexed to its report on the session.

UNCITRAL was established as an organ of the UN General Assembly to promote the harmonization and unification of international trade law. The model law was created by UNCITRAL to provide a model for countries to evaluate, assess, and modernize their procurement laws and practices, and to develop legislation in order to facilitate these reforms. Specifically, '[t]he Model Law presents several procurement methods so as to enable the procuring entity to deal with the varying circumstances likely to be encountered by procuring entities. This enables an enacting State to aim for as broad an application of the Model Law as possible. As the rule for normal circumstances, the Model Law mandates the use of tendering, the method of procurement widely recognized as generally most effective in promoting competition, economy and efficiency in procurement, as well as the other objectives set forth in the Preamble. For the exceptional circumstances in which tendering is not appropriate or feasible, the Model Law offers methods other than tendering' (Model Law, §. D. 13, 33 *I.L.M.* 445, 447–448).

Further, '[t]he Model Law is intended to provide all the essential procedures and principles for conducting procurement proceedings in the various types of circumstances likely to be encountered by procuring entities. However, it is a 'framework' law that does not itself set forth all the rules and regulations that may be necessary to implement those procedures in an enacting State. Accordingly, the Model Law envisages the issuance by enacting States of 'procurement regulations' to fill the procedural details for procedures authorized by the Model Law and to take account of the specific, possibly changing circumstances at play in the enacting State—without compromising the objectives of the Model Law' (Model Law, §. C. 11, 33 *I.L.M.* 447).

Thus, the model law adopts a 'menu of options' approach to procurement law, and advises enacting states to promulgate, as necessary, implementing regulations that take into account the different circumstances in that state. However, the integrity of the model law is preserved.

[72] World Bank, *Governance: The World Bank's Experience with Governance* (World Bank, 1991), p. 35, Box 1.15.

[73] *Ibid.*

Further, the model law is conceived of as a 'framework law'. The drafters urge states enacting the model law (or provisions thereof) to promulgate, as necessary, implementing regulations that take into account the different circumstances in that state.[74] This maintains the integrity of the model law as an international model law, yet provides the necessary flexibility with which to adapt it to the specific needs of the enacting state. Thus, enough flexibility is retained within the structure of such legal models to make them truly useful in developing new contextual norms.

Another important example of establishing an international contextual norm is the Agreement on Trade-Related Aspects of Intellectual Property Rights (TRIPS).[75] TRIPS establishes a comprehensive framework for protecting and enforcing intellectual property rights on an international scale. With regard to copyright protection, for example, parties who infringe upon the rights of legitimate copyright holders must cease reproducing a work, or derivative works which reproduce significant elements of the original work, and must pay damages.

A national approach which may also serve as a model in developing contextual norms is the US Uniform Commercial Code (UCC). The UCC provides a national model that articulates consistent rules or 'blackletter law' dealing with secured transactions and other related commercial issues. The UCC adopts a menu of options approach insofar as the practice of one state is contrasted with, and incorporated into, the practice of another. Thus, a state has choices which it may exercise within the framework of the UCC which enhance its flexibility in developing laws best suited to that state's particular commercial needs. Thus, the independent commercial practices of various states in the United States are constantly being cross-fertilized by contributing to and being incorporated into the UCC framework.[76] If this approach is taken at an international scale, different legal models can be devised for addressing asset securitization, mortgages, bankruptcies, and other legal issues underlying secured lending transactions.

---

[74] See United Nations Commission on International Trade Law, *supra* n. 71, p. 447.

[75] Reprinted in (1994) 33 *I.L.M.* 1197.

[76] See D. Levy, 'Contract Formation Under the UNIDROIT Principles of International Commercial Contracts, UCC, Restatement and CISG', (1998) 30 *Uniform Commercial Code L.J.* 249. See also M.J. Bonell, 'The UNIDROIT Principles of International Contracts: Why? What? How?' (1995) 69 *Tul. L. Rev.* 1121; A.M. Garro, 'The Gap-Filling of the UNIDROIT Principles in International Sales Law: Some Comments on the Interplay Between the Principles and the CISG', (1995) 69 *Tul. L. Rev.* 1149; H. Veytia, 'The Requirement of Justice and Equity in Contracts', (1995) 69 *Tul. L. Rev.* 1191; L.O. Baptista, 'The UNIDROIT Principles for International Commercial Law Project: Aspects of International Private Law', (1995) 69 *Tul. L. Rev.* 1209; F. Ferrari, 'Defining the Sphere of Application of the 1994 "UNIDROIT Principles of International Commercial Contracts"', (1995) 69 *Tul. L. Rev.* 1225; G. Parra-Aranguren, 'Conflict of Law Aspects of the UNIDROIT Principles of International Commercial Contracts', (1995) 69 *Tul. L. Rev.* 1239; F.K. Juenger, 'Listening to Law Professors Talk About Good Faith: Some Afterthoughts', (1995) 69 *Tul. L. Rev.* 1253.

Thus, a menu of options approach may create a flexible framework of legal choices. Inasmuch as a basket of currencies is used in determining the artificial value of Special Drawing Rights used by the IMF to determine member quotas, it may be possible to develop a 'basket of laws' in developing a concrete, pragmatic approach to resolving development law questions. In other words, the commercial practices of France may be a useful model for Romania, whereas the commercial practices of Germany may provide useful insights to Thailand. Or the lending practices of the Grameen Bank in Bangladesh may provide a useful microfinance model for Côte d'Ivoire, which may be trying to encourage decentralized rural finance for women.

Of course, this is not to say that if the menu does not provide a choice then it must be discarded as an option. The menu simply provides structured choices from which deviations may be made. Moreover, the menu may be added to or deleted from, depending on the relative successes (or failures) of certain development options or strategies. Thus, the menu of options should be dynamic and responsive to the lessons learned from the development experiences of the participating countries.

The 'menu of options' approach exemplified by the UNCITRAL model law is an important means of furthering the development law process. The central idea behind this approach is not to take a balkanized view of development law principles, but to realize that certain models, typologies, regional applications and the like may hold valuable lessons for other countries. By creating a systemic approach based on models, and variants thereon, a certain integrity to the development of legal systems may be developed over time. This is not to resuscitate the 'legal imperialist' law and development approach which took account only of Anglo-American legal traditions, but to make legal systems development more pluralist in its vision and application. After all, the needs of Côte d'Ivoire in rural banking may be closer to Bangladesh than to France.

Building an international consensus is extremely important in this context. For example, the International Organization of Securities Commissions has been considering the capital adequacy standards for securities firms. In its deliberations, it has articulated the specific terms of acceptable market risks, clearance and settlement needs, liquidity and other important issues.[77] This type of legal discussion is extremely important in order to develop the 'plumbing' of globalized emerging capital markets. Moreover, such an international consensus on international regulation of private securities firms may provide the launching pad for creating a 'menu-based' model for international securities law. Over time, consensus-building may lead to the development of contextual norms in the area of commercial legal practices. Indeed, the seminal work of UNCITRAL, UNIDROIT and other international efforts may already be leading us in that direction.

---

[77] See International Organization of Securities Commissions, 'Technical Committee Report on Capital Adequacy Standards for Securities Firms', (1991) 30 *I.L.M.* 1018.

Finally, development law may need to adopt some absolute norms in order to impose international legal discipline in certain areas. An absolute norm has been described as:

a norm that provides identical treatment to all countries and does not require or permit consideration of factors that vary between countries... No bright line thus exists between absolute and contextual norms... Absolute norms have the capacity for being very precise... Precision is often desirable as a general matter because of easier application, more predictable outcomes, and [a] lower risk of manipulated, unprincipled third-party decisionmaking.[78]

Absolute norms should be applied, for example, to protect fundamental, inalienable human rights, such as the right to be free from torture and cruel and inhuman treatment. Of course, as discussed earlier, there may need to be a redefinition of which international human rights are 'fundamental', but certainly there should be satisfactory international accord to impose some absolute norms in the human rights arena. The struggle to define internationally accepted absolute norms which permit imposing international trade sanctions for environmental offences[79] and human rights violations,[80] however, is just beginning.

Absolute norms are applied equally to all international actors, and individual circumstances are not taken into account in the same way that the application of a contextual norm would require. Torturing prisoners, for example, may be considered a violation of an international human right that is not legally justifiable. Therefore, the prohibition of this type of conduct would be absolute. Absolute norms represent the 'bottom line' of international legal norms, below which no conduct is permissible.

In sum, the substantive principles of development law are grounded in the mutuality of obligation and equitable participation in development. Further effort needs to be dedicated to developing new, contextual legal norms using a menu-based model format as a starting point.

4.   ENFORCING LEGAL NORMS: AN INSTITUTIONAL FRAMEWORK FOR DEVELOPMENT LAW

The enforcement of contextual norms may be done by pursuing one of three courses of action: conciliation (the parties negotiate their dispute

---

[78] D.B. Magraw, *supra*, n. 2, p. 76.

[79] See generally C. Feddersen, 'Focusing on Substantive Law in International Economic Relations: The Public Morals of GATT's Article XX(A) and "Conventional" Rules of Interpretation', (1998) 7 *Minn. J. Global Trade* 75; M. Meier, 'GATT, WTO and the Environment: To What Extent Do GATT/WTO Rules Permit Member Nations to Protect the Environment When Doing So Adversely Affects Trade?', (1997) 8 *Colo. J. Int'l & Pol'y* 241.

[80] See generally R. Bhala, 'Fighting Bad Guys with International Trade', (1997) 31 *U.C. Davis L. Rev.* 1; N.A.F. Popovic, 'In Pursuit of Environmental Human Rights: Commentary on the Draft Declaration of Principles of Human Rights and the Environment', (1996) 27 *Colum. Hum. Rts. L. Rev.* 487.

privately); litigation (bringing a justiciable claim in a court or forum of competent jurisdiction for the formal resolution of disputes); or arbitration (the parties voluntarily submit to the decision-making of a third party). These options are certainly available now to the stakeholders in the development process, but this discussion will be devoted to outlining a new institutional framework for development law.

The success of the development equation rests on three pillars: the exchange of capital, commodities, and technology. The WTO has established an institutional framework for two out of the three pillars by establishing the substantive law of trade and intellectual property rights, and by establishing an enforcement mechanism for both.[81] An annex to the Agreement establishing the WTO sets forth the rules and procedures governing the settlement of disputes, and also lists the trade agreements covered by its scope.[82] Moreover, there is a WTO agreement on the trade of information technology products.[83]

The WTO may be viewed as a latecomer to the scene. Originally, the formation of three organizations was contemplated in 1942: the International Bank for Reconstruction and Development, the International Monetary Fund, and the International Trade Organization. The World Bank and the IMF resulted from the conference which took place in 1944 in Bretton Woods, New Hampshire. (The World Bank and the IMF are thus often collectively referred to as the 'Bretton Woods institutions'.)

Parallel negotiations were held in Havana, Cuba to form the International Trade Organization which was not formally established, but which survived in a truncated form known as the General Agreement on Tariffs and Trade (GATT). The GATT was not an institution similar to the IMF and the World Bank, but rather a forum in which to discuss (and resolve) international trade issues. It was the passage of the Final Act of the Multilateral Trade Negotiations (the Uruguay Round) of the GATT in 1994 that finally resulted in the establishment of the WTO.

The purpose of this text is not to critique the efficacy or relative success of the WTO, but simply to state that the WTO provides a mechanism for its members to agree to principles of trade law, intellectual property and technology-related matters. The WTO also provides a forum, through the Dispute Settlement Body (DSB), for dispute resolution among its members. The WTO's dispute resolution function was emphasized in a decision issued by the Appellate Body of the WTO in deciding an appeal brought by India against the United States.[84]

---

[81] See Agreement Establishing the Multilateral (World) Trade Organization, reprinted in (1994) 33 *I.L.M.* 13.

[82] See General Agreement on Tariffs and Trade—Multilateral Trade Negotiations (The Uruguay Round): Understanding on Rules and Procedures Governing the Settlement of Disputes, reprinted in (1994) 33 *I.L.M.* 112.

[83] See World Trade Organization: Agreement on the Implementation of the Ministerial Declaration on Trade in Information Technology Products, reprinted in (1997) 36 *I.L.M.* 375.

[84] WTO Appellate Body, *United States—Measure Affecting Imports of Woven Wool Shirts and Blouses From India* (AB-1997-1), 25 April 1997. Doc. available on Westlaw database, WTO-DEC, 1997 WT/DS33/AB/R/Corr. 1, pp. 13–14.

The underlying Dispute Settlement Panel report concluded that the US restraint on imports of woven wool shirts and blouses from India violated Articles 2 and 6 of the Agreement on Textiles and Clothing (ATC) which, in effect, nullified and impaired India's benefits under the ATC. In upholding this decision, the Appellate Body stated that:

Article 3.7 of the DSU [Understanding on Rules and Procedures Governing the Settlement of Disputes] explicitly states:
> The aim of the dispute settlement mechanism is to secure a positive solution to a dispute. A solution mutually acceptable to the parties to a dispute and consistent with the covered agreements is clearly to be preferred.

Thus, the basic aim of dispute settlement in the WTO is to settle disputes.[85]

In fact, the DSB's rulings 'shall be aimed at achieving a satisfactory settlement of the matter in accordance with the rights and obligations under this Understanding and under the covered agreements' and further, that the '[r]ecommendations and rulings of the DSB cannot add to or diminish the rights and obligations provided in the covered agreements'.[86] In addition, the WTO recognizes that the 'dispute settlement system of the [WTO] is a central element in providing security and predictability to the multilateral system'.[87] The DSB has also established a standing Appellate Body which hears appeals of decisions issued by DSB-established panels on disputes.[88]

The function of the DSB is quite different from that of the Bretton Woods institutions. The DSB acts as a neutral international body that is empowered, *inter alia*, to resolve legal disputes arising among its members concerning international agreements, understandings and protocols that WTO members have adopted, and that the WTO has incorporated.[89] In other words, the DSB has been delegated the adjudicatory function of resolving legal conflicts that arise pursuant to these agreements among WTO members. Thus, the WTO, through the DSB, administers and oversees compliance with the substantive legal principles that the WTO has adopted as a body, and adjudicates disputes arising therefrom.

The WTO, while resolving disputes which may arise between its sovereign members, does not provide a forum for private dispute resolution. (Private parties do, however, often lobby their respective sovereign governments to bring matters before the WTO when they feel that their private interests are affected by the trade practices of another country.) Further, the WTO does not hear disputes which may arise between its members and the WTO itself. Nevertheless, the public international law aspects of two of the three pillars (i.e., trade and technology) are addressed, in principle, by the WTO.

---

[85] *Ibid.*, p. 13.
[86] See §§ 3.4, 3.2 of the General Agreement on Tariffs and Trade *supra* n. 82, p. 115.
[87] *Ibid.*, §3.2, p. 115.
[88] *Ibid.*, §17.1, *et seq.*, p. 123.
[89] See General Agreement on Tariffs and Trade, *supra* n. 82.

On 12 December 1997, more than 70 members of the WTO successfully concluded negotiations for a multilateral agreement to cover 95 per cent of all trade related to financial services, banking, insurance, securities and financial information.[90] This new protocol was to be open for governments to accept until 29 January 1999, the agreement entering into force on 1 March 1999, at the latest.[91]

By way of contrast, there is no mechanism for addressing capital transfer issues that arise from the official lending practices of the World Bank and the IMF. In addition, there is no international protocol which members of these institutions have agreed to which sets forth the substantive legal principles of sovereign lending practices of the Bank and the IMF. The only option open to IMF and World Bank members is to seek conciliation of their disagreements, if any, with the lending institution in question. There are no institutional means for seeking redress for any disputes, as such, regarding the enormous capital transfers which take place in furtherance of development purposes.[92]

Most importantly, the 'law-making'[93] function of the World Bank and the IMF in terms of requiring internal policy changes, governance changes, macro-economic reforms, and institutions-building in its official borrowers

---

[90] WTO, 'Successful Conclusion of the WTO's Financial Services Negotiations', Press Release No. 86, 15 December 1997, available on internet at http://www.wto.org/wto/new/press86.htm., p. 1.

[91] *Ibid.*, pp. 1–2.

[92] The Articles of Agreement of the International Bank for Reconstruction and Development, Art. IX(a), provides that questions regarding the interpretation of the Articles of Agreement shall be submitted to the Executive Directors of the World Bank. Members of the Bank may refer a decision made by the Executive Directors concerning interpretation of the Agreement to the Board of Governors, whose decision in the matter shall be final. (See Arts. IX(b) and V, §2(b)(iv).)
   The same basic institutional arrangements regarding interpretation of the Articles of Agreement of the IMF, and appeals of executive directors' decisions to the IMF Board of Governors, are set forth in Art. XXIX of the IMF's Articles of Agreement. However, this arrangement is limited to decisions regarding the interpretation of the Articles of Agreement of each institution, and therefore, is very narrow in scope. This text argues for the ability to appeal all decisions of the executive directors of the Bretton Woods institutions, without limitation with regard to content.
   Both the World Bank and the IMF provide for an arbitration of disagreements which may arise between a member and the respective institution under three circumstances: when the member has withdrawn from the institution in question, and 'during the permanent suspension of the Bank' or 'during the liquidation of the Fund'. (See Art. IX(c) of the Bank's, and Art. XXIX of the IMF's Articles of Agreement.) These articles call for the establishment of a tribunal of three arbitrators, one appointed by the member, one by the respective institution and one by the Permanent Court of International Justice or other such authority.
   Although this establishes a means for sovereign members to arbitrate disputes they may have with either institution, there still remains a serious gap. This text addresses questions raised by current members in good standing, and not those raised by a member who has withdrawn from membership, or in a situation where either the World Bank or the IMF is dissolving.

[93] See J. Cahn, *supra* n. 3, p. 167. Perhaps this function can be better termed the 'law-giving' function of the Bretton Woods institutions, since these institutions are not responsible for actually legislating such changes into effect in the borrower country.

is truly phenomenal. Although the World Bank's Articles of Agreement provide that the Bank shall not interfere with the political affairs of any of its members,[94] the Bank exercises wide latitude in this area. The World Bank's General Counsel has interpreted this provision to mean that as long as governance issues are related to economic development, Bank-imposed conditionality on governance issues in furtherance of development purposes is acceptable.[95] Thus, by imposing complex matrices of conditionality, the IMF and the World Bank often require sovereign borrowers to agree to change their macro-economic, legal and institutional frameworks. Sovereign members are often required to make profound structural changes to comply with World Bank 'conditionality' before any financing is made available to it.

Similarly, the conditionality imposed by the IMF's structural adjustment programmes, as Korea's brief example illustrates, can require profound structural changes. These changes may affect the manner of governance, may require the passage of new legislation and may require that public and private industries and government agencies be fundamentally restructured. Under the IMF's structural adjustment programme, for example, Korea is required to pass legislation to consolidate its financial sector supervisory function into one government agency.[96] This small example demonstrates the profound impact that IMF-imposed conditionality may have on governance options of the affected country.

In fact, such changes need not be limited to financial sector reform, but may extend to other governance issues, such as controlling corruption in the host country. The conditionality imposed by the IMF, the World Bank and other bilateral agencies, can be very detailed and quite burdensome. The governance function of the World Bank and the IMF—the manner in which these changes are agreed to and implemented—lies outside public scrutiny, in both the country of the sovereign borrower and in the international community generally. Whether such changes in governance are good, bad or indifferent is not the real subject of this comment. The cause for concern here is that the power of the IMF and World Bank to effect changes in the governance of its members is unaccounted for.[97]

Accountability, an important constitutional principle of development law, can be encouraged by considering the following options. For example, since the World Bank Inspection Panel may investigate 'requests' brought in relation to adjustment credits issued by the World Bank,[98] the scope of

---

[94] See Articles of Agreement of the International Bank for Reconstruction and Development, Art. I, §10.

[95] See J. Cahn, *supra* n. 3, p. 163, n. 20. See also I. Shihata, 'The World Bank and "Governance" Issues in its Borrowing Members', in *The World Bank in a Changing World* (F. Tschofen and A.R. Parra (eds.), 1991), pp. 79–80.

[96] IMF, *supra* n. 42, p. 1.

[97] See J. Cahn, *supra* n. 3, pp. 164–165.

[98] See Inspection Panel, Request No. 8, 'Bangladesh: Jute Sector Adjustment Credit, Inspection Panel', *Annual Report* (1 August 1996 to 31 July 1997), p. 13.

its investigatory authority can be enlarged to include the structural adjustment activities of the IMF. (Of course, the World Bank Inspection Panel should be renamed accordingly, and may be known simply as the 'Joint Inspection Panel' or the 'Bretton Woods Inspection Panel'.) By expanding its coverage to jointly cover the Bank's and the IMF's structural adjustment activities, the Inspection Panel is the first step in investigating the potential complaints brought by participants in the development process.

However, investigating these complaints is not enough. Although this is a very important step towards making development more participatory in nature, the Inspection Panel is only authorized to investigate. It is not a law-making, administrative body with independent enforcement powers like an administrative tribunal. The Panel is only empowered to render factual findings, not legal opinions. Delegating investigative power to an independent panel is an important first step, but it still does not adequately address the underlying need for accountability. Even if official action in response to these investigations is taken by the Executive Board of the IMF, this may still not be legally adequate. The only 'remedy' that a borrower has against the IMF is to continue to negotiate further to reach an acceptable solution, which may not always be politically feasible.

For example, the IMF used the procedures set forth in its emergency financing mechanism (EFM) to speed the hastily concluded stand-by arrangement for Korea.[99] What if this line of credit were denied to Korea? What if Korea wanted to question the terms under which such credit was made available to it? What if implementation questions regarding the conditionality agreed to by Korea under the agreement arose during the course of the project?[100] At this point, neither Korea nor private parties affected by the adjustment programme have any means (or any forum) in which to challenge the validity of this agreement, or the discrete actions taken pursuant to it.

---

[99] See Emergency Financing Mechanism, *supra* n. 45, pp. 156–160. This document provides, in relevant part, that: 'The emergency procedures would be expected to be used only in rare circumstances that represented or threatened to give rise to a crisis in a member's external accounts requiring immediate response from the Fund. Identification of such an emergency would be based on an initial judgment by management, in consultation with the Executive Board, that the member was faced with a truly exceptional situation threatening its financial stability, and that a rapid Fund response in support of strong policies was needed to forestall or to contain significant damage to the country itself or to the international monetary system, it being understood that the potential for spillover effects would be an important element of the Board's final judgment'. *Ibid.*, p. 158.

[100] Implementation questions can become quite problematic, since the emergency procedures of the Fund specify that: 'The conditions for activation of emergency procedures would include the readiness of the member to engage immediately in accelerated negotiations with the Fund, with the prospect of early agreement on—and implementation of—measures sufficiently strong to address the problem. Prior actions normally would be expected'. Emergency Financing Mechanism, *supra* n. 45, p. 158.

Thus, the interpretation of this clause regarding the implementation of measures deemed 'sufficiently strong' is an open question, and one for which the member country has no redress in the event of an adverse decision by the IMF Executive Board.

This creates an accountability gap with the IMF, and thereby violates a constitutional principle of development law.[101] As discussed above, the scope of the World Bank Inspection Panel can be enlarged to include investigations of adjustment credits made by the IMF; as an institutional response, this is not sufficient. There should be an independent, adjudicatory body empowered to render legal opinions on the legal validity of such complaints. Leaving this to the discretion of the executive boards of the World Bank and the IMF still leaves an accountability gap.

Before an independent body can be established to adjudicate capital transfer disputes arising between the World Bank, the IMF, and the respective members, the legal principles and procedural practices underlying the sovereign lending practices of these institutions need to be fully articulated. This may be a propitious time to initiate such a discussion since the policy groundwork is already being established. For example, at a recent meeting held at Davos, Switzerland, hundreds of government leaders, financiers, and investment bankers, economists, industrial leaders and others convened to discuss how to avoid another Asian currency crisis by formulating rules on foreign bank lending.[102] In other words, serious discussions are taking place on whether to implement capital controls by limiting or discouraging the flow of short-term loans to developing countries. Short-term capital flows are now being recognized as a precipitating factor for financial disaster as in the Asian currency crisis.[103]

In more concrete terms, taxing short-term loans with maturities of one year or less, or offering tax deductions for loans of one year or more, provides disincentives for short-term lending, and incentives for long-term investment.[104] These and other proposals for instituting capital controls to be implemented by the IMF are currently under serious consideration.

---

[101] Indeed, the IMF's 'accountability gap' is very wide in certain circles. For example, the IMF has fallen from favour with the political right as an institution which is 'the enemy of free markets'. See P. Passell, 'Economic Scene: The I.M.F. must go, critics say, but who will cope with crises?', *New York Times*, 12 February 1998, p. D2. The political left have also roundly criticized the IMF for taking a 'one-size-fits-all approach to financial distress', and for inflexibly insisting on debt repayments from economically struggling economies, making the IMF into little more than a 'collection agency for international bankers'. *Ibid.* Thus, W.B. Wriston, the former Chairman of Citicorp, concluded that the IMF was 'ineffective, unnecessary and obsolete'. *Ibid.*

   In light of the IMF's failure to predict and contain the Asian currency crisis of late 1997-early 1998, it has lost part of its political credibility. Although none but the most radical of free market ideologues believe that the world monetary system can function without the watchdog function of the IMF, the secrecy which surrounds its proceedings and its dogmatic and authoritarian prescriptions for macro-economic reform may have to change in response to a new political climate. Indeed, Mr. Passell reports that, "[f]irst among the demands of the I.M.F.'s newly empowered critics is an end to the secrecy that shrouds everything from routine country status reviews to emergency bail-out plans." *Ibid.* The following discussion suggests a novel approach to resolving the underlying accountability and credibility crisis being faced by the IMF now.

[102] L. Uchitelle, 'I.M.F . May Be Closer To Lending-Curb Idea: Critics Warn of Free-Market Tampering', *New York Times*, 3 February 1998, p. D4.

[103] *Ibid.*

[104] *Ibid.*

Additionally, observers seem agreed on the need for instituting stronger financial monitoring, surveillance, and rating systems for developing nations' monetary systems.

The real policy conflict stems from the view that such capital controls, while possibly warranted where a developing nation is exiting from short-term financial crises, actually interfere with free global markets. Further, many fear that capital controls of this type may inhibit such a country from making long-term macro-economic adjustments, by keeping its economy hobbling along. These are precisely the issues that should be faced and resolved by the international financial community. Indeed, the successful resolution of such issues may fundamentally affect the future role and continued viability of the IMF.

Perhaps a special, joint annual meeting of the IMF and World Bank can be arranged to consider the passage of a protocol setting forth the legal principles for making capital transfers by the Bretton Woods institutions to their sovereign members. This protocol should be submitted for acceptance by the Executive Directors of the IMF and the World Bank, respectively. The Articles of Agreement of each institution may need to be amended accordingly, so that IMF and World Bank executive board decisions can be appealed in this manner. Once the protocol is adopted, the next step of establishing an institutional framework to adjudicate the rights of the parties flowing from the substantive legal principles set forth there in can be pursued.

An independent adjudicatory body with certain enforcement powers, initially called the Capital Transfer Appellate Board (CTAB), should be established in order to formally adjudicate disputes between the Bretton Woods institutions and their members. The function of the CTAB would be to help ensure accessibility, transparency and accountability in the development process. The skeletal framework for such an institution is proposed in the Annex, *infra*.

The CTAB should adjudicate such rights, liabilities and remedies arising from the protocol, and other relevant legal sources, on a problem-driven basis. In other words, the legal opinions generated by the CTAB should respond to the specific questions brought for its judicial determination by members of the Bretton Woods institutions. Thus, the substantive law which is created through this independent adjudicatory process will be problem-driven, rather than an abstract process.

An important distinction should be made at the outset insofar as the CTAB provides a forum for sovereign nations to appeal executive board decisions issued by the IMF and the World Bank, respectively. Why should any redress be provided to sovereign members of these institutions, and why is this important? Currently, sovereign members have no right of redress for IMF or World Bank executive board decisions, with a limited exception of appealing executive board interpretations of their respective Articles of Agreement to the Board of Governors.[105] However, the issue here is not decisions related to

---

[105] See e.g., Articles of Agreement of the International Bank for Reconstruction and Development, Art. IX(a); and Articles of Agreement of the International Monetary Fund, Art. XXIX.

the Articles of Agreement of these institutions, but their decisions to approve financing and implemention of development assistance.

In order to provide further clarification of this matter, let me first state that the CTAB is *not* designed to give sovereign governments the means for escaping, avoiding or nullifying agreements that have been entered into with the IMF and the World Bank. Structural adjustment programmes are especially painful in the short-term, and it requires a steely political will to fully implement such measures. The temptation to wriggle out of these commitments must be strong. The CTAB does not provide the means to abrogate commitments to implement structural reform measures undertaken by a host government.

The CTAB appellate process is designed to address the potential accountability gap insofar as the executive decisions of the IMF and the World Bank are not subject to scrutiny, and cannot be effectively questioned. The governance function of these institutions is currently wielded without any safeguards, and the CTAB is designed to make this function more transparent and accountable to the sovereign party affected by such decisions. It is *not* meant to provide a convenient way out for sovereign nations which do not want to follow through with structural adjustment measures. The CTAB is thus designed to provide a forum to sovereign members of the Bretton Woods institutions to appeal executive board decisions.

Private claimants now have access to the World Bank Inspection Panel, whose jurisdiction arguably should be expanded to cover IMF activities. Similar to the WTO practice where private claimants may lobby their respective sovereign government to appeal decisions to the DSB, the same option should be made available for private claimants seeking appellate review by the CTAB. Thus, private interested parties should be free to lobby their respective sovereign government to bring an appeal before the CTAB. Regardless of such lobbying by private parties, however, bringing an appeal before the CTAB is a political matter for the host government as only a sovereign member may appeal an IMF or World Bank executive board decision.

The CTAB has been conceived as an appellate body (rather than an arbitration board) since its function will be to resolve discrete appeals of decisions issued by the executive boards of the IMF and the World Bank, respectively. Indeed, the scope of the discretion which may be exercised by these executive boards is impressive. The Executive Directors of the IMF and the World Bank, for example, are authorized to decide policy matters, interpret their respective Articles of Agreement, and approve all financing for loan and credit proposals.[106] Therefore, all capital transfers, whether in

---

[106] See Articles of Agreement of the International Bank for Reconstruction and Development, Art. V, §4(a), which specifies that the Executive Directors 'shall be responsible for the conduct of the general operations of the Bank'. Articles of Agreement of the International Monetary Fund, Art. VII, §3(a), specifies that the Fund's Executive Directors shall be responsible for 'conducting the operations of the Fund'.

Further the World Bank's Executive Directors are empowered to issue interpretations of its Articles of Agreement (see Art. IX), and the Fund's Executive Directors are given the equivalent authority to interpret its Articles of Agreement (see Art. XXIX). See also J. Cahn, *supra* n. 3, p. 185.

the form of loans, credits, currency purchases, or other types of financing, must be approved, in principle, by the executive boards of these institutions. If these decisions may be appealed to the CTAB, as proposed herein, the scope of the appellate jurisdiction of the CTAB will be very wide, if not all-inclusive of the corporate acts of these institutions.

It is also important that all such executive decisions should be subject to review by the CTAB, regardless of whether such decisions deal with structural adjustment financing, loans or credits. The jurisdictional question that was raised by World Bank management with regard to the mandate of the Inspection Panel to investigate claims relating to adjustment credits, has been resolved in favour of giving the Panel inspection authority over such matters.[107] The same jurisdictional scope should be accorded to the CTAB.

It is important that the CTAB possess sufficient enforcement powers to be truly effective. Initially, the CTAB should be accorded the power both to make declaratory judgments and to grant injunctive relief on a limited basis in exceptional circumstances. This would mean, for example, that a provision in the conditionality matrix appealed by a sovereign member may be declared null and void by the CTAB and struck from the under-lying loan document or letter. This element of the conditionality matrix would be rendered a nullity, and the financing would proceed without requiring compliance with it, unless otherwise directed by the CTAB. The remainder of the agreement, as severable from the stricken provision, would remain intact and unaffected by the CTAB decision. The legal opinion of the CTAB would not, however, affect any remedies which might otherwise be available to the IMF or the World Bank.

In order for the CTAB to consider such an appeal, certain bases for an appeal must be demonstrated by the sovereign member. The proposed jurisdictional bases for bringing such an appeal are the following:

(1) that the IMF or the World Bank, in making or implementing the executive decision in question, failed to follow their respective policies or procedures with respect to an act or omission committed by either institution;

(2) that an act or omission required of a member by the IMF or the World Bank violates the member's laws, rules, procedures, or public policy;

(3) that any act or omission required of the member by the IMF or the World Bank violates the terms or conditions of a valid international agreement entered into, or other obligation incumbent upon, such a member;

(4) that any act or omission required of the member by the IMF or the World Bank, and duly agreed to by such member, cannot be carried out due to unforeseeable, changed circumstances, other than a change in government or official policy made subsequent to such an agreement being entered into.

---

[107] See Inspection Panel, *supra* n. 98, p. 13.

Of course, these jurisdictional grounds for bringing an appeal may be changed or refined as the practice of the CTAB develops over time.

Parties bringing appeals must demonstrate to the satisfaction of the CTAB that negotiation with the relevant institution, or cancellation of the underlying financing, are not feasible options. This should eliminate the bringing of appeals by members which are best suited to a negotiated solution. Nevertheless, it is recognized that negotiations may not be successful in all cases, especially since the World Bank 'tends to adopt a take-it-or-leave-it stance' in its negotiations.[108] This may be even more true of the IMF.

Finally, with regard to amending the proposed draft protocol establishing the CTAB, amendments should be made by the CTAB itself following a notice and comment period. Interested parties should be permitted to comment on proposed amendments to the draft protocol in accordance with the rules for doing so as established by the CTAB.

The CTAB, as proposed here, is designed to provide a means and a forum for holding the IMF and the World Bank accountable for their corporate decisions. Yet the IMF's sphere of influence extends far into the international financial community. As Chapter 3 will discuss in further detail, there is strict mutual cooperation between the IMF, the World Bank, bilateral donor institutions acting through the Paris Club and private creditors acting in consortium independently or through the London Club. Multilateral financing, bilateral debt rescheduling and 'new money' infusions from private banks will only be made available if an IMF stand-by arrangement is in place with the sovereign government in question. Thus, the host government's standing in the international finance community hinges on whether the IMF makes its pivotal decision to agree to a stand-by arrangement with the host government. This is the crucial first domino which must fall if other international financing is to be made available to the host government.

In light of the above, therefore, accountability should extend beyond the IMF and the World Bank. Since so many decisions to provide development-related financing hinge on an IMF executive board decision, downstream decisions made by regional banks, bilateral lending institutions, and private commercial creditors should be made more transparent and open. These institutions should also be held accountable for their financing decisions. Accordingly, the scope of the CTAB's jurisdiction should be expanded to reflect this.

Since World Bank structural adjustment and sectoral loans are institutionally linked so closely to IMF financing, my recommendation is to group the IMF and the World Bank together for a test run. If the prototype CTAB for the IMF and the World Bank goes well over an initial period of two years, then its jurisdiction can be expanded to the next level which should include regional lending institutions such as the EBRD (Europe), the IDB (Latin America and the Caribbean), the African Development Bank (Africa)

---

[108] J. Cahn, *supra* n. 3, p. 183, quoting a World Bank report (the 'Wapenhaus Report') reprinted in World Bank, *Portfolio Management Task, Effective Implementation: Key to Development Impact* (World Bank, 1992), Annex B, p. 3.

and the Asian Development Bank (Asia). These institutions should accede to the protocol and the agreement establishing the CTAB. Such signatories should be given leave to enter any amendments that may be appropriate to their institutional framework, articles of agreement or constitutions.

Two years following the addition of regional banks, the bilateral donor community should also enter the picture by acceding to the protocol and the agreement establishing the CTAB. (An Agreed Minutes of Meeting at the Paris Club at a special meeting convened for this purpose can be arranged to prevent unnecessary duplication of effort.) Two years hence, the private creditors (leading commercial banks in international lending syndicates, in other words) can also accede to the protocol, and be signatories to a special annex to the protocol drafted for this purpose. This way, private creditors who require that IMF stand-by arrangements be in place before additional commercial financing will be made available to the sovereign debtor will also be held accountable for their actions.

Thus, the sovereign nations who are profoundly affected by the multi-dimensional nature of international borrowing practices shall have an independent forum in which to challenge the discrete, yet interrelated, decisions made by the international creditor community along the lines suggested above. The purpose of this proposal is not to suggest more litigation for the sake of litigation, but to open up development-related, international financing to new accountability standards. Individual sovereign governments must exercise their discretion in not bringing spurious claims, and the CTAB must be vigilant about not entertaining frivolous and disruptive appeals. The CTAB appellate process should be regarded by all parties as an extraordinary right to appeal where further negotiation is pointless.

The above proposal is directed at providing greater parity and mutuality of obligation by the various parties entering into international financing commitments. It is not intended to provide the institutional means for bringing international development financing to a dead halt. Clearly, this would not serve the special interests of any party, least of all those of developing countries. The CTAB is meant to provide a concrete, institutional framework in which to discuss capital transfer practices and policies, reach an international consensus thereon and create a problem-driven body of substantive law flowing therefrom.

5. CONCLUSION

In conclusion, why should we be concerned about establishing development law as a separate field of legal inquiry? The need for doing so is dictated by the urgency with which legal systems now need to react to fast-moving current events. There is an absence of an existing legal framework in which to consider questions such as the Asian currency crisis which has been unfolding since the late summer of 1997, and whose repercussions are still being felt globally. This is not simply a question for economists, but one for lawyers as well. Lawyers must react to the changing economic needs by forging legal solutions which support resolutions of complex development questions.

If lawyers fail to react, law will be left out of the development equation, and that it is too high a risk to take. This is particularly true if a Rule of Law regime is to be implemented, maintained and strengthened over time on a worldwide basis. If not, then there will be increasing discordance between the laws and legal systems of the world, and the important and complex development needs that such laws are intended to support. In light of the new legal needs posed by the globalization process, existing laws may become so inadequate or contradictory that the current legal scheme may risk systemic failure and collapse. The time to act decisively in formulating the new tenets of development law is now.

In light of the above discussion, what critical components of development law are missing? First, there needs to be some overall understanding and acceptance of the constitutional principles of development law: openness, transparency, accessibility and accountability.

Secondly, the international legal community must come to terms with the substantive principles of development law: mutuality of obligation, the duty of cooperation, fair dealing, and the right to participatory development. In giving this basic framework substance and meaning, the international community needs to work towards the development of new contextual norms on a variety of subjects, not the least of which are the substantive legal principles of capital transfers in support of development which are made available by the Bretton Woods institutions and other financiers.

Finally, the institutional framework for enforcing such rights under development law, and the constructive rules of engagement need to be strengthened. The investigatory powers of the World Bank Inspection Panel need to be refined and enlarged to include the adjustment programmes of the IMF. In addition, in order to support the mutuality of obligations among the members of the Bretton Woods institutions, an adjudicatory body such as the CTAB needs to be formed in order to make the institutions accountable for their governance function. In the end, the aim is to make the development process more accessible to sovereign participants, and more accountable to the ultimate end-beneficiaries of the development process.

Part II
Structural Legal Reform

3. International Borrowing

Part II, Structural Legal Reform, will explore three separate areas of international finance which are fundamentally interconnected. This Part concentrates on legal reforms within the financial sectors of developing countries. Financial sector reform is extremely important in terms of integrating developing nations into a global economy.

The discussion will explore certain notions of law and legal regulation of trade, capital investment, and economic development underlying such reforms. Chapter 3 will address international borrowing practices and the resulting debt crisis. The strategies and specific tactics of resolving the debt overhang of the developing world—a critical impediment to long-term development—will be analysed, along with future prescriptions for debt relief.

Chapter 4 will review recent trends in privatization. The withdrawal of the state from productive sectors of the economy has been a key strategy for development during the past decade. The implications of changing the role of the state from being a provider of basic goods and services to that of being a regulator of the economy will be discussed. Additionally, the manner in which privatizations are being accomplished also provides valuable insights into what strategies are working, for whom, and why. Innovative techniques for small and large-scale privatizations will be addressed in this context.

Finally, strengthening the private sector in developing countries and creating emerging capital markets will be explored in Chapter 5. Many emerging capital markets are rethinking strategies for financing their development needs, and are beginning to rely more heavily on private capital markets. Thus, Part II should provide the reader with an overall view of key developments in financial sector reform, particularly as such reforms have been influencing legal changes in developing countries and transitional economies.

1. THE SOVEREIGN DEBT CRISIS

A principal cause of underdevelopment is the lack of access to capital.[1] Whereas industrialized nations have mobilized capital savings and

---

[1] B. Boyd, 'The Development of a Global Market-Based Debt Strategy to Regulate Private Lending to Developing Countries', (1988) 18 *Georgia J. Int'l and Comp. L.* 461 at 464.

investments over the course of centuries, the picture has been very different for developing countries.[2] In the colonial era, profits were not reinvested in developing country enterprises or returned to local investors as dividends—they were expatriated to investors in European nations. The failure to reinvest profits in developing country economies resulted in the severe undercapitalization of developing country enterprises. Moreover, the failure to incorporate developing economies into the international monetary system skewed their incipient financial markets.

Capital accumulation is very difficult in cash-poor economies. This has been particularly true of developing economies producing agricultural and other basic commodities. Often, global prices for such commodities were set at artificial, non-market rates and the commodities sold at devalued prices on world markets. Thus, there was little opportunity to generate foreign exchange by developing countries which produced exportable raw materials and other goods. Moreover, since much of the industrial manufacturing was done in the North, little emphasis, if any, was placed on generating value-added commodities in the resource-rich but technology-poor South.

What little cash and foreign exchange may be available in cash-depleted developing economies is generally used to pay for imported goods in order to meet basic needs, and for external debt servicing. Since there was little capital accumulation in most developing countries, there was very little capital mobilization through savings (China being a notable exception to this). In light of the fact that capital markets were underdeveloped, or non-existent, in most developing countries, stock market investment was generally not available as an option of creating capital wealth.

Yet, developing countries need large amounts of capital investment to finance development undertakings. Since indigenous capital mobilization is so difficult, developing countries have had no other option but to attract capital investment from industrialized nations. Developing nations have several options for doing so, including: (1) negotiating for foreign aid on a grant basis; (2) borrowing from 'official' sources such as multilateral organizations (like the World Bank), or borrowing from bilateral donors (such as the United States, United Kingdom or France); (3) negotiating loans from private commercial banking sources (such as Citibank); (4) attracting foreign direct investment (FDI); or, (5) attracting foreign portfolio investment (FPI) in the form of equity investments (e.g., shares in mutual funds or direct equity holdings in private companies in the developing country).[3]

Since development projects often have such heavy capital investment needs, the option of foreign aid is not an attractive one. Foreign assistance

---

[2] Certain scholars, such as André Gunder Frank and other dependency theorists, argue that many developing economies were drained of capital during the colonial era. See A.G. Frank and J. Cockcroft, *Dependence and Underdevelopment: Latin America's Political Economy* (Anchor Books, 1972). See also P. Sweezy, *The Theory of Capitalist Development* (Oxford University Press, 1942).

[3] B. Boyd, *supra* n. 1, p. 465.

tends to make small amounts of heavily conditioned aid available for jointly-agreed uses. Moreover, much of the assistance tends to be programmed for making technical assistance, rather than unrestricted sources of capital, available to the developing country in question.

Foreign direct investment is a desirable form of investment principally because it establishes a medium- to long-term relationship between the investor and the developing country. Indeed, FDI may be catalytic in improving the attractiveness of the sector and country involved. However, this form of investment requires close supervision and oversight from entrepreneurs in industrialized countries. In addition, in the past, FDI was often resisted by many developing countries, on political grounds when making financial dealings and accounts accessible to foreign and/or local investors was considered too risky a proposition.

Rather than opening their economies to foreign investors, many developing countries through the 1950s to 1970s instituted protectionist policies, shielding their economies from outside access. Many Latin American and other developing countries reformulated their development strategies in accordance with the reasoning of dependency theorist, Raul Prebisch.[4] Prebisch argued that developing countries mainly produced and exported raw materials and unprocessed commodities, and that the prices of such commodities were artificially depressed or devalued on world commodities markets. Therefore, developing countries' economies tended to deteriorate over time. Prebisch argued that the world free trade system was inherently biased against the developing world, and contributed in a systemic way to perpetuating its underdevelopment.

Following this logic, many Latin American countries, such as Argentina, Brazil, Colombia and Peru, developed import substitution and other protectionist policies in the 1970s. These and other developing countries, including India and South Korea, imposed stiff trade barriers and tariffs behind which to protect and cultivate infant industries in order to compete with industrialized nations.[5] In addition, many formerly foreign-owned industries were nationalized by developing countries following their independence.[6] But despite such policies, and the distrust or unease that many developing countries may have felt concerning foreign direct investment, FDI nevertheless continued to be the dominant means of transferring capital between industrialized nations and developing countries during the 1950s and 1960s.[7] However, there was an abrupt change in lending patterns following the 1973 oil shock.

The wealthy oil-exporting countries (principally Arab nations) earned much of their cash revenues in US dollars which were deposited in dollar-denominated 'petrodollar' accounts in US and European commercial banks.

---

[4] *Ibid.*, p. 466.
[5] *Ibid.*, p. 496, n. 23. See also R. Prebisch, *Change and Development—Latin America's Great Task* (1971); Jova, 'Private Investment in Latin America: Renegotiating the Bargain', (1975) 10 *Tex. Int'l L. J.* 455 at 470–473.
[6] B. Boyd, *supra* n. 1, p. 466.
[7] *Ibid.*, pp. 466, 467.

The glut of hard currency reserves in these commercial banks encouraged them to seek borrowers who would pay interest on loans. This would enable these commercial banks to profit from this excess liquidity. Although private commercial banks had been wary of lending to the developing world, the 1973 oil shock forced them to re-evaluate their lending portfolios. Commercial banks began to look seriously at developing countries as potential borrowers.[8]

Recycling petrodollars in the global economy by lending to sovereign borrowers in the developing world eased the recessionary conditions of the West which had been caused, in part, by the oil shock.[9] Syndication fees in multi-lender sovereign loans accrued as an immediate profit to the lead banks in the syndications, further enhancing the attractions of making sovereign loans.[10] By 1976, foreign direct investment had shrunk to 20 per cent of net capital inflows to developing countries while in the same period, commercial lending outstripped official aid sources as the principal means of funding development.[11]

In an effort to reverse the effects of the worldwide recession, the US Federal Reserve Board raised interest rates in the United States. This had a two-pronged effect: first, it made US dollar deposits more attractive, thereby exacerbating capital flight from the developing world. Secondly, the cost of servicing commercial loans which charged floating interest rates increased substantially as the value of the US dollar appreciated.[12] Since commercial loans to developing countries were made on 'hard', market-based terms rather than 'soft' or concessionary terms, this meant that the interest rates and maturity terms of commercial loans were negotiated at market rates. Thus, interest payments on these commercial loans increased exponentially as a result of the US interest-rate hike.

Although oil prices fell in response to the worldwide recession and the reduced demand for oil, that did not improve the overall economic condition of oil-importing developing countries. As a result of the recession, the demand for developing country exports fell correspondingly, cutting off potential revenue sources for these countries.[13] Moreover, the drop in oil prices adversely affected oil-exporting countries such as Nigeria, Mexico, and Venezuela, which lost an important source of hard currency earnings with which to service their debt.[14]

---

[8] *Ibid.* See also A. Santos, 'Beyond Baker and Brady: Deeper Debt Reduction for Latin American Sovereign Debtors', (1991) 66 *New York U. L. Rev.* 66 at 73; E. Carrasco and R. Thomas, 'Encouraging Relational Investment and Controlling Portfolio Investment in Developing Countries in the Aftermath of the Mexican Financial Crisis', (1996) 34 *Col. J. Transnat'l L.* 539 at 550.

[9] B. Boyd, *supra* n. 1, pp. 467, 468.

[10] A. Santos, *supra* n. 8, p. 73.

[11] World Bank, *World Development Report* (1988), pp. 27–29. See also E. Carrasco and R. Thomas, *supra* n. 8, p. 550.

[12] A. Santos, *supra* n. 8, pp. 72–73. See also E. Carrasco and R. Thomas, *supra* n. 8, p. 551.

[13] R. MacMillan, 'The Next Sovereign Debt Crisis', (1995) 31 *Stan. J. Int'l L.* 305 at 311; see also V. Tanzi, 'Fiscal Policy Responses to Exogenous Shocks in Developing Countries', (1986) 76 *Am. Econ. Rev.* 88 at 89–90.

[14] B. Boyd, *supra* n. 1, p. 472.

Although the debt crisis of the 1980s was caused by a number of significant external economic factors, it was also due to a failure of bank regulation in industrialized countries. Additionally, commercial loan proceeds were mismanaged by developing countries. First, commercial banks in industrialized countries relaxed their lending standards, since they were under the mistaken impression that should debt servicing problems arise, the central banks of the sovereign borrowers would make up for any shortfall. In other words, commercial bank lenders believed that it was impossible for sovereign borrowers to default on their loans.[15]

By paying insufficient attention to their overall loan exposure and the risks involved in lending to developing countries, commercial lenders simply recycled petrodollars. The banks later realized that their failure to exercise adequate supervision over the use of these funds for sovereign lending purposes was a mistake. Supervised lending based under terms of 'conditionality', which required developing countries to meet specific economic targets and institute policy-based reforms, was a duty delegated to the IMF.[16] This soon led to a vicious cycle of unrestricted commercial lending to sovereign borrowers, followed by painful periods of structural adjustment by the borrowing country.

Throughout the 1980s, many developing countries relied heavily on foreign commercial loans to meet their domestic import demands, especially for oil imports. Rather than using the loan proceeds to strategically support export industries, much of the loan proceeds were devoted to inefficient state-owned enterprises which failed to generate profits domestically or abroad, thus further increasing the reliance of developing countries on foreign imports.[17] This had disastrous consequences, since paying for imports and meeting increased debt servicing obligations drained sovereign debtors of their foreign exchange reserves. These reserves were, in fact, desperately needed for investment in strategic, export-oriented sectors of the economy. Investing in capital equipment and technology in critical sectors could have boosted exports, thereby increasing foreign exchange reserves and strengthening the economy.

Soon, developing nations were faced with a crushing burden of external debt, overvalued currencies and inflationary conditions, as well as severe

---

[15] *Ibid.*, p. 469. See also L. Buchheit and R. Reisner, 'The Effect of the Sovereign Debt Restructuring Process on Inter-Creditor Relationships', (1988) *Uni. Ill. L. Rev.* 493 at 496, n. 6. The authors point out that the lack of information concerning sovereign borrowers available to commercial lenders contributed to the debt problem. In other words, it was nearly impossible for commercial lenders to gauge whether sovereign borrowers had become overextended, without knowing how much credit other banks had extended to the debtor country or to its public enterprises.

[16] C. Lichtenstein, 'Aiding the Transformation of Economies: Is the Fund's Conditionality Appropriate to the Task?' (1994) 62 *Fordham L. Rev.* 1943 at 1947, writes that: 'The Fund is an exemplar of the theory of familial relations called "tough love". The Fund will promise the availability of funds, but the applicant country must demonstrate that it will embark on policies that, in the Fund's view, will enable the applicant country to repay the borrowing as soon as possible. Moreover, the Fund has sought to enforce the applicant's adherence to the agreed-upon economic policies by dribbling out its loans'.

[17] A. Santos, *supra* n. 8, p. 74.

fiscal deficits, rising real interest rates and domestic capital flight. These conditions were compounded by the belt-tightening policies of industrialized nations which reacted to the recession by cutting down on foreign imports. Thus, dwindling exports in a recessionary world market left developing countries with fewer foreign exchange reserves to meet their debt servicing requirements.[18]

Certainly, there was enough blame to go around, from adverse external economic conditions, to quick profit-making without adequate bank regulation, to the short-sighted use of commercial loan proceeds by developing countries[19]—the commercial creditors were by no means all to blame. The developing world's (particularly Latin America's) heavy dependence on foreign capital to finance imports, rather than expand export-oriented industries, also led to a critical shortfall in foreign exchange with which to service debt obligations. Internal and external factors contributed to the impending crisis and by 1982 there was a major debt crisis.

2.   THE MEXICAN DEBT CRISIS: PHASE I

The sovereign debt crisis formally began on 22 August 1982, when Mexico declared a moratorium on its debt repayments, announcing that it could no longer service its external debt.[20] Mexico's external debt exceeded $80 billion, over 30 per cent of which fell due in 1982, and the country had exhausted its foreign exchange reserves. Mexico informed the International Monetary Fund, the US Secretary of the Treasury, and the US Chairman of the Federal Reserve Board that it could no longer service its external debt.[21] This was the first indication of the impending debt crisis. Brazil, Venezuela, Argentina, the Philippines and Chile all followed in short order with similar debt crises.[22]

---

[18] See J. Asherman, 'The International Monetary Fund: A History of Compromise', (1984) 16 *Int'l L. and Pol.* 235.

[19] Commercial borrowing by developing countries during this time frame was a window of opportunity in terms of unprecedented access to international lenders. Essentially, the loans did not prescribe the uses the loan should be applied to. In other words, there was no 'conditionality' attached. Rather than investing in capital improvements in export-oriented industries, much of the loan proceeds were used to pay deficit accounts of non-performing SOEs. In Mexico's case, almost half of the funds borrowed in 1981 were expatriated abroad, rather than invested in-country. See J. Asherman, *supra* n. 18, p. 297. However, Ms Asherman concludes that, 'On the whole, however, the developing nations invested their borrowings in growth oriented industries.' *Ibid.*

[20] L. Buchheit, 'Sucretisation and Original Sin', (September 1990) *Int'l Fin. L. Rev.* 21; A. Santos, *supra* n. 8, p. 66; see also E. Carrasco and R. Thomas, *supra* n. 8, p. 551; Schirano, 'A Banker's View', in W. Eskridge, Jr., (ed.), *A Dance Along the Precipice: The Political and Economic Dimensions of the International Debt Problem* (1985), p. 20.

[21] S. Cohen, 'Give Me Equity or Give Me Debt: Avoiding a Latin American Debt Revolution', (1988) 10 *Uni. Penn. J. Int'l L.* 86 at 94–95.

[22] E. Carrasco and R. Thomas, *supra* n. 8, pp. 551, 571–572; see also L. Buchheit, 'You'll Never Eat Lunch in this Conference Room Again', (April 1992) *Int'l Fin. L. Rev.* 11. By July 1983, over 40 countries had applied for debt reschedulings. J. Asherman, *supra* n. 18, p. 295.

The conditions which precipitated the debt crisis are fairly simple to understand, although the ramifications of the crisis itself are more complex. The following discussion will examine the strategic responses to the sovereign debt crisis by the IMF, the US Treasury Department and commercial lenders.

Sovereign debt problems were initially handled on a case-by-case basis by commercial bank lenders and the IMF. During the initial phase of the crisis, from 1982 to 1985, the United States had no official debt policy, relying instead on commercial bank creditors and the IMF to resolve the crisis on an *ad hoc* basis.[23] The inadequacy of this initial response contributed to the subsequent 1994–95 Mexican debt crisis, which ultimately necessitated a $50.8 billion bail-out package by the US government.

From 1982 to 1985, the immediate response to the sovereign debt crisis was to impose a policy of 'containment'[24] which had three separate components: (1) rescheduling; (2) commercial lending of 'new money' loans; and (3) the imposition of IMF adjustment programmes. The 'containment' policy allowed debtor countries to continue to service their external debt, but had a slightly panicked edge to it since US and European commercial banks were dangerously over-exposed in their sovereign borrower debt portfolio. The first priority, therefore, was to avoid an international banking collapse.

2.1 Rescheduling

A sovereign debt crisis is created when a country's net inflow of foreign exchange is insufficient to meet its external debt burden. Generally, such liquidity crises are dealt with through such means as rescheduling or forgiving certain debt obligations, reducing imports and stimulating exports, or by further borrowing from foreign sources.[25]

In the initial stages, the sovereign debt crisis was regarded as a liquidity crisis rather than an insolvency crisis.[26] In other words, the crisis was seen as being a short-term cash shortage that could be remedied through fast-paced economic growth. Increased exports would generate the foreign exchange needed to allow debtor countries to resume their loan repayments. No one anticipated that such economic growth would stall indefinitely in some cases, or not materialize at all in others.

When a sovereign debtor is unable to meet its debt servicing requirements, the potential default on the underlying loan affects all syndicated lenders. (Syndication simply means that several private commercial bank creditors have lent their funds to one borrower through a single loan document.) In cases where a loan default is imminent, the debtor country usually approaches the lead bank (usually with the participation of the

---

[23] P. Power, 'Sovereign Debt: The Rise of the Secondary Market and Its Implications for Future Restructurings', (1996) 64 *Fordham L. Rev.* 2701 at 2709.

[24] B. Boyd, *supra* n. 1, pp. 475–476.

[25] L. Buchheit, 'The Capitalization of Sovereign Debt', 1988 *Uni. Ill. L. Rev.* 401.

[26] R. MacMillan, *supra* n. 13, p. 322.

IMF, the implications of which will be explored later) to help renegotiate the terms of the syndicated loan in question.

The syndicated banks form a steering or advisory committee, generally composed of 10 to 14 banks, to renegotiate the terms of repayment of the original loan instrument. *Pari passu* clauses which may appear in the original debt instrument ensure that all creditors are treated equally.[27] However, the number of parties involved in rescheduling sovereign debt can be unmanageable for large loan syndications. For example, in the case of Mexico's 1982 debt crisis, Mexico had more than 500 commercial lenders of record.[28]

In the initial stage of the debt crisis, commercial banks rescheduled loans with maturity dates falling due within one year, which meant that rescheduling took place every year.[29] It quickly became clear, however, that the debt crisis would not be resolved within a year or two, so multi-year rescheduling agreements were entered into. The first such agreement to be negotiated concerned Mexico's external public sector debt with maturities of up to five years, which was rescheduled over a period of 14 years.[30] Parallel restructuring agreements were concluded for each underlying syndicated loan, but all the parallel agreements may have been contained in a single document.[31]

Under US banking law, principal payments may be rescheduled to decrease overall debt service amounts, and loan maturity dates may be lengthened, but interest payments on the loan must be kept current. This means that interest payments must be made within 90 days of the due date.[32] Should interest payments lapse for more than 90 days, the debt may be declared 'non-performing' and be charged against the bank's reserves. This write-off will be reflected on the asset side of the bank's balance sheet. Once loan reserves are exhausted, there is a corresponding reduction in the bank's earnings. If bank earnings are insufficient to sustain the loss, then the

---

[27] B. Boyd, *supra* n. 1, p. 507. *Pari passu* clauses simply ensure that all creditors will be treated equally and rateably in the event that the loan is paid by the debtor. In other words, the repayment will be equally shared by all the syndicated lenders in accordance with the percentage of the loan made by each individual lender.

  Other clauses which may appear in the original debt instrument also ensure the equal and fair treatment among the lenders, and may include such provisions as sharing clauses (all creditors share the funds originating from repayment, set-offs or secured interests); mandatory prepayment clause (each creditor is entitled to a rateable portion of a prepayment of the loan that is paid earlier than contemplated by the loan or rescheduling agreement); cross-default clause (a default of the instant loan agreement may be called if the debtor defaults on another loan to a third party); and negative clause (prohibits the debtor from granting security interests on its assets or property in favor of third parties).

[28] L. Buchheit and R. Reisner, 'The Effect of the Sovereign Debt Restructuring Process on Inter-Creditor Relationships', (1988) *Uni. Ill. L. Rev.* at 505–506.

[29] C. R. Ebenroth, 'The Changing Legal Framework for Resolving the Debt Crisis: A European's Perspective', (1989) 23 *Int'l Lawyer* 629 at 633.

[30] *Ibid.*, p. 633.

[31] *Ibid.*, p. 635.

[32] See R. MacMillan, *supra* n. 13, p. 321; M. Monteagudo, 'The Debt Problem: The Baker Plan and the Brady Initiative: A Latin American Perspective', (1994) 28 *Int'l Lawyer* 59 at 62; see also T. Link, 'The Value of Bank Assets Subject to Transfer Risk', (1984) 23 *Colum. J. Transnat'l L.* 75.

bank's net worth will be reduced accordingly.[33] Therefore, if the loan is actually 'written off', the profitability of the bank's operations will suffer commensurately, thus gradually eroding its capital base. In the worst case scenario, this may lead to the bank's insolvency and, finally, its bankruptcy.

More importantly, rescheduling debt does not 'forgive' any portion of the debt; it simply extends the period within which repayment must be made in order to enable the borrower to repay the loan. Thus, the original rate of interest on the loans in question was not reduced by the commercial banks. Since most interest payments were at 'floating' market rates, rather than at fixed concessional rates, the strong US dollar in the mid-1970s added to the volatility of the equation.

The immediate concern of commercial banks was to preserve the income stream generated by interest payments on the loan. In order to avoid defaults on interest payments, commercial banks soon realized that quick infusions of new money would be necessary in order for sovereign debtor countries to keep making current interest payments. Moreover, US commercial banks knew that US bank regulators would not penalize them for lending additional money to sovereign borrowers. This would enable foreign borrowers to make current interest payments on the original loan.[34] Thus, US bankers adopted a policy of 'throwing good money after bad'.

2.2 New money lending

'New money' loans were aimed at filling the financing gap,[35] thereby enabling the debtor country to meet its balance-of-payments shortfall. The new money loans took into account any additional official funds (made available by multilateral banks or bilateral donors) that would help ease the credit squeeze. However, another problem immediately appeared. Although many banks had participated in the syndicated lendings to sovereign borrowers

---

[33] M. Monteagudo, *supra* n. 32, p. 62. During the period for restructuring sovereign loan agreements, banks had a general reserve fund called the Allowance for Loan Losses, or the loan-loss reserve. (*Ibid.*, p. 65.) The loan-loss reserve was considered to be part of the bank's capital and surplus so that a deduction made against the reserve resulted in a corresponding loss to the bank's capital.

Under the US International Lending Supervision Act, 12 U.S.C. §§3901–12 (1988), a special reserve called the Allocated Transfer Risk Reserve (ATRR) was established. The ATRR is not part of the general capital and surplus of the bank, but is established with regard to specific loans which are officially classified according to the amount of country risk assessed by the Interagency Country Exposure Review Committee. These country risk classification levels range from strong, moderately strong, weak, substandard, value-impaired and loss. (*Ibid.*, pp. 65–66.) The ATRR must also be established with respect to a specific loan that is past due in interest or principal for over 90 days. Once a loan is subject to the ATRR, the interest income from the loan, if any, cannot be reported as bank income, and has the same effect as writing down the loan. (*Ibid.*, p. 65.) See also L. Buchheit, 'Alternative Techniques in Sovereign Debt Restructuring', (1988) *Uni. Ill. L. Rev.* 371, 379–381; C. Lichtenstein, 'The US Response to the International Debt Crisis: The International Lending Supervision Act of 1983', (1985) 25 *Va. J. Int'l L.* 401.

[34] J. Burlock, 'Legal Implications of Interest Rate Caps on Loans to Sovereign Borrowers', (1985) 17 *New York U. J. Int'l L. and Pol.* 543 at 549–551.

[35] A. Santos, *supra* n. 8, p. 75.

during the 1970s, not all had the same degree of exposure. Whereas larger banks with maximum exposure had a vested interest in funding new money to enable the debtor country to continue interest payments, this dire need was not necessarily shared by smaller banks in the lending syndicates.

Smaller banks (or, at least, banks with minimal exposure on sovereign loans) showed a natural reluctance to extend additional credit to nearly insolvent sovereign debtors.[36] This became increasingly problematic where the concurrence of smaller bank was critical to the equation. Many loan documents contained restrictive covenants ensuring that all creditors be treated equally, receiving *pro rata* shares of loan repayments made by the borrower. Some restrictive clauses also required unanimity among the syndicated lenders before the loan instrument could be amended.

For example, a sharing clause in the original loan agreement might require that disproportionate payments to one creditor be shared amongst the other creditors. This created a 'free rider' problem, insofar as the smaller creditors could benefit from the loan packaging arranged by larger creditors and the IMF. Lee Buchheit has commented that:

In the context of sovereign debt restructuring, a free rider is a bank which desires to be paid interest on its credit exposure to a sovereign borrower but which declines to participate in the new financings that effectively fund those interest payments. From the standpoint of the sovereign borrower, such a bank wants to ride on the bus which keeps interest payments current, but apparently does not fancy buying a ticket. Even worse, the sovereign's other lenders, whether official or commercial bank, may see themselves as indirectly paying for a fellow creditor who wants the benefits, but does not wish to share the burdens that attend consensual debt workouts.[37]

Thus, the *quid pro quo* became amply clear since all new money financing (or so-called 'bridge loans') were to be used to service current interest payments falling due in the rescheduling consolidation period. Smaller banks were made to choose between the risk of being cut out of the equation and being forced to list the loan in question as 'non-performing', on the one hand, or financing new money loans on the other hand. Smaller

---

[36] L. Buchheit, *supra* n. 33, pp. 374, 375: 'The verb "invite" when used to describe a request directed to a commercial bank to participate in a new money loan, is euphemistic. . .Any bank that flirts with the idea of *not* participating is reminded that the proceeds of the new money loan will be used largely (if not entirely) to pay current interest due on commercial bank debt'.

[37] L. Buchheit, 'Unseating Free Riders', (September 1989) *Int'l Fin. L. Rev.* at 14. This article first appeared in the September 1989 Issue of International Financial Law Review. http://www.lawmoney.com. The author also suggests various approaches to the 'free rider' problem, including, the 'scorched earth' policy where the majority lenders exchange their interest in the original loan agreement for a parallel facility which requires their participation in a new financing, thereby leaving the so-called 'free riders' with the basically worthless original loan agreement. Another approach would be to pass an amendment to the loan agreement preventing 'free riders' from assigning their interests, or charging stiff fees for such assignments. Amending sharing clauses permitting the non-pro rata share of repayments would require the unanimous agreement of all lenders, including the free riders, whose possibilities of being repaid under the loan may become nil under this arrangement.

banks must have felt this was a choice between Scylla and Charybdis. As the debt crisis struggled on, the yearly or biannual exercise of rescheduling debt owed by nearly insolvent sovereign debtors was beginning to exhaust the parties involved.

2.3 IMF structural adjustment

Apart from new money lending designed to help sovereign debtors repay interest due on their loans, the long-term 'structural adjustment' of their economies also became a factor in the rescheduling process. The IMF began to play a pivotal role in debt restructurings from 1982 onwards,[38] assuming a role in providing funds to ease the repayment crunch by helping its members meet their external debt obligations and, thus, easing the liquidity crisis.

An IMF structural adjustment programme is intended to address the underlying macro-economic problems of the debtor country. A structural adjustment programme agreement was generally concluded in the form of a standby, extended fund, or enhanced credit arrangement in which clear and rigorous economic performance criteria were set out. The legal authority to make stand-by commitments to its member nations is contained in Article I(v) of the IMF's Articles of Agreement.[39] If economic indicators set forth in the stand-by arrangement are not met by the sovereign borrower, and economic growth falters, the availability of new financing may be jeopardized.[40] These 'arrangements' do not have the status of international agreements,[41] and generally do not require ratification by the parliaments of developing countries.

As the debt crisis continued throughout the mid-1980s, it became increasingly clear that the IMF neither had sufficient resources to cover the shortfall in sovereign lending to Latin America, nor did it wish to become

---

[38] R. MacMillan, *supra* n. 13, p. 317. For a discussion of the IMF and structural adjustment 'conditionality', see 'A Survey of the IMF and the World Bank: Sisters in the Wood', *The Economist*, 12 October 1991; see also C. Lichtenstein, *supra* n. 16, p. 1949.

[39] The section provides, in relevant part, that: 'The purposes of the International Monetary Fund are to give confidence to members by making the general resources of the Fund temporarily available to them under adequate safeguards, thus providing them with the opportunity to correct maladjustments in their balance of payments without resorting to measures destructive of national or international prosperity'. Art. I (v), Articles of Agreement of International Monetary Fund, adopted 27 December 1945, 60 Stat. 1401, T.I.A.S. 1501, 2 U.N.T.S. 39, 20 U.S.T. 2775, 29 U.S.T. 2203, as amended. See also C. Lichtenstein, *supra* n. 16, p. 1946.

The World Bank also engages in structural adjustment lending and while the legal authority for doing so is less clear, the 'special circumstances' exception provided in the World Bank's Articles of Agreement is relied on for this purpose. See J. Levinson, 'Multilateral Financing Institutions: What Form of Accountability?' (1992) 8 *Am. U. J. Int'l L. and Pol'y* 47 at 49–50.

[40] J. Gold, 'Financial Assistance by the International Monetary Fund, Law and Practice', *IMF Pamplet Series* No. 27 (2d edn., 1982), pp. 11–24.

[41] A. Jayagovind, 'The Financial Facilities of the IMF: Development Dimensions', in *The Right to Development in International Law* 353 at 355.

the lender of last resort.[42] Thus, as a precondition to making IMF loans (or stand-by arrangements) available for a sovereign debt workout, the IMF began requiring that commercial banks make new monies available.[43] In order to avoid these types of debt crisis occurring in the future, commercial lenders were now required to provide new financing to the debtor country before the IMF will approve the underlying structural adjustment programme, and an associated structural adjustment loan. Therefore, 'involuntary lending' by commercial banks became a standard feature of these debt workouts.

The reciprocality of the arrangements between the commercial banks and the IMF also became a standard feature. The IMF would only approve a structural adjustment programme (and loan) if the bank creditors provided new commercial lending. The commercial banks, on the other hand, conditioned their new loans based on IMF approval of an adjustment programme. In addition, the IMF structural adjustment programme required the sovereign debtor country implement quite severe economic stabilization and liberalization measures very quickly. The entire rescheduling process became a circular one where IMF-imposed austerity measures on the debtor country were conditioned on new commercial loans being in place, and new money lending was conditioned on an approved IMF structural adjustment programme being in place.[44]

IMF adjustment programmes share a number of features that address balance-of-payments crises. IMF-mandated macro-economic adjustment may include, for example: (1) devaluing the currency, thereby encouraging exports and inhibiting imports; (2) cutting subsidies, including agricultural support for farmers; (3) eliminating price controls; (4) reducing the government's fiscal deficit by sharply cutting back government expenditure; (5) raising tax revenues; (6) reducing government-funded social programmes; (7) privatizing certain industries or sectors; and (8) liberalizing trade and attracting new foreign investment.

IMF structural adjustment programmes are meant to provide short-term supervision, and are not expected to remain in place in perpetuity. Indeed, once the initial economic targets of economic stabilization, currency devaluations, eliminating price controls and subsidies, restricting the money supply and reducing government expenditures have been met, IMF austerity measures have been fairly ineffective in stimulating long-term economic growth.[45]

IMF economic stabilization measures usually also include sharp cutbacks in imports to stop the drain on foreign exchange reserves. This generally means that capital equipment imports from industrialized nations drop

---

[42] R. MacMillan, *supra* n. 13, pp. 318–319.

[43] C. Farnsworth, 'A Dramatic Change at the IMF', *New York Times*, 9 January 1983 at C10.

[44] R. MacMillan, *supra* n. 13, pp. 320. See also J. Gold, 'Relations Between Banks' Loan Agreements and IMF Stand-By Arrangements', *Int'l Fin. L. Rev.* (September 1983) at 28; P. Power, *supra* n. 23, p. 2712.

[45] L. Buchheit, *supra* n. 33, pp. 376–377. See also Kahn and Knight, 'Do Fund Supported Adjustment Programs Retard Growth?' *Fin. and Dev.* (December 1985) at 30.

significantly. Since these capital imports can be used to support fledgling export industries in developing countries, the cut-back on imports tends to further stall the growth of export-oriented sectors. This, in turn, tends to reduce gross domestic product levels. Moreover, sharp reductions in government spending tend to lead to recessionary conditions.[46]

The human cost of adjustment policies can be measured in terms of sharply increased unemployment levels, reductions in real wages, and drastically reduced social services to the most vulnerable segments of the population, namely, women, children and the disabled.[47] Rioting in Venezuela in 1989, in protest over the government's austerity measures, left over 300 people dead.[48] IMF structural adjustment programmes are no laughing matter.

It has been suggested that if commercial lenders need some 'comfort' in terms of making additional lending available to sovereign borrowers, this should take some form other than an IMF structural adjustment programme which remains in place indefinitely.[49] Conditioning *all* debt rescheduling by commercial creditors (including those rescheduling private commercial debt under the auspices of the London Club), and by official creditors (acting through the Paris Club), on the imposition of an IMF structural adjustment programme has been overly burdensome on developing countries. The cartelized nature of commercial and official lending has given creditors an unfair advantage in negotiating loan agreements and reschedulings.

Over time, it became clear that the IMF's strategy for imposing austerity measures in an attempt to stabilize, liberalize and restructure debtor nations' economies was too short-sighted. Macro-economic imbalances were seen only in the narrow context of the debtor country alone, and not in terms of the macro-adjustment of world economic conditions. For example, devaluation of developing country currencies is often advocated by the IMF as a means of promoting the free convertibility of the currency, increasing exports and decreasing imports. However, many developing countries rely heavily on exporting raw materials and commodities, the demand for which is not necessarily increased by lower export prices. Thus, the efficacy of devaluing the currency of developing countries has been questioned in certain cases.[50]

In addition, while cutting food subsidies and other basic services is intended to reduce government deficits and stabilize the economy, it does not take into account the social and political impact of such cuts and social services. Imposition of IMF austerity measures led to riots in Peru, Egypt, Ghana and Brazil.[51] Also, these measures did not take into account the fact that trade protectionism and decreased production in

---

[46] A. Santos, *supra* n. 8, p. 76.

[47] B. Boyd, *supra* n. 1, pp. 477–478.

[48] 'After 32 Years of Democracy, Fears of a Coup in Venezuela', *New York Times* (10 August 1990) at A3.

[49] L. Buchheit, *supra* n. 33, p. 377.

[50] J. Asherman, *supra* n. 18, p. 264, n. 166.

[51] *Ibid.*, p. 288, n. 284.

industrialized nations severely cut back on export markets available to developing countries.[52]

The IMF's short-sighted view of structural adjustment problems is somewhat predictable. Lord John Maynard Keynes, head of the British delegation to the 1944 Bretton Woods Conference, lost a critical argument to Harry Dexter White, representing the US Treasury. Keynes argued that the burden for balance-of-payments adjustments should be borne equally by surplus nations as well as deficit nations.[53] Keynes suggested that surplus nations could open their markets to imports from trade deficit countries, and spend their surplus foreign currency.[54] This would reduce the need for debtor nations to make painful adjustments in terms of devaluing their currencies, reducing fiscal deficits, and cutting social services.

Harry Dexter White, however, successfully argued that the burden of correcting any disequilibrium in the international monetary system should fall squarely on the shoulders of debtor nations. He reflected the US position that creditor (or surplus) nations should not be required to adjust their economies or revalue their currencies, even if this meant a long-term net flow of capital resources from economically weaker nations to stronger nations.[55]

Devaluation of their currencies (by adjusting the exchange rate) was viewed with suspicion by most surplus countries, who were wary of creating conditions leading to inflation and unemployment.[56] Surplus nations wished to keep, rather than spend, their excess foreign currency reserves, and shared White's belief that adjustment should be borne by deficit nations. Since White won that argument, the policies of the IMF and the World Bank, created as a result of the 1944 Bretton Woods Conference in New Hampshire, have reflected that position ever since. This ultimately culminated in an ongoing debt crisis of enormous proportions.

The initial response of 'containment' from 1982 to 1985 provided some initial relief to the debt crisis. During that period, over $140 billion in commercial loans were rescheduled, and the IMF provided $31 billion in

---

[52] *Ibid.*, p. 289.

[53] *Ibid.*, pp. 236, 245, 254, 271. Ms Asherman severely criticizes the IMF policy of requiring adjustments of deficit countries, but not surplus countries, as making such adjustment, by necessity, 'harsher'. Unless surplus nations are required to make adjustment as well, she suggests that structural adjustments will continue to be 'destructive of national and international prosperity'. *Ibid.*, p. 301. See also R. Mikesell, 'The Bretton Woods Debates: A Memoir', in *Essays in International Finance*, No. 192 (March 1994) at p. 13. Mr Mikesell, an economist from 1942–47 in the US Treasury Department, Division of Monetary Research, gives a personal account of the debates surrounding the creation of the Bretton Woods institution, in particular, his personal account of the interaction between Lord Keynes and Harry Dexter White.

[54] See J. Asherman, *supra* n. 18, pp. 245–246.

[55] *Ibid.*, p. 271. See also Articles of Agreement of the International Monetary Fund (22 July 1944), 60 Stat. 1401, T.I.A.S. No. 1501, 2 U.N.T.S. 39, reprinted in *III The International Monetary Fund 1945–1965* (J.K. Horsefield (ed.) 1969), p. 8.

[56] J. Asherman, *supra* n. 18, p. 271.

structural adjustment loans to 72 developing countries.[57] 'Involuntary lending' by commercial banks accounted for an additional $27 billion in new money.[58] The balance-of-payments deficit for the developing world declined from $110 billion in 1982, to $44 billion in 1985. A $50 million trade deficit in 1982 of developing countries actually grew to a trade surplus of an astonishing $7 billion in 1985.[59]

The provision of new money by commercial banks enabled sovereign debtors to meet current interest payments falling due within the period of rescheduling, but it was self-serving. Commercial banks needed to provide new money to assist sovereign debtors to meet current interest payments thereby avoiding bank failures, or worse, an imminent collapse of the entire international banking system. Commercial banks did not want to create a 'moral hazard' by reducing or forgiving the debt obligations of sovereign borrowers. This would have had the effect of penalizing other debtors who were servicing their debt obligations, and further reducing the credit-worthiness of sovereign debtors who were not.

In the long run, however, additional new money loans only worsened the debt load of the borrowers. The undeniable fact was that the under-lying balance-of-payments problems of debtor countries were being exacerbated by incurring additional debt. Developing countries' foreign reserves continued to be depleted to service their burgeoning national debts, while the downstream impact of IMF austerity measures was beginning to be expressed in increasing social unrest and unstable political conditions.

The containment policy was short-sighted, in that it treated the debt crisis as a short-term cash flow problem, without seeing the long-term issues with regard to sustained economic growth and solvency. As such, the initial response to the debt crisis merely provided the means for commercial banks (acting in concert with the IMF) to negotiate additional time in which to build up their reserves, or dispose of their sovereign debt holdings as quickly as possible.[60]

Mexico's debt rescheduling negotiations in 1984, which involved approximately $50 billion in public sector debt, were resolved by the extension of an IMF enhanced stand-by credit arrangement.[61] The relative futility of rescheduling debt, issuing new money loans, and imposing harsh IMF austerity measures, became clear as the debt crisis persisted. Stop-gap measures only exacerbated the situation. The underlying problems needed to be addressed in a strategic fashion; the failure to do so was ultimately to lead to a far deeper debt crisis.

---

[57] B. Boyd, *supra* n. 1, p. 477.

[58] *Ibid.*

[59] *Ibid.*

[60] *Ibid.*, p. 478.

[61] L. Buchheit, 'Comity, Act of State, and the International Debt Crisis: Is There an Emerging Legal Equivalent of Bankruptcy Protection for Nations?' *ASIL Proceedings*, 79th Annual Meeting (25 April 1985) at 135.

3. STRATEGIC APPROACHES TO RESOLVING THE DEBT CRISIS

3.1 The Baker Plan

The failure of 'gap' financing to meet loan repayment terms by sovereign debtors became apparent by 1985. Continuing high real interest rates, the reluctance of commercial banks to provide additional new monies, and weak commodity prices all contributed to this failure.[62] In response to the continuing debt crisis, the United States proposed a new policy, which was announced by the then Secretary of the Treasury, James Baker, at the joint annual meeting of the IMF and the International Bank for Reconstruction and Development in Seoul, Korea, on 9 October 1985.[63]

The so-called 'Baker Plan' proposed the following: (1) to provide official support to finance debt repayment; (2) to provide additional commercial bank 'new monies'; and (3) to condition such increased lending levels on the adoption of market-based policies by the recipient sovereign nations. The Baker Plan did not offer a new approach, but merely continued the containment strategy that had been pursued by commercial banks and the IMF since 1982. The Baker Plan simply expanded what had been an *ad hoc* containment policy into a more structured, strategic approach.

The Baker Plan initially addressed 15 countries (the 'Baker Fifteen'), 10 of which were in Latin America. The Baker Plan called for $9 billion in official loans from multilateral banks (primarily the World Bank), and bilateral donors (primarily Japan) over a three-year period from 1985 to 1988.[64] Additionally, commercial banks were asked to lend $20 billion over the same time period.[65] The proposal was predicated on the belief that restructuring the economies of the most heavily indebted nations along market-oriented lines would create a strong internal economy, thereby resolving the debt crisis.

Unfortunately, despite its good intentions, the Baker Plan did not work as planned. Instead of net cash inflows, the Baker Fifteen experienced capital outflows. Servicing the loans extended by international financial institutions (such as the World Bank) resulted in a net outflow from these countries of $4.32 billion, between 1985 and 1988.[66] Although commercial banks did extend new lending that exceeded the $20 billion requested under the Baker Plan over a three-year period from 1985 to 1988, the net capital outflow in interest payments for 1988 alone exceeded this amount.[67]

---

[62] A. Santos, *supra* n. 8, p. 76.
[63] James Baker, III, 'Statement', *Treasury News*, 8 October 1985 at 9, reprinted in D. Dicke (ed.) *Foreign Debts in the Present and a New International Economic Order* (1986), p. 291. See also P. Power, *supra* n. 23, p. 2714.
[64] R. MacMillan, *supra* n. 13, p. 326, n. 112.
[65] *Ibid.* See also A. Santos, *supra* n. 8, p. 76.
[66] A. Santos, *supra* n. 8, p. 77.
[67] *Ibid.*

In fact, the position of sovereign debtors was more precarious in 1985 than it had been in 1982.[68]

When Citicorp, the largest lender to the developing world, announced in May 1987 that it was setting aside $3 billion in loan-loss reserves—a full quarter of Citicorp's total debt holdings[69]—this was an acknowledgement that the debt crisis had gone beyond the limits of the Baker Plan. By increasing the ratio of its capital to its loan-loss reserves, Citicorp would eventually be better able to absorb future losses, and maintain a stronger bargaining position with sovereign borrowers.[70] Citicorp and other commercial banks drastically reduced their exposure to potential sovereign debtor default.[71] This was a clear signal that the debt crisis needed to be dealt with by seeking long-term resolutions that went beyond mere adjustment of bank balances.

3.2   The Brady Initiative

James Baker's successor as Secretary to the US Treasury, Nicholas Brady, announced his 'Brady Initiative' in a speech he gave on 10 March 1989. The Brady Initiative proved to be a momentous turn of events in the debt crisis.[72] This was the first time that the US government lent its official support for voluntary debt reduction (in both principal and interest). More importantly, the United States withdrew its objections to using IMF and World Bank official credits to facilitate such debt reductions.[73]

The Brady Initiative offered a way of 'securitizing' sovereign loans by converting commercial loans into bonds.[74] These bonds, which later became known as 'Brady bonds', pooled together all the commercial bank loans owed by a sovereign debtor, repackaged them, and offered them to the public as bonds.[75] The proceeds generated from the sales of these bonds were then used to retire the original debt. The sovereign debtor makes interest payments on the bonds to an indenture trustee, and those payments are later distributed to the bondholders.[76] Thus, the Brady Initiative allowed the original debt instrument to be transformed into bond obligations, thereby releasing the sovereign debtor from endless rounds of debt reschedulings.

The choices available under a Brady Initiative 'menu of options' were: (1) direct cash buy-backs of the debt by the sovereign debtor; (2) the exchange of the original debt for Brady bonds or so-called 'exit' bonds at a

---

[68] L. Buchheit, 'The Evolution of Debt Restructuring Techniques', (August 1992) *Int'l Fin. L. Rev.* 10 at 11.
[69] *Ibid.* See also M. Monteagudo, *supra* n. 32, p. 67.
[70] M. Monteagudo, *supra* n. 32, pp. 67–68.
[71] *Ibid.*, p. 68.
[72] N. Brady, Remarks to the Brookings Institute and Bretton Woods Conference on Third World Debt, 10 March, 1989.
[73] L. Buchheit, 'The Background to Brady's Initiative', (April 1990) *Int'l Fin. L. Rev.* at 2.
[74] P. Power, *supra* n. 23, p. 2720.
[75] *Ibid.*
[76] *Ibid.*

below-market rate of interest ('par bonds') or, alternatively, exit bonds with a lower face value but at the market rate of interest ('discounted bonds'); or (3) temporary interest rate reduction bonds.[77]

Par bonds have the same face value as the existing debt, but have a discounted, fixed rate of interest of 6.25 per cent.[78] Discounted bonds were discounted by 35 per cent from the original face value of the debt, but charged a market rate of interest (generally a spread of 13–16 per cent over the London Interbank Offered Rate (LIBOR).[79] Temporary interest rate reduction bonds are bonds that have a below-market rate of interest for a specified number of years, at the conclusion of which the interest rate reverts to the market rate.[80] If the option chosen (e.g., buy-back or exit bond) reduces the interest or principal amount of the original loan, then the difference between the original book value and the new discounted value of the loan is calculated as a loss. That difference, in theory, is chargeable against the commercial bank's loan-loss reserve.[81]

The most common form of Brady bonds were bonds issued at the same face value as the original principal amount, but with a reduced, fixed rate of interest. These bonds normally mature thirty years from the date of conversion, much longer than normal market maturities.[82] Thus, the concessionality element is found in the reduced rate of interest and the long maturity length. Additionally, Brady bonds are generally collateralized by the sovereign debtor, who agrees to purchase zero-coupon US Treasury bonds (or comparable securities). Cash for the interest due on the Brady bonds for the first 12 to 18 months is also usually paid in advance by the sovereign debtor at the time of the transaction.[83]

Thus, the Brady Initiative contemplated that commercial banks would agree to modest reductions in the principal and/or interest of loans made to sovereign debtors. In exchange for the debt reduction, 'enhanced credit' would be provided by the IMF, the World Bank, and perhaps by certain bilateral donors such as the Japanese. The net result of the Brady Initiative was that commercial lenders were able to set aside a certain portion of the loans in anticipation of the enhanced credit support provided by multilateral/bilateral sources. Of course, only countries that had adopted, or were well on their way to adopting, market-based policies of economic growth would be eligible to participate in the new programme.

---

[77] A. Santos, *supra* n. 8, p. 78, n. 95. See also L. Buchheit, 'Overview of the Four Debt Reduction Programs: Mexico, Costa Rica, the Philippines, and Venezuela', in R. Reisner, E. Cardenas and A. Mendes (eds.), *Latin American Sovereign Debt Management: Legal and Regulatory Aspects* (1990), p. 81; M. Monteagudo, *supra* n. 32, p. 73.

[78] M. Monteagudo, *supra* n. 32, p. 72.

[79] *Ibid.*

[80] L. Buchheit, *supra* n. 77, p. 81.

[81] *Ibid.*

[82] P. Power, *supra* n. 23, p. 2721.

[83] *Ibid.* Certain Brady bonds are not collateralized. So-called 'stripped' Brady bonds are not collateralized by any security interest in the principal or interest of the original loan that is being converted. *Ibid.* p. 2722.

Within a few weeks of Secretary Brady's announcement, Mexico approached its commercial bank advisory group to negotiate a single, integrated debt reduction proposal to provide it with immediate and significant debt relief.[84] Out of its total outstanding debt of $70 billion, the Mexico agreement covered approximately $54 billion in short- and long-term debt owed by Mexico.

Mexico's proposal gave commercial banks one of three options: (1) exchange the loans for exit bonds at a 35 per cent discount at a market rate of interest; (2) exchange the loans for exit bonds at face value, but with a reduced, fixed rate of interest of 6.25 per cent; or (3) provide new money over a four-year period at a market rate of interest for an amount equal to 25 per cent of the amount owed to the bank by Mexico.[85]

As collateral for the bonds, Mexico pledged US government zero coupon bonds which, upon maturity, would be equal to the principal amount of the new exit bonds. Additionally, a cash amount for the interest payments on the new bonds for an 18-month period was also offered as collateral.[86] Mexico's commercial creditors opted for debt reduction (of both principal and interest) with only a modest new money component. However, in light of the fact that Mexico's current account deficit in 1989 alone was $5.5 billion, the Brady Initiative, while laudable, was still not enough to resolve Mexico's debt crisis.[87]

Moreover, certain countries faced a significant financing 'gap' which meant that new money as well as debt reduction must be negotiated at the same time in order to keep such countries from falling into arrears on current interest payments falling due. This was the situation confronted by the Philippines during 1989–90 following a period of impressive economic growth, but where debt reduction was also sorely needed to consolidate such gains.

The Philippine government reached an agreement with its commercial bank advisory committee in August 1989 with two significant components. First, new financing was arranged through the issuance of 'transferable bonds' which would be sold to the Philippines' commercial bank creditors.[88] Secondly, the Philippine government arranged a debt buy-back of over $3.1 billion, or 20 per cent of its short- and medium-term external debt, from its commercial bank creditors who did not wish to purchase the transferable bonds.[89] The buy-back was steeply discounted and sold for cash by the Philippine government at 50 per cent of its face value. The Philippine government's single debt buy-back eliminated a good portion of the country's external debt and, in addition, the conversion of loans into exit bonds met the new financing needs of the Philippines.[90]

---

[84] L. Buchheit, *supra* n. 73, p. 2.
[85] 'Mexico and Banks Agree on Debt Accord Language', *New York Times*, 14 September 1989, p. D6.
[86] L. Buchheit, *supra* n. 77, p. 83.
[87] A. Santos, *supra* n. 8, p. 80.
[88] L. Buchheit, *supra* n. 73, p. 3.
[89] *Ibid.*
[90] *Ibid.*

Following the Mexican debt conversion in 1990, Costa Rica, Venezuela, Uruguay, Argentina and Brazil all followed suit by converting their loans into Brady bonds.[91] Brazil sold $3 billion of unsecured 30-year bonds in exchange for Brady bonds, reducing its future interest payments by at least $160 million.[92] Bulgaria, Ecuador, Panama and Peru are expected to execute Brady bonds in the near future.[93] The Brady Initiative marked a sea-change in the thinking of the US government in terms of permitting the use of official assistance in support of debt and debt service reduction.

However, the Brady Initiative did not provide a long-term solution to the worldwide debt crisis. The Brady debt reduction scheme of providing $20 billion in IMF/World Bank resources, and $4.5 billion provided by the Japanese, was insufficient to reduce, collateralize or guarantee developing country debt which, in Latin America alone, amounted to $7 trillion in 1987.[94] The reluctance of commercial banks to provide new money under the Brady Initiative also meant that a significant source of capital was now less available to developing countries.

However, the Brady Initiative was the beginning of the official recognition by the US government that an element of debt forgiveness needs to be an integral part of any long-term solution to the debt crisis. But, perhaps more importantly, it was the first concrete step in terms of converting 'non-performing' syndicated loans into securitized debt assets in the form of Brady bonds.

The Brady Initiative also gave a window of time to US and other commercial banks in which to recapitalize their reserves to better absorb loan losses. It also provided the means by which commercial lending institutions could convert debt from a non-performing liability to a securitized asset. However, the Brady Initiative did not go far enough. The debt overhang, and the constant depletion of foreign exchange reserves to service external debt, continued to impede development efforts.

4.   TACTICAL APPROACHES TO RESOLVING THE DEBT CRISIS

The following section will examine specific tactics for dealing with the debt crisis, namely debt exchanges (or swaps), the securitization of debt through the issuance of exit bonds, and special financing techniques such as co-financings and growth facilities.

---

[91]   P. Power, *supra* n. 23, p. 2722.
[92]   P. Truell, 'Brazilians Sell $3 Billion of Unsecured 30-Year Debt: Brady Bond Exchange is Well Received', *New York Times* 25 November 1997, p. D8.
[93]   P. Power, *supra* n. 23, p. 2723.
[94]   A. Santos, *supra* n. 8, p. 79.

4.1 Debt-for-debt exchanges

Beginning in 1982, a small market for inter-bank trading of sovereign debt assets began to develop.[95] For example, if a bank wanted to consolidate its portfolio of loans in Mexico in exchange for another bank's portfolio in the Philippines, an inter-bank 'swap' could be arranged.[96] These informal inter-bank arrangements gradually developed into a secondary market for trading sovereign debt. This market developed over time, in final recognition of the fact that certain debts would never be collected in the full amount of their face value. Sovereign debt was being traded at a discount, the discount reflecting, in part, the eventual likelihood of repayment. In other words, the deeper the discount, say, 20 cents on the dollar, the less likely it is that the debt will ever be repaid.

Purchasing discounted sovereign debt in a 'swap' attracted several different types of players. By repurchasing its own debt in a debt 'buy-back', a sovereign debtor could avoid future interest payments (and the drain on its foreign reserves), and reduce its overall debt liability. The lending bank would also realize an immediate return, albeit heavily discounted from the original face value of the loan. A debt buy-back liquidates the loan, and permits the lending bank to remove the loan from its portfolio.

Interestingly, the principal means of debt reduction under the Brady Initiative has been by way of debt-for-debt exchanges, rather than cash buy-backs by debtor nations.[97] Discounted bonds, par bonds and temporary interest rate reduction bonds were all classified as debt-for-debt exchanges under the Brady Initiative.[98] In fact, if cash buy-backs by sovereign debtors had been attempted, such buy-backs may have triggered restrictive covenants in the original loan agreements.

Box 3.1: Examples of restrictive clauses
Examples of restrictive clauses which may have been contained in the original loan documents include: sharing (requiring the unanimous consent of all creditors), mandatory prepayment (prohibiting the borrower from paying one instrument of indebtedness before the others), *pari passu* (requiring the debtor to treat all creditors equally, thereby preventing the creation of senior indebtedness), cross-default (the default of one loan agreement triggers the default of another, unrelated loan), and negative pledge (restricting or preventing the borrower's ability to pledge assets or revenues in favour of one creditor without also doing the same for the other creditors).

For example, if the original loan agreement contained a sharing clause, it would have forced the debtor nation to obtain the unanimous consent of all the creditors before amending the agreement. This meant that a single

---

[95] M. Monteagudo, *supra* n. 32, p. 68. See also S. Sperber, Note, 'Debt-Equity Swapping: Reconsidering Accounting Guidelines', (1988) 26 *Colum. J. Transnat'l L.* 377.
[96] P. Power, *supra* n. 23, p. 2715.
[97] L. Buchheit, 'Exchanging Places', (May 1991) *Int'l Fin. L. Rev.* 13.
[98] *Ibid.*, p. 14.

creditor could withhold consent for any Brady-type transaction, potentially holding the entire debt restructuring process hostage. Debt-for-debt exchanges avoided this possibility in a very clever way.

The debt-for-debt exchange first came into being in Mexico's debt restructuring agreement, entered into in 1987.[99] By offering to issue new debt instruments in exchange for outstanding credits, Mexico was negotiating for greater flexibility with its creditors. Under the terms of the restrictive clauses contained in the original loan agreements, if the new debt instruments had a 'weighted life to maturity' equal to or longer than the outstanding loans, Mexico would not have been obliged to make its offer to exchange the debt to all its creditors on an equal basis.[100] If the new debt instruments had a weighted life to maturity less than the outstanding loans, then Mexico would have been required to treat all of its creditors equally and make the offer available to them all. Thus, by offering new bonds with a weighted life to maturity that was equal to that of the original loans, Mexico avoided the operation of restrictive clauses contained in the original loan agreements.[101]

Therefore, by using debt-for-debt exchanges, restrictive covenants in the original loan instrument did not necessarily apply to the new 'exit' bonds being issued. A sovereign debtor, for example, could pay off certain debtors before others. This meant that creditors were no longer being treated equally. This also gave sovereign debtors the leverage to work outside the confines of the Banking Advisory Committee.[102]

4.2 Debt-equity swaps

Foreign investors interested in purchasing equity became very interested in secondary market trading of sovereign debt. Many transnational corporations also became interested in debt-equity swaps, whereby a foreign corporation uses its dollar-denominated funds to purchase sovereign debt at a discount on the secondary market. The commercial bank would then extinguish the underlying debt, and the corporation could exchange the debt instrument with the central bank of the sovereign debtor for local currency. The local currency is then applied towards equity (share) purchases in private companies or in state-owned enterprises which are in the process of being privatized. If a debt-equity swap is involved in an SOE privatization, then the initial purchase by a foreign investor may be in the form of a joint venture, a joint-stock company, or some preliminary form of a public-private partnership.

Generally, local currency proceeds generated by a debt-equity swap are exchanged for the local currency equivalent to the face value of the original debt. Thus, if $100 worth of debt is bought for $80 in hard currency, it is exchanged for the equivalent of $100 worth in local currency. By purchasing sovereign debt at a discount on the secondary market, and exchanging it for equity shares in a local enterprise, the foreign corporation becomes a direct equity participant in the local economy.

---

[99] *Ibid.*, p. 13.
[100] *Ibid.*
[101] *Ibid.*, p. 14.
[102] *Ibid.*

The release of local currency into the local economy pursuant to a debt-equity swap has to be carefully tranched, however. Too much local currency flooding the market will cause inflationary conditions. However, this can be avoided by immediately converting the debt instrument into an equity holding, without monetizing the debt into local currency.[103] Critics have argued that these types of swaps do not bring in new foreign direct investment, but this may be a viable strategy for initially attracting foreign investors to the local economy.

Apart from corporations interested in debt-equity swaps, non-profit organizations have also expressed a strong interest in debt conversions. Many organizations, beginning with the Conservation International's debt-for-nature swap in Bolivia in 1987,[104] have used local currency proceeds to finance conservation activities or biodiversity protection. The non-profit organization purchases the dollar-dominated debt at a discount, and redeems the debt instrument for local currency. (The hard currency price of the debt may even be donated by a third party based on tax write-off considerations.) Generally, the non-profit organization bargains for the local currency equivalent of the full face value of the debt which is paid by the central bank of the developing country.[105]

Box 3.2: Roundtripping

With regard to debt-equity swaps, restrictions are usually imposed by the developing country's central bank to prevent 'roundtripping'. Roundtripping uses a debt-equity swap to purchase debt at a discount, and exchange it for local currency. The local currency is then reconverted into hard currency and repatriated out of the country. This not only leads to a loss of the developing country's foreign currency reserves, but also contributes to the expatriation of flight capital out of the country.

The foreign corporation profits from the swap by taking advantage of the discount to obtain more local currency. In other words, the swap enables the foreign investor to acquire more local currency than is available through a straight exchange of hard currency at normal foreign exchange rates. Currency speculators have also showed an interest in secondary market debt conversions, buying steeply discounted debt in hopes that the discount would improve, thus permitting the speculator to profit from the difference. Clearly, the sovereign debtor needs to regulate or restrict unlimited arbitrage opportunities made available through the vehicle of debt-equity swaps.

Source: P. Power. 'Sovereign Debt: The Rise of the Secondary Market and its implications for Future Restructurings', 64 *Fordham L. Rev.* 2718.

---

[103] A. Vernava, 'Latin American Finance: A Financial, Economic and Legal Synopsis of Debt Swaps, Privatizations, Foreign Direct Investment Law Revisions and International Securities Issues', (1996) 15 *Wis. Int'l L. J.* 89 at 96.

[104] M. Chamberlin, M. Gruson and P. Welschek, 'Sovereign Debt Exchanges', in D. Bradlow (ed.), *International Borrowing: Negotiating and Structuring International Debt Transactions* (3rd edn, 1994), p. 533.

[105] P. Power, *supra* n. 23, pp. 2718–2719.

The local currency proceeds are then used in support of in-country, agreed-upon uses. Moreover, such swaps need not be limited to debt-for-nature uses, but have many creative outlets in support of education, the arts, historic preservation, etc. These debt conversions are referred to as 'debt-for-development' swaps.

Thus, debt-equity swaps help reduce the debt overhang of developing countries, liquidate non-performing debt from the loan portfolios of commercial banks, and transform public debt into private equity holdings. Since there are no formal reporting requirements for secondary debt trading, official records of the amounts being traded do not exist; however, the World Bank estimated that secondary market sovereign debt sales approximated $7 billion in 1986.[106] By 1993, that amount had grown to $273 billion.[107]

Despite these impressive figures, Chile, Mexico, the Philippines and perhaps a handful of other developing countries have only exchanged $10 billion in the face value of sovereign debt in debt-equity swaps, of which Chile accounts for roughly a third. Chile reduced its debt stock by 10 per cent through debt-equity swaps.[108] By 1986, debt-equity swaps had liquidated a mere $5 billion out of the staggering $800 billion in developing country debt.[109] Although debt-equity swaps are an innovative technique for the transformation and reduction of debt, they are by no means a panacea.

4.3   Securitization of debt

Another novel feature of the Brady Initiative was the transformation of sovereign debt into bonds. This debt-for-debt exchange is different from a debt-equity swap, since the debt is not being traded for an equity investment in a developing country enterprise. Rather, the original debt is traded at a discount for a negotiable instrument (e.g., a bond). In other words, the debt is 'securitized'. These so-called Brady bonds or exit bonds permit the commercial bank to 'exit' from the loan instrument as well as the country risk of the loan. (Under the Brady Initiative, the risk of non-payment is now assumed by the IMF or the US government, through enhanced credit guarantees.)[110] The swapping of sovereign debt for high-yielding securities in managing the debt crisis has met with mixed success.[111]

Another approach to securitizing debt is to transfer the loan assets to a third party who then 'pools' the assets, and sells the pass-through interests to outside investors.[112] The discount of the loans could also be 'passed through' to the ultimate investor, making the security an attractive investment vehicle.

---

[106] P. Power, *supra* n. 23, p. 2719.

[107] *Ibid.*

[108] B. Boyd, *supra* n. 1, pp. 481–482. For a general discussion of debt-equity swaps, see L. Maktouf, 'Some Reflections on Debt-for-Equity Conversions', (1989) 23 *Int'l Lawyer* 909.

[109] B. Boyd, *supra* n. 1 at 484.

[110] M. Monteagudo, *supra* n. 32, p. 72.

[111] For a discussion on the 1988 Morgan Guaranty/Mexican Plan to securitize Mexican foreign debt holdings by issuing US Treasury zero coupon notes and various 'junk bond' schemes, see R. Plehn, 'Securitization of Third World Debt', (1989) 23 *Int'l Lawyer* 161.

[112] L. Buchheit, *supra* n. 33, p. 395.

This type of 'Fannie Mae' investment (see Box 3.3)[113] may greatly expand the potential number of investors (i.e., bondholders), but the large number of bondholders may prove to be unwieldy in the event that the underlying debt has to be restructured.[114]

Box 3.3: Securitizing debt

Securitization of loans began in 1970 when the Government National Mortgage Association (GNMA, or 'Ginnie Mae'), a federal agency, began issuing tradeable securities based on residential mortgages insured by the Federal Housing Administration or the Veterans Administration. GNMA (along with the Federal National Mortgage Association (or 'Fannie Mae'), and the Federal Home Loan Mortgage Corporation (or 'Freddie Mac')) generally purchases highly secure loans issued by banks, savings and loans, thrifts and other financial institutions, and pools the loans into an insured bond or other type of security.

Pooling loans of developing countries can be quite difficult, especially since the sovereign risk involved may not be insurable, unless OPIC, the US Treasury, the World Bank or the IMF agrees to do so. Additionally, a reserve fund held in escrow until the LDC bonds are paid off may also provide insurance against default, to make the bonds more attractive to purchasers.

The bonds can also be diversified by pooling the sovereign loans of several developing countries, e.g., Brazil, Argentina and Venezuela. Or, if the underlying loans are purchased by a multilateral debt reduction facility, and thereafter restructured and forgiven, in part, securitization may become easier.

Source: A. Puchala Jr, 'Securitizing Third World Debt', (1989) 1 *Colum. Bus. L. Rev.* 137; D. Leebron 'First Things First: A Comment on Securitizing Third World Debt', (1989) 1 *Colum. Bus. L. Rev.* 173.

4.4 Special financing techniques

Cofinancing is another means of providing enhanced credit or guarantees of debt instruments. Under a cofinancing arrangement, commercial banks lend in conjunction with official loans extended by the World Bank or other official donors. The official creditor may extend a loan in a separate credit agreement or pursuant to a parallel credit agreement with the commercial banks.[115] The enhanced credit portion of the loan may be 'blended' with the market rates offered by the commercial lenders to make the entire financing package slightly more concessional in nature.

A sovereign borrower can also refinance its debt by issuing capital market instruments. Once these securities are purchased by third parties,

---

[113] A. Puchala, Jr., 'Securitizing Third World Debt', (1989) 1 *Colum. Bus. L. Rev.* 137 ; D. Leebron, 'First Things First: A Comment on Securitizing Third World Debt', (1989) 1 *Colum. Bus. L. Rev.* 173.

[114] R. MacMillan, *supra* n. 13, p. 67.

[115] R. MacMillan, *supra* n. 13, p. 384. See also M. Stumpf and W. Debevoise, 'Overview of Techniques: Raising New Money, Growth Facilities, Cofinancing and Collateralized Borrowings', in D. Bradlow (ed.), *International Borrowing: Negotiating and Structuring International Debt Transactions* (3rd edn.) (1994), p. 522.

the sale proceeds can be used to retire outstanding debt or existing 'new money' loans. The advantage of this approach is that the sovereign borrower can directly raise funds from international capital markets by issuing its own securities.[116] Assuming, however, that the underlying debt restructuring is satisfactory, and the sovereign borrower does not fall foul of restrictive covenants in existing debt instruments, this could be a constructive means of recovering its financial health.

Another means of recovering from severe balance-of-trade imbalances is to use stand-by credit 'facilities' which operate on a revolving fund basis. These credit or 'growth' facilities were developed in response to the increasing alarm being expressed by sovereign borrowers concerning IMF adjustment programmes. These structural adjustment programmes, originally conceived as emergency measures to 'jump start' an economy, were becoming long-term strait-jackets. Thus, a proposed solution was to tie disbursements from a credit facility as the sovereign borrower met specific, agreed-upon economic targets.[117]

Box 3.4: Credit facilities

In most cases, initial funding for the credit facility is deposited in a special account in the central bank of the borrowing country. Funds from the facility are disbursed by the central bank once agreed-upon, eligible trade transactions are completed. Once the foreign creditor is paid, the funds must be redeposited in the central bank special account, or used to fund another trade transaction. In addition to trade transactions, agreed-upon investment (or capital) projects can be used so that the sovereign borrower can draw down from the stand-by credit facility once internal benchmarks under the programme have been met.

Source: R. MacMillan, 'Towards a Sovereign Debt Work-Out System', (1995) 16 *N. W. J. Int'l L. & Bus.* 57 at 67.

Further, where a developing country is heavily dependent on one or two commodities (such as oil) to generate foreign exchange, a loan facility may be 'indexed'. This means that the amount which can be drawn down under a new money commitment is linked to the international market price for that commodity. In Mexico's case, the IMF stand-by arrangement provided for IMF contingency payments in the event that the export price of Mexico's oil fell below $9 per barrel. The availability of new money would be correspondingly reduced if the price of Mexican oil rose to above $14 per barrel. As additional financial support, commercial bank lenders were asked to help fund a $1.2 billion 'contingent investment support

---

[116] L. Buchheit, *supra* n. 33, pp. 396–397.
[117] R. MacMillan, *supra* n. 13, pp. 57, 67. See also M. Stumpf and W. Debevoise, 'Overview of Techniques: Raising New Money, Growth Facilities, Cofinancing and Collateralized Borrowings', in *International Borrowing: Negotiating And Structuring International Debt Transactions*, p. 522.

facility' from which Mexico could draw down funds in the event of slipping oil prices.[118] However, this type of indexing has been criticized insofar as it does not encourage the sovereign borrower country to make necessary macro-economic adjustments.[119]

All this having been said, commercial lenders and multilateral banking institutions need to come to terms with the fact that market-based commercial lending for certain countries, or for certain sectors in particular developing countries, is simply not workable. More realistic targets for debt repayment by developing countries need to be negotiated in seeking a long-term resolution of the debt crisis.

5.   THE MEXICAN DEBT CRISIS: PHASE II

Mexico's oil boom of the late 1970s and early 1980s was expected to give it a real chance at economic self-sufficiency leading to economic prosperity. Heavy international borrowing from commercial banking institutions was supported by a belief (on both sides) in the surging growth of Mexico's economy based on its oil exports. However, when oil prices slipped, and floating interest rates moved up relentlessly, Mexico was left with dwindling foreign reserves with which to service its ever-increasing international debt. The bubble burst in August 1982 when Mexico depleted its available foreign currency reserves, thus initiating the debt crisis of the 1980s.

Painful adjustment measures followed, including a decline in real wages, unemployment and slow economic growth.[120] Mexico began dismantling its protectionist policies of tariffs and import restrictions which had been intended to bolster the growth of incipient domestic industries. Between 1982 and 1987, the Mexican government devalued the peso, liberalized trade and investment under the North American Free Trade Agreement (NAFTA), relaxed exchange controls, and began privatizing SOEs, including commercial banks.[121]

The increase in the US prime rate by nearly three percentage points between 1993 and 1994 made US capital markets more inviting for international investors. Moreover, US investors began investing more heavily in US markets. The high US interest rates attracted Mexican flight capital as well.[122] By 1994, foreign capital investment in Mexico was drying up. This left Mexico with a choice between raising the interest rate to attract dwindling foreign investment into the country, or devaluing the peso. Since Mexico let its stand-by arrangement with the IMF lapse in 1993, it was less restricted in making a choice in the matter. Despite the urging of the US

---

[118] L. Buchheit, *supra* n. 33, pp. 387–388.
[119] See C. R. Ebenroth, 'The Changing Legal Framework for Resolving the Debt Crisis: A European's Perspective', (1989) 23 *Int'l Lawyer* 649.
[120] W. Lovett, 'Lessons from the Recent Peso Crisis in Mexico', (1996) 4 *Tulane J. Int'l and Comp. L.* 143 at 148.
[121] E. Carrasco and R. Thomas, *supra* n. 8, p. 558.
[122] *Ibid.*, p. 561.

Treasury Department to devalue the peso,[123] Mexico did not, opting instead to raise the interest rate.[124]

However, in order to assure nervous international investors about the stability of Mexican investments, Mexico issued nearly $5 billion in *tesobonos*, short-term, dollar-indexed securities, repayable in pesos. The risk of any foreign exchange rate movement is absorbed by the Mexican government rather than the investor.[125] *Tesobono* debt grew 10 times as a result.[126]

Unfortunately, following the election of President Ernesto Zedillo on 21 August 1994, Mexico's political fate caught up with it. Beginning with the assassination of Jose Francisco Ruiz Massieu, second in command to President Zedillo,[127] the political condition of Mexico deteriorated. Mexico's political climate worsened as internal unrest in the Chiapas region developed in December 1994.[128]

On 20 December 1994 the Mexican Finance Minister announced a 14 per cent devaluation of the peso, but the next day President Zedillo announced that the peso would be allowed to float.[129] The peso entered a free fall, devaluing 15 per cent over the course of the next day alone, and devaluing 54 per cent by March 1995.[130] By the end of December 1994, $4 billion in capital had exited Mexico, and capital reserves plummeted.[132] Short-term, portfolio investors, faced with a drop of 15 per cent or more in the value of their investments, redeemed their Mexican stocks and bonds, rather than permitting the securities to roll over.[133]

Although Zedillo's government took immediate stabilization measures such as freezing wage and price increases for 60 days, the peso devaluation continued.[133] Health, education and food subsidies were cut from government budgetary allocations, and 40 per cent of the population slipped below the poverty line. Moreover, the constant peso devaluations and high interest rates were causing hyperinflationary conditions.

Faced with an imminent collapse of the Mexican economy, and the real possibility that Mexico would default on payments due on outstanding *tesobonos*, the US government intervened, announcing an $18 billion emergency stabilization package for Mexico on 2 January 1995. The package consisted of $9 billion from the United States, $1 billion from Canada, $5 billion from the Bank for International Settlements (BIS), and $3 billion from foreign commercial banks.[134] But the foreign exchange drain on Mexico's reserves continued, despite this emergency rescue package.

---

[123] *Ibid.*, p. 562, n. 127.
[124] *Ibid.*, p. 562.
[125] *Ibid.*, pp. 562–563 and nn. 131–32.
[126] *Ibid.*, p. 563.
[127] *Ibid.*
[128] W. Lovett, *supra* n. 120, p. 154.
[129] *Ibid.*
[130] E. Carrasco and R. Thomas, *supra* n. 8, pp. 564–565.
[131] *Ibid.* at 563. See also A. DePalma, 'Crisis in Mexico: The Overview with Peso Freed, Mexican Currency Drops 20% More', *New York Times*, 23 December 1994), p. A1.
[132] E. Carrasco and R. Thomas, *supra* n. 8, p. 566.
[133] *Ibid.*, p. 565.
[134] *Ibid.*, p. 567.

On January 12, 1995, the Clinton Administration proposed a $40 billion loan guarantee programme. However, the plan required Congressional approval[135] and met with political resistance in response to the adverse impact the proposed bail-out would have on US jobs. Shrinking export markets for US goods following a devaluation of the Mexican peso were a further cause for concern. Others in Congress were more concerned with illegal immigration and drug trafficking, while still others were reluctant to require US taxpayers to provide relief to wealthy investors who had lost their investments in Mexican securities markets.[136]

In light of the mounting political resistance to the emergency bail-out, and the likelihood of its failure to gain Congressional approval, the Clinton Administration reformulated the plan so that Congressional approval would not be required. The subsequent $50 billion loan package was comprised of the following: (1) $20 billion in US loans and loan guarantees funded by the Treasury's Exchange Stabilization Fund; (2) $18 billion from the IMF (or 600 per cent of Mexico's IMF quota); (3) $10 billion from the BIS; and (4) $3 billion from commercial banks.[137] In exchange for the bail-out package, Mexico agreed to and announced a new IMF austerity programme on 9 March 1995, which imposed strict economic targets restricting domestic credit, the internal money supply, fiscal spending by the government and foreign borrowing.[138]

Repayments of the US loans and loan guarantees were collateralized by oil revenues generated by PEMEX (Petroleos Mexicanos), the state-owned oil refinery.[139] Oil export revenues, less operating costs, were deposited directly into a separate account in the Federal Reserve Bank of New York. The oil exports proceeds facility set up under this arrangement required Mexican notification to and consultation with the US Treasury Department if its oil export income dropped below agreed levels.[140] These oil export proceeds would have been automatically seized by the US government if Mexico defaulted on its loan obligations to the United States.

The $20 billion in loans and loan guarantees comprising the US portion of the Mexican emergency loan package was advanced in six agreements. The

---

[135] *Ibid.* See also Tim Carrington, *et al.*, 'Quick Fix: Clinton Hastily Drops Mexican Rescue Plan, Gives New Aid Instead', *Wall Street Journal*, 1 February 1995), p. A1.

[136] See E. Carrasco and R. Thomas, *supra* n. 8, pp. 567–568.

[137] *Ibid.*, p. 568. The Exchange Stabilization Fund (ESF), established by §.10 of the Gold Reserve Act of 1934, 31 U.S.C. §5302, as amended, permits the purchase and sale of US dollars to stabilize the US currency, and may also be used for short-term loans to other countries without Congressional approval. The use of the ESF loans, which operates as a revolving account, is limited to a six-month period based on a presidential determination that emergency circumstances warrant such a use. *Ibid.*, p. 568, n. 176. See also P. Wertman, 'The Mexican Support Package: A Survey and Analysis', (August 1995) 5 No. 9 *Mex. Trade and L. Rep.* 19 at 22–23; C. Lichtenstein, 'The Mexican Crisis: Who Should Be a Country's Lender of Last Resort?' 10 *Fordham Int'l L. J.* at 1771.

[138] E. Carrasco and R. Thomas, *supra* n. 8, p. 568, and n. 177.

[139] Patricia Wertman, 'The Mexican Support Package: A Survey and Analysis', (September 1995) 5 No. 9 *Mex. Trade and L. Rep.* at 9. Proceeds of oil exports from PEMEX and its two subsidiaries, PMI Comercio Internacional S.A. de C.V., and PMI Trading Ltd., were deposited into the same special account. *Ibid.*

[140] *Ibid.*, p. 13.

US-Mexico Framework Agreement (the so-called 'umbrella agreement') was signed on 21 February 1995.[141] These funds were to be used to assist Mexico in stabilizing its foreign exchange and to ease the volatility of its short-term debt markets. The Framework Agreement was designed to help Mexico move from short-term financing to longer-term financing, and had helped retire $16 billion in *tesobonos* by the end of 1995.[142] The Framework Agreement remained in effect for a year, and was renewable for six months thereafter. There were five additional financing agreements which must be in accord with the Framework Agreement.[143]

Despite the gravity of the debt crisis and the seriousness of its immediate consequences, Mexico made a remarkable recovery and floated a $1 billion two-year floating rate bond issue on 10 July 1995.[144] These bonds carried a spread of 5.375 per cent over LIBOR.[145] Banks were given an opportunity to earn a modest 0.25 per cent fee for subscribing to the issue or redeeming the note for face value by buying a share interest in a Mexican bank or an SOE undergoing privatization.[146] The issue was oversubscribed, attracting buyers in European, Asian and American markets. In addition, Mexico re-entered international capital markets without drawing down on any US loan guarantees.

On 16 January 1997, in a signing ceremony at the White House, the Mexican government repaid the $13.5 billion it owed the United States, a remarkable three years ahead of schedule.[147] The early repayment helped Mexico save about $100 million per year in interest payments that would otherwise have been payable to the US Treasury.[148]

Although this discussion will not address the impact that the Mexican debt crisis had on other Latin American economies, particularly Argentina and Brazil, the human cost to Mexico alone was high. The Mexican Labour Secretary estimated that close to six million Mexicans lost their jobs,[149] and the depletion of savings to support their families has impoverished many Mexicans. Moreover, the privatization process undertaken as part of the structural adjustment effort contributed to a widening of the gap between the rich and the poor.

What are the lessons to be learnt from the Mexico debt crisis? First, it is important to distinguish Mexico's debt crisis of the 1980s from the peso crisis of the 1990s. By the mid-1990s, Mexico's economy was more competitive

---

[141] P. Wertman, *supra* n. 139, p. 20.

[142] *Ibid.*, p. 15.

[143] Those additional agreements include: (1) the Medium-Term Exchange Stabilization Agreement (Feb. 21, 1995); (2) the Guarantee Agreement (Feb. 21, 1995); (3) the North American Framework Agreement (Apr. 26, 1994); (4) the Exchange Stabilization Agreement (26 April 1994); and (5) the Temporary Exchange Stabilization Agreement (4 January 1995). P. Wertman, *supra* n. 139, p. 20–21.

[144] P. Wertman, *supra* n. 139, p. 12.

[145] *Ibid.* See also E. Carrasco and R. Thomas, *supra* n. 8, p. 569, n. 184.

[146] P. Wertman, *supra* n. 139, p. 12.

[147] D. Wessel and C. Torres, 'Mexico Will Close Out Its Debt to US: Earlier Repayment Marks Both Livelier Economy, Access to Bond Markets', *Wall Street Journal*, 16 January 1997, A10.

[148] *Ibid.*

[149] E. Carrasco and R. Thomas, *supra* n. 8, p. 570.

and less protectionist. Although painful structural adjustments had had to be absorbed by Mexico in the interim, it did create a more balanced and competitive economy.

Secondly, although the first debt crisis was caused, in part, by heavy dependence on external borrowing, the second crisis was precipitated by Mexico's heavy reliance on foreign portfolio investment. Portfolio investment usually takes the form of cross-border stock market purchases of highly liquid, high-yielding debt and equity securities. These purchases are made by foreign individual (retail) investors, or by large foreign institutional investors. The nature of portfolio investment is that such capital investment flows are highly volatile and may be quickly reversed.

High domestic interest rates are generally what attract large-volume investment flows, in the first instance. However, this may ultimately prove to be counterproductive, since high interest rates may dampen domestic borrowing and stifle the growth of export-oriented industries. (High foreign capital inflows may also contribute to inflationary conditions and decreased internal rates of savings.)[150]

Moreover, emerging markets are especially vulnerable to the volatility of portfolio investment. Outflows of portfolio investment can be potentially destabilizing, if not devastating to an emerging market economy. These outflows of portfolio investment may be sudden and unanticipated if the cause lies in external economic factors. For example, a rise in US interest rates may persuade US investors to invest at home rather than abroad.

Portfolio investment is also very sensitive to internal political and economic conditions in the developing country, as demonstrated by the run on the peso following political assassinations and other turmoil in Mexico.[151] Capital outflows may also occur in response to another emerging capital market coming 'on-line'. Thus, portfolio investment can be highly unpredictable.

Although restructuring the economy to provide a solid industrial and export base, and liberalizing the trade and investment scheme are important components in creating a stable economy,[152] excessive reliance on foreign portfolio investment to finance development is dangerous. The impact of foreign currency flows has to be contained within the framework of the economy so that the nation is not held hostage to the vagaries of foreign portfolio investors.

Enrique Carrasco and Randall Thomas argue forcefully that Mexico should encourage 'relational investment' or, in other words, FDI.[153] Relational investors bear the risk of their investment (unlike portfolio investors), and tend to stay vested in the developing country in the long-run. A developing

---

[150] *Ibid.*, p. 576.

[151] *Ibid.*, p. 563.

[152] A. Vernava, 'Latin American Finance: A Financial, Economic and Legal Synopsis of Debt Swaps, Privatizations, Foreign Direct Investment Law Revisions and International Securities Issues', (1996) 15 *Wis. Int'l L.J.* 89 at 112. Mexico rewrote its investment law by legislation effective on 1 January 1994, eliminating, *inter alia*: (1) the need for advance approvals on certain types of transactions; (2) restrictions on the movement of investment capital in and out of Mexico; and (3) eliminating controls on the repatriation of earnings on capital.

[153] E. Carrasco and R. Thomas, *supra* n. 8, pp. 579–582.

country can better control the entry and exit of such investors, unlike portfolio investors whose presence in or departure from the economy can be effected instantaneously by a retail stockbroker executing a trade in New York, London or Sydney. Further, by orienting FDI investment towards management and long-term growth issues, there is less volatility and more focus on the development of the enterprise being invested in. For example, FDI may facilitate technology transfers, may open up new markets, and impose more rigorous standards for corporate governance of the local enterprise.

This, of course, leads us right back to where we started. Many post-independence developing countries resisted FDI as a form of economic 'imperialism', and placed greater emphasis on encouraging and protecting domestic industries. Perhaps there truly is nothing new under the sun, and developing nations should consider reformulating the terms of this familiar dilemma. By encouraging strategic, long-term, illiquid, management-oriented FDI investments, a developing nation fosters its own integration into a global economy. This requires that developing countries reassess the importance of safeguarding certain industries and sectors from foreign ownership, management and oversight. If developing countries can be assured that the veil of colonialism has lifted for them, then this may provide a window of opportunity to seek out new development options and partnerships.

Mexico's example is a warning that heavy reliance on international borrowing from commercial sources, or dependence on volatile portfolio investments, can lead the economy to boiling point. While the US bail-out of Mexico was based on strategic US political considerations, these considerations are unlikely to be similarly compelling for other developing nations, or even for Mexico for a second time.[154] Thus, Mexico's example may not establish a model, but can be used to draw important lessons and gain valuable insights for the future.

The Mexican debt crisis did change international monetary management in a very important respect. Based on the urging of US Treasury Secretary, Robert Rubin, at the G-7 meeting in 1995, the IMF set aside emergency funds so that emergency loans would not be so dependent on American financing possibly requiring Congressional approval.[155] Thus, the Mexican fiscal crisis has left a lasting imprint on the global financial scene.[156]

As a footnote to this discussion, the IMF approved a $1 billion emergency loan to the Philippines on 20 July 1997, to help stabilize the Philippine peso.[157] The IMF's Executive Board approved the Philippine government's request to draw down on an existing $600 million loan programme, and an additional

---

[154] D. Sanger, 'Treasury Chief Rules Out US Move To Rescue Asian Economies', *New York Times*, 27 October 1997, p. A8.

[155] S. Erlanger, To Ease Crisis, I.M.F. Makes Philippines Emergency Loan, *New York Times*, 21 July 1997), p. A1.

[156] Moreover the consequences of Mexico's debt crisis are still being felt. Opposition politicians (and other critics) in Mexico are accusing the Mexican government of supporting the local political elite since the government will not release the names or identities whose unpaid loans have been bailed out by the government following the peso devaluation in 1994. See S. Dillon, 'The Debate on Banks Gets Nasty in Mexico', *New York Times*, 7 August 1998, p. A7.

[157] *Ibid.*

line of credit for $435 million.[158] This $1 billion loan to the Philippines is dwarfed by the $17.8 billion loan to Mexico, but it demonstrates the IMF's much more rapid response time to such crisis situations.

The IMF also needed to react quickly in Thailand's case following its currency devaluation. This occurred after the Thai government decided to 'delink' its currency from the US dollar and other hard currencies, on 2 July 1997.[159] The economic conditions leading up to the devaluation of the Thai currency are complex and stemmed, in part, from borrowing heavily from foreign sources (mainly in relation to speculative real estate projects). Unpaid loans began to accumulate and interest rates rose, causing the Thai economy to slow down.[160] Since stock portfolios were earning less, this prompted overseas investors to sell off Thai stock, which culminated in a general financial and political crisis.[161]

In desperation, the Thai government dismissed the country's central bankers, and turned to the IMF which organized a $17.2 billion rescue package, which included a $1 billion bridging loan extended by the Swiss-based Bank for International Settlements, $250 million of which will be provided by the US Treasury Department's Exchange Stabilization Fund.[162] In exchange for the financial bail-out, the IMF required Thailand to agree to strict fiscal controls such as higher taxes, and to close financial institutions that have made unrepaid loans.[163]

The Thai crisis turned out to be part of a larger regional economic maelstrom. When the dollar rose in early 1998, the East Asian 'tiger'

---

[158] *Ibid.*

[159] E. Gargan, 'The Thai Slump at Ground Level', *New York Times*, 19 September 1997, available on internet at http://search.nytimes.com/search/daily (last visited on 13 August 1998). See also 'Many Asian Stock Markets Fall Sharply: Currencies Also Lower; Trading Rule Change by Malaysia Faulted', *New York Times*, 29 August 1997, p. C2. By 21 August 1997, the Thai baht had dropped in value by over 20%. See D. Sanger, 'First Part of Thai Bailout Is Authorized by the I.M.F.: $4 Billion Loan to Stem the Currency Crisis', *New York Times*, 21 August 1997, p. D2.

[160] 'Many Asian Stock Markets Fall Sharply: Currencies Also Lower; Trading Rule Change by Malaysia Faulted', *New York Times* , 29 August 1997, p. C2.

[161] *Ibid.* See also E. Gargan, 'The Thai Slump at Ground Level', *New York Times*, 19 September 1997, available on internet at http://search.nytimes.com/search/daily.

[162] *Ibid.* See also D. Sanger, 'The Overfed Tiger Economies', *New York Times*, available on internet at http://search.nytimes.com/search/daily. See also D. Sanger, 'First Part of Thai Bailout Is Authorized by the I.M.F.: $4 Billion Loan to Stem the Currency Crisis', *New York Times* , 21 August 1997, p. D2.

[163] Sanger, 'First Part of Thai Bailout Is Authorized by the I.M.F.: $4 Billion Loan to Stem the Currency Crisis', *New York Times* , 21 August 1997, p. D2. However, the IMF's role in the Thai financial crisis has been sharply criticized by observers who urge that the IMF's prescription to Thailand to devalue its currency was a 'poison pill' which started the Asian financial crisis. See S. Forbes, 'Be Wary of Bailing Out the IMF', *Washington Times*, 27 July 1998, p. A19. Mr Forbes argues that when a country will not defend its currency, the currency effectively collapses causing rampant inflation, wages reduced in value by one-half, bankruptcy, unemployment and a precipitous rise in political and ethnic tensions. Further, he urges that the IMF's cut-off of social safety nets, including food and other subsidies, can be calamitous for the people living in the affected economy. He thus urges strict adherence to four cardinal principles: sound money, low taxes, the rule of law, and restricted bureaucratic interference with running businesses, along with eliminating all tax-free incomes for IMF employees. *Ibid.*

economies were forced to increase their interest rates.[164] Most fought valiantly to defend their currencies, but serious competition from China and shrinking export markets for their goods meant that their currencies needed to be devalued in order to lower the costs of production for exports.[165] This in turn meant that the short-term borrowing binge from 1993–96 in support of long-term investments in real estate, and other non-export sectors,[166] was a financial crisis in the making. Rental income from real estate ventures, for example, was being earned in local currency, but dollar-denominated loans in support of these investments had to be repaid in hard currency by converting devalued currencies.[167]

Beleaguered by currency crises stemming from a variety of complex reasons, the Philippine, Indonesian, Malaysian, Singaporean, Thai, South Korean, and Hong Kong stock markets crashed, necessitating emergency bail-out packages for Thailand ($17.2 billion); Indonesia ($22 billion); and South Korea ($20 billion).[168] International investors panicked, withdrawing $1.4 billion in two days alone in October 1997 from international equity funds. (This amount represents about 4 per cent of the total $380 billion held by such funds.)[169]

Now that massive dollar-denominated debts must be paid back in devalued local currencies, the East Asian economies of Thailand, Malaysia, the Philippines and Indonesia are feeling squeezed. The IMF-led prescription for economic recovery is to follow Mexico's example by exporting goods that are now cheaper on the world market because of the drop in domestic currency value.[170] The price that Mexico paid, and that these other East Asian economies can expect to pay, is a severe recession.[171]

---

[164] 'Many Asian Stock Markets Fall Sharply: Currencies Also Lower; Trading Rule Change by Malaysia Faulted', *New York Times*, 29 August 1997, p. C2.

[165] J. Sachs, 'The Wrong Medicine for Asia, *New York Times*, 3 November 1997, p. A30.

[166] *Ibid.*

[167] *Ibid.*

[168] A. Pine, 'Unsettled Markets: US to Join the IMF Rescue of Indonesia Asia: Its $3 Billion Contribution is part of a $22-Billion Contingency Package', *Los Angeles Times*, 31 October 1997, p. D1. See also J. Burton, 'Korean Pride Battered by Plea for $20bn IMF Rescue', *Financial Times*, 22 November 1997, p. 3.

[169] T. Smart, 'Money Flowing Out of Global Mutual Funds', *Washington Post*, 31 October 1997, p. G1. See also S. Pearlstein, 'At Economic Summit on Asia, A Search for the "Right" Policy', *Washington Post*, 21 November 1997, p. G1.

[170] P. Lewis, 'For Asia, Austerity and Exports: Seeing Mexican Parallel, Economists Stress Market Freedom', *New York Times*, 9 September 1997, p. D3. Robert Rubin, Secretary of the US Treasury also suggests that central banks in developing countries disclose financial information concerning their activities in currency markets. See D. Sanger, 'Asia's Economic Tigers Growl at World Monetary Conference: Say Opening of Markets Hands Wall Street Too Much Power', *New York Times*, 22 September 1997, p. A1. Secretary Rubin also suggested that commercial banks should report their non-performing loans. See D. Sanger, 'Rubin to Press Central Banks to Disclose Financial Data', *New York Times*, 19 September 1997, p. C5. (Japan's failure to do so resulted in a crisis of failing banks which had to be closed, discussed in Chapter 4.)

[171] P. Lewis, 'For Asia, Austerity and Exports: Seeing Mexican Parallel, Economists Stress Market Freedom', *New York Times*, 9 September 1997, p. D3.

East Asian economies need to worry about something else as well. China has devalued its currency by 35 per cent against the US dollar since 1994,[172] and received $52 billion, or about one-fifth of all private capital flows to developing countries during 1997.[173] The price of China's exports over the past three years has fallen by 25 per cent,[174] posing some very tough competition for other East Asian economies.

Even at this early stage, it is becoming clear that the close cooperation between government and industry, and the long-term investment planning for critical sectors of the economy, which were long considered to be strengths of the East Asian tigers, also meant less transparency and accountability.[175] The underregulation of capital markets in these emerging markets has also been a systemic problem.[176]

In order to avoid the moral hazard posed by such financial crises requiring international rescue plans, US Treasury Secretary Robert Rubin has urged that more financial information be disclosed by the governments of emerging market economies.[177] Secretary Rubin has specifically urged that central and commercial banks should report their financial assets and liabilities, urging that such disclosure could prevent future financial crises by warning creditors and investors of impending financial squeezes.[178]

Indeed, the IMF has proposed an early-warning system to ward off economic crises which is targeted at 23 emerging capital economies, including Brazil, China, South Korea, Malaysia, Mexico, Peru and Thailand, which borrow most heavily from international capital markets.[179] IMF officials now urge developing nations to publish periodic financial reports providing accurate information on inflation, the money supply, and foreign exchange reserves so that economic warning signs can be detected early on.

At the time of writing, the Asian financial crisis is still unfolding and thus, it may be somewhat premature to draw lessons from the recent

---

[172] Observers of China's economic scene argue that further devaluation is unlikely.
See S. Faison, 'Even as Asians Worry, China is Unlikely to Devalue', *New York Times*, 11 August 1998, p. D4.

[173] *Ibid.*

[174] *Ibid.*

[175] 'Asian Economies: More Myth Than Miracle? New Problems Causing Some of Region's Nations to Rethink Reliance on Japanese Model', *Washington Post*, 25 November 1997, p. A1.

[176] J. Sachs, 'The Wrong Medicine for Asia', *New York Times*, 3 November 1997, p. A30.

[177] D. Sanger, 'Asia's Economic Tigers Growl at World Monetary Conference: Say Opening of Markets Hands Wall Street Too Much Power', *New York Times*, 22 September 1997, p. A1.

[178] D. Sanger, 'Rubin to Press Central Banks to Disclose Financial data', *New York Times*, 19 September 1997, p. C5. Secretary Rubin has also urged the Thais to follow the IMF's prescriptions for economic recovery. While acknowledging that such measures will cause enormous hardships on the Thai people, Secretary Rubin nevertheless attributed such difficulties to the financial crisis itself rather than to IMF-backed reforms.
See M. Landler, 'Rubin Hoping Thais Back Requirements of the I.M.F.', *New York Times*, 1 July 1998, p. A9.

[179] 'IMF Proposes Plan for Early Warning of Economic Crises', *Wall Street Journal*, 12 February 1996, p. C18.

events. However, certain analytical conclusions are already being set drawn by the IMF as well as its critics. The IMF attributes the Asian financial crisis not to macro-economic imbalances but to systemic weakness in the financial and banking systems of the affected East Asian countries, as well as to poor governance in general.[180] Poor governance covers the lack of transparency in financial dealings (particularly by the respective governments involved), 'crony capitalism', and poor supervision of banking and financial systems.

In response, the IMF has made $35 billion of its own financial resources available to support the Indonesian, Korean and Thai economies, and mobilized over $77 billion in additional resources for these countries. The IMF has moved quickly to institute structural financial reforms, including tightening monetary policies to ease the balance-of-payments crunch, closing non-viable financial institutions, and addressing poor governance issues by urging liberalization of capital markets and insisting that governments disengage from businesses.[181]

The IMF's approach, while laudable in intent, has nevertheless been the subject of serious criticism. In particular, its insistence on tightening fiscal controls by slashing government spending has ignored the fact that most of the affected East Asian economies had budget surpluses (not the usual developing country malaise of huge government deficits), high savings accumulations and relatively low inflation.[182] The huge currency devaluations may not have served the region well unless there is a prompt recovery in these economies. While 'crony capitalism', combined with under-regulated banking systems, are elements in a contagion that has affected Russia, Mexico and Australia,[183] IMF prescriptions have not been fully effective in containing it. There is a new recognition of and emphasis on the importance of social safety nets and on the role of Japan in absorbing exports from the affected East Asian economies.[184]

Moreover, there is a very real political danger underlying the Asian currency crisis. Unless a full recovery is made by these economies soon, there is a significant risk of derailing the process of economic and political liberalization in the region. The Second World War was preceded by rampant inflation and economic chaos, together with a sharp increase in nationalism and fascism. Commentators have warned that Europe's past should not become East Asia's future.[185] The interests of supporting a globalized effort to encourage economic and political liberalism, heavily underwritten by Japanese efforts to stabilize the region economically, may prove very important in light of a potential power shift to China. In any

---

[180] 'The IMF's Response to the Asian Crisis', 27 July 1998, available on http://www.imf.org/External/np/exr/facts/asia.HTM (last visited on 13 August 1998).
[181] *Ibid.*, pp. 2–3.
[182] See F. Zakaria, 'Will Asia Turn Against the West?', *New York Times*, 10 July 1998, p. A17.
[183] *Ibid.*
[184] *Ibid.* See also P. Blustein, 'Rubin Heads Home After Prescribing Bitter Medicine for Asia', *Washington Post*, 2 July 1998, p. E1.
[185] See F. Zakaria, *supra* n. 182, p. A17.

case, East Asian countries provide an important role model in their reliance on export expansion which has dramatically alleviated poverty and increased national wealth—a model which is at stark variance from the socialist models followed by other developing nations such as India, Brazil and Egypt.[186]

6.   THE DEBT CRISIS IN PERSPECTIVE

Although the debt crisis of the 1980s is over, debt-related problems for developing countries persist. This section will address possible approaches and options for resolving debt-related problems for the developing world.

First and foremost, it is important to recognize that a sustainable, long-term solution to the debt problem is to generate trade surpluses that will allow the servicing of external debt. There does not seem to be any way of avoiding the fact that international trade is the basis for maintaining stable flows of foreign exchange reserves. These reserves may be used to service debt obligations and, more importantly, may also be used to finance critical inputs into the economy in the form of capital equipment, technology, and access to international markets. While import substitution and the protectionist policies of the past held nationalistic allure, simply meeting domestic needs (without producing exportable goods) will not generate the volume of hard currency needed to regenerate and strengthen the economies of developing countries. Global integration is a fact of life, and ignoring this reality to serve short-term political priorities is a dangerous undertaking.

Incurring debt should be regarded as a legitimate strategy for economic growth, but the reasons for incurring international debt, the purposes for which the debt will be used, and the sources and type of debt to be incurred are all critical political considerations that must be made in a disciplined fashion. Otherwise, relying on international commercial credit to finance imports without simultaneously building up an export base, as we have seen in the case of Latin American countries, is an invitation to disaster.

Developing countries can source their capital needs by three principal means: by obtaining loans, by issuing bonds or by attracting equity investment. If debt obligations are to be incurred, there are two principal sources of international lending: commercial banks and multilateral development banks. As the previous discussion illustrates, the fallacies of relying too heavily on either source can cause severe imbalances to a developing country economy. Although debt workouts are inevitable, ultimately, they are unsatisfactory. Indeed, the decade of the 1980s has been termed the 'lost decade for development',[187] in large part because the debt crisis wastefully consumed so much time, resources and energy.

---

[186] *Ibid.*
[187] E. Carrasco and R. Thomas, *supra* n. 8, p. 553. See also B. Ngenda, 'Comparative Models of Privatization: A Commentary on the African Experience', (1995) 21 *Brooklyn J. Int'l L.* 179.

If equity, along with bond financing is also chosen as a pathway to financing development, then developing countries will need to make disciplined decisions on how to balance and structure FDI investment as well as portfolio investment. Both avenues of equity investment have their uses and priorities. Developing countries need to craft strategies which reflect their national priorities and development goals, and sequence various options for attracting capital investment wisely. This is no mean task, and it requires that the existing debt overhang also be taken into account.

6.1   A critique of IMF structural adjustment

In dealing with the international debt question, the principal actors (i.e., developing countries, commercial banks, multilateral institutions and the United States), need to refocus the debt question along different lines. First, all debtor countries cannot be treated equally, for a number of reasons. The composition and competitiveness of their economies differ, their past credit histories and present creditworthiness vary, and their overall development objectives differ tremendously. For example, many East Asian countries are considered to be very strong international economic actors with a different set of goals and priorities than most other developing nations; most Eastern European countries are considered to be 'in transition' to becoming market-based economies, whereas many sub-Saharan countries have deeply entrenched political and economic problems that cannot be smoothed away with structural adjustment programmes.

Secondly, IMF structural adjustment programmes are designed to operate solely within a single country context. However, this ignores the fact that developing country economies do not function in isolation, but are an integral parts of a much wider and more complex economic fabric. By dogmatically insisting that certain macro-economic adjustments be made in isolation from global economic developments, the IMF's approach can be very short-sighted and, in some instances, has been doomed to failure.

IMF conditionality is predicated on the notion that the panacea for all economic woes is to resolve the balance-of-payments crisis by: (1) depreciating the currency and making it freely convertible; (2) cutting subsidies, including agricultural supports, and eliminating price controls and ceilings; (3) reducing the government's fiscal deficit by curbing government expenditures and raising tax revenues; (4) reducing social programmes for the poor, women and children, the elderly and other vulnerable social groups; (5) privatizing certain industries or sectors; and (6) liberalizing the trade and investment scheme to permit freer cross-border movement of capital. IMF officials often urge developing countries in crisis to improve their domestic fiscal deficits by removing price distortions, opening up competition and deregulating the economy.

A critique of structural adjustment lending must focus on the following concerns. First, too much policy influence is exerted by the IMF/World Bank, and this infringes on the bargaining position of developing nations. Secondly, there is too little regard for external economic factors that are outside the control of developing countries (e.g., the oil shock of the late 1970s, or raising the prime rate of interest by the US Federal Reserve).

Thirdly, and perhaps most importantly, there is too little regard for the social and political impact of structural adjustment on the poor. Indeed, structural adjustment reforms often threaten the political survival of the ruling party that is entrusted with enacting drastic economic reforms. Thus, IMF structural adjustment programmes focus on external economic indicators in a complete vacuum, with little or no consideration being paid to the social, political or human impact of such programmes.

In fact, structural adjustment can have alarming social consequences, as evidenced by a precipitous drop in child immunizations and birth weights, and the simultaneous rise in infant mortality, child malnutrition, illiteracy and school drop-out rates, as reported by UNICEF.[188] Adjustment policies assume their harshest form at the cost of the weakest and most vulnerable groups in society. Moreover, poor coordination between multilateral and bilateral institutions often results in confusion and duplicative policy-based lending programmes which may be at cross-purposes with each other. The narrow objective of correcting trade imbalances has not served poorer developing countries well. Indeed, by imposing harsh conditionality on developing countries, the IMF accentuates inequalities between the developed and the developing worlds.[189]

The IMF's 'cookie-cutter' approach to debt-related problems has been perpetuated by bilateral donors as well as commercial creditors. An IMF

---

[188] UNICEF, *Adjustment with a Human Face: Protecting the Vulnerable and Promoting Growth*, Vol. I (G.A. Cornia, R. Jolly, F. Stewart (eds.) (Clarendon Press, 1987).

[189] It should be noted that structural adjustment programmes do not strictly apply to industrialized nations, for several reasons. First, when the Kennedy Administration proposed in 1961 that it might seek access to IMF resources, the response was to form the G-10, composed of the United States, the United Kingdom, France, Germany, Japan, Canada, Italy, the Netherlands, Belgium and Sweden. The G-10 of the most highly industrialized nations agreed to form the IMF General Arrangement to Borrow in 1961 (and still continuing today) permitting G-10 members only to borrow short-term credit supplied by other G-10 members to overcome currency fluctuations or problems. No 'conditionality' is attached to the General Arrangement to Borrow. See J. Asherman, *supra* n. 18, pp. 269–270. Thus, G-10 nations are not subject to structural adjustment programmes as long as they have access to the General Arrangement.

Secondly, the US tends to avoid the General Arrangement, preferring to use currency swaps made available by the central banks of other nations and completely outside the rubric of the IMF, in order to overcome any short-term currency problems. *Ibid.*, p. 270. Finally, an IMF member can draw up to roughly 25% of its membership quota, which is known as a reserve tranche drawing. Anything above this level is known as a credit tranche drawing made under a stand-by arrangement with conditionality attached. A. Jayagovind, *supra* n. 41, 'The Financial Facilities of the IMF: Development Dimensions', in *The Right to Development in International Law*, p. 355.

Further, the membership quotas contributed by G-10 countries are significantly higher than those contributed by developing nations. Since borrowings within the quota (or reserve amount) are not subject to adjustment programmes this, in effect, means that developing countries tend to be subject to adjustment programmes more often than fully industrialized nations. J. Asherman, *supra* n. 18, at 272. On the other hand, drawings made by developing countries generally exceed their quota, and are made subject to performance criteria in ensuring repayment of the IMF loan. Thus, developing countries do not have access to the General Arrangement to Borrow, open-ended currency swaps, or to unconditioned borrowings from the IMF.

structural adjustment programme *must* be in place before related IMF loans
or World Bank structural adjustment or sectoral loans can be made, or even
before 'new money' commitments will be extended by commercial bank
lenders. Further, no debt rescheduling by official creditors acting under the
auspices of the Paris Club, or by commercial lenders acting through the
London Club, will take place before an IMF structural adjustment programme is in place. This stringent and cartelized type of conditionality
turns the debt resolution process into a vicious circle.

Structural adjustment goals are both legitimate and extremely important.
However, correcting balance-of-payments imbalances in a vacuum has been
counterproductive in many cases. The 'one-size-fits-all' structural adjustment philosophy needs to be modified to take into account the important
differences in economic conditions, history and culture, and in the
respective development goals of IMF borrower nations. A more gradualist
approach needs to be taken to avoid the human and political costs of
imposing an economic discipline that requires the recipient country to
produce more than it consumes, to export more than it imports, and to save
and invest more than it spends.

In response to these criticisms, the IMF has become more lenient in terms
of extending the period for repayment of its loans by borrower nations, and
has been more sensitive in terms of addressing social safety net issues
before requiring that draconian, short-term economic adjustments be
made.[190] Although there has been a gradual movement of the Bretton
Woods institutions towards reform and giving structural adjustment a
'human face', there needs to be a fundamental reassessment of the underlying structural adjustment philosophy.

6.2   Resolving the debt crisis: short and long-term options

For certain middle-income developing countries, access to capital markets
should be a short to medium-term objective, depending on the strength of
their economies. Upon completing appropriate debt work-outs, 'decoupling'
IMF conditionality for these middle-income countries should be the
appropriate next step.[191] In other words, commercial lending to 'graduating'
developing countries should go back to what it was before the debt crisis:
unconditioned commercial lending. The debt crisis, both in terms of its
magnitude and its prolonged time frame, led to the mutual reinforcement of
commercial banks' and IMF agendas. It is time to let go of the debt crisis of
the 1980s, so as not to relive it in the future.

Preparing low-income, heavily indebted countries for integration into
global markets also has to be an important priority for industrialized
nations. If large segments of very poor societies are left behind, this will
polarize a newly emerging global community and result in continuing

---

[190] B. Rajagopal, 'Crossing the Rubicon: Synthesizing the Soft International Law of the IMF
and Human Rights', (1993) 11 *Boston U. Int'l L. J.* 81. See also C. Lichtenstein, *supra* n. 16,
p. 1943.

[191] A. Santos, *supra* n. 8, pp. 94–95.

political instability. This instability will, in time, give rise to the increased likelihood of military coups, authoritarian regimes and nuclear proliferation, and may finally result in certain nation-states imploding (e.g., Somalia, Sudan, Liberia, Afghanistan, Rwanda and Burundi).

This may be an opportune time to consider restructuring the World Bank's lending portfolio, in light of radically different global conditions and development policies. The World Bank has strayed from its original role of providing guarantees and limited loan participation along with private investors, and now almost exclusively makes loans as a principal lender from its own capital reserves.[192] Thus, the World Bank should consider going back to its original mandate of providing enhanced credit to developing nations.

This could mean establishing two categories of World Bank lending: (1) enhanced credit facilities for middle income countries (in the form of World Bank guarantees, cofinancing or limited loan participation); and (2) IDA loans for the most severely indebted countries as the lender of last resort.

For the first category, the World Bank would provide 'additionality' in the form of enhanced credit and other measures, including technical assistance. This financing should be designed to encourage middle income countries to become creditworthy on commercial lending terms, and facilitate their return to full participation in international capital markets. Additionally, commercial lending in this category should not be 'tied' or 'linked' to structural adjustment programmes.

For the second category, this would mean abolishing all non-IDA loans (or simply completing the loans outstanding, and not making any additional loans on non-IDA terms). This policy would hopefully discourage lending in support of SOEs and other public sector borrowing by developing countries. By financing IDA loans only through the use of World Bank resources, and by using the IMF's Enhanced Structural Adjustment Facility (ESAF) lending where appropriate, the World Bank does, in fact, become the lender of last resort.

The second category of loans would apply to the many low-income countries which are heavily dependent on official development assistance.[193] For example, the growth potential for many sub-Saharan countries remains discouraging because of limited international demand for their export commodities. Further, their inability to attract FDI or financing on commercial terms adds to their desperate need for multilateral financing and access to concessional credit. Thus, for the most heavily indebted countries whose economic futures are bleakest, the World Bank is often the lender of first, not last, resort. And, for IDA-only countries (in other words, for the lowest-income countries which are eligible for IDA loans), the conditionality imposed under IMF-directed structural adjustment programmes may be

---

[192] M. Hurlock, 'New Approaches to Economic Development: The World Bank, the EBRD, and the Negative Pledge Clause', (1994) 35 *Harv. Int'l L.J.* 345 at 362.

[193] See E. Stern, 'Prospects of Development Financing in the 1980s', (1982) 32 *Am. U. L. Rev.*, 145 at 147–148, 150.

appropriate. Of course, there is room to modify such structural adjustment programmes along the lines discussed above.

Thus, appropriate debt exiting tactics, including debt relief where necessary, may rid middle-income countries of their debt overhang. The next phase should establish two tracks of lending, one leading to the other: first, enhanced credit for middle income countries; secondly, concessional (IDA-only) loans for severely indebted countries until they are gradually readied for borrowing money on commercial market lending terms. The following discussion will discuss these options in greater detail.

6.3   A menu of options for middle income countries

Middle income countries, while still in need of debt relief measures (of the type contemplated by the Brady Initiative, for example), should creatively make use of the menu of options available to them to effectively write down their debt. The previous discussion addressed securitization and collateralization of debt as well as specific techniques such as swaps, cofinancing, on-lending and indexed facilities, which will not be repeated here.[194] Formulating a menu of options for debt and debt service reduction is critical in encouraging the continued economic growth of middle-income countries. Additionally, economic growth through capital investment in emerging capital markets is an important factor as well, and will be addressed in Chapter 5.

However, just as debtor nations have to be treated differently, so do lenders. The restrictive clauses found in many loan agreements are designed, as in the case of *pari passu* and sharing clauses, to ensure the equal treatment of creditors. Each creditor is thus guaranteed that it will receive its *pro rata* share of loan repayments. Other restrictive clauses such as negative pledge, mandatory prepayment and cross-default clauses, ensure that the interests of unsecured creditors are not subordinated to other lenders who enter into subsequent loan agreements with the same borrower. These types of restrictive clauses tend to exert a prospective or injunctive effect on future indebtedness by prohibiting the borrower from pledging assets or revenues to subsequent creditors. Alternatively, the borrower may be penalized for its prepayment of the loan, or deemed to be in default if the borrower defaults on another, unrelated loan.

The equal treatment of all creditors is a critical legal assumption that has been changed by the debt crisis of the 1980s. The debt-for-debt approach of the Brady Initiative changed the legal effect of sharing and negative pledge clauses by permitting the debtor to repay its creditors in a preferential, selective way.

In addition, the menu approach of the Brady Initiative requires each commercial bank creditor to choose a menu option. The options can be tailored to

---

[194] See S. Claessens, *et al.*, 'Market-Based Debt Reduction for Developing Countries: Principles and Prospects', (1990) World Bank Paper No. 16.

permit each bank to meet its own capital, tax and other constraints. This encourages efficiency and coordination between syndicated lenders, and tends to minimize free-rider problems. In the final analysis, however, choosing from a menu of options means that the conservative and orthodox legal notion of treating all creditors equally has been vitiated.

The inclusion of restrictive clauses, such as the negative pledge clause, in loan agreements by the World Bank in the context of sovereign lending can severely affect the borrower country's ability to obtain additional financing. This is especially the case where the sovereign borrower owns a great deal of capital assets and needs to pledge the use of these assets in secured lending arrangements with other creditors. Although the pledge of sovereign assets may technically be a breach of contract and entitle the multilateral lender to seek an acceleration of payment on the original loan, or to seize the pledged assets, this 'right' is rarely, if ever, exercised.[195] This would lead to the politically awkward situation where the World Bank may foreclose its loans, and end up seizing the assets of its member countries. The World Bank and other multilateral lenders have granted waivers from negative pledge clauses, but the utility of such restrictive clauses in sovereign loan agreements, and their continued inclusion therein, should be carefully re-examined.

6.4 Additional approaches to debt relief

An additional approach to resolving the debt problems of developing countries would be to monetize debt repayments to the World Bank or bilateral donors in local currency. If local currency were used rather than hard currency (i.e., foreign exchange reserves generated by exports), the most heavily indebted nations could ease their debt burden. The local currency repayments could be deposited in a special account in the central bank of the debtor country and programmed for agreed uses with the multilateral bank or bilateral donor. Potential uses for local currency would be to support human resource development, education, and developing non-traditional exports and markets.

A more structured approach would be to set up an endowment or special trust fund to oversee the uses of the local currency. Rather than replenishing the capital stock of the World Bank, the local currency generated could be used in-country for purposes agreed with the World Bank. Alternatively, the local currency deposits could be used to support internal government fiscal deficits.[196] To avoid the inflationary impact of such deposits, the local currency could be 'sterilized' or simply taken out of circulation in accordance with IMF structural adjustment measures. This way, the drain on outgoing

---

[195] M. Hurlock, *supra* n. 192, pp. 349–350, 356.

[196] It is unlikely that such local currency deposits could be securitized by issuing Treasury-like bonds denominated in local currency. The sales of such bonds to local pension funds or institutional investors would only generate additional local currency and create inflationary conditions, or result in worthless bonds.

foreign exchange is halted, and external debt repayable in hard currency becomes internal debt repayable in local currency.

The precedent for doing so lies in the Enterprise for the Americas Initiative (EAI)[197] enacted in 1990 and 1992, providing limited debt relief for eligible Latin American countries. EAI provides that eligible Latin American and Caribbean countries whose governments are democratically elected, which do not support international terrorism, and which co-operate in international drug trafficking matters, may be eligible for debt forgiveness.

Upon entering into an Americas Framework Agreement, the debtor country deposits principal repayments, in US dollars, into a special account. Interest payments are to be deposited in local currency into an interest-bearing Americas Fund account. The local currency is held in that account until disbursed for programmed uses in conservation, the sustainable use of natural resources linked to local community development or child develop-ment activities. Based on an appropriation by the US Congress of $90 million, the Bush Administration forgave $611.1 million owed by six countries in Fiscal Year 1993.[198]

By 1995, the United States had forgiven over $2.3 billion owed to it by the most heavily indebted nations.[199] Despite the modest progress made in the last decade, it is clear that the political obstacles to debt relief for the most heavily indebted countries are highly problematic. Before debt relief can become a feasible option for the poorest, most heavily indebted countries, there has to be a new political awareness of the stakes involved. As previously discussed, the possibility of these countries slipping into intractable poverty and political instability makes them high-risk targets for military or fundamentalist take-overs, terrorism, or even political disintegration and genocide. Therefore, debt relief should be seen as a political opportunity to stabilize economies and avoid potential calamities.

6.5   Debt relief for the most heavily indebted nations

In returning to my original proposition, the past decade has shown that debtor countries cannot be treated equally. Imposing market discipline on heavily indebted nations such as sub-Saharan countries has not been successful.[200] Structural adjustment reforms, such as eliminating subsidies and market distortions, correcting interest rates and other measures, are difficult to implement, even in industrial nations. These types of market

---

[197] See Jobs Through Exports Act of 1992, Pub. L. no. 102–549, §602(a), 106 Stat. 3664 (1992), as codified as amended, at 22 U.S.C. §2430, *et seq.*

[198] J. Sanford, 'Foreign Debts to the US Government: Recent Rescheduling and Forgiveness', 28 *Geo. Wash. J. Int'l L. and Econ.* at 372.

[199] *Ibid.*, pp. 389–390.

[200] J. Levinson, 'Multilateral Financing Institutions: What Form of Accountability?' (1992) 8 *Am. U. J. Int'l L. and Pol'y* 47 at 48.

corrections are especially burdensome in developing countries, which often have unstable and vulnerable economic and political systems together with endemic poverty.[201] Therefore, rather than focusing narrowly on correcting balance-of-payments imbalances, macro-economic reforms should be more broadly directed at export market creation (perhaps by developing non-traditional exports for regional trade),[202] poverty reduction and human resource development. Additionally, programmes which address the development of human capital should, *inter alia*, address democracy and governance issues.

It is unclear whether foreign aid or policy-based lending that conditions grant assistance and loans on meeting agreed economic targets or policy changes are a successful means of promoting sustainable growth in very poor societies. The dismal results after five decades of development efforts do not inspire much confidence. Therefore, a 'Sub-Saharan Africa Marshall Plan' may not be the best approach. What is clear is that such societies are ill-equipped to absorb the structural reforms imposed on them by the IMF and the World Bank. Perhaps they lack sophisticated markets, civil societies or a democratic political fabric but, in any case, this type of approach is simply not working.

For heavily indebted countries, debt relief seems to be the only remaining option. Becoming hostage to the repayment of non-performing debt does not help stabilize or strengthen their economies. The actors in the international debt scene fall into two camps: those in favour of debt relief, and those opposed to it. The camp in favour of debt relief, particularly for heavily indebted nations (referred to in some circles as the 'Fourth World'), believe that oppressive debt repayment schedules stifle short- and long-term economic growth.

The opponents of debt relief are very powerful. Debt forgiveness has long been resisted by the US Treasury Department, the US Federal Reserve Board and US commercial bankers, as well as by official lending institutions.[203] The argument against debt relief is persuasive, since it would create a moral hazard by penalizing countries that have been repaying their debt, damage the sovereign debtor countries' future credit ratings and weaken world financial markets. Additionally, it would force commercial bank lenders to incur heavy losses and impede the opening up of new channels of credit to sovereign borrowers, who may be forced to operate on an unworkable cash-only basis. Finally, it would provide no real incentives for sovereign borrowers to adopt and implement better economic and fiscal policies.[204] Notwithstanding these powerful arguments, the case for constructive debt relief will be explored in the next section.

---

[201] E. Stern, *supra* n. 193, pp. 152–153.
[202] For a scathing critique on the failure of African trading regions or areas, see M. wa Matua, 'Why Redraw the Map of Africa', (1995) 16 *Mich. J. Int'l L.* 1113 at 1170–1175.
[203] J. Sanford, *supra* n. 198 at 353.
[204] B. Boyd, *supra* n. 1, p. 485, n. 123.

6.6 Bilateral debt relief: the US example

The passage of the Federal Credit Reform Act of 1990[205] changed the method of calculating and forgiving US government loans and loan guarantees. Before the passage of the Federal Credit Reform Act, one dollar appropriated by the US Congress was necessary in order for a US government agency to forgive one dollar's worth of debt. Beginning in 1992, section 661a(5) of the Federal Credit Reform Act changed this by requiring US government agencies to calculate the 'net present value' of a debt obligation owed to the US government, rather than using the debt's face or book value. Factors such as the likelihood of default, the interest rate and maturity period are also taken into account in determining the debt's net present value.[206] The equivalent amount of the *present net value* of the debt sought to be forgiven must be appropriated for the fiscal year in which debt relief is sought.

Much of developing country sovereign debt is heavily discounted because the debtor is unable to repay the debt. This means that the present net value of such debt is far less than its actual face value. Thus, a dollar's worth of current fiscal year funds can relieve several dollars' worth of old, non-performing debt. Current year appropriations must be set aside for debt relief purposes, and that amount is charged against the US agency's operating account. Thus, debt relief becomes a political choice.

Performance-based disbursements on loans is an important means for supporting foreign policy objectives. Further, conditioning debt relief on meeting specified economic or political targets is also a strategic tool in enforcing policy goals. Transforming non-performing and uncollectable debt into 'grant' assistance through debt forgiveness is not as costly to the US taxpayer as it was in the past, and may serve important policy considerations. Moreover, debt relief may also serve the interests of debtor nations by relieving them of their repayment obligations, enhancing their future borrowing power and enabling donor countries to extend more credit to them.

For example, from 1990 to 1995, the US government forgave $12.93 billion in debts owed to it by sovereign borrowers, of which Egypt, Poland and Jordan accounted for over 70 per cent of the total amount.[207] In 1990, $6.7 billion in military debt owed to the US by Egypt was cancelled, together with 70 per cent of the $3.8 billion owed by Poland. In 1994,

---

[205] Pub. L. No. 101–508, 104 Stat. 1388, 1388–610 (1990), codified as amended, 2 U.S.C. §661 (Supp. V 1994).

[206] 2 U.S.C. §661a(5)(B). In other words, the below-market interest rate and the long maturity periods (both reflecting the concessionality element in these loans) decrease the overall present net value of the debt. The concessionality element, in combination with the debtor country's inability to pay, further decreases the value of the debt and, in effect, increases the discount on the debt.

[207] J. Sanford, *supra* n. 198, p. 363. The author gives a detailed description of the terms of debt forgiveness to these countries, their relationship to Paris Club reschedulings and to structural adjustment requirements.

the US cancelled $99 million owed to it by Jordan. Although debt relief served US strategic interests *vis-à-vis* these particular countries, 'conditionality' was imposed before forgiveness would be granted (see Box 3.5).[208] Poland, for example, was required to pursue certain economic reforms.[209]

Box 3.5: Countries indebted to the United States

The four countries most heavily indebted to the US are all sub-Saharan African countries which do not have functional governments. (It is a little too early to tell about Laurent Kabila's government in the Congo, formerly Zaire.) The option of writing off the debt may seem attractive, although Vietnam may also provide an interesting contrast. Left-over Commodity Credit Corporation debt, P.L. 480 debt for food aid, and miscellaneous USAID and EximBank loans lapsed when Saigon fell on April 16, 1975. However, these loans were rescheduled, in part, and forgiven, in part, 22 years later in 1997. Rescheduling these loans was a precondition to commencing foreign aid to Vietnam. The US may wish to wait also for the final outcome of the above-named countries that are the most heavily indebted to it but it will, no doubt, be a long wait. Meanwhile, there is little, if any debt service on a cumulative debt of these four sovereign debtors amounting to $2.81 billion.

Source: J. Sanford, 'Foreign Debts to the U.S. Government: Recent Rescheduling and Forgiveness', 28 *Geo. Wash. J. Int'l L. & Econ.* 387 at 388.

Apart from the special considerations relating to Egypt, Poland and Jordan, the US has also passed legislation appropriating $14 million to use in Paris Club reschedulings (see Box 3.6)[210] to help the most heavily indebted countries.[211] By 1992, 28 countries which were eligible for debt reduction through the Paris Club owed a total of $4.08 billion to the United States.[212] Over half of this amount was owed by four countries: Liberia, Somalia, Congo (Zaire) and Sudan.[213] The other 24 countries owed $1.27 billion.

The remaining 24 countries owed a total of $83.6 billion in 1992 to official creditors (i.e., multilateral and bilateral donors), owing the US less than 2 per cent of the total.[214] Therefore, forgiving this debt may be as insignificant for the United States as it is for the debtor nations. Debt service of the amount owed to the United States is also insignificant, since most of these heavily indebted counties choose to service multilateral (official) debt owed to the World Bank, rather than the United States or other bilateral

---

[208] §. 579(a) of the Foreign Operations, Export Financing, and Related Programs Appropriations Act, 1991, Pub. L. No. 101–513, 104 Stat. 2045 (1990).
[209] J. Sanford, *supra* n. 198, pp. 387, 388.
[210] §. 570 of the Foreign Operations, Export Financing, and Related Programs Appropriations Act, 1994, Pub. L. No. 103–87, tit. II, 107 Stat. 931 (1993).
[211] Ibid. pp. 359–360.
[212] J. Sanford, *supra* n. 198, p. 387.
[213] *Ibid.*
[214] *Ibid.*, p. 390.

donors. This way, these debtor countries remain eligible for future World Bank loan disbursements. Thus, the US bilateral approach, while highly political in nature, gives a concrete example of how debt relief can still be a politically viable option.

Box 3.6: Paris Club reschedulings

A Paris Club meeting is normally initiated at the request of the debtor country, and a rescheduling will only be considered if an IMF stand-by arrangement is already in place. The objective of the meeting is to ensure that all official creditors are treated equally for debt repayment purposes, and that preferential treatment of one at the expense of the others does not take place.

Rescheduling debt, however, does not forgive it; it merely changes the timing of the repayment schedule to better enable the debtor country to meet its debt obligations. Generally, the debtor nation reschedules payment of debt that had already fallen in arrears, and maturities falling due in the con- solidation period, or 12–18 months immediately following the execution of the rescheduling agreement. These Paris Club loan rescheduling agreements are called 'agreed minutes'.

Both principal and interest may be rescheduled, but debt payments becoming due after the consolidation period, or due after a specific date known as the contract cut-off date, may not be rescheduled. Between January 1980 and September 1993, 60 countries negotiated 204 agreed minutes rescheduling $210 billion in sovereign debt.

Source: J. Sanford, 'Foreign Debts to the U.S. Government: Recent Reschedulings and Forgiveness', 28 *Geo. Wash. J. Int'l L. & Econ.* 359 at 359–360.

6.7   Bilateral debt relief through Paris Club rescheduling

Most official debt, that is developing country sovereign debt which is owed to bilateral donors such as the United States, France, Germany and other OECD countries, is rescheduled under the auspices of the Paris Club when default is imminent on the underlying loan(s).[215] The Paris Club is an informal, inter-governmental meeting that is hosted in Paris by the French Ministry of Finance. The IMF, the World Bank, the OECD and the UN Conference on Trade and Development have observer status.

Based on a G-7 meeting in Toronto in June 1988, the Paris Club approved a plan for limited debt forgiveness. The menu of options, known as the Toronto Terms, permitted forgiveness of up to one-third of the debt owed, lower interest rates and longer rescheduling terms. By September 1990, the Paris Club had approved the Houston Terms permitting longer debt repayment terms, and the exchange of up to 10 per cent of market-rate debt through debt swaps.

---

[215] Non-Paris Club creditors include China, Russia, Saudi Arabia and Libya. See A. Boote and K. Thugge, 'Debt Relief for Low-Income Countries and the HIPC Initiative', IMF Working Paper No. 24 (March 1997), p. 19, n. 2, and chart.

Although the Paris Club rejected the UK proposal of the Trinidad Terms in July 1991 which would have cancelled two-thirds of all outstanding debt stock, rescheduling the remaining one-third over 25 years, it did accept the Enhanced Toronto Terms (also referred to as the 'London Terms') in December 1991, permitting official lenders to cancel up to 50 per cent of outstanding eligible debt owed by sovereign borrowers. In December 1994, the Paris Club agreed to the 'Naples Terms', which will be addressed later in this text, permitting the cancellation of up to 67 per cent of eligible debt.

6.8 Multilateral debt relief

The World Bank is in the process of reassessing its views and policies concerning official development assistance (ODA) debt. Although the International Development Association (IDA) was formed in 1960 as part of (or rather, as a programme of) the World Bank group to make concessional lending available to the poorest members, it soon became clear that IDA loans were insufficient to address the capital needs of the poorest countries.

The World Bank designed the Special Programme of Assistance (SPA) in 1983 in order to help relieve the debt crisis. By 1987, the IMF, the World Bank and IDA concentrated SPA resources on debt-distressed countries, particularly sub-Saharan nations. Increased IDA disbursements and reflows (i.e., repayment of interest and principal on such loans) for structural adjustment lending, credits from the IMF's Enhanced Structural Adjustment Facility, cofinancing with other donors, and certain debt relief measures were made available through the SPA.

The World Bank also set up the Special Facility for Africa (SFA) in 1985 in order to provide bilateral donors with the means of cofinancing structural adjustment-based lending to sub-Saharan countries. Additionally, the World Bank established the Debt Reduction Facility in 1989 with an initial funding of $100 million to be contributed by the World Bank, the IMF, the African Development Bank, and bilateral donor contributions.[216] The Debt Reduction Facility has already extinguished over $981 million in external commercial debt (principal only), and over $500 million in interest and arrears on such commercial debt.[217] Debt reduction operations have been concluded for Bolivia, Guyana, Mozambique, Niger, Sao Tomé and Principe, Sierra Leone, Uganda and Zambia.[218] This new aid will be condi-

---

[216] J. Sanford, *supra* n. 198, p. 400, n. 276. Ernest Stern points out that the World Bank's lending ratio is extremely conservative since its outstanding and disbursed loans cannot exceed its capital reserves. This may need to be reexamined in forging new means of addressing the debt question. See E. Stern, *supra* n. 193, p. 151.

[217] World Bank Policy Research Bulletin, Vol. 4, No. 5, *Debt Reduction Facility*, available on internet address: http://www.worldbank.org/dec/Publications/Bulletins/ PRB/vol4no5.htm (last visited on 28 July 1998).

[218] Additional countries approved for debt reduction include: Albania, Ethiopia, Nicaragua, Guinea, Mauritania, Senegal, Tanzania and Vietnam are being prepared for facility operations, and Cameroon, Congo, Honduras and Togo are under consideration. See World Bank Policy Research Bulletin, Vol. 4, No. 5, *Debt Reduction Facility*, available on internet address: http://www.worldbank.org/dec/Publications/Bulletins/PRB/vol4no5.htm.

tioned on making structural adjustment reforms and obtaining similar debt relief from other donors, and is designed to help relieve the debt servicing burdens of the most heavily indebted countries.

Debt reduction takes place through cash buy-backs of discounted commercial debt, with a certain amount of the facility's resources being available for collateralizing debt exchange transactions. There is, however, a clear emphasis on short-term balance-of-payments corrections through structural adjustment measures without providing actual debt relief. Apparently, the SFA has been designed to avoid writing off any debts with the World Bank that might otherwise negatively impact on the Bank's credit rating.[219]

6.9   The HIPC initiative

Finally, in September 1996, the World Bank and the IMF jointly proposed the Heavily Indebted Poor Countries (HIPC) initiative. In recognition of the fact that the traditional means of dealing with the debt overhang of developing countries, including structural adjustment programmes, Paris Club debt reschedulings, bilateral donor debt forgiveness, and new money loans by commercial creditors, have not provided a comprehensive, enduring solution to the debt question, the HIPC initiative has been approved.[220]

The HIPC initiative provides for a three-stage process whereby the developing country enters into a three-year programme of policy reforms and uses the Paris Club's Naples Terms to relieve up to 67 per cent of outstanding, eligible bilateral debt. After the completion of the first stage, a decision point will be reached with regard to the applicant's eligibility under the HIPC initiative, based on a Debt Sustainability Analysis prepared by World Bank and IMF staff. If the effort to date has been successful, the debtor country exits, and is not eligible for further debt relief under the HIPC initiative. (Borderline cases are given additional time to reach the decision point.) To date, Benin, Bolivia, Burkina Faso, Guyana, Mali and Uganda have established three-year track records under the Naples Terms.[221] Additionally, an HIPC initiative package for Uganda in excess of $700 million has already been approved. (See Text Box 7.)

If the Paris Club reschedulings under the Naples Terms have been deemed to be insufficient, then a final determination will be made with regard to the eligibility of the country to participate under the HIPC initiative. Additional debt relief may be provided by Paris Club creditors

---

[219] P. Blustein, 'Debt Relief for Poor Nations Weighed', *Washington Post*, 15 September 1995, p. F3.

[220] World Bank, *The HIPC Debt Initiative,* available on internet address: http://www.worldbank.org/html/extdr/faq/97631.htm (last visited on 13 August 1998). See also A. Boote and K. Thugge, 'Debt relief for Low-Income Countries and the HIPC Initiative', IMF Working Paper, No. 24 (March 1997).

[221] A. Boote and K. Thugge, 'Debt Relief for Low-Income Countries and the HIPC Initiative', IMF Working Paper No. 24 (March 1997), p. 22.

up to 80 per cent under the Lyons Terms, with comparable debt relief provided by commercial creditors as well.

If, in addition to bilateral and commercial debt relief, the debt sustainability point of the applicant country is not achieved, then there is an additional mechanism. The World Bank has set up the Multilateral HIPC Trust Fund, initially funded with $500 million from the World Bank, which will be administered by IDA (see Box 3.7).[222] The HIPC Trust Fund will either prepay or purchase part of the debt owed to a multilateral creditor (i.e., the World Bank, the IMF, or a regional multilateral development bank such as the African Development Bank), or pay the debt as it becomes due. The IMF will also provide grants or highly concesssional loans from its Enhanced Structural Adjustment Fund (ESAF)-HIPC Trust, established in February 1997. These funds will be made available only to cover debt service owed to the IMF.

Box 3.7: HIPC package to Uganda

The World Bank approved an HIPC package to reduce Uganda's debt by $338 million, of which $160 million was to be provided by the World Bank. The HIPC package was to be delivered by April 1998, reducing Uganda's debt level by $700 million in nominal terms, and enabling it to exit from the debt rescheduling process. The three-year interim time period was reduced by the Executive Boards of the World Bank and the IMF to one year, in recognition of Uganda's 'exceptional record' of economic and social reforms.

Source: World Bank Press Release No. 97/1324-S (23 April 1997).

The HIPC Trust Fund provides encouraging new progress in adopting a comprehensive, strategic approach to resolving the debt crisis, and permitting developing country participants to exit from the debt rescheduling process on a permanent basis. It is too early to measure the success of such an undertaking, but it does give hope for the future.

In conclusion, this discussion is meant to provide an historical perspective on the debt crisis and its impact on development. This discussion is also meant to provide some insight on possible approaches to be considered in ameliorating, and finally resolving, the debt overhang of developing countries. A menu of options should be used constructively and flexibly by debtor countries, and policy changes should be considered and implemented by creditor countries. Clearly, a partnership between the two is necessary if the debt question is to be resolved in the near future.

---

[222] World Bank Press Release No. 97/1324-S, 23 April 1997.

4. Privatization

This chapter will explore the implications of privatization as a development strategy. In particular, specific techniques of privatization and their most advantageous application within a developing country context will be discussed. Finally, the impact of privatization on emerging capital markets, an important trend for the future will be considered.

The reader may have been overwhelmed by the recent level of attention given to privatization efforts taking place in Eastern Europe, Latin America and Asia. Global privatization activities seem to be proceeding at a frenzied pace. More than 100 countries have privatized selected state-owned enterprises (SOEs), generating revenues in excess of $80 billion in 1994–95 alone.[1] In terms of dollar value, 57 per cent of all privatizations in 1995 took place in Latin America, and 18.7 per cent took place in Eastern Europe and Central Asia.[2] However, the reasons why privatization is being pursued with such enthusiasm may not be quite clear. This discussion will attempt to give a 'big picture' analysis of privatization as a strategic tool in the development process.

Privatization simply means the transfer of ownership or control of enterprises or assets from the government to private individuals or entities. Privatization is the opposite of nationalization, which is the transfer of ownership of assets and productive enterprises from private owners to the government.[3] As the following discussion will highlight, privatization has many profound implications. Most importantly, perhaps, the privatization process can be instrumental in transforming the role of the state from that of being a provider of goods and services to being a regulator of commerce and private enterprise.

The withdrawal of the state from the productive sectors of the economy (e.g., oil production, mineral extraction, transportation, power, water use) requires a fundamental reorientation in the underlying notions of governance. The privatization process can be catalytic in helping the state

---

[1] P. Guislain, *The Privatization Challenge: A Strategic, Legal and Institutional Analysis of International Experience* (World Bank, 1997), p. 1.

[2] International Finance Corporation (IFC), *Privatization: Principles and Practice* (Lessons of Experience Series, No. 1, IFC and World Bank, 1995), p. 9. Privatizations in Africa and the Middle East were only a minimal percentage of the total amount. *Ibid.*

[3] A. Chua, 'The Privatization-Nationalization Cycle: The Link Between Markets and Ethnicity in Developing Countries', (1995) 95 *Colum. L. Rev.* 223 at pp. 226–227; IFC, *supra* n. 2, p. 13. See also P. Guislain, *supra* n. 1, p. 10.

redefine its responsibilities towards the populace it governs. A change in a developing state's approach towards governance may have many varied and complex practical implications. For example, debt management, taxation, the development and viability of the private sector, the creation of legal regulations and regulatory institutions, corporate governance, and a rule of law regime may all be affected by the privatization process. Although it is not possible to address the full implications of privatization in all contexts, the following discussion will attempt to put certain aspects of privatization into perspective.

1.   NATIONALIZATION V. PRIVATIZATION

As mentioned earlier, privatization is at the opposite end of the spectrum from nationalization. Nationalization of private assets has often been associated with a certain ideological outlook and idealism in the 1950s and 1960s following independence movements in the developing world. Nationalization has often coincided with periods of renewed interest in public policy and governance issues generally. Privatization, on the other hand, tends to follow periods of disillusionment with such ideals, and typically leads to a retreat to the private pursuit of material gain.[4]

Nationalization has often been associated with inward-looking policies such as import tariffs and trade protectionist measures. Economic protectionism, in general, is designed to foster the growth of nascent industries in order to ensure self-sufficiency in developing countries. Therefore, imports from the outside world are discouraged. In contrast, privatization is much more outward-looking. Private entrepreneurs may be motivated to seek joint ventures with foreign firms and to explore new markets for capitalist expansion. Thus, there seems to be a unity of opposites between nationalization and privatization. However, it is important to remember, as Amy Chua points out, that 'in developing countries, privatization and nationalization cannot, respectively, be equated with idealism and self-interest'.[5]

Further, Professor Chua contends that developing countries tend to oscillate between nationalization and privatization, supporting her theory with case studies and anecdotal evidence from Latin American and South-east Asian countries.[6] For example, Mexico began nationalizing its industries around 1917, privatized beginning in 1940, nationalized again beginning in 1958, and began privatizing yet again in the mid-1980s.[7]

Similarly, Malaysia followed a fairly laissez-faire policy from its independence in 1957. However, increasing ethnic tensions led to the adoption of the New Economic Policy (NEP) in 1971. The NEP set aside minority ownership interests for the ethnic Malay population (Bumiputras) in private enterprise undertakings and education. The subsequent decline in Malaysia's economy

---

[4] A. Chua, *supra* n. 3, p. 258.
[5] *Ibid.*
[6] *Ibid.*, pp. 256–259.
[7] *Ibid.*, pp. 230–237.

by 1980 spurred the government to institute a massive privatization programme. The government's privatization scheme nevertheless preserved NEP
goals by permitting foreign ownership of Malaysian enterprises, but
stipulating that at least 70 per cent of the enterprises must be owned by
Malaysians; 40 per cent of which may be owned by non-Bumiputra
Malaysians, and 30 per cent of which must be owned by the Bumiputra.[8]

Indeed, there does seem to be a degree of truth in the contention that
developing countries seem to move in cycles between nationalization and
privatization. Post-independence nationalization movements were often
fuelled by a heady reaction to decades, if not centuries, of foreign domination.
Reclaiming national assets and resources, formerly 'expropriated' by foreign
powers, helped formalize the independence of new nations. Moreover, by
transferring the ownership of foreign-owned private enterprises to the public
sector, the entire population became automatically vested, at least nominally,
in the economic production and survival of the newly independent country.
Further, nationalization helped legitimize the goals of independence by
making everyone a stakeholder in the new order.

Apart from ideological or sentimental reasons for nationalization, there
were more practical considerations behind the nationalization process during
the 1950s and 1960s. In the aftermath of the post-independence era, there may
have been no real choice than to nationalize critical export industries and
industrial sectors of national importance. The domestic private sector may
have been too weak, or even non-existent, in many developing countries, to
actually support the type of sophisticated economic activity required in
producing consumer goods and services on a national scale. Such goods and
services would have had to be of exportable quality in order to generate
foreign exchange through international sales.

Moreover, borrowing from commercial sources by private, indigenous
companies may not have been feasible immediately after independence. In
such instances it may have been a risky proposition to stake the country's
future on private sector support of the economy. Thus, the state may have
been the only national actor capable of borrowing from international
sources, engaging in international trade and commerce on a broad enough
scale to meet national import/export needs, and undertaking large capital
infrastructure projects such as power, telecommunications, waste water
disposal and transportation to serve the public.

Further, since World Bank lending is only available to its member
governments (and to private parties whose borrowing is supported by sovereign guarantees extended by a member state), this also tended to reinforce
the economic power of the state and the benefits of nationalization. This
policy is common to other multilateral lending institutions besides the World
Bank. In 1990, for example, 98 per cent of all Asian Development Bank loans
were made to member governments, or to parastatals whose loans were
supported by sovereign guarantees.[9] In light of the fact that the World Bank

---

[8] *Ibid.*, pp. 246–47; see also C. Adam and W. Cavendish, 'Background' in K.S. Jomo (ed.),
Privatizing Malaysia: Rents, Rhetoric, Realities (1996), p. 14.
[9] D. Newberry, 'The Role of Public Enterprises in the National Economy' (Institute for Policy
Reform, Working Paper Series No. 45, May 1992), p. 3.

will not make loans to private parties without sovereign guarantees, this provided an additional incentive for developing states to borrow directly from multilateral banking sources, especially since most of these governments were reluctant to guarantee private obligations.[10]

Although for many Western policy-makers nationalization is inextricably intertwined with the idea of socialism, this association can be very misleading.[11] Of course, nationalization may superficially resemble a 'socialist' redistribution of national assets to the public, and may also conveniently fit into the rhetoric of empowering the working classes in relation to the entrepreneurial, capitalist classes. However, for most developing countries, nationalization was not directed at bringing about a Marxist revolution,[12] but rather was aimed at realizing two completely different goals: to end foreign domination and control of economic assets and to achieve economic self-sufficiency. The confusion of nationalist sentiment for Marxist ideals during the Cold War era has been most unfortunate.

Professor Chua also argues that ethnicity has been a second, important factor in nationalization programmes. In other words, during times of privatization (generally during periods of economic expansion and prosperity), certain ethnic groups tend to do better than others. Thus, nationalization can also be directed at domestic groups, not just foreign corporate interests. Nationalization is a means of 'levelling the playing field' by usurping private profits and profit-making from a domestic economic elite (and, in the case of many Latin American countries, from a social, cultural and intellectual elite as well).[13]

In Latin America, the 'ethnic' backlash against the ruling political and social elite with clear ties to European and/or American antecedents is a further expression of the desire to remove the influence of 'foreigners' from the local culture.[14] For some South and South-east Asian as well as African cultures, certain nationalization efforts have been directed towards ethnic minorities. Such minorities may have been targeted despite their presence in the 'indigenous' culture for many generations.

In those instances, therefore, the 'foreigner' is perceived as someone who is ethnically distinct, rather than a representative of a former colonizer as such.[15] This has been especially true of efforts to rein in Chinese entrepreneurs in Malaysia, Indonesia, Thailand and Burma (Myanmar),[16] as well as Idi Amin's campaign to rid Uganda of Africans of Indian origin in the

---

[10] W.W. Baer and M. Birch, 'Privatisation and the Changing Role of the State in Latin America', (1992) 25 *N.Y.U.J. Int'l. L. & Pol'y* 1 at 6.

[11] A. Chua, *supra* n. 3, pp. 261–262.

[12] See e.g., *ibid.*, p. 262.

[13] *Ibid.*, p. 272. The sociological implications and potential causes explaining why certain ethnic groups become economically dominant regardless of the cultures in which they are harboured is explored in J. Kotkin, *Tribes* (Random House, 1993). The reasons why certain ethnic minorities are 'accepted' and others retain their 'foreignness' is outside the scope of this discussion, but is another layer of complexity that the law is ill-adapted to handle.

[14] A. Chua, *supra* n. 3, pp. 276–277.

[15] *Ibid.*, pp. 271–272.

[16] *Ibid.* at pp. 269–270. This is also true of the attempts to curtail the economic success of Indians living in Malaysia, Sri Lanka and Kenya, for example.

late 1970s. Thus, past nationalization efforts have been directed at eliminating (or neutralizing) the 'foreigner', whether within or without the 'indigenous' culture. The anti-foreign, protectionist, and inward-looking character of certain nationalization efforts can be very thinly veiled.

The continual contraction and expansion between nationalization and privatization in many developing countries can be difficult to understand, particularly in instances where nationalization efforts have had disastrous consequences, as in Tanzania, Zambia and other African countries. Nationalization has, in some cases, led to the creation of a 'predatory' state,[17] rather than one designed to embody the ideals of equity, participation and opportunity. Inefficient SOEs, mounting external debt, capital flight, the failure to develop robust export-oriented industries are but a few reasons which all account for a gradual economic decline. Corruption from within, and the failure of the state to deliver on the ideals of nationalization, has often led to wide-scale disillusionment.

Alienation from the nationalization process and its underlying ideals can spur a movement towards privatization. However, privatization attempts may be followed by the state reasserting its political power by nationalizing industries and privately-owned assets.[18] The return to renationalization, despite its proven track record of failure to produce economic prosperity and self-sufficiency, starts the cycle over again.

The movement back and forth between nationalization and privatization points to a deeper underlying cause: the desire to seek equilibrium between our outward-looking and inward-looking natures. On the one hand, privatization encourages the entrepreneur to seek linkages with the outside world, whether it be in the form of joint ventures, technology transfers, developing new regional and international markets, or creating innovative advertising campaigns for international markets.

Indeed, in an information age where marketing and sales can be done via internet and other electronic or satellite transmissions, the ethnicity of the two parties transacting business becomes less and less relevant. Thus, privatization tends to soften (and may finally eradicate) the differences in ethnic or national origin, religion, age, gender, disabilities, and all other immutable human characteristics. By trivializing such differences, capitalism on an international scale offers the first real glimpse into a truly global culture where cultural differences are immaterial. The specificity of different cultures may be rendered obsolete in the final equation.

Nationalization may be seen as a backlash against the idea of 'foreignness', however it is perceived. It is legitimate to ask in this context why certain ethnic groups, while present in recipient cultures for generations, are not perceived as 'indigenous' cultures. Unfortunately, that query lies outside this text. It may be argued, however, that nationalization efforts speak to the desire to remain within the confines of national culture. National culture can be given seemingly arbitrary limits and defined in

---

[17] D. Lal, 'The Political Economy of Economic Liberalization', (1987) 1 *World Bank Econ. Rev.* 273 at 277.

[18] A. Chua, *supra* n. 3, pp. 264–265.

such a way as to exclude others, whether they are perceived as a foreigner within or without.

If foreign entrepreneurs are targeted, then this exclusionary tendency is expressed in economic terms by setting up protectionist measures such as international trade barriers of various kinds. This protects the national culture from foreign intervention and domination on the international or macro-level. If, on the other hand, ethnic minorities are the implicit subject of nationalization, this may be a form of cultural protectionism on the national or micro-level. Thus, nationalization efforts can be seen as a form of protectionism against foreign intervention from without, or ethnic economic domination from within. Nationalization may, therefore, be viewed as an attempt to 'level the playing field' ethnically between peoples, whether they are inside or outside the culture. There may, in fact, be an element of fear and anxiety implicit in such a strategy.

The purpose of this discussion is not to condemn nationalization as a short-sighted and inappropriate strategy for development. What has been remarkably absent in the literature, to date, is a discussion of how to achieve a new equilibrium between the two very strong impulses of nationalization and privatization. Rather than reinventing the wheel time and time again, should a new synthesis be sought out? Or does the onset of the information age render nugatory any nationalization impulse? Is it possible to achieve a balance between preserving 'indigenous' cultures and participating in a new global culture?

While capitalism may be the only viable means of economic production for the foreseeable future, it seems that certain cultures and ethnic groups will inevitably be favoured in this process. This is hardly a new idea—Max Weber laid the foundation for this type of thinking in the early 1900s with his view that the Protestant Ethic supported the creation and preservation of strong capitalist institutions.[19] However, privatization does *not* provide equal opportunities to all peoples in their quest to achieve material prosperity.

In fact, privatization and expanded opportunities for capitalist activities tend to exacerbate implicit ethnic tensions. In many instances, certain racial groups (e.g., the Chinese, Indians, Jews and Arabs) tend to achieve a disproportionate amount of economic success in a more liberalized economy.[20] So, while privatization opens up new opportunities for the unencumbered pursuit of capitalist ideals, the danger of exacerbating underlying ethnic conflicts in this process is very real.

The next logical question is whether the state should intervene in assisting certain ethnic groups to achieve economic parity with others. This, of course, opens up the discourse on the relative merits of 'affirmative

---

[19] M. Weber, *The Protestant Ethic and the Spirit of Capitalism* (T. Parsons (trans.)), (Scribner, 1958).

[20] See A. Chua, *supra* n. 3, pp. 284, 303. Generally, the peoples that succeed at capitalism are not the ones urging nationalist measures to be taken by the government. The issue of preserving 'culture' is framed differently for those who succeed within a capitalist framework: they can create or participate in a new global culture, or pursue their own culture without feeling threatened by others.

action' type policies which attempt to boost the standing and opportunities of certain groups over others. As may be expected, the NEP and other national policies aimed at restricting ownership along ethnic lines have been severely criticized (primarily by neo-classical economists, who object to such government interference with free market principles). However, there has been insufficient time to properly judge the efficacy of such policies. NEP-like policies, for example, may be an attempt to 'level the playing field', but a lifespan of less than 25 years for such policies is unlikely to render any permanent change.

In the final analysis, viewing privatization in a vacuum is both self-serving and self-defeating. The preservation and propagation of culture (however narrowly defined) is a very important factor in any development story. Ignoring the impulse to preserve culture (or national identity), however this is defined, may be politically risky, especially where a backlash cannot be anticipated or controlled.

As the following discussion will endeavour to prove, liberalizing developing country economies by eliminating trade barriers to the outside may, indeed, be necessary in order to compete effectively in international markets. Thus, certain developing countries may need to give serious consideration to whether nationalization and protectionist measures on the macro-level are appropriate development strategies at their stage of development.

Developing states may additionally need to decide whether to give disadvantaged ethnic and minority groups a preferential stake in the privatization process. The more marginalized certain ethnic or racial groups become, the greater the potential for ethnic conflict and political destabilization. (The conflagrations in Rwanda, Burundi and the former Yugoslavia are grim reminders of how serious a danger ethnic conflicts can be.) But if such preferences are to be given, how is this to be accomplished? Are set-asides and other measures appropriate and viable in this context? These are all controversial questions within the development process, and there are no simple answers.

2.   CHANGING THE ROLE OF THE STATE

The previous discussion described certain historical reasons giving rise to the strong economic role of post-independence governments of many developing countries. The absence of a strong private sector was, in most cases, the primary reason for the *de facto* assumption of this role by the state.[21] Additionally, policies of nationalization and import-substitution based industrialization also fuelled the development of a strong public sector.[22]

---

[21] W. Baer and M. Birch, *supra* n. 10, pp. 5–7.

[22] See *ibid.*, p. 3. Import substitution was an industrialization policy that emphasized the domestic production and consumption of goods. These goods generally had been previously imported, usually under preferential trade relations with former colonial powers, and import-substitution was directed at producing economic self-sufficiency.

Government-directed planning policies tended to emphasize the creation and support of heavy industries, mineral and oil extraction, and large public works in sectors deemed by the state to be critical to the national interest.[23] From the 1950s to the 1970s, many developing countries adopted policies where the state owned, controlled and managed key enterprises as well as important sectors including agriculture, telecommunications, petrochemicals, banking, hotels, airlines, air and seaports, telecommunications and tourism.

Finally, as mentioned earlier, a critical source of investment capital came not from commercial banking sources, but from multilateral banking sources such as the World Bank which required sovereign guarantees be in place before loan approvals would be granted. Thus, all these factors contributed to the development of a burgeoning public sector that provided large-scale employment opportunities. This, in turn, helped popularize the ruling party in power who could provide stable sources of public sector employment to its constituents.

However, the state-led approach to economic growth, and the import-substitution policies adopted by many Latin American, Caribbean, African and Asian countries, began to unravel in the early 1970s. The creation of state monopolies in those countries led to many inefficient practices.[24] The monopolistic status of SOEs was reinforced by establishing market entry barriers, thereby discouraging private sector competition for the production of the same goods and services.

The lack of a profit motive for most SOEs also meant that there was no real incentive to produce export-quality products and services efficiently. Redundant employees added to the inefficiencies of SOEs, and tended to encourage corrupt practices and rent-seeking.[25] The ineffective regulation of SOEs by the state also meant that environmental controls, fiscal discipline and accountability were absent.

State resources were also budgeted 'off-line' in support of SOEs in the form of hidden subsidies, tax holidays, exemptions from paying utility bills and customs duties. Thus, carrying the debt load of inefficient SOEs added to the budget deficit of the government. With the debt crisis of the early 1980s, many developing nations became desperate to finance their foreign exchange needs with additional borrowing from international sources.[26]

The rationale for privatization under these circumstances is immediately obvious.[27] Government expenditure in support of nonprofitable SOEs will be reduced in time by eliminating subsidies and other price supports. In time, reduced government deficits lowers the government's overall debt burden.[28] This tends to lower inflationary pressures on the economy and

---

[23] *Ibid.*, p. 5.
[24] B. Ngenda, 'Comparative Models of Privatization: A Commentary on the African Experience', (1995) 21 *Brooklyn J. Int'l L.* 179 at 179–180.
[25] See W. Baer and M. Birch, *supra* n. 10, pp. 13–14.
[26] *Ibid.*, pp. 11–12. See also B. Ngenda, *supra* n. 24, pp. 179–180.
[27] See IFC, *supra* n. 2, pp. 1–2.
[28] W. Baer and M. Birch, *supra* n. 10, p. 17.

stabilize economic conditions. As a result, the government can begin reallocating tax revenues, and ensure that its fiscal funds will not be disproportionately spent on keeping inefficient SOEs afloat. Moreover, by creating new, taxable, private corporate entities, the tax base may actually broaden over time.[29]

Further, eliminating trade barriers to foreign investors and companies on an international level, and dismantling market entry barriers on a domestic level tends to strengthen competition. Increased competition may eventually lead to new foreign investment, technology transfers and an increased number of firms. Indeed, it is important not to transform public monopolies into private ones through the privatization process.[30]

Attracting new investment (domestic and foreign) also means that there is a renewed potential for export development, and creating new international markets. In the end, privatization should result in better quality, lower-priced goods and services with export potential which will generate foreign exchange revenues. In addition, privatization may actually provide increased employment opportunities by introducing better technology, opening up new markets and creating new investment opportunities.

Moreover, the recapitalization of SOEs through the private sales of shares usually provides fresh funds for making capital improvements, introducing new technology, and training workers to be more efficient. Eliminating excessive bureaucracy and reducing the number of redundant employees also tends to make the overall enterprise more profitable, and more responsive to market demands in the long-run.

Privatization is, however, always a *political* process that involves critical decision-making by the government of the developing country.[31] In essence, privatization is a process which is initiated, controlled and implemented by the state. The transfer of government-owned assets and productive enterprises to private hands is an important and complex decision. Reducing the size of the public sector has immediate economic and political consequences, especially in developing economies which have historically been heavily dependent on the public sector for the provision of goods, services and employment.

In many African countries, the public sector has been exploited for political patronage purposes, thus perpetuating the political power and survival of the ruling elite.[32] Reducing the power base for such leaders often means making personal sacrifices. Since privatization inevitably raises the spectre of lay-offs of redundant employees, sacrifices may be required of more than just the ruling political elite. Thus, an important lesson of experience with privatization is that it will not succeed unless there is the political will to make it succeed. Imposing privatization programmes and goals from the outside is a meaningless exercise unless the broad-based polity within the developing country wishes privatization to succeed.

---

[29] *Ibid.*, p. 18. (Note, however, that tax revenues could be less than the revenues generated if the state still owned the enterprise.)

[30] See *ibid.*, p. 17. See also B. Ngenda, *supra* n. 24, p. 182.

[31] IFC, *supra* n. 2, p. 1.

[32] B. Ngenda, *supra* n. 24, pp. 179–180.

Box 4.1: Privatization

The political objectives of the state in initiating a privatization programme, for example, may include one or more of the following: (1) seeking budgetary relief from keeping unprofitable, heavily debt-ridden SOEs afloat; (2) reallocating tax revenues for purposes other than maintaining SOEs in their current condition; (3) increasing the efficiency of SOEs by providing cheaper, better-made goods and more efficient services for public use and consumption; (4) fostering more competitive and productive enterprises; (5) removing market entry barriers to permit foreign competition, or encouraging foreign participation in the privatization process; (6) breaking up public monopolies; or (7) supporting the development of the private sector and encouraging public participation in the privatization process.

Privatization also offers an opportunity for the state to change the nature of its governance. The state can and should use the privatization process as an opportunity to redefine and clarify its responsibilities to the governed. Redrawing the line between the public and private sectors requires clear and well-thought out government policy determinations on which industries should be privatized, and which should remain in the public sector, and why.

Thus, privatization may liberate the state by allowing it to move away from the direct production of goods and services and towards the regulation of commerce, international trade, and the environment. Privatization permits the state to move out of the productive sectors of the economy and move towards regulating the economy.

The government may also use the privatization process to set new political and economic priorities. Tax revenues, for example, can more easily be devoted to social safety net issues, capital infrastructure development and human resource development. The state can also begin to devote more energy to providing greater accountability and transparency in governance. Thus, privatization may reduce the size of the public sector, but the role of the state in the privatization process cannot afford to remain static.

Of course, privatization is a far more complex question in the so-called transitional economies of Eastern Europe and the former Soviet Union.[33] Whereas most Latin American, Caribbean, African and Asian countries have a certain legal infrastructure and institutional framework on which to base a privatization programme, transitional countries face the complex challenge of first having to develop such a framework, before the privatization process may commence. Rather than focusing on ways in which to improve the imperfections and shortcomings of the privatization framework of developing countries, let us first turn to the challenges faced by transitional countries undergoing the privatization process.

---

[33] See generally G. Bogdan, 'The Economic and Political Logic of Mass Privatization in Czechoslovakia and Poland', (1996) 4 *Cardozo J. Int'l and Comp. L.* 43. Eastern and Central European countries began transitioning towards becoming democratic, market-driven societies in late 1989. *Ibid.*, p. 43. By 1991, the Soviet Union had disintegrated into 15 sovereign states. *Ibid.*

The influence of Anglo-American neo-classical economists in devising prescriptions for the economic recovery of Eastern Europe and the former Soviet Union has been heavily criticized.[34] Nevertheless, the three-pronged policy directive to these countries issued by Western economists and consultants was clear: liberalization, stabilization and privatization.[35] Despite disagreements concerning the sequencing of these economic reforms, most economists believed that they should be undertaken simultaneously, rather than sequenced one after the other.[36]

Liberalization simply means the elimination of market constraints on the free flow of commerce, e.g., removing tariffs, export and price controls, market barriers.[37] Stabilization involves macro-economic policy changes, usually along the lines of making balance-of-payments adjustments, controlling inflation, restricting the money supply and devaluing the currency.[38]

Liberalization and stabilization tend to make transitional economies more responsive to the demands of traditional market-driven forces, but privatization is what truly transforms centrally planned (or socialist) economies into functioning market economies. Privatization moves state ownership of productive enterprises and industries into private hands, thereby abolishing a state-directed, planned economy which is impervious to market forces.[39]

Unfortunately, the implementation of a 'Big Bang' or 'shock therapy' involving the simultaneous deregulation of the economy, macro-economic adjustments, and privatization led to rampant inflation, unemployment and higher prices of imports in transitional economies.[40] Not only were major economic reforms quickly implemented, but a full-fledged, immediate transition to democratic, civil societies was also expected by Western donors, policy-makers, multilateral institutions and consultants. Moreover, the economic and political prescriptions for transforming these societies were grounded on a narrowly-based 'modernization' approach of Western advisors. The underlying idea was to recreate transitional societies in the

---

[34] P. Brietzke, 'Designing the Legal Frameworks for Markets in Eastern Europe', (1994) 7 *Transnat'l Lawyer* 35 at 35–38; G. Bogdan, *supra* n. 33, pp. 46–47; P. Murrell, 'Privatization Versus the Fresh Start', in V. Tismaneanu and P. Clawson (eds.), *Uprooting Leninism, Cultivating Liberty* (1992); J. Kornai, *The Road to a Free Economy—Shifting From a Socialist System: The Example of Hungary* (1990); J. Kregel, *et al.* (eds.), *The Market Shock: An Agenda for Socio-Economic Reconstruction in Central and Eastern Europe* (1992); G. Kolodko, 'From Recession to Growth' in *Post-Communist Economies: The Expectations Versus Reality*, (1993) 26 *Communist and Post-Communist Stud.* 123.

[35] P. Rutland, 'Privatization in East Europe: Another Case of Words That Succeed and Policies That Fail?' (1995) 5 *Transnat'l L. and Contemp. Probs.* 1 at 2. See also J. Sachs, *Poland's Jump to the Market Economy* (1993).

[36] P. Rutland, *supra* n. 35, pp. 2–3.

[37] *Ibid.*, p. 4; W. Philbrick, 'The Task of Regulating Investment Funds in the Formerly Centrally Planned Economies', (1994) 8 *Emory Int'l L. Rev.* 539 at 541.

[38] P. Rutland, *supra* n. 35, p. 4; W. Philbrick, *supra* n. 37, p. 541.

[39] P. Rutland, *supra* n. 35, pp. 4–5.

[40] W. Philbrick, *supra* n. 37, pp. 540–541.

image of the post-modern, democratic, market-driven nation-state modelled principally on the Anglo-American experience.[41]

Indeed, the failure to perceive the essentially European character and history of these transitional economies, and ignoring their aspirations to join the EU, revealed the short-sighted approach of many US-based advisors.[42] Many Eastern European nations have legal customs and codes which follow the civil law (rather than common law) tradition embodied in the French or Austro-German civil codes.[43] Imposing a strict, almost dogmatic, form of Anglo-American liberal capitalism created artificial tensions, further complicating and delaying the transition process.[44]

The transition to democratic capitalism could have been eased, in some cases, by using European models of social democracy.[45] Scandinavia, Germany and Holland, for example, have mixed economies incorporating a large degree of socialist-type state planning that more closely resemble post-communist states.[46] The neo-classical, Anglo-American economic and legal perspective tends to emphasize the Hobbesian role of the lone individual in a deregulated 'free' market economy. However, this viewpoint is predicated on notions and institutions that have not taken root in transitional societies.

The neo-liberal approach may always remain foreign to these societies, which have vastly different histories, institutions and social values. In any case, rather than plunging into the cold waters of 'shock therapy', a more gradualist, Europeanized approach to economic and structural legal reform may have served post-communist, transitional societies better. Despite the shortcomings of neo-liberal approaches to privatization issues, however, the twin economic and political goals of achieving a transformation into market-based, democratic societies has been adopted wholesale by post-communist states.[47]

The next section will examine a form of mass privatization (or 'popular capitalism') to effect this transition. The following case study of the Czech Republic's voucher programme will discuss the large-scale distribution of vouchers to all eligible Czech citizens as a means of privatizing state-owned assets and enterprises.

3.   PRIVATIZATION STRATEGIES AND TACTICS

Many considerations may be relevant in formulating a privatization strategy, including 'corporatizing' SOEs into appropriate legal forms, passing

---

[41] See P. Brietzke, *supra* n. 34.

[42] *Ibid.*, pp. 58–60.

[43] *Ibid.*, p. 48.

[44] *Ibid.*, pp. 38–40. See also P. Rutland, *supra* n. 35, p. 3.

[45] P. Brietzke, *supra* n. 34 at 62. See also R. Dahl, 'Social Reality and "Free Markets": A Letter to Friends in Eastern Europe', *Dissent* (1990) at 224, 227.

[46] P. Brietzke, *supra* n. 34, p. 62.

[47] P. Rutland, *supra* n. 35, p. 4.

Box 4.2: Privatization campaigns

Many different legal mechanisms may be employed in privatization campaigns. These approaches may be roughly divided into several categories:

(1) denationalization (making a public or private offering of all or a portion of the shares of the SOE being privatized);

(2) mass privatization (issuing vouchers or coupons representing limited ownership interests in SOEs being privatized, or setting up public auctions or tenders using sealed bids to sell SOEs);

(3) restructuring (breaking up an SOE into its subsidiaries or component parts, which may be especially useful in fragmenting vertically integrated monopolies such as a port authority or an airline);

(4) liquidation and dissolution (selling the assets of the SOEs through auctions, negotiated bids or negotiated contracts; additionally, bankruptcy proceedings or receiverships may be involved in this process);

(5) changing the ownership *or* management of an SOE (management or employee buy-outs, worker cooperatives, leases, management contracts, or concessions may be employed);

(6) debt-equity swaps (exchanging or 'swapping' the commercial debt of an SOE for an equity position in a newly privatized entity by an interested investor).

Any of these privatization methods may be used simultaneously with each other, or appropriately sequenced, in a combined campaign for privatization.

---

new legislation, and ensuring that an appropriate regulatory framework is in place.[48] There has been sustained academic and practical scrutiny of various progressive steps needed in order to formulate a privatization framework.[49] Rather than describing (and reiterating) these abstract considerations, however, this section will examine two case studies: voucher privatization in the Czech Republic and pension fund privatization in Chile. These case studies are designed to highlight certain issues with regard to privatization efforts undertaken in the last decade. In addition, specific privatization techniques which may be appropriate in countries with poorly developed capital markets will be discussed.

3.1 The Czech voucher programme

Mass privatization (or popular capitalism) was instituted in the Czech Republic as a means of pushing through important economic and political reforms. Speed was of the essence, since Czech policy-makers (and their international advisors) feared that the longer privatization took, the weaker the resolve to make economic reforms would become.[50]

Mass privatization was effected via the distribution to eligible citizens of vouchers or coupons representing shares (i.e., equity interests) in the SOEs

---

[48] See P. Guislain, *supra* n. 1, pp. 15–32.

[49] See e.g., P. Guislain, *supra* n. 1.

[50] G. Bogdan, *supra* n. 33, pp. 59, 60.

being privatized. The public sale of SOEs could then proceed directly through public auctions, or indirectly through the use of investment funds. These investment funds trade the privatization vouchers for shares in the companies being privatized, functioning like Western-styled mutual funds.

Voucher privatization was a way of killing two birds with one stone. The wide dissemination of shares of privatized SOEs meant that the average person could become engaged and share in the economic fortunes of the new private sector. The transparency of the voucher method, and the distribution of shares by democratic means, prevented the entrenched elite (or *nomenclatura*) from surreptitiously acquiring the assets of SOEs scheduled for privatization. Thus, voucher privatization was meant to create a diverse, new private sector using democratic principles.

The Czech government initiated a phased privatization programme, the first phase of which involved the transfer of state property to municipalities.[51] In the second phase, 100,000 individual properties were restored to their pre-1948 owners.[52] These properties were principally comprised houses, small shops and factories.[53] The third phase, which was launched in February 1991, involved a small privatization campaign. In this phase, five-year leases on about 22,000 shops and workshops were auctioned to Czech (i.e., non-foreign) private bidders.[54]

Finally, the Czechoslovak Federal Assembly passed an Act on the Conditions of Transfer of State Property to Other Persons (referred to as the 'Large-Scale Privatization Law') on 22 February 1991.[55] The law took effect on 1 April 1991 and directed the Federal Ministry of Finance to issue investment coupons or vouchers for a nominal price of about 1,000 crowns, or $35, to every Czechoslovakian citizen over 18 years of age.[56] Each voucher booklet was worth 1,000 'investment points'.[57]

Voucher-holders were entitled either to bid in public auctions directly for shares of Czech SOEs being privatized, or to invest their vouchers in one of nearly 400 private investment funds.[58] If the Czech investor chose an investment fund, the fund would exchange the vouchers or 'investment points' for shares in the joint-stock companies being privatized. The investment fund would then issue its own shares to the individual investor.[59] The actual monetary value of the shares being purchased through the use of

---

[51] R. Ceska, 'Privatization in the Czech Republic—1992' in A. Böhm and M. Simoneti (eds.), *Privatization in Central and Eastern Europe 1992* (UNDP, CEEPN, 1993), pp. 84, 88.

[52] *Ibid.*, pp. 89–90.

[53] P. Rutland, *supra* n. 35, p. 11.

[54] *Ibid.*, p. 11.

[55] G. Bogdan, *supra* n. 33, p. 50. The Czech Large Privatization Law was later supplemented with the Decree on the Issuance and Use of Investment Coupons, adopted 5 September 1991, and the Law on Investment Companies and Investment Funds, enacted on 28 April, 1992. *Ibid.*, p. 52. These laws were designed to regulate the activities of investment funds which were prohibited from owning more than 20% of the shares of any company.

[56] *Ibid.*, p. 50; W. Philbrick, *supra* n. 37, p. 554; P. Rutland, *supra* n. 35, p. 12.

[57] G. Bogdan, *supra* n. 33, p. 50.

[58] W. Philbrick, *supra* n. 37, p. 554.

[59] *Ibid.*, p. 554; R. Ceska, *supra* n. 51, p. 99.

'investment points' was later determined through the secondary trading of the shares on the Prague Stock Exchange.[60]

The first wave of voucher privatization took place on 18 May 1992, when the shares of nearly 1,500 companies were sold.[61] Apparently, there was little interest in the voucher programme until January 1992 when several investment funds offered to purchase voucher coupons for up to 15 times their original cost, payable one year following the transfer of actual shares in the privatizing SOE.[62] The first wave officially ended on 31 January 1993, after five rounds of bidding had taken place.[63] The shares of the privatized companies were actually distributed in May 1993.[64]

The second tranche began with the distribution of voucher booklets in late 1993, with actual bidding beginning in March 1994.[65] The second wave of voucher privatization was limited to about 900 Czech firms. (It should be noted that Slovak firms did not participate, since the federal union of Czechoslovakia had broken up in 1992.) Shares were distributed in early 1995, and nearly 80 per cent of the Czech economy was transferred to private ownership through the voucher privatization programme.[66] Although the Czech voucher programme was generally hailed a success, the voucher method of mass privatization did not actually help raise additional capital for heavily indebted and undercapitalized enterprises.[67]

However, the mass privatization method ensured that vouchers were widely distributed among the Czech population. The IMF initially warned against the risk of diffusing the ownership of privatized companies to so many individuals, rendering effective shareholder control nearly impossible.[68] This, however, was a specious objection, since shareholder ownership in many large international companies is widely diffused. Moreover, by 1992, 72 per cent of the vouchers distributed were invested with 220 Czech investment funds.[69] By the end of the second wave of voucher privatization in 1994, 64 per cent of all investment points were invested with investment funds.[70] Thus, the voucher method created strong institutional investors in the form of Czech investment funds.

In fact, criticism of the Czech voucher privatization programme centres on the concentration of investment points in the hands of nine investment funds who control about 50 per cent of the total investment points.[71] Seven

---

[60] W. Philbrick, *supra* n. 37, p. 554.

[61] P. Rutland, *supra* n. 35, p. 12; G. Bogdan, *supra* n. 33, pp. 50–51.

[62] S. Bell, *Sharing the Wealth: Privatization Through Broad-Based Ownership Strategies* (World Bank Discussion Paper No. 285, 1995), p. 14.

[63] D. Triska, 'Voucher Privatization in Czechoslovakia—1992' in A. Böhm and M. Simoneti (eds.), *Privatization in Central and Eastern Europe 1992* (UNDP, CEEPN, 1993), pp. 104, 112.

[64] P. Rutland, *supra* n. 35, p. 12.

[65] *Ibid.* at p. 12; G. Bogdan, *supra* n. 33, p. 51.

[66] G. Bogdan, *supra* n. 33, p. 51.

[67] P. Rutland, *supra* n. 35, p. 12.

[68] *Ibid.*, p. 12; W. Philbrick, *supra* n. 37, p. 558. See also G. Pohl, *et al.*, *Creating Capital Markets in Central and Eastern Europe* (World Bank Tech. Paper No. 295, 1995), p. 7.

[69] P. Rutland, *supra* n. 35, p. 12.

[70] W. Philbrick, *supra* n. 37, p. 562.

[71] G. Bogdan, *supra* n. 33, pp. 52–53.

of these nine investment funds are state-owned Czech banks and insurance companies which have become shareholders in the newly privatized entities.[72] The fear that the small number of large investment funds may lead to oligopolistic and potentially anti-competitive business practices has already been voiced.[73]

Moreover, since so many of the former SOEs are heavily indebted to these banks and financial institutions, there is a conflict of interest since the banks are consequently reluctant to force these privatized firms into bankruptcy.[74] For these banks, this could mean writing off the bad debts of former SOEs, and being left holding worthless securities in dissolved firms. In addition, the investment funds themselves are quite illiquid since the underlying shares may be equity interests in nearly bankrupt SOEs.[75] This means that private investors are not easily able to liquidate their shares in investment funds.

In order to successfully privatize the state-owned banks which manage the Czech investment funds, several sequenced steps need to be taken. First, these banks need to negotiate debt work-outs on the loans they made to the SOEs, whose stock they now own through the investment funds. Once this is completed, the banks need to restructure their own portfolios in preparation for privatization.[76] To date, Czech banking reform efforts have met with mixed results.[77]

Despite the Czech government's attempt to regulate investment funds, there has been a significant lack of capable investment fund management.[78] Inexperienced fund managers were tempted to make misleading or confusing misrepresentations concerning vouchers to unsophisticated investors. Nevertheless, it is important to recognize how young Czech investment funds are. Whereas new securities laws and the creation of an effective regulatory environment of investment funds may still be in the works, these funds nevertheless offer an excellent means of mobilizing equity capital from local investors.

In fact, investment funds have been instrumental in mobilizing the 'under the mattress' type of savings, and encouraging equity participation in the private sector by broad segments of the population. Investment funds also offer diversified ownership in many different enterprises, which

---

[72] *Ibid.*, pp. 52–54.

[73] See J. Coffee, Jr., *Investment Privatization Funds: The Czech Experience* (World Bank, Policy Research Dep't., Transition Economics Div., 1994).

[74] G. Bogdan, *supra* n. 33, p. 54; P. Rutland, *supra* n. 35, p. 13.

[75] G. Bogdan, *supra* n. 33, p. 54. See also W. Philbrick, *supra* n. 37, p. 570.

[76] G. Bogdan, *supra* n. 33, p. 54. Clearly, the Glass-Steagall Act would prevent US banks from becoming equity stakeholders in the companies they have lent to; however, Mr Bogdan suggests that the Czech government may wish to follow the type of corporate governance established under the German system where banks do control investment companies. *Ibid.* This is another example where US models may not be appropriate in the privatization process in Eastern European countries.

[77] L. Takla, 'The Relationship Between Privatization and the Reform of the Banking Sector: The Case of the Czech Republic and Slovakia' in S. Estrin (ed.), *Privatization in Central and Eastern Europe* (1994), p. 154.

[78] W. Philbrick, *supra* n. 37, pp. 564, 569–570.

reduces the individual investor's risk. Further, once fund management becomes more sophisticated, these investment funds will become an easily accessible source of expert investment advice. Detractors should remember that the glass is be half full as well as half empty.

The principal lesson that the Czech experience may hold for other developing countries considering privatization options is that mass privatization may be effected in both a speedy and transparent manner. If the Czech-type voucher scheme for enfranchising the population in the private sector is opted for, then it is important to examine the relationship between the nominal and the market worth of the vouchers issued. The Czech government allowed the Prague Stock Exchange to make this valuation, but for those countries without secondary markets (i.e., stock exchanges or over-the-counter exchanges) in place, this may be problematic.

China, for example, announced on 2 September 1997 that it would 'privatize' 10,000 of the nation's 13,000 large and medium-sized enterprises, having reached the conclusion that these enterprises could no longer be supported by the government.[79] Of course, the Chinese government is avoiding the phrase 'privatization', and planning for ordinary people buying shares of stock in public enterprises in a form of 'public ownership'.[80]

Chinese leaders will have to confront the massive and complex legal, organizational and labour issues involved in this version of a 'socialist market economy', especially since tens of millions of jobs may be at stake.[81] However, since at least 700 of the most successful Chinese companies are listed on the Shanghai and Shenzhen stock exchanges, and some are traded on the Hong Kong and New York stock exchanges, there may be some market depth to absorb new entrants in the foreseeable future.[82]

Certain cautionary notes based on the Czech privatization scheme should be considered. For example, it may be wise for the government involved in privatization to protect against the likelihood of a concentration of voucher/stock ownership by investment funds. A concentration of ownership by bank-owned investment funds may undermine the continued economic stability of the Czech banking system is grave indeed. Therefore, certain safeguards against anti-competitive behaviour in stock acquisition may need to be put in place even before the shares are publicly released.

Moreover, the regulation of such investment funds in terms of disclosure requirements, licensing brokerage activities, protecting against insider trading, capital requirements, liquidity, and other related issues also need to be carefully considered and planned before the investment funds are created. But in retrospect, the Czech example proves that a fairly quick and effective transfer of ownership from the government to the private sector

---

[79] S. Faison, 'In Major Shift, China Will Sell Industries', *New York Times*, 12 September 1997, p. A1.
[80] *Ibid.*
[81] *Ibid.*
[82] S. Faison, A Great Tiptoe Forward: Private Enterprise in China, *New York Times*, 17 September 1997, p. A1.

can be made which encourages broad public participation, the development of local institutional investors, and mobilizes local sources of capital into newly created equity markets.

3.2   Pension plan privatization in Chile

Chile's political and economic fortunes changed forever when General Augusto Pinochet overthrew the Allende government in a bloody coup in 1973.[83] The privatization of Chile's national pension scheme has been chosen to illustrate the potential downstream benefits privatization programmes may have on capital markets.

Pinochet's authoritarian government rode roughshod over any objections voiced by interest groups, and began instituting free market economy reforms in 1980. Among his reform package was the wholesale privatization of SOEs.[84] Pinochet's Minister of Labour and Social Security, José Piñera, successfully transformed Chile's pay-as-you-go pension system (of a type still used in the United States), into a system of privately funded and managed individual retirement accounts.[85] Ultimately, pension fund privatization and reform proved to be instrumental in Chile's economic recovery.[86]

On 4 November 1980, Pinochet created a new system of individual retirement pensions where today each worker makes mandatory contributions of 13 per cent of their wages into a private pension fund.[87] These pension plans (now numbering about 20) are known as Adminstradoras de Fondos de Pensiones (AFPs). AFPs are capitalized by individual worker contributions in what is known as a 'defined contribution system'.[88] These AFP accounts follow the worker from job to job and, at retirement, the savings can be used either directly or to purchase an annuity.[89] Self-employed workers have the option of joining an AFP, but are not required to do so.[90]

The AFPs are private entities functioning much like mutual funds, but are heavily regulated by the state. The government guarantees a minimum pension to retirees to cover his or her subsistence costs, and requires that AFPs take minimal market risks in protecting the savings of pensioners. As of February 1997, the AFPs' $30 billion portfolio was invested in the following manner: 40 per cent of all pension assets were invested in Government-backed debt; 25 per cent in interest-bearing bank deposits; and 35 per cent in Chilean stocks.[91] Over the last 15 years, AFPs have averaged a 13 per cent return over inflation.[92]

---

[83] M. Paskin, 'Privatization of Old-Age Pensions in Latin America: Lessons for Social Security Reform in the United States', (1994) 62 *Fordham L. Rev.* 2199 at 2207.

[84] *Ibid.*, p. 2207.

[85] P. Passell, 'How Chile Farms Out Nest Eggs: Can Its Private Pension Plan Offer Lessons to the U.S.?' *New York Times*, 21 March 1997, p. D1.

[86] M. Paskin, *supra* n. 83, p. 2207.

[87] *Ibid.* at p. 2207; P. Passell, *supra* n. 85, p. D4. (In 1983, the required contribution was 10%. See M. Paskin, *supra* n. 83, p. 2207.)

[88] P. Passell, *supra* n. 85, p. D4.

[89] *Ibid.*

[90] M. Paskin, *supra* n. 83, p. 2207.

[91] P. Passell, *supra* n. 85, p. D4.

[92] *Ibid.* M. Paskin, *supra* n. 83, p. 2208.

An unexpected gain in privatizing the pension fund system was the jump in the domestic savings rate, from 16 per cent in 1980 to 28 per cent in 1997.[93] Individuals may increase the amounts in their pension accounts by simply contributing more from their current wages. This has the additional advantage of providing pensioners with greater tax-deferred savings. The increased pension savings means that this capital is being mobilized by investing in current government securities as well as in private stocks and bonds traded on the Santiago stock market.

In 1985, the Chilean law on pension funds was changed to permit AFPs to invest up to 30 per cent of their holdings in the equity of private companies.[94] The diversification of AFP portfolio holdings into private equities and bond holdings, currently constituting 35 per cent of total holdings, is also an improvement over the old system which only permitted investments in government securities.[95] Thus, investors are able to assume more risk by acquiring equity stakes in private companies where the potential for returns is greater than returns from government securities. For future pensioners trying to create 'nest eggs' to fund college tuition for their children or support ageing parents with special medical and other needs, or who are simply trying to build a more secure financial future for themselves, diversified investments in their pension plans can be a plus.

AFPs became the largest institutional purchasers of the shares of Chilean SOEs that were privatized between 1985 and 1990.[96] The significant amount of savings being captured by AFPs has spurred the development of capital markets in Chile as well.[97] The pension funds invested by AFPs have contributed to a boom on the Chilean stock market.[98]

The transformation of the pension plan system into a defined contribution system in which workers make individual contributions to a private pension fund of their choice is very significant. It means, in effect, that the Chilean government is no longer required to support current pensioners on social security-type tax withholdings. Further, the government is able to move out of directly providing pension plans for retirees, and into regulating the private industry that does so. Thus, the Chilean government has now assumed a public watchdog role.

The picture is not entirely rosy—there are economic inefficiencies which arise from the heavy marketing campaigns used by AFPs to attract new pensioners. Since workers can change their pension fund every six months, the competition to keep old contributors and attract new ones can be fierce. In fact, one-third of all contributors switch their pension accounts every year.[99] Although a large percentage of overhead costs may be devoted to free gifts and introductory offers to attract new pensioners, the competitive

---

93 P. Passell, *supra* n. 85, p. D1.

94 P. Guislain, *supra* n. 1, p. 79.

95 M. Paskin, *supra* n. 83, p. 2209.

96 P. Guislain, *supra* n. 1, p. 79. See also E. Rubinstein, 'The Other Path', *Nat'l Rev.*, 30 April 1990, p. 16.

97 P. Passell, *supra* n. 85, p. D4.

98 M. Paskin, *supra* n. 83, p. 2209.

99 P. Guislain, *supra* n. 1, p. 79.

nature of AFPs means that they are forced to react to market demands, and cannot afford to be complacent.

Since the Chilean government guarantees a minimum level of pension, it is possible that a decline in investment return levels may put pressure on the government to subsidize pensions. In fact, for the first time, in 1995 AFPs made negative real returns of 2.5 per cent.[100] Despite this recent decline in AFP earnings, Chile's deficit with regard to social security payouts has fallen by a remarkable two-thirds.[101]

Most importantly, a good macro-economic environment of reduced government expenditures, controlled inflation levels, and reduced tax distortions have all added to the success of private pensions in Chile.[102] Workers were given strong incentives to save. Additionally, low inflation rates meant that capital market investments retained their value, thereby decreasing the likelihood of capital flight. Interestingly, these pension plan reforms were instituted under Pinochet's military dictatorship. However, in 1990 Chile adopted a democratic form of government.[103]

The Chilean case study illustrates two important points: first, by investing in private pension funds, workers provide for their own retirement security without being reliant on government support or intervention. And secondly, by mobilizing domestic savings by investors, and encouraging the growth of institutional investors, Chilean capital markets were both broadened (by the number of new participants) and deepened (by capturing greater savings). In other words, Chile's economic recovery was more or less self-financed. Chile's example is now studied as a model by other Latin American countries

---

[100] *Ibid.*

[101] *Ibid.*

[102] The same types of issues faced by Chilean government officials in reforming its pension system are being faced by other developing countries. Zambia, for example, has statutory pension schemes for private sector employees (Zambia National Provident Fund, the largest pension fund); for civil servants, military personnel and teachers (Civil Service Pension Fund); and for local government employees (Local Authorities Superannuation Fund). However, there is no single government regulatory agency overseeing these funds. There are also two non-statutory pension schemes: the Zambia State Insurance Corporation which manages about 75 private pensions funds, and the Mukaba Pension Fund which is owned and managed by the Zambia Consolidated Copper Mining Company, a Zambian SOE.

Zambians are facing complex design issues such as choosing between: (1) defined benefit schemes which assure pensioners of guaranteed retirement benefits; (2) defined contribution schemes where there are no predefined government obligations to provide a certain level of benefits or, (3) a pay-as-you-go scheme where payroll social security-like taxes are collected, but there is no relationship between the amount collected and what is paid out in benefits (the system used in the United States). Negative rates of returns on the funds, the inability to support pensioners, and indiscriminate government 'borrowing' from pension plans have all created a weak pension system in Zambia which badly needs systemic reform: C. Bailey, *et al.*, *Reforming Pensions In Zambia: An Analysis of Existing Schemes and Options for Reform* (World Bank, 1997).

[103] J. Briggs, 'A Political Miracle', *Forbes*, 11 May 1992, p. 108. Although it is convenient to argue that strong macro-economic conditions create a foundation for, and may even precipitate, a democratic revolution, this argument, while tempting, is beyond the scope of this limited discussion.

(e.g., Colombia, Peru and Argentina)[104] seeking new strategies to fuel their economic growth.

AFPs demonstrate that institutional investors can be a strong catalyst for capital market development even if stock market listings are limited. By investing in government commercial paper and other government-backed securities, institutional investors add a great deal of stability to financial markets. Moreover, by privatizing AFPs and allowing them to invest in the shares of private companies, local capital markets are both broadened and deepened. Rather than continue the pensioners' dependence on government taxation and budgetary allocations, private pension plans relieve the government of this responsibility while still preserving a very important social safety net.

In comparing the Chilean model of private pension funds with the Czech model of private investment funds following a mass privatization programme, it is clear that institutional investors can add to the depth and stability of domestic capital markets. Institutional investors can be instrumental in capturing and mobilizing domestic savings and investing these savings in domestic capital markets. Thus, by encouraging private sector development, the state is able to assume a strategic role in private sector and capital market development. Government participation in privatization thus becomes a strategic intervention in a sustainable public–private partnership.

3.3 Non-traditional privatization methods

A commonly cited reason for the scarcity of privatization opportunities in many developing nations is the absence of capital markets.[105] Although this may affect an initial public offering (IPO) of the stock of an SOE being privatized, it is by no means an absolute impediment to privatization. In fact, the privatization of the National Commercial Bank in Jamaica, discussed below, is a clear-cut example of the successful use of IPOs even where capital markets are shallow or non-existent.

However, privatization will not succeed in a policy vacuum, as the Chilean example demonstrates. In other words, if the macro-economic framework is not conducive to financial sector development, privatization alone will not improve the economic condition of the country. Thus, macro-economic reforms (e.g., positive real interest rates, controlling the government deficit, maintaining low inflation, and encouraging a freely convertible currency)[106] may all be critical factors in ensuring that equity investments in local enterprises will retain their value over time.

Other macro-economic prescriptions may include reducing government-directed credit towards certain industries or sectors, making credit available on market terms, removing excess reserve requirements for central and

---

[104] See e.g., IFC, *Investment Funds in Emerging Markets: Lessons of Experience, No. 2* (World Bank and the IFC, 1996), p. 46.
[105] N. Zank, *et al.*, *Reforming Financial Systems: Policy Change and Privatization* (Greenwood Press, 1991), p. 3.
[106] *Ibid.*, p. 2.

commercial banks, lifting interest rate ceilings, and creating a functional bank supervisory and regulatory framework.[107] Without these important financial sector reforms, privatization has little chance of succeeding. In addition, tax reform, removing market barriers to foreign and domestic competitors in the banking and securities industries, and establishing a clear and coherent framework of government supervision through independent bank examiners may also be required.[108]

Privatization, as discussed earlier, can be accomplished by a number of different, but complementary, mechanisms tailored to the government's political and economic objectives (see Box 2). In fact, most privatization programmes in Africa and other parts of the developing world make use of several different methods of privatization, thus, maintaining a diversified privatization portfolio. This section will explore alternative means of privatizing state-owned enterprises in countries with poorly developed capital markets (see Box 4.3).[109]

Of course, if the developing country does have deep and broad, functioning capital markets (as in Chile), then IPOs may be used to publicly float the shares of an SOE to be privatized. A prospectus is issued, the par values of the classes of stock being offered are set, and the shares are sold to the public.[110] Alternatively, more sophisticated developing countries may seek access to international equity and bond markets in order to finance their privatization activities. However, in developing countries with poor capital markets, privatization may need to be sequenced. Thus, certain pre-privatization steps need to be planned and executed, as discussed below.

---

[107] *Ibid.*

[108] Deregulating banking activities within an overall framework of liberalizing the economy can be a very effective tool in financial sector reform, but only if banks are adequately supervised by an independent agency. Ideally, banks should strive to be self-regulatory (as in the German system), but this requires that bank staffs be well-trained and fairly sophisticated. *Ibid.*, p. 52.

[109] *Ibid.*, p. 26.

[110] *Ibid.*, pp. 58–61. See also SRI International, *Worldwide Experience in Alternative Privatization Financing Methods*, prepared for USAID (1996), p. II-13. Of course, this description is an oversimplification. There are several, important steps that must be taken before privatization may take place. First, the past financial performance of the entity being privatized has to be audited to determine the financial health of the enterprise. If the SOE is in bad financial shape, it may be wiser to negotiate its sale to a private party, or enter into a management contract or lease to try to make its operations profitable in the short-term.

Secondly, corporatizing the SOE into a legal form is an important step whereby it may be merged with another SOE to help improve its performance, or simply make its equity available for public sale. Finally, restructuring the SOE by transferring or writing off bad loans or debts, dissolving non-performing portions of the SOE, or fragmenting it into smaller units for sale to the public are all pre-privatization steps that have to be implemented by the government.

Once the SOE is readied for an IPO, then certain protections for new stockholders have to be instituted so that an accurate record of their names, registration of stock certificates, and resales of shares are duly recorded. Byelaws governing shareholder voting, payment of dividends and corporate governance issues must also be addressed. Additionally, the stocks must be issued, valued and priced. Once the prospectus is prepared by investment bankers and lawyers and is made available to the public, it is often a useful tool in marketing the shares to the public.

Box 4.3: Government intervention in the financial sector
Government intervention in the financial sector by directing that credit
be allocated to certain sectors of the economy, while successful in several
East Asian countries, has been disastrous in many other developing countries.
Such policies have resulted in the creation of large portfolios of non-
performing loans made to SOEs. Government-imposed requirements, specify-
ing that banking institutions and pension funds may only purchase
government securities, have helped underwrite government indebtedness, but
have also had the effect of crowding out the private sector. In addition,
outmoded legal systems which impede bank collection of overdue debt, or
which have inadequate bankruptcy, collateralization, securitization and
foreclosure laws and procedures, further complicate an inefficient financial
system.

Source: N. Zank *et al*, *Reforming Financial Systems* (Greenwood Press, 1991), p. 26.

3.4 Pre-privatization preparation

Before initiating a programme for privatization, the government needs
to consider several factors in preparing the SOE for privatization:
(1) corporatizing the SOE, thereby changing its legal form to permit
privatization; (2) restructuring the enterprise by liquidating or selling
certain non-performing assets (rather than selling shares of the SOE);
(3) fragmenting the SOE into smaller units that are more conducive to
public sales, especially important in large monopolistic concerns; or
(4) writing off or transferring its bad debts to another SOE or government-
owned holding or trust company.

Alternatively, the government may consider entering into management
contracts or leases to try to increase the SOE's profitability before attempting
a public sale. Under a management contract, there is no transfer of ownership to a private management company by the state. The state bears all
commercial risks and assumes all liabilities in keeping the SOE in operation.
The management contractor is paid a fee by the state to manage the SOE
(regardless of profitability), in the hope of making the enterprise more
profitable and attractive to private investors.

A lease, on the other hand, is a different arrangement whereby the lessee
pays a fee to the state for managing the SOE for a specified period of time.
This may be a first step in privatization as the private lessee may be given
an option to purchase shares in the SOE in tranches. For example, the lessee
may be given the option of purchasing 10 per cent of the SOE's shares
after the first year, thereby acquiring the company in 10 years' time.
Alternatively, depending on the financial condition of the SOE, it may be
better to simply declare bankruptcy and dissolve the SOE, rather than
trying to privatize it.

Before initiating privatization, the government needs to identify clearly
its objectives in privatization, and to develop a menu of flexible options in
carrying out its privatization programme. Such a menu should include one
or more of the following options: (1) private sales, (2) management or
employee buy-outs, (3) IPOs, (4) mass privatization, (5) debt-equity swaps,

and (6) issuing government bonds or guaranteeing private corporate bonds. These options are discussed below.

3.5   Meeting government objectives in the privatization process

The government of a developing country interested in initiating a privatization programme may have many different, and even conflicting, objectives in the privatization process. The discussion below will examine a few possible goals in planning a successful privatization programme: speed, transparency, and encouraging capital market development.

3.6   Speed in the privatization process

3.6.1   *Private sales*

If speed is of the essence, then the government may wish to pre-qualify buyers in a private sale of the SOE being privatized. In particular, if technology transfers or some other kind of commercial partnership is sought, then foreign capital firms who are willing to stake risk capital in the privatizing company may be good partners to seek out. A private placement involving a limited group of investors can be particularly useful where the government is seeking specific managerial expertise, technology transfers, or access to international markets, and the interested investors have proven track records in these areas.

Private sales of shares can be arranged through direct negotiations or through competitive bidding. Competitive bidding may take place through a government-issued tender for private bids, or through public auctions. Public auctions, of course, ensure transparency in the privatization process, and deflect criticisms that the 'family jewels' are being sold to foreign interests in secret deals. If, however, the nature of the SOE requires a sophisticated investor (such as a foreign joint venture by the local telecommunications firm), public auctions may be unsuitable.

In some cases, the government may wish to consider initially entering into a limited joint venture with a foreign firm (who may acquire perhaps 20 per cent of the SOE's equity), followed by a public offering of the balance of the shares once a certain level of profitability has been achieved. Initially, therefore, the government would create a 'joint stock' company representing a public–private partnership between the government and a private concern, followed by a complete divestiture of the government's shares in the SOE.

Private placements of shares mean that legal and transactional costs may be reduced since determining the share value, and disclosing the financial condition of the SOE being privatized to a private investor, may be easier. However, the actual time involved in negotiating such a sale may vary depending on the complexity of the deal.

3.6.2   *Bond and equity financing of private sales*

If a private sale is being negotiated between the government and an interested buyer, financing questions will arise immediately. The purchaser in a private sale of the equity of an SOE may finance the transaction by using debt financing, equity financing or a combination of the two. If debt financing is the preferred option, the buyer will simply enter into a loan to purchase the equity of the SOE in a so-called leveraged buy-out (i.e., where credit is used to finance the transaction). This means that the purchaser must have access to international banking institutions to negotiate a loan, if domestic banking sources are insufficient to finance this type of transaction.

However, caution must be exercised in this matter. If the purchaser stakes the SOE's equity and assets as collateral for the loan, in the event of a loan default, these assets may be seized by or forfeited to the lending insti-tution.[111] This means that the SOE will be effectively dissolved. Therefore, the government may wish to insist that the private (foreign) purchaser seeks a loan from outside sources using separate collateral.

Alternatively, another type of debt financing is to issue bonds. In other words, the purchaser may issue bonds (representing a form of indebtedness) that can be floated domestically or, if domestic bond markets are not well-developed, sold internationally. Where bond markets are not well-developed, banks are usually required to underwrite, distribute and guarantee repayment of such bonds.[112] The bonds can be purchased domestically by the general public or by local institutional investors (e.g., local pension plans or mutual funds).

Bond markets can mobilize domestic savings (particularly if local pension plans or domestic institutional investors are available to purchase the bonds). However, a bond issuance is usually appropriate only where large sums of money need to be raised in order to effect a sale of an SOE. The fairly complex financial, accounting, and legal structuring is costly, and may affect the speed with which the private sale is carried out. Therefore, the underlying financing for a private sale must be carefully evaluated to judge whether this transaction meets the government's demand for a speedy sale of the SOE.

A second type of financing which may be used is equity financing, whereby the shares of the SOE being privatized are acquired in tranches by the private purchaser. This is particularly valuable where the SOE is being 'recapitalized' or additional shares are being issued pursuant to the private sale. Recapitalization is especially valuable where the SOE has insufficient working capital and needs capital investment to update its machinery, technology, market delivery systems, etc. Since equity holdings represents the private purchaser's ownership in the SOE, it increases the purchaser's stake in the company. Depending on the identity and nationality of the private purchaser, the amount of equity made available for purchase can be a delicate political question.

---

[111] SRI International, *supra* n. 110, p. III–27.
[112] *Ibid.*, pp. VII–68, 69. The lead underwriter (usually a merchant or investment bank) generally forms a consortium of other banks to spread the risk of the bond issuance. The bonds are then offered to potential (local) investors, much in the same way as an initial public offering of stock.

If the SOE itself is heavily indebted, then debt work-outs for the SOE may be the government's first priority. If, however, a private investor is lined up to purchase the equity of the SOE, then a hybrid of debt-equity financing may be considered. Debt-equity swaps permit an investor to purchase the sovereign debt at a discount and exchange it for an equity position in the newly privatized SOE. Generally, such investors tend to be foreign firms with access to hard currency. Thus, a debt-equity swap enables the government to reduce its external debt overhang while privatizing an SOE.

The Ministry of Finance and, even more importantly, the central bank of the developing country, are critical players in this type of debt-equity swap negotiation since they are responsible for setting the rules governing such swaps. Further, if the government is anxious to avoid the issuance of private bonds (which may need to be guaranteed by the government), debt-equity swaps may be preferable to issuing private bonds or other debt instruments.

3.6.3   *Management and/or employee buy-outs*

Alternatively, if the government wants to make a speedy transition to the private sector, but independent buyers are not available, a management and/or an employee buy-out may be the best option. Of course, this type of sale lacks transparency since only the managers/workers of the enterprise (or 'insiders') are eligible to purchase its equity. However, the 'captive audience' of the management/workers have a vested interest in the economic success of the privatized entity, and may be highly motivated in buying and reforming the SOE.

The government may also be able to achieve other objectives by setting aside at least part of the sale of an SOE through a worker buy-out. For example, labour opposition to privatization, (mainly fuelled by fear of redundancies), may be contained by offering worker ownership in the privatizing SOE on discounted or preferential terms. This preferential access to equity ownership may appease some of these fears, as well as foster cooperation between the government and the SOE. (Otherwise the government might run the risk of worker sabotage or theft of SOE assets while the privatization process is ongoing.)

A management/employee buy-out (M/EBO) may be appropriate in small SOE privatizations where there are no independent buyers interested in investing in the enterprise. Since most workers have limited capital, and limited access to capital resources such as domestic banks, capital venture funds, credit unions and other financial intermediaries, these M/EBOs tend to be highly leveraged transactions. In other words, the government may be required to finance a portion of the buy-out.

In most M/EBO privatizations, a special equity issue is subscribed to exclusively by managers and workers wishing to buy shares in the SOE. This can be an important means of recapitalizing the SOE. The equity shares are usually heavily discounted, and may be purchased directly with cash. Since workers tend to be cash-poor, buy-outs are generally leveraged through a loan. In some cases, the SOE's assets are used as collateral for a loan. In considering financing options, the government may provide access to subsidized credit (e.g., low-interest loans) for workers, instalment payments for equity purchases deducted directly from workers' pay, vouchers to purchase shares, or leases whereby workers lease the SOE in exchange for an equity interest in it (see Box 4.4).[113]

Box 4.4: The case of ECOM

ECOM, a Chilean computer firm, was acquired by its workers who formed a corporation and organized a $1.5 million financing package. The workers negotiated loans from their pension accounts, and an additional loan from CORFO, a state holding company. The loans were guaranteed by shares in the workers' cooperative and by the assets of the computer firm. The workers/owners have reaped impressive results by changing the wage scales, selling disposable assets, and leasing the original office space, while moving to less expensive premises.

Source: 'Chile—No Going Back', *The Economist*, 3–9 June 1995, pp. 17–19.

Normally, corporatization of the workers into an independent corporation, holding company, worker cooperative, or non-incorporated membership association takes place before privatization takes place. The worker cooperative buys the special share issue using cash contributions by workers and the proceeds of a loan that it enters into. This loan may be collateralized with shares in the worker corporation and the SOE's assets itself.

The US model of employee stock ownership plans (ESOPs) may be very useful in this context. The ESOP borrows a loan from a bank, and uses the loan proceeds to acquire shares in the SOE. The SOE (rather than the ESOP) pays back the loan by deducting certain amounts from worker salaries on a biweekly or monthly basis. However, in the event of non-payment or default, the bank has no recourse against the individual workers. ESOPs are a regulated trust-like instrument similar to a pension fund where the bank lending to an ESOP receives tax advantages for doing so. It is important that tax incentives are in place, however, before a similar device is used in other countries.

The example in Box 4.5[114] demonstrates that cash infusions in the privatization process are important to the viability of the undertaking, and for many cash-poor countries, foreign participation is the only viable means of sourcing adequate capital. Once again, this raises the nationalization-privatization dilemma which can only be resolved by the developing countries on its own terms.

On the other hand, M/EBOs can be very successful if they are well-structured. For example, in 1990 the Hungarian State Property Agency (SPA) decided to privatize a computer software firm in Hungary.

---

[113] See 'Chile—no going back', *The Economist*, 3–9 June 1995, pp. 17–19.
[114] SRI International, *supra* n. 110, p. V–48. See also *Privatization in Africa: Lessons and Opportunities* (Price Waterhouse and Associates, 1994).

Employees were assigned 'points' based on seniority and on their performance in the firm to determine their eligibility to purchase shares in the firm.
About 10 per cent of the company's shares were set aside for employee
purchases at a 95 per cent discount, and an additional 15 per cent of the
shares were made available at 50 per cent of the face value.[115]

Box 4.5: The case of ZPA

The importance of financing an M/EBO is very important, not only in seeking
ways to recapitalize the SOE, but also in ensuring that the privatization will be
successful. For example, the Zambia Privatization Agency (ZPA) received
proposals for M/EBOs for 15 out of 19 SOEs being divested of government
ownership. Several bids were returned to the offerors because the financing
arrangements were inadequate.

Several offerors responded by submitting revised bids which included the
participation of foreign investors. These revised bids were rejected by ZPA on
the grounds that foreign interests would gain a controlling interest in the
SOEs. As of February 1996, no MBOs had been concluded.

Source: SRI International, *Lessons Learned for Worldwide Privatization Experience in
Alternative Privatization Financing Methods* (prepared for USAID, February 1996), p. V–48.

Despite these heavily discounted shares, employees were still unable to
pay cash for share purchases. So, the SPA instituted an instalment plan
permitting employees to purchase shares over a three-year period. By 1993,
over 50 per cent of the firm had been acquired by its employees.[116] This
example demonstrates that subsidized rates and instalment plans for
employee stock purchases may be necessary in order for M/EBOs to become
a viable way to privatize.

3.6.4 Mass privatization

Mass privatization is another way of ensuring a wholesale transfer of state
assets to the private sector. Generally, mass privatization such as voucher
privatization models used in the Czech Republic, Poland, Romania, Russia
and Kazakhstan are only suitable when privatization is being contemplated
on a very large scale. Although voucher privatizations have been effective
devices for Eastern European and Central Asian countries, such mass
privatizations have been viewed with suspicion in African countries.[117]

The speed of mass privatization is key, and the success of such a
programme is wholly dependent on the political, economic, legal, regulatory
and institutional environment in which it takes place. A supportive climate
for mass privatization should have the following elements:

---

[115] OECD, *Trends and Policies in Privatization*, Vol. 1, No. 3 (1994). See also SRI International,
    supra n. 110, p. V–47.
[116] *Ibid.*
[117] B. Ngenda, *supra* n. 24, p. 181.

- *Political will*, including top political leadership as well as a commitment from the general public to participate in the mass privatization process and make it a success. Public support can only be mustered through aggressive publicity campaigns and widely disseminated public information on the availability of vouchers, the steps in the privatization process, and the location and times of public auctions, if scheduled.
- *Technical support* is particularly important since privatization involves complex legal, banking, accounting, and other consultant expertise. Pricing the assets and valuing the stock of privatizing SOEs is a difficult process that requires foresight and judgment.
- *Legal infrastructure* so that property ownership rights, transfers and enforcement of such rights are established well before privatization begins. In addition, corporatizing the legal forms of SOEs, as well as instituting rules of corporate governance, may be critical steps in the privatization process. Training government bureaucracy, lawyers, judges and other professionals to meet the demands of a market-driven economy also requires tremendous institutional and technical support.
- *Regulatory regimes* generally need to be restructured in most developing and transitional economies in order to accommodate a new Rule of Law regime. In many cases, for example, monopolistic or oligopolistic concerns have to be dismantled and anti-competitive protections have to be removed. Often regulatory agencies have to be established to oversee the entire process, ensure market competition and remove market entry barriers. Additionally, new environmental concerns may also need to be addressed, and may require that appropriate regulations be legislated.
- *Financial sector reform* is also critical, since the financial sector supports important linkages between domestic capital mobilization and the sales of SOE shares.[118] Financial sector reforms in bank supervision and regulation, and the creation of new financial intermediaries such as credit unions, micro-enterprise institutions, and other financial institutions and products, may need to be instituted.

3.7 Transparency in the privatization process

Of course, mass privatization, apart from its speed, also ensures transparency in the privatization process. Vouchers are made available to all eligible participants and the transfer of ownership is quick. Public auctions, sealed bidding, and the public sales of SOE assets in liquidation or related bankruptcy proceedings (sometimes referred to as 'stripping'),[119] are also very transparent means of transferring ownership from the government to private owners.

---

[118] OECD, *Mass Privatization: An Initial Assessment* (1995).
[119] B. Ngenda, *supra* n. 24, p. 182.

Another accessible, equitable and transparent means of privatizing SOEs is by making an initial public offering (IPO). Public flotations of stock are usually only appropriate for companies that are large, well-managed and profitable. Since IPOs—from legal, investment banking, and accounting standpoints—are technically complex transactions, the transaction costs and the time involved generally need to be carefully justified before initiating an IPO.

Although IPOs have been criticized as a limited option for countries that do not have well-developed capital markets, in Jamaica, Pakistan, India and other developing countries IPOs have been heavily oversubscribed. If the publicity campaign is geared appropriately, there may be quite a bit of 'money-under-the mattress'-type savings that potentially can be mobilized into the formal financial sector. Although functioning stock markets may not be a necessary precondition to a successful IPO, accumulated domestic savings are a critical factor.[120]

In 1986, for instance, the Jamaican government sold 51 per cent of the shares of the National Commercial Bank (NCB) in a public offering of $16.5 million.[121] The public offering took place over a 10-day period, from November to December 1986, following an intensive publicity campaign. Shares could be obtained from post offices, and the prospectus was reproduced, in its entirety, in the national newspaper one week prior to the offering.[122] Over 30,000 individuals and institutions applied for applications, and the offering was oversubscribed by 170 per cent.[123] Over 170,000 NCB shares were traded for the first time on the Jamaican Stock Exchange on 23 December 1986. Although the initial share price proved to have been seriously undervalued, the government nevertheless collected $16.5 million in revenues from this extremely successful IPO, which still serves as a model today.

The Jamaican example demonstrates that a successful IPO may take place even in the absence of a well-developed capital market. Careful and detailed planning, adequate publicity and information campaigns, wide distribution and easy share access, together with the provision of credit, where appropriate, are all important factors for a successful IPO in a developing country context. The lack of capital market development is not an insurmountable obstacle to initial public offerings or other means of privatization (such as voucher schemes). In fact, IPOs can ensure transparency, thus building public trust in, and access to, the overall privatization process.

3.8   Encouraging capital market development

Another important government objective in the privatization process is encouraging the growth of capital markets and ensuring broad-based

---

[120] SRI International, *supra* n. 110, p. II–13.
[121] N. Zank, *et al., Reforming Financial Systems: Policy Change and Privatization, supra* n. 10, p. 125.
[122] *Ibid.*, p. 132.
[123] *Ibid.*, p. 134.

ownership of the equity in the productive enterprises of a developing coun-tries. Although the lack of capital markets is often cited as an impediment to public stock flotations or to public offerings of bonds,[124] the Jamaican example demonstrates that a well-orchestrated and planned IPO can be very successful, and can deepen emerging financial markets.

Moreover, the role of institutional investors, such as the investment funds in the Czech Republic, and the pension funds in Chile, also adds to the depth and liquidity of capital markets. These financial intermediaries provide the individual retail investor with the means of diversifying his/her portfolio, and of benefiting from investment advice from experienced fund managers. Moreover, domestic institutional investors are often reliable purchasers of the shares of SOEs being privatized. This is an important factor, since inter-national buyers of such equity may be difficult to source. Thus, the government may wish to create an institutional investor framework before beginning large-scale privatizations of SOEs.

Investment funds or mutual funds[125] can be set up specifically for privatiz-ation purposes. These funds can buy large blocks of shares of SOEs being privatized, and then sell the shares to individuals, functioning much like a mutual fund. Alternatively, if the voucher method is being used, then indivi-duals can purchase shares in investment funds with vouchers, and the investment funds then bid for shares in SOEs on behalf of the investor.

Privatization trust funds are often used in African countries (e.g., Tanzania, Uganda, Kenya) to 'warehouse' or 'park' shares in SOEs, to be sold to the public at a later date. These types of funds act as a bridge by removing SOE shares from direct government control. The shares are managed through a private trust, thus temporarily removing from government control the shares in question.

Zambia has an ambitious privatization programme, and plans to divest its ownership in some 150 SOEs over the next five years. Majority equity owner-ship in these SOEs are often reserved for strategic private investors.[126] A maximum of 30 per cent equity interest in these SOEs may by offered through IPOs floated on the Lusaka Stock Exchange.[127] Minority shares are reserved for interested Zambian stockholders and are 'parked' in a trust fund.

In fact, the Zambian government has passed legislation and regulations to establish the Zambian Privatization Trust Fund (PTF) under a five-year trust deed. The PTF, itself an SOE, acquires shares in privatizing SOEs, and

---

[124] B. Ngenda, *supra* n. 24, p. 182.

[125] Mutual funds or unit trusts are usually open-ended stock portfolios meaning that shares can be liquidated into cash upon demand. Moreover, mutual funds do not generally participate in the management of the company whose shares are being held by the fund. In contrast, closed-ended funds such as venture capital funds or investment trusts involve more management control and involve high-risk investments. See SRI International, *supra* n. 110, p. VI-52–53.

[126] See S. Bell, *Sharing the Wealth: Privatization through Broad-Based Ownership Strategies* (World Bank Discussion Paper No. 285, April 1995), p. 27.

[127] *Ibid.*

holds them for local shareholders during the transitional period.[128] Further, share prices for minority shares being held for local investors are deeply discounted. In fact, Zambians may receive bonus shares and have access to instalment plans for share purchases.

Although the government has issued a ceiling on the number of minority shares that individuals or local institutions may purchase, at the end of the transitional period and the expiration of the trust, any remaining shares will be sold or distributed free of charge. Thus, the Zambian privatization plan involves the innovative use of a privatization trust fund which transfers control of minority shares to a government holding company. Additionally, incentives and discounts are provided to the local investors in order to facilitate share purchases.

The examples discussed above illustrate potentially effective methods of privatization in a developing country working without the benefit of well-established capital markets. Developing country governments should plan their privatization activities from a menu of options that are tailored to the specific industry, enterprise or sector being privatized. The above examples illustrate that there are many techniques which may be used to privatize an enterprise, including M/EBOs, voucher schemes, IPOs and private placements. These options, perhaps in conjunction with each other or sequenced properly, can effect a privatization that is efficient, speedy, transparent, and less painful a transition than originally anticipated. Careful and meticulous planning, while not ensuring an absolute degree of success, can rationalize the privatization process and optimize it as a tool available to the developing country government.

The influence of privatization on emerging capital markets will be further explored in the next chapter.

---

[128] *Privatization in Africa: Lessons and Opportunities* (Price Waterhouse and Associates, 1994).

5.   Emerging Capital Markets

This chapter will examine emerging capital markets, the reasons for their emergence, and potential future trends in their development. First of all, it examines which countries are considered to be emerging capital markets, and the extent of their relative importance in an increasingly global economy. Secondly, this chapter looks at what types of strategic planning and decision-making need to be undertaken by developing countries in order to structure their respective capital markets, and how choices should be made between encouraging mobilization of domestic savings and providing incentives for foreign direct investment.

Finally, why should lawyers be concerned with what is essentially an economic trend? Are legal and regulatory regimes in need of systemic reform in order to respond to the development of new emerging capital markets? This chapter provides an analytical framework in which to consider options on how to structure emerging capital markets, and offers a perspective on formulating legal and regulatory regimes in support thereof.

1.   AN OVERVIEW

A significant change in perspective with regard to developing countries is reflected in a subtle change in terminology. The terms discussed in the introduction—'Third World', 'lesser developed country', 'LDC', or even 'developing country', are becoming passé. The new term is 'emerging capital market'.

The transition from 'developing' country to 'emerging capital market' is a new and extremely important one and reflects an overall change in the view of development. Emerging market economies are now perceived as offering a wealth of opportunity in terms of trade, technology transfers and direct foreign and portfolio investment. Emerging capital markets offer the foreign investor the potential for profit, and although most of these economies are located in the developing world (e.g., Brazil, Mexico, India, Indonesia), investing in these economies no longer conforms to the traditional notion of 'development' whereby assistance is provided to poorer nations. This chapter will discuss the legal implications of significant private capital flows to poorer countries. These relatively new flows of capital are catalytic in making a final transition from being a developing country to becoming an to emerging market economy.

The new terminology of 'emerging capital market' means that the country in question is in transition from poverty to prosperity, wielding new economic power and, if desired, political and military power, too. But who actually belongs to the new international club of emerging capital markets? According to the World Bank, the 'Big Five' emerging economies are China, India, Indonesia, Brazil and Russia.[1]

The World Bank is predicting that the Big Five emerging economies are set to become economic powerhouses, doubling their share of world imports and exports in the next 25 years.[2] The rosy outlook for developing countries, including sub-Saharan countries, is bolstered by stable market conditions and a tremendous influx of foreign capital and technology into these emerging markets.[3] Emerging market economies have made a critical transition, at least in the eyes of Western commentators and observers, that will fundamentally alter the course that these countries take in the next decade.

Private capital flows have now surpassed public financing to the developing world, and constituted about 80 per cent of the total net flows in 1996.[4] Foreign direct investment (FDI) to developing countries increased from 12 per cent of global FDI in 1990, to 38 per cent in 1995.[5] However, private investment has been very selective, with 18 developing counties receiving over 90 per cent of all private capital flows from 1990 to 1994,[6] as follows:

In fact, foreign investors have been investing $60–$70 billion every year in East Asia since the mid-1990s—some two-thirds of all money invested in the developing world during that time period.[8]

To put this change in investment patterns into perspective, public financing (i.e., official development assistance (ODA) from multilateral banks and bilateral donors and other official sources) totalled $5.6 billion in 1970. In contrast, private investment (i.e., commercial bank loans, FDI, private bonds and foreign portfolio investment) amounted to just slightly more, totaling $5.8 billion in 1970. A decade later in 1980, public capital flows amounted to $35.1 billion, while private flows jumped to $53.3 billion. In 1990, private investment in the developing world came to about

---

[1] World Bank, *Global Economic Prospects and Developing Countries* (1997). See also R. Stevenson, 'World Bank Report Sees Era of Emerging Economies: New Giants Include Brazil, India and Russia', *New York Times*, 10 September 1997, p. D7; R. Chote and M. Suzman, 'Developing Economies Gain Pace', *Financial Times*, 10 September 1997, p. A1. (Ironically, Russia has slipped from superpower status to that of an emerging market.)

   Jeffrey Garten, the Dean of the Yale School of Management, declares in his book *The Big Ten: The Big Emerging Markets and How They Will Change Our Lives* (1997), that the rising stars are China, Mexico, Brazil, Argentina, India, Indonesia, Poland, South Africa, South Korea, and Turkey.

[2] R. Stevenson, *supra* n. 1, p. D7. See also R. Chote and M. Suzman, *supra* n. 1, p. 1; World Bank, *supra* n. 1.

[3] R. Stevenson, *supra* n. 1, p. D7.

[4] World Bank, *Managing Capital Flows in East Asia* (1996), p. 6.

[5] *Ibid.*, p. 5; see also World Bank, *Debt Tables* (1996), p. 7.

[6] World Bank, *supra* n. 4, p. 6.

[7] *Ibid.*, p. 18, n. 5.

[8] D. Sanger, 'The Overfed Tiger Economies', *New York Times*, available on internet at http://search.nytimes.com.search.daily (last visited in July 1997).

Table 5.1:   Private investment in developing countries

	Country	% of private investment
1	China	24
2	Mexico	12.4
3	Korea	7.2
4	former Soviet Republics	7.1
5	Argentina	6.6
6	Malaysia	6
7	Portugal	5.7
8	Brazil	4.7
9	Thailand	4
10	Turkey	3.3
11	Venezuela	2.5
12	Hungary	2.3
13	Iran	2.2
14	India	1–2
15	Chile	1–2
16	Indonesia	1–2
17	Philippines	1–2
18	Poland	1–2[7]

$30 billion, with official development assistance amounting to nearly $65 billion.[9] By 1992, public flows had dropped to $55 billion, but private flows had shot up to $100.3 billion, double the total public investment made that year. By 1994, public investment had further dropped to $48.6 billion, whereas private capital flows exceeded $158.8 billion.[10] Now, official aid has dropped to $45 billion, whereas, private investment has expanded exponentially to $245 billion.[11]

The IMF estimates that foreign direct investment is the biggest component of private investment in Asian, Latin American and Eastern European countries, amounting to $100 billion in 1996, up from $48.8 billion in 1993.[12] In comparison, net foreign portfolio investment (FPI) in these economies was a modest $43.2 billion in 1996.[13] Thus, private financing (primarily in the form of FDI, FPI and private bonds) has far outstripped public financing to the developing world, which has far-reaching implications.

The sea change from public financing to private capital flows to the developing world (albeit to selected countries) is a dramatic shift which merits some analysis and discussion. Two principal causes for this shift

[9] D. Sanger, 'Asia's Economic Tigers Growl at World Monetary Conference: Say Opening of Markets Hands Wall Street Too Much Power', *New York Times*, 22 September 1997, p. A1.
[10] See Table 1.1 of the World Bank, *supra* n. 4, p. 5.
[11] *Ibid.*
[12] B. Wysocki, Jr., 'Distant Echoes: Asian Woes Will Take a Toll on Economies Around the World', *Wall Street Journal Europe*, 31 October 1997, p. 1.
[13] *Ibid.*

require consideration in this context. First, the debt crisis of the 1980s deeply shook the confidence of both commercial lenders and sovereign borrowers in the viability of syndicated commercial lending to developing countries. The increased reluctance in recent years to pursue commercial lending by sovereign borrowers has led to a revitalized interest in bond financing.

Secondly, developing country capital markets have been deepened and strengthened by privatization activities taking place in those countries. Privatization of state-owned enterprises has led to a new reliance on equity financing. Thus, bond and equity financing (rather than commercial lending or ODA) has been shaping the emerging capital markets. The new strength of the emerging capital markets in the developing world is dramatically changing the patterns of investment flows. This also means that the state's role in supporting its capital finance needs is being radically transformed in many important ways.

1.1 The failure of sovereign borrowing

Commercial lending to sovereign borrowers was spurred on in the late 1970s, in part because of low yields on US and European investments.[14] Additionally, as discussed in Chapter 3, many US and European commercial banks, then flush with petrodollar deposits after the oil shocks of 1976 and 1979,[15] began lending heavily to developing nations. Commercial bankers accumulated massive portfolios of sovereign loans in the belief— misguided, as it later turned out—that it was impossible for sovereign borrowers to default on their loan obligations. The debt crisis of the early and mid-1980s proved that this was not the case.

Most of the commercial bank lending which took place during the 1970s and 1980s was in the form of syndicated bank loans. The nature of syndicated commercial bank lending is important, for several reasons. First, commercial lending is not generally subject to securities laws of either the borrowing or lending parties. This meant that the precise nature of the economic conditions under which such borrowing was taking place, including significant cross-border risks,[16] the amount of overall debt exposure of the borrower country, and the regulation of such lending, was left uncomfortably vague and indeterminate.

Secondly, syndicated commercial lending was usually in the form of five-to-ten year, US dollar-denominated loans made on the basis of floating interest rates. Generally speaking, the floating interest rates were set at a spread of 50–500 basis points above the London (or Singapore) Inter-

---

[14] L. Buchheit, 'Cross-Border Lending: What's Different This Time?' (1995) 16 *N.W. J. Int'l L. & Busi.* 44 at 46.

[15] *Ibid.*, p. 47.

[16] Cross-border risks may include, for example, exchange rate movements, political risk in the form of *coups d'état*, rebellions, war and other political instability, nationalizations or expropriations, corruption and rent-seeking, and tariffs, customs duties, tax and regulatory regimes which discriminate against foreign investors. See L. Buchheit, *supra* n. 14, p. 48. These risks are difficult to assess at the outset of making sovereign loans since this information may not be publicly available or disclosed through the course of negotiating for the loan.

bank Offered Rate (LIBOR or SIBOR).[17] The sovereign borrower assumed both interest rate and exchange rate risks. However, repayment of the loan was expected regardless of whether the rates move upward, although this could potentially jeopardize the financial condition of the borrower.[18] The rise in LIBOR in the early 1980s created a tremendous debt service burden on sovereign borrowers, precipitating the debt crisis of that decade.[19]

In response to the debt crisis, sovereign debt owed to commercial lenders was rescheduled, as supplemented by limited debt relief granted under the US Treasury Department's Brady Initiative as discussed earlier. Many developing countries, notably Mexico, entered into destructive boom-and-bust cycles in which enormous amounts of commercial lending supported consumer (rather than capital) import needs. The inability of sovereign borrowers to make debt service payments resulted in the imposition of painful IMF structural adjustment programmes, strict belt-tightening and recessionary economic conditions.[20]

Thus, commercial lending to sovereign borrowers had built-in limitations, particularly insofar as private commercial lending itself is neither transparent nor well-regulated. Additionally, shifts in a floating interest rate could make loan repayments problematic. Potential defaults on the loans (or non-repayment in general) spurred the need to enter into multi-year rescheduling agreements. These repetitive and painstaking exercises eventually exhausted the parties involved. And finally, sovereign lending was often tied to boom-and-bust cycles of economic growth and retrenchment, making development goals even more illusory.

At the same time as overheated sovereign lending was taking place, sovereign borrowers also made limited use of publicly-issued debt instruments (principally in the form of bonds). International bond markets were not so affected by the international debt crisis of the 1980s since developing country bonds were relatively few in number. Moreover, such bonds were rarely rescheduled, since the resulting debt relief would be fairly minimal to the bond-issuing country.[21]

As a result of the debt crisis, commercial lending has somewhat fallen from favour as a method of financing developing countries' capital needs. Unsecured, syndicated commercial bank loans have been replaced by the new favourite: developing country bonds.[22] These bonds have the relative advantage of being fixed-rate (rather than floating rate) instruments. In addition, they are not easily subject to debt rescheduling

---

[17] World Bank, *supra* n. 4, p. 23.

[18] *Ibid.*, p. 23.

[19] L. Buchheit, *supra* n. 14 at 51. See also Lindert, 'Response to Debt Crisis: What is Different About the 1980s?' in B. Eichengreen and W. Wynne (eds) *International Debt Crisis in Historical Perspective* (1989), pp. 229–234.

[20] See generally F. Dawson, *The First Latin American Debt Crisis* (1990).

[21] L. Buchheit, *supra* n. 14, p. 49. Professor Buchheit notes that Costa Rica is an exception from this rule since it rescheduled its bonds in 1982. *Ibid.*, p. 48, n. 16 citing 'Costa Rica: A Case History' in D. Suratgar (ed.) *Default and Rescheduling* (1984), pp. 149–50 and S.M. Yassukovich, 'Eurobonds and Debt Rescheduling', *Euromoney*, January 1982, p. 61.

[22] L. Buchheit, *supra* n. 14, p. 49.

exercises. Moreover, country bonds are subject to securities laws (and legally mandated public disclosure requirements). Finally, they are less susceptible to being 'offloaded' to fill the offshore, secret bank accounts of corrupt developing country officials.

Of course, there are disadvantages, insofar as bondholders may be less manageable than commercial bankers because of their numbers, their more diverse interests, and the greater likelihood that they will file lawsuits instead of rescheduling the terms of the bonds.[23] However, it is unlikely that international bondholder dissatisfaction will trigger IMF intervention; it is far more likely that the bonds will simply be sold by the bondholders. The capital outflows from such bond sales may, in fact, lead to serious market-based repercussions, which may destabilize the developing country economy. IMF conditionality, therefore, is gradually being replaced by market-driven investor behavior which both punishes and rewards the relative economic performance of emerging capital markets.

1.2   The impact of privatization on capital market development

Between 1988 and 1994, over $110 billion in state revenues was generated by the sales of SOEs in developing countries.[24] Revenues from SOE 'fire sales' peaked at $26 billion in 1992, dropping somewhat to $21 billion in 1994.[25] Viewed in terms of total revenue generated by privatization, Latin America leads with 57 per cent followed by East Asia with 20 per cent, and Eastern Europe and Central Asia with 14 per cent for this time period.[26] There was relatively little privatization activity in Africa and the Middle East.[27]

From 1988–94, foreign direct investment accounted for about 42 per cent of the total in privatization revenues generated, amounting to almost 40 per cent of the overall FDI in Eastern Europe and Central Asia.[28] The FDI generated through privatization activities amounted to just over 15 per cent in the Latin America region; however, these percentages can be misleading, since the former Soviet bloc had very little FDI to begin with. (Indeed, under the constitution of the former USSR, foreign ownership of Soviet property was illegal.)[29]

---

[23] *Ibid.*, pp. 53–54.
[24] L. Bouton and M. Sumlinski, 'Trends in Private Investment in Developing Countries: Statistics for 1970–95' (IFC Discussion Paper No. 31. 1996), p. 5. These figures are derived from the World Bank's Privatization database which includes statistics on sales of state-owned property and assets to the private sector through public offers (e.g., IPOs), direct sales, concession and licensing agreements and joint ventures. The database excludes information on voucher sales and divestitures. *Ibid.*, p. 5, n. 4.
[25] *Ibid.*, p. 5.
[26] *Ibid.*
[27] *Ibid.*
[28] *Ibid.*, p. 7.
[29] See W. Frenkel and M.Sukhman, 'New Foreign Investment Regimes of Russia and Other Republics of the Former U.S.S.R.: A Legislative Analysis and Historical Perspective', (1993) 16 *Boston C. Int'l & Comp. L. Rev.* 321 at 338.

Chapter 4 discussed the importance of domestic savings mobilization, and the means for doing so through institutional investors. Chile's example of privatized pension plans, and the Czech example of mass privatization through a voucher scheme effectively demonstrate the power of local institutional investors to create, strengthen and deepen local capital markets. Once institutional players are in place, they often become the eager buyers of equity stakes in local SOEs which are scheduled for privatization by the government.

Thus, privatization, if properly sequenced, can become self-financing with very little foreign participation. This is not to say, however, that FDI has no place in privatization. Private placements and joint ventures may be very useful in forging new relationships to increase productivity, updating technology for processing goods, and creating new international markets.

Of course, privatization alone is not enough. A World Bank study has found that the simultaneous implementation of five components of economic reform is important to the overall success of the privatization programme.[30] Those individual components are divestiture, competition, 'hard' budgets, financial sector reform, and changing the institutional relationship between SOEs and the government.[31] The study found that 'hardening' budgets by eliminating direct and hidden subsidies,[32] eliminating directed credits (i.e., government allocations to particular enterprises, industries, or sectors), making credit available on market-based commercial terms, and eliminating monopoly prices, were all critical factors to success.

In sum, the failure of international borrowing practices to yield the type of development results hoped for, and the dramatic increase in privatization activities in developing countries, have both supported a surge of

---

[30] It should be noted that the World Bank also played a critical role in encouraging public sector growth in developing countries. If, for example, the borrower is not itself a government agency, then the member government must provide a government guarantee to the World Bank on the loan. See D. Sanger, *supra* n. 9, p. A1. This has meant, in effect, that private loans are not sourced from the World Bank since member governments have generally only been willing to guarantee the borrowings of SOEs or parastatals. *Ibid.* Thus, World Bank lending tends to reinforce the role of the state as a primary economic actor.

Additionally, the World Bank has been a very conservative lender, requiring that $1 in loans be supported by an equivalent $1 in the World Bank's capital reserves. No leveraging is permitted. See E. Stern, 'Prospects of Development Financing in the 1980s', (1982) 32 *Am. U.L.Rev.* 145 at 147–148, 151.

[31] World Bank, *Bureaucrats in Business*, Executive Summary (1996), pp. 2–3. The study found that Chile, Korea and Mexico obtained the best privatization results; Egypt, Ghana and the Philippines had mixed results; and India, Senegal and Turkey achieved the poorest results.

[32] Hidden subsidies are often difficult to gauge since they may take the form of:

- loans made at below-market interest rates with reduced principal or interest rates (which may be 'forgiven' if unpaid);
- tax exemptions or tax holidays;
- exemptions from paying customs duties;
- rent-free use of state-owned land and buildings;
- preferred access to bidding on government contracts; and,
- government-imposed requirements that the manufactured output be purchased by other SOEs.

interest in private bond and equity financing. Sovereign borrowing and public financing from official donors and multilateral banks, while still useful, are becoming outmoded instruments of international finance as the developing world becomes more financially integrated with global capital markets.

The practical limitations of sovereign borrowing, as discussed earlier, illustrate two points: the unsuitability of using sovereign borrowing to sustain long-term development, and the inability of most developing states to effectively manage capital resources.[33] The shift in geopolitical politics has signalled a change in ODA policies of most Western donor nations. Depending on the vagaries of official assistance from multilateral and bilateral institutions in a post-Cold war era is not, therefore, a totally reliable means of supporting long-term capital needs. In fact, shrinking ODA budgets may leave developing countries with no other choice than to seek development financing from international capital markets. In fact, the entry of developing countries into global finance markets may be viewed as a much-needed and welcome breath of fresh air.

2.   STRUCTURING CAPITAL MARKETS IN DEVELOPING COUNTRIES

2.1   The role of a financial system in emerging capital markets

A financial system captures domestic savings and mobilizes these savings into capital markets and other means of productive investment.[34] Capital investment helps local enterprises create goods and services more efficiently, thereby stimulating economic growth.[35] A domestic financial system has three vital components: savings (capital formation), borrowing (extending credit), and financial intermediation between the two.[36] Without functioning capital (equity) and credit (loan) markets, a developing country will be little more than a barter economy.

The 'capitalization' or 'monetization' of savings in the formal sector is extremely important. Otherwise, savings are accumulated in many developing countries in the form of real estate, gold or other precious minerals, cattle or livestock, or offshore investments which represent capital flight from the country.[37] The retention and investment of savings in

---

[33] A World Bank study states rather dramatically that, 'Seventy years of socialism have yielded overwhelming proof of Adam Smith's views that market forces are more efficient in solving most production and distribution problems than large organizations and administrative controls.' G. Pohl, *et al.*, *Creating Capital Markets in Central and Eastern Europe*, World Bank Tech. Paper No. 295 (1995), p. 3.
[34] See USAID Policy Paper: 'Financial Market Development' (USAID, 1988), p. 2.
[35] *Ibid.*
[36] N. Zank, *et al.*, *Reforming Financial Systems: Policy Changes and Privatization* (Greenwood Press, 1991), p. 11.
[37] See USAID *supra* n. 34, p. 8.

domestic capital markets is critical, and the government should provide the incentives and the means for doing so.

It is important, therefore, that a domestic financial system provides the means of mobilizing capital through the development of a capital market (i.e., the means for trading the equity of private enterprises). Trading the shares of private enterprises in secondary (i.e., stock) markets provides the means for creating broad-based ownership of the productive enterprises in a developing country, and for creating individual capital wealth. In addition, financial systems are part of the 'formal' sector. In other words, financial systems are heavily state-regulated, subject to legal regulation and taxation and transparent.

If financial systems are not healthy and trusted by its users, the 'informal' financial sector (comprised of family-oriented lending, moneylenders, pawn-shops, unofficial middlemen and even organized crime)[38] will take over the basic function of providing credit. The unregulated nature of this type of lending activity tends to lead to abuses such as higher than market interest rates, draconian repayment terms and the illegal seizure of collateral. This type of financial activity, by virtue of its secretive nature, remains in the informal sector, and outside public scrutiny, oversight, and taxation.

2.2   Macro-economic impediments to capital market formation

The next section will explore certain means of creating capital markets in developing countries. However, before strategies and policies in support of capital market formation are discussed, certain macro-economic impedi-ments may exist which prohibit the creation of sustainable capital markets. These impediments are an integral part of the picture, and must be constructively dealt with in creating a solid foundation for a well-functioning capital market.

First, the role of the government in the overall financial sector must be carefully assessed. For example, many developing countries have official government policies to encourage the use of 'directed credit'. This means, essentially, that credit resources are channeled towards certain banks, sectors, or borrowers, based largely on political considerations.[39] This tends to distort local financial markets, since market conditions are distorted by political agendas. This can, and very often does, result in misallocation of credit resources and misuse of subsidized credit, thereby undermining the strength and reliability of financial institutions.[40] Thus, moving away from a command-type of financial market with heavy government intervention and towards market-determined credit use is generally encouraged.[41]

Another issue which may be relevant in this context is that of govern-ment-imposed interest rate ceilings. Interest rate ceilings, if at issue in the first place, 'cap' the amount of interest chargeable for a certain loan. No

---

[38] N. Zank, *et al.*, *supra* n. 36, p. 22.
[39] See USAID *supra* n. 34, p. 14.
[40] *Ibid.*
[41] See e.g., *Ibid.*

matter how well-intentioned the policy behind interest rate ceilings may be, this policy has fairly predictable, and negative, downstream effects. Since the administrative costs of lending to small, rural, or disadvantaged borrowers cannot be recouped by passing on a higher interest rate, this discourages financial institutions from making loans to small and medium-size entrepreneurs. Ultimately, small and medium-size enterprises with specific credit needs are unable to access credit from formal financial institutions, and turn to the informal market for credit. Thus, removing ceilings on interest rates, if they exist, may be an important step in creating a conducive environment for financial market development.

Another government-led reform which may be necessary to create the groundwork for capital market development is to remove overly burdensome and excessive bureaucratic impediments such as high collateral requirements, administrative controls, explicit or implicit taxes on financial transactions and excessive paperwork requirements. Streamlining credit application processes and simplifying access to credit are important to encouraging broad-based public participation in capital market development.[42] Apart from removing excessive government red tape, the government may also need to reconsider its role in regulating financial markets.

In other words, the host government may wish to structure certain interventions in the market. For example, deposit insurance, if not widely available, may need to be instituted. Other investor protections in accordance with market needs may also need to be implemented. Perhaps most importantly, the government's regulatory and supervisory responsibilities with regard to banking and financial institutions need to be carefully reconsidered and revised, as discussed later in this chapter. Appropriate enforcement mechanisms and institutions may also need to be set up so that securities, banking and other relevant laws and regulations are adequately enforced. Unless adequate enforcement of the legal and regulatory framework takes place, investors and borrowers will lose confidence in the financial system and revert to informal finance markets for their capital needs.

2.3   Steps towards capital market formation

Domestic resource mobilization has often been overlooked in developing countries.[43] These countries may have relied on their domestic treasury revenues, or sourced credit from outside sources such as foreign commercial banks, multilateral institutions, or bilateral donor agencies. In fact, if donor-supported loans are readily accessible on concessional terms, there is little incentive for the government to make domestic capital mobilization a priority.[44]

---

[42] Other factors in addition to directed credit, interest rate ceilings on deposits and loans, and taxation which may inhibit the growth of stable and transparent capital markets include: exchange controls, market entry barriers in the banking industry, and heavy reserve requirements. *Ibid.*, pp. 6, 16, 17.

[43] N. Zank, *et al.*, *supra* n. 36, p. 26.

[44] *Ibid.*, p. 34.

Nevertheless, the domestic savings of private individuals are a critical source of funds for local banks and banking institutions which can then on-lend these funds to borrowers.[45] Thus, the developing country should ensure that its policies and banking practices encourage domestic savings mobilization.[46] Once these savings are captured by the formal financial market, market-oriented credit needs can be met from a local resource base. The previous discussion on market impediments to savings mobilization (e.g., directed credit, taxation) are all issues that must be dealt with in an effective manner by the government if the incipient financial market is to be strengthened and deepened.

For the foreseeable future, domestic savings will continue to be more important than foreign investment, thus, domestic savings mobilization should be encouraged.[47] In this regard, tax incentives (such as tax-deferred savings accounts), and other attractive savings vehicles need to be established to entice domestic investors to access the formal financial market. Thus, the developing country may need to launch new forms of investment vehicles (e.g., money market funds, government securities, investment funds or clubs) in order to attract investors. Financial intermediaries who can handle new savers and investors may also need to be set up or strengthened. Such local institutions may include credit unions, pension plans, and other local financial institutions that can make savings and investment products easily accessible to the individual investor. The objective, of course, is to facilitate savings mobilization, create investment opportunities with maximum returns and involve the public to the greatest extent possible.

2.4   Capital market development: components and sequencing

Developing countries face a series of critical decisions on how to structure their capital markets in order to meet their financing needs.[48] The initial decision centres on formulating an appropriate (and dynamic) mix between domestic and foreign sources of financing. First, the government must decide, in partnership with other important financial players, on its approach to debt financing.

Commercial bank loans are still expected to be the major source of debt financing for developing countries in the immediate future.[49] However, commercial lending can be tailored, for example, towards financing the short-term importation of capital equipment, perhaps in conjunction with foreign joint ventures that are intended to revamp local industries. Official assistance, on the other hand, often makes training and policy reform measures part of the 'conditionality' imposed for the credits or grants

---

[45] See USAID *supra* n. 34, p. 3.
[46] Economic Development Institute of the World Bank, *Securities Market Development: A Guideline for Policymakers* (1997), pp. 1–7.
[47] See *ibid.*, pp. 2–3.
[48] See e.g., *ibid.* at p. 16 (Zambia case study) which sets forth an analytical plan of action for securities market development.
[49] G. Pohl, *et al., supra* n. 33, p. 3.

extended by international donors. Therefore, it is logical to use ODA to support long-term macro-economic policy reform agendas, institution-building and strengthening, and legal and institutional reforms.

Secondly government must formulate policies to develop equity capital markets, and may need to design and fund institutional support for such development. This may involve establishing financial and tax incentives for domestic savings mobilization, setting up local institutional investors (e.g., private pension plans, mutual funds, investment funds, private equity and venture capital funds),[50] and instituting a well-thought out plan for financial sector reform.

For example, from 1979 to 1982, the Chinese government borrowed a total of $10.6 billion from commercial banks.[51] In the period 1981–90, the government began issuing government bonds and making shares in local corporations available for purchase by domestic investors, purely in an effort to mobilize domestic savings.[52]

At the same time, the Chinese government opened up industrial, tax-free zones along the coastal areas, and offered other tax-based concessions to attract foreign investors. The government started to encourage FDI. In 1983 FDI amounted to $0.6 billion; by 1991, FDI reached $4.4 billion. FDI in China increased exponentially to $27.5 billion in 1993 and $33 billion in 1994, making China the undisputed leader of the developing world in attracting FDI.[53]

Despite initial delays in formulating a legal framework and a regulatory regime in support of functioning stock markets, the Chinese government opened two securities exchanges, in 1990 and 1991, in Shanghai and Shenzhen, respectively. The two stock exchanges offered two parallel tracks of investments.[54] 'A' shares are exclusively for domestic shareholders, including, as of 1994, domestic pension funds acting as institutional investors. 'B' shares are available only to foreign investors.

Additionally, from 1994 onwards, 16 companies listed 'H' shares on the Hong Kong Stock Exchange, and five companies have listed 'N' shares on the New York Stock Exchange (NYSE). Both 'H' and 'N' shares may be traded on

---

[50] It should be noted, however, that venture capital funds have generally not been instrumental to stock market development in the United States or in other countries. In fact, well-established stock markets tend to precede venture capital activities. Investment bankers who invest in high technology stocks generally create limited markets for high-risk undertakings, only after a dynamic capital market is already established.

Venture capitalists typically support a company with a new technology or process but with little know-how on how to finance, market or produce it. The collective experiences of bilateral donors such as USAID, and multilateral banks such as the International Finance Corporation, tend to support the conclusion that investing ODA in venture capital portfolio investment is not an effective means of supporting emerging capital market development. See generally USAID, *The Venture Capital Mirage: Assessing USAID Experience with Equity Investment* (USAID Program and Operations Assessment Rep. No. 17, August 1996), pp. 5, 13, 21.

[51] World Bank, *supra* n. 4, p. 61.

[52] *Ibid.,* pp. 61–62.

[53] *Ibid.,* p. 62.

[54] *Ibid.,* p. 62. (See Table 2.5 and Box 2.1, pp. 28 and 22, respectively.)

the NYSE.[55] The two parallel tracks of 'A' and 'B' stocks were expected to be eliminated when China's currency became fully convertible.[56]

Thus, the Chinese have adopted a progressive model of sequencing the following components: (1) sovereign borrowing; (2) domestic savings mobilization; (3) creating local institutional investors; (4) attracting FDI, permitting limited foreign access to Chinese stock markets; and, (5) finally permitting strong domestic companies to list their stocks for trading on the NYSE. This sequencing (including parallel track development of certain types of capital market components) demonstrates the incremental, and successful, nature of capital market development in China. All facets of internal and external financing are being thoroughly exploited on China's pathway towards global financial integration.

The lesson that this may hold for other developing nations is to adopt a well-sequenced plan for capital market development from a diverse menu of options. Commercial lending, official development assistance, and international capital market-based financing can all be complementary elements in a strategy that meets an individual country's capital financing needs.

Of course, internal savings mobilization cannot be overlooked in this process. Experience shows that sovereign borrowing from commercial banking institutions cannot be a substitute for domestic savings mobilization. By creating equitable opportunities for local investors to save and invest their earnings, the government can create a foundation for broad-based economic savings, investment and growth.

The government may also need to encourage the growth of local institutional investors in this context. For example, there may need to be tax-based incentives for individual and institutional investors to capitalize their savings in a growing domestic capital market. Local pension plans, mutual funds and other investment vehicles, for example, may later become instrumental in the ultimate success of privatization schemes, and help deepen local capital markets over time.

In sum, creating an open, transparent, and well-regulated domestic savings capital market is a critical government undertaking. Market transparency and the smooth execution of trades are both key in creating domestic investor confidence. Investor confidence in local capital markets will help stem the flow of capital flight, if that is a serious problem.

3.   FOREIGN INVESTMENT IN EMERGING CAPITAL MARKETS

With regard to foreign sources of financing, several options are open to most developing countries. Careful choices need to be exercised in deciding

---

[55] *Ibid.*, p. 71, n. 2. See also L. Cao, 'The Cat that Catches Mice: China's Challenge to the Dominant Privatization Model', (1995) 21 *Brooklyn J. Int'l L.* 97.
[56] World Bank, *supra* n. 4, p. 62.

which strategic approach best suits a country's needs. Foreign sources of financing include: official development assistance, in the form of loans and grants from multilateral or regional development banks and bilateral donors and private capital flows.

Private capital flows can, of course, be sourced from foreign commercial banks willing to lend to the developing country, as discussed earlier. Commercial lending is essentially 'untied' foreign exchange that may be used for any capital need that the sovereign borrower sees fit to apply it to. (In contrast, ODA is concessional financing which is 'conditioned' on the recipient country meeting certain benchmarks or other agreed-to reforms.) If, however, commercial financing is used to support capital import needs to update technology and equipment, it may be quite useful in the short-term.

Nevertheless, there are some inherent dangers which make commercial bank financing somewhat problematic. First, there are few means available to the sovereign borrower to protect itself against exchange rate and interest rate fluctuations. The risks of these fluctuations are not assumed by the commercial bank lenders, but by the sovereign borrower.

Secondly, interest and exchange rates may move upwards (or downwards), depending on external global economic movements outside of the country's control, or on macro-economic conditions within the country which may take time to resolve. Loan repayment amounts may fluctuate in accordance with exchange or interest rate movements, becoming quite volatile over time. Thus, while commercial bank financing is an attractive means of obtaining external financing, it should be used selectively by developing countries, to avoid heavy reliance on it and risking the pitfalls of the past.

Other sources of private capital flows include FDI—a time-honoured technique for recapitalizing enterprises—and seeking out new partners, technologies and markets. Additionally, international bond and equity markets are now becoming attractive financing options. Foreign portfolio investment is a surprising newcomer to the scene, but the volatility of capital flows (and outflows) necessitates a degree of stability and absorptive capacity in the developing country before FPI financing should be attempted. These options for structuring developing country capital markets are explored below.

3.1   Foreign direct investment

FDI is foreign equity investment in an enterprise (or project) which is either directly owned by a foreign entity, or owned jointly by a foreign investor and local entrepreneurs.[57] Unlike commercial bank loans, however, the foreign investor shares the risks of the enterprise—one of the chief advantages to FDI, from the recipient country's perspective—and is entitled to a percentage of the profit generated by the commercial enterprise.[58]

FDI, as mentioned earlier, is also a means for the host country to acquire more advanced technologies, updated equipment and capital goods, and

---

[57] *Ibid.*, pp. 24–25.
[58] *Ibid.*

access to new international markets. Management and employee skills may also be upgraded through additional training and working with export markets. FDI may also provide additional working capital and liquidity for the enterprise. Since no benefits inure to the foreign investor until the venture yields profits, the investment tends to be long-term in nature and less volatile in comparison to portfolio investment.[59]

The primary disadvantages of FDI are decreased management control, and the ownership of local enterprises by foreign interests. The potential 'recolonization' effect of FDI is a political factor which may have to be dealt with by the developing country in question. If the foreign partner eventually sells the enterprise to local investors, the profit-producing initial investment can be regarded as being catalytic in nature. Nonetheless, the eventual repatriation of profits by the foreign investor may deplete the developing country of its foreign exchange earnings.

There has been a tremendous boom in FDI in East Asia, capturing 54 per cent of all FDI in 1994, with China being the largest recipient.[60] Latin America followed, capturing 25 per cent in FDI flows, with Eastern Europe and Central Asia garnering 10 per cent.[61] The Middle East and North Africa registered 5 per cent of net FDI private capital flows, with sub-Saharan Africa capturing 4 per cent, and South Asia obtaining 2 per cent of global FDI invested in 1994.[62]

Apart from attracting the most FDI as a region, East Asia is notable in another regard. Much of the FDI comes from intra-regional countries, including Japan and China.[63] An important legal development in many East Asian countries has been the clear definition of property rights allowing foreigners to own local assets as well as equity in a broad range of companies.[64] In fact, many of these newly industrializing economies, including Korea, Malaysia and Taiwan, offer incentives to foreign investors such as guaranteeing repatriation of profits, and tax relief measures.

It may be wiser, however, to focus on leveling the playing field by eliminating all distortions and preferential treatment of foreign investors.[65] Eliminating trade barriers is clearly a painful, but necessary, process. The experience of developing countries over the last 50 years has demonstrated that international trade protectionism is a self-defeating policy in the long-run. Economic isolationism and internal market distortions have led to bitter IMF prescriptions and painful market corrections.

China is beginning to discover how politically difficult it is to eliminate trade barriers. Indeed, China's membership in the World Trade Organization, which the Clinton Administration hoped to have secured by October 1997, is still pending. In order to be admitted to the WTO, members must agree to

---

[59] *Ibid.*, p. 82.
[60] *Ibid.*, pp. 27, 28.
[61] *Ibid.*, p. 27.
[62] *Ibid.*, p. 27.
[63] *Ibid.*, p. 29.
[64] *Ibid.*, p. 28.
[65] *Ibid.*, pp. 32, 31.

produce exports which are free of government subsidies, and to permit imports to compete against local goods on commercially viable terms.[66] In order to comply, China needs to eliminate tariffs, quotas, subsidies and other trade barriers, potentially creating a serious unemployment problem until the transition can be completed. Clearly, China's adoption of internationally imposed norms will take longer than expected.

Just as creating a level playing field is important internationally, it is equally important nationally. As the discussion in Chapter 4 on privatization pointed out, creating a level playing field among ethnic minorities or disadvantaged segments of the population (who may actually be in the majority, as in Malaysia), may need to be an important government priority. It seems paradoxical perhaps to liberate market forces on an international scale, but to selectively favour certain groups on the national level. This contradiction can be rationalized by arguing that market-based policies should not have the effect of marginalizing certain segments of the population. Economic disempowerment will, no doubt, later translate into political disenfranchisement. This will, in time, lead to political unrest.

Schisms in the social fabric are a predictable consequence of unrestrained market forces, and this may lead to political instability, or worse. Thus, the inequities created by capitalist market forces need to be mitigated in order to ensure equity and equitable opportunities within a developing society. Internal reforms should be considered in order to avoid deepening any gaps between certain segments of the population. Otherwise, certain social and cultural strata may be lost in the process, and in the new millennium, no one should be regarded as dispensable.

3.2   Financing private infrastructure projects

An important and growing area for private foreign investment in developing countries is cross-border financing of capital infrastructure projects. Such projects are being actively pursued in various sectors such as telecommunications, transportation and roadways, seaports, airports, water and sewage treatment, and power (e.g., hydroelectric, gas, coal-fired). Capital infrastructure involves the arteries of commerce, providing vital linkages both intra-country and internationally in the manufacture, distribution and sale of goods.

The need for such capital infrastructure development and improvement is clear—the antiquated and decaying roads, communication networks, and power generation facilities in many developing countries are completely inadequate to support their current population needs. In most cases, the lack of adequate infrastructure is a key impediment, slowing the development process and inhibiting economic growth. For example, in 1991, daily black-outs lasting 6–10 hours in the Philippines cost an average of $1 billion in lost economic output. Largely due to the commitment of President Ramos' Administration, these black-outs were virtually eliminated by 1995.[67]

---

[66] 'China's Resistance to Fair Trade', *New York Times*, 5 August 1997, p. A24.
[67] IFC, *Financing Private Infrastructure: Lessons of Experience* (1996), p. 1.

There is clear evidence that more countries, more sectors (and subsectors), private actors, and more varied sources of financing are involved in the complex, evolving picture of private infrastructure growth. The International Finance Corporation, a member of the World Bank Group, reported that the estimated private financing of new projects nearly doubled from 1993 to 1995, increasing from $17 billion to over $35 billion.[68]

The number of countries involved in this significant trend is, however, limited. In 1993, nine countries, namely, Argentina, Colombia, Hungary, India, Malaysia, Mexico, Pakistan, the Philippines and Thailand, accounted for 99 per cent of international private infrastructure loans.[69] By 1995, these nine countries, along with Indonesia and Turkey, accounted for 97 per cent of all such loans.[70] Thus, international private interest in infrastructure development is limited in scope to countries which are considered to be emerging capital markets.

In fact, the IFC has categorized three strata of countries, based on its experience in this area: (1) a group of 10–15 countries including Argentina, Chile, Hungary, Malaysia, Pakistan and the Philippines where the political will for creating an institutional framework for privatized infrastructure is attractive to foreign financiers; (2) some 20–25 developing countries including India, Indonesia, Turkey and Latvia which need further political commitment to making regulatory changes in order to sustain systemic reform in infrastructure sectors; and (3) developing countries which must first muster the political commitment to begin tackling issues related to policy and regulatory change, and increasing their financial creditworthiness.[71]

Private participation in infrastructure and introducing competition in infrastructure sectors such as transportation, telecommunications and power means implicitly that some form of privatization is contemplated. Many developing countries, as discussed in Chapter 4, followed policies of nationalization, resulting in infrastructure sectors that are wholly government controlled and owned.

Once again, the first and most critical component to any discussion on a proposed private participation in infrastructure is a clear, serious political commitment by the government to institute the necessary legal, regulatory and institutional changes. This translates into a complex agenda of competing needs and priorities relating to increasing the creditworthiness of the infrastructure sector or industry being opened up to private participation and financing; attracting foreign investors (as co-sponsors); establishing new regulatory frameworks including new rules relating to more transparent and open competitive international bidding; government liberalization of the tariff; tax and regulatory structures in place; addressing labour issues, and developing capital markets, thus encouraging private ownership of such enterprises. The complexity and diversity of these needs is immediately apparent.

---

[68] *Ibid.*, p. 2.
[69] *Ibid.*
[70] *Ibid.*
[71] *Ibid.*, pp. 10–11.

The government of a developing nation which is considering this type of agenda has many options in developing a coherent approach to its infrastructure needs. For example, it may wish to pursue leasing or management contract options in a specific enterprise in order to make it more profitable; or the government may need to effectively restructure the enterprise by breaking it up into component units. Some units of an SOE may be more profitable than others, and more suitable for immediate privatization.

Longer-term planning and restructuring (or liquidation) may be necessary for less-profitable components of an integrated enterprise. (For example, it may be wise to disaggregate or unbundle an enterprise such as a seaport, perhaps by separating stevedoring from other functions, or for telecommunications, by separating long distance from local service, and local service into urban and rural markets.) Further, divestiture of the government interest in a national enterprise may take place through 'build-own-operate' or 'build-own-transfer' approaches, whereby operation (or ultimately, the ownership of an enterprise) is shifted to private hands.[72]

The IFC has discovered that attracting private financing in support of capital infrastructure ventures is more dependent on 'risk perceptions' than on actual income levels of the subject country.[73] Since project finance is very complex and involves long-term commitments from the government and the project sponsors, the political and economic risks associated with the developing country are important factors in determining whether private cross-border financing can be successfully attracted.

Ironically, perhaps, developing countries with higher risk factors tend to have more foreign financing—in part, since their domestic capital markets tend to be underdeveloped.[74] Besides commercial bank financing, domestic capital markets along with new sources of financing such as insurance companies, local pension funds, official lending institutions and export credit agencies have created a dynamic picture. Nevertheless, mobilizing finance, especially from commercial sources, remains difficult for most developing countries. Only 50 or so international commercial banks are active in project finance in developing countries, and they tend to be cautious lenders.[75] Equity investors in such projects normally expect returns of 15–20 per cent on their limited recourse investment.[76]

Financing is more easily mobilized if the host country has a clear legal framework with transparent procurement and bidding rules and concession contracts which provide adequate security packages for the lenders.[77] Additionally, international arbitration clauses providing for the arbitration of disputes at the International Chamber of Commerce or the International Centre of Investment Disputes may prove important.

---

[72] R. Sarkar, 'The Role of Bilateral Financing Supporting Capital Infrastructure Development', in D. Campbell (ed.), *The Globalization of Capital Markets* (Kluwer Law, 1996).

[73] IFC, *supra* n. 67, p. 21.

[74] *Ibid.*, p. 56.

[75] *Ibid.*, p. 58.

[76] *Ibid.*

[77] *Ibid.*, p. 50. Such security packages often consist of a mortgage over the project's real property or fixed assets, share pledges by the sponsor, and share retention agreements. *Ibid.*

Other means of enforcing contract provisions may also be an important negotiating point.

Other issues which may become important before financial closure can be reached are foreign exchange convertibility questions, repatriation of profits and the setting up of offshore escrow accounts, eliminating subsidized tariffs, and issuing adequate guarantees for the actual contractual performance of state-owned utilities.[78] Financial closure (i.e., when the sponsors, host government and the financiers reach an agreement in principle on the financial and corporate structure of the project finance undertaking), is a critical juncture in the process. Often closure is impeded by inadequate policy, contractual, and asset security protection for outside lenders. Yet the participation of such private financiers is key if important capital infrastructure sectors are to be adequately developed in emerging capital markets.

3.3 International bond and equity markets

A recent World Bank study concluded that most developing countries tend to prefer debt over equity financing, despite fairly limited corporate bond markets in those countries.[79] The cost of international debt financing may be cheaper in the short-term, and international debt markets may offer lower interest rates and longer maturities than those available domestically in emerging markets.[80] (Korea, Thailand, and China are currently the largest East Asian issuers of bonds.)[81] Issuing equity is often disfavoured, as there are strong disincentives to floating corporate stock in international markets. Strict disclosure requirements under securities laws applicable both locally and abroad, for example, often deter family-owned businesses from entering international equity markets to raise capital.

International bond instruments include Eurobonds and Yankee bonds. Eurobonds are generally unregistered securities which are underwritten by an international syndicate.[82] Yankee bonds are US dollar-denominated bonds issued by foreign underwriters, and traded in the foreign bond market in the United States.[83] Another option is to use Euroconvertible bonds, which are debentures that can be converted into equity if certain preconditions are met.

Raising equity on international capital markets is an option which is becoming increasingly attractive to developing country companies. Developing country firms seeking to raise equity for their companies are now beginning to look beyond local securities exchanges, and are seeking

---

[78] *Ibid.*, p. 51.
[79] J. Glen and B. Pinto, *Debt or Equity? How Firms in Developing Countries Choose*, International Finance Corporation, Discussion Paper No. 22 (1994), p. 27.
[80] *Ibid.*, p. 24.
[81] World Bank, *supra* n. 4, pp. 37–38.
[82] *Ibid.*, p. 37.
[83] *Ibid.* Likewise, yen-denominated bonds are referred to as Samurai bonds; UK bonds as Bulldog bonds; Netherlands as Rembrandt bonds; Spain as Matador bonds; and (former) Hong Kong and Singapore bonds as Dragon bonds.

international buyers of their equity shares. By floating equity instruments in foreign capital markets, these developing country firms gain a much wider access to international investors who may be interested in diversifying their risk. Certain emerging market economies (particularly in East Asia) have strong, highly profitable local companies which are capable of directly raising equity funds in international capital markets.

Several different types of equity instruments are available for purposes of raising equity. American Depository Receipts (ADRs) are US-dollar denominated, registered securities representing ownership interests in shares of LDC companies being held in trust by a depository institution.[84] The depository institution is usually a bank which actually issues the ADRs which are publicly traded on the New York Stock Exchange, NASDAQ and AMEX.[85] Global depository receipts (GDRs) are similar to ADRs, but may be placed in non-US as well as US capital markets in several hard currencies.

Both ADRs and GDRs are publicly-traded securities which must be registered with the US Securities and Exchange Commission (SEC). The SEC requires issuers to meet strict guidelines on publicly disclosing financial and corporate information on a periodic basis. Although both types of depository receipts are subject to US securities laws, GDRs traded in the United States are subject to rule 144A of the US Securities and Exchange Act of 1933, and may only be purchased by qualified institutional investors.[86]

Additionally, depository receipts listed on a stock exchange must meet all applicable listing requirements. Since many developing country firms are closely held corporations or family businesses not wishing to disclose financial and other information publicly, such firms often opt for over-the-counter (OTC) trading of their securities, rather than listing their securities on major securities exchanges. OTC trading may be regarded as the first step towards full international securities trading.[87] In sum, developing country firms are increasingly able to list their securities in US and other foreign stock exchanges through registered, depository receipts.

3.4   Foreign portfolio investment

Whereas FDI tends to indicate foreign investor support for the entry of developing countries into international markets for exportable, consumer-oriented goods, FPI often is seen as an indication that emerging capital markets have matured and come of age. FPI is often the last stage in a developing country's final integration into global finance markets.

---

[84] J. Glen and B. Pinto, *supra* n. 79, p. 20.
[85] World Bank, *supra* n. 4, p. 37.
[86] *Ibid*.
[87] J. Glen and B. Pinto, *supra* n. 79, p. 21.

FPI can take many forms. Foreign portfolio investors (generally institutional investors in Europe and North America) may purchase public or private corporate bonds (i.e., debt instruments) from developing countries. Alternatively, FPI investors may buy equities (i.e., stock) of private corporations, usually pooled together and held by mutual funds or country funds, and traded in secondary (stock) markets.

FPI (particularly if based on secondary market trading of already-issued shares) may not actually increase the amount of equity invested in the particular stock being traded.[88] Further, FPI may not add to the foreign exchange reserves of a developing country in the way that FDI provides immediate hard currency recapitalization or investment.[89]

Moreover, FPI investors tend to be quite skittish and very concerned with the income stream generated by their investments. Although foreign portfolio investors, if purchasing equity stakes, do assume some of the risk of such investments, they tend to be very concerned about the security of such investments. FPI, therefore, can be volatile, since portfolio investors 'tend to vote with their feet',[90] and capital outflows can lead to unstable market conditions in non-performing countries.[91]

The Mexican fiscal crisis of 1994–94, discussed earlier, contains certain illustrative points that can be made in an FPI context. In the first instance, Mexico's high interest rates were an attraction to short-term capital from abroad. However, the use of foreign exchange inflows to finance consumer (rather than capital) goods proved short-sighted. When the peso was devalued, investors immediately responded by exchanging their peso holdings to US dollar investments, thereby depleting Mexico's foreign exchange reserves.

The subsequent flotation of the peso, on 22 December 1994, saw the peso go into freefall. This eroded not only domestic investor confidence, but also international investor confidence in the stability of Mexican securities. Moreover, issuing short-term bond instruments (*tesobonos*) that were pegged to the US dollar was a very risky exercise. As foreign investor confidence eroded, *tesobonos* were not rolled over but were cashed in, further depleting Mexico's foreign exchange reserves, and deepening Mexico's fiscal crisis.

Nevertheless, FPI to Mexico from 1990–94 amounted to 47 per cent of global FPI for that period, far outstripping China's FPI at 8.7 per cent.[92] The reversals of these capital inflows during the Mexican fiscal crisis

---

[88] World Bank, *supra* n. 4, p. 35.
[89] *Ibid.*
[90] *Ibid.*, p. 90; see also G. Pohl, *et al.*, *supra* n. 33, p. 17.
[91] Economic Development Institute of the World Bank, *supra* n. 46, pp. 6-8–6-9. The authors suggest that as much financial information as possible be made available to foreign investors through financial intermediaries in order to prevent investor panic. *Ibid.*
[92] World Bank, *supra* n. 4, p. 61.

demonstrates how volatile FPI can be. International perceptions of a developing country's broad financial and political health can quickly influence foreign investor behaviour.

In part, the attractiveness of emerging capital markets is based on the perceived stability of its macro-economic and overall political conditions. FPI outflows (and even inflows) can wreak havoc on countries with vulnerable or unstable macro-economic or political conditions. In the end, emerging capital markets may face market-based (rather than IMF-dictated) conditionality, both punishing and rewarding a developing economy for its economic policies and political behaviour.[93]

Although encouraging FPI is a far easier means of rasing foreign-based capital than seeking out foreign partners in FDI-type of arrangements,[94] there are inherent dangers in portfolio investments. These risks should be carefully assessed before the more sophisticated FPI financial instruments and markets are sought out. In particular, the developing country should ensure that it has achieved a sufficient degree of depth and liquidity in its capital markets. This market depth is necessary in order to absorb the shocks of both inflows and outflows of capital investment.

Finally, as a cautionary note, developing countries should not be side-tracked from encouraging domestic savings mobilization, and the development of indigenous institutional investors, while pursuing FPI investors. If utilized successfully, however, FPI can be the last step in a 'coming of age' in terms of the sophistication, depth, and global integration of developing country capital markets.

Structuring capital markets is a time-consuming and difficult process. It requires the creative use of a menu of financing options which should be carefully tailored to meet the country's needs and capabilities. Each financing option has specific advantages and disadvantages, and the appropriate context for their use needs to be carefully gauged before any given option is hastily pursued.

Although the flexible use of financing options is critical to capital market development, it will not be successful in the final analysis unless macro-economic conditions are reformed in support of capital market growth. Institution-building (e.g., forming credit unions, pension funds, investment funds) is critical in order to mobilize domestic savings. It is clear that the government needs to take an active role in creating an enabling environment in which these new institutions may thrive. Equally importantly, the government needs to establish a legal and regulatory framework so that new financing, policy and institutional changes can be sustained.

---

[93] *Ibid.*, p. 90.
[94] *Ibid.*, p. 35.

4. A LEGAL AND REGULATORY FRAMEWORK FOR EMERGING CAPITAL MARKETS

The withdrawal of the government from the productive sectors of the economy through privatization or other measures does not mean that the government no longer has a role to play in these sectors. Productive sectors of the economy naturally include agriculture, heavy industry, transportation, power generation, telecommunications and many others. By delegating responsibility for the primary production, distribution, and export of goods and services to the private sector, the government may refocus its attention on other issues. Government officials may then consider devoting its budgetary and human resources to these other priorities.

In the financial sector, the state can focus on regulating markets, enforcing legal and regulatory regimes, and creating and reinforcing important institutions. The discussion below will focus on reforms of the financial sector, a critical component of the productive economy of any developing nation. As discussed earlier, the financial sector performs a vital function by intermediating between savings mobilization and extending credit for economic development. Without effective intermediation between the two needs, capital will not circulate effectively, and this will ultimately inhibit broad-based economic growth and investment.

In terms of creating a successful legal and regulatory framework for emerging capital markets, developing countries need to consider establishing the following:

(1) a clear, well-defined legal structure of laws governing share owner-ship and transfer, rules on foreign investment and ownership, protection of minority shareholder interests, prohibiting insider trading and addressing other transparency issues, and disclosure and reporting requirements;[95]

(2) laws and regulations setting forth appropriate enforcement mechan-isms for violations of any of the above areas, and legal institutions to enforce (or mediate) such rights;[96]

---

[95] An appropriate legal infrastructure would also include the following areas of law: company law (defining limited liability, shareholder rights and corporate governance); banking law (facilitating the prompt settlement of banking transactions); commercial code (defining the rights and obligations of parties in contractually based transactions); contract law (enforcing the rights and obligations of parties to a contract); secured transactions (defining the rights to collateral); tax law (providing for transparent and equitable taxation); bankruptcy law (addressing the rights of creditors and collateral-holders) and competition law (prohibiting anti-competitive and collusive business practices). See generally R. Strahota, 'Securities Regulation in Emerging Markets: Issues and Suggested Answers' (Securities Exchange Commission, 1997), unpublished memorandum on file with author. See also Economic Development Institute of the World Bank, *supra* n. 46, pp. 2–11, 3-9, 3–10.

[96] The goal of a regulatory regime should be to create transparent and orderly markets where the settlement of securities transactions takes place promptly and accurately. Additionally, securities market regulation needs to provide for the full and fair disclosure of market information to investors in order to avoid fraudulent and deceptive conduct. See R. Strahota, *supra* n. 95, pp. 2–3.

(3) an effective market infrastructure for completing market transactions through computerized trades, clearing and settling accounts and balances,[97] auditing and accounting corporate balance sheets which meet international standards, and clear reporting and disclosure mechanisms;[98]

(4) appropriate tax and other incentives to mobilize capital resources and provide adequate incentives to invest.[99]

This is a complex and highly interrelated undertaking where the laws, regulations, and institutions must smoothly intersect in mutual support of one another. Conflicting rules and procedures will only confuse investors and erode their confidence and, '[a]t the end of the day, a capital market is only as good as it is perceived by its investors'.[100]

Financial regulation by the government (e.g., an independent government agency or body) is extremely important in order to ensure investor confidence in the financial markets of the developing country. Otherwise, the risk of capital flight, strengthening informal financial markets, and interventions by organized crime, is all too great. In addition, the likelihood of attracting FDI or FPI decreases accordingly.

Principles of contract law, property law, and secured transactions (relating to collateralization, for example) may need to be reformulated in order to support a modern market economy. If this legal infrastructure is outmoded based on 'received' legal traditions dating back to the developing country's colonial experience, or if it does not exist in the first instance as in many transitional economies, a certain amount of legal restructuring needs to be done.

A functional company (or corporate) law code which defines basic corporate structures, the fiduciary duties and liabilities of office bearers, the ways in which various classes of stock may be issued, and the means of effecting mergers and joint ventures, is of critical importance in this context. It is also important for corporate laws to address shareholder voting rights, disclosure, auditing and reporting requirements as well as other relevant corporate governance issues. Corporate tax treatment, too, needs to be rationalized and clarified.

Bankruptcy laws, regulations and courts may also need to be established to permit the dissolution of non-performing firms and the orderly distribution of assets to their creditors. Debt work-outs and other related issues

---

[97] Clearing is the process by which the number, identity, and price of the shares, the date of the transaction, and the identity of the buyer and seller, are verified. Settlement refers to transferring payment to the seller, and legal ownership to the buyer. See G. Pohl, *et al.*, *supra* n. 33, p. 14. See generally Economic Development Institute of the World Bank, *supra* n. 46, pp. 4-24–4-34.

[98] For example, what should the reporting requirement be, how much information should be disclosed and on what periodic basis? Whom should this information be made available to for review, comment and regulation?

[99] World Bank, *supra* n. 4, p. 99. See also Economic Development Institute of the World Bank, *supra* n. 46, pp. 7–8 (Mauritius case study).

[100] G. Pohl, *et al.*, *supra* n. 33, p. 6.

may also be important, particularly if privatization is being contemplated as an intermediate step in an economic reform programme. Thus, it is important to have a coherent and consistent legal framework for establishing efficient corporations, issuing equity (and protecting shareholder rights), and dissolving troubled firms.

The government needs to determine the scope of its authority to regulate financial markets.[101] In other words, it needs to decide whether it will regulate stock exchange transactions, broker-dealer transactions effected through licensed financial intermediaries, over-the-counter transactions, public offerings as well as private placements of equity, government commercial paper, and other investment vehicles. These are all important decisions to make in setting up a regulatory scheme. Registration, disclosure, and licensing requirements are important considerations which will affect the enforcement mechanisms imposed for violations. For example, are civil penalties or fines sufficient, or do criminal sanctions for securities fraud also need to be considered? What should be the responsibilities and liabilities of corporate directors and officers?

Apart from deciding which types of activities are to be regulated, the government also needs to decide how much regulation it will undertake itself and how much it will delegate to self-regulatory organizations (SROs).[102] SROs may include private sector organizations such as stock exchanges, associations of broker-dealers, clearing agencies (such as a depository or clearing house), an association of investment companies or advisors.

The self-regulatory roles which SROs should assume in terms of licensing brokers, regulating and disciplining the conduct of its members, and the confidence which the public and the government chooses to place in such SROs are important factors to consider before setting up a regulatory framework. Thus, the government, in partnership with new financial intermediaries, must carefully define the government's responsibilities and priorities, to ensure market transparency and efficiency, and provide a reliable regime for enforcing investors' rights. In fact, much of the legal groundwork may need to be in place before capital market development can proceed.

4.1 Prudential regulation of emerging capital markets

Apart from making the legal infrastructure coherent and user-friendly, so to speak, developing country policy-makers must also make critical decisions on how to set up the capital market infrastructure. Section 2, above, discussed different components of structuring a capital market

---

[101] Capital market efficiency can suffer from too much regulation as well as from too little. See Economic Development Institute of the World Bank, *supra* n. 46, pp. 3–6.

[102] For example, the government may wish to delegate its authority, in part, to SROs in order to share the costs of regulation, and take advantage of SRO expertise in the area. *Ibid.*, pp. 3–7.

(e.g., commercial bank loans, FDI, bond and equity issues, and FPI). An even more basic question that developing countries must face is precisely how to structure their financial system.

Western states offer two models which may be of use in this context. First, the German-Japanese model is a bank-based system where banks (both private and government-controlled) both lend to and own large productive enterprises. Corporate decision-making (e.g., financing entrepreneurial undertakings, making loans, acquiring other subsidiaries) is done by banks who are both owners of and lenders to the firms involved. Thus, bankers are in a position to make critical financing decisions for, and may exercise a high degree of managerial control over, the enterprises which are owned by the banks.

This so-called 'control-oriented'[103] model of finance is closer in structure to many command economy systems of finance. Disclosure rules may be relaxed since the decision-makers are 'in-house', as opposed to public shareholders. Moreover, a bank-based financial system does not require a large supportive industry comprised of market-makers, brokers, organized stock exchanges, lawyers and financial consultants.[104] These related industries are critical to the smooth operation of the financial sector in the Anglo-American system of finance, discussed below.

An obvious drawback to the 'control-oriented' finance model is the potential conflict of interests involved in lending to an enterprise which is owned by the bank extending the loan. This creates problems related to 'circular ownership' or, in other words, where the banks own the enterprises who own the banks. As a result of the firms being so closely held, the banks may be reluctant to write-off loans, force the enterprise to restructure itself by selling subsidiaries, or to force the company to liquidate assets to pay its creditors.

The financial health of the enterprise may directly affect the bank's own portfolio, and its annual earnings on that portfolio. This is a problem, for example, that is faced by prominent Czech banks, discussed in Chapter 3, which own the seven largest investment funds in the country. (The Czech Republic may be second only to Japan in the prominence of its core investors.)[105] Thus, in a 'control-oriented' system, there may be considerable reluctance to force an enterprise to make changes along market-driven principles.

An additional problem arises when banks also act as investment advisors to the enterprises that they lend to. This may lead to a potential conflict of interest problem if the bank is advising companies on whether to issue securities. Undue influence may be exercised by banks on deciding how to structure the company's equity or debt financing.[106] The end result may not necessarily be in the company's best interest.

---

[103] G. Pohl, *et al.*, *supra* n. 33, p. 7.
[104] *Ibid.*
[105] *Ibid.*
[106] Economic Development Institute of the World Bank, *supra* n. 46, pp. 1–9.

Thus, the conflicts of interest described above may deter banks in a control-oriented financial system from making unpopular, but necessary, financial decisions.

Another serious concern with bank-based financial systems is that the banks who own controlling shares in certain enterprises can use their influence, in effect, to create monopolies.[107] In other words, if a bank owns a substantial number of enterprises within a certain industry, the bank could encourage collusive, predatory and anti-competitive practices. If, for example, the bank encourages the firms which it owns to engage in collusive price-setting at lower than market prices, these firms could force other firms out of the industry, and then later raise their prices. If these firms successfully establish an oligopolistic stance in the industry, they have effectively eliminated their competition.

Thus, the concentrated power of banks in a bank-based system can be subject to criticism, and can be further compounded if the banks are self-regulated. Although the government may exercise some oversight over the activities of banks and other financial institutions, this oversight may be limited. The finance industry in bank-based systems is generally expected to be fairly self-regulating. Professional associations are expected to assume responsibility for certifying professionals in the industry and maintaining a code of ethics. However, a lack of close government (or independent) scrutiny may lead to anti-competitive business practices in the banking industry, such as limiting the number of new market entrants, and creating banking cartels.[108]

Indeed, there are warning signs that all may not be well with the control-oriented banking system. The Hokkaido Takushoku Bank, one of Japan's 20 largest banks, collapsed on 18 November 1997, under the weight of its bad loans.[109] This bank failure was the first indication of the Japanese government's reluctant willingness to let market forces reshape Japan's financial landscape. The remaining assets of the Hokkaido Takushoku Bank were transferred to the North Pacific Bank in an orderly merger where a failing bank was rolled into a stronger one.[110] This recent bank failure followed closely on the heels of the closure of Nissan Life Insurance Company and Sanyo Securities.[111] Yamaichi Securities Company, the fourth largest brokerage firm in Japan, also went out of business on 24 November 1997, after 100 years of business.[112] Thus, certain market-driven changes are beginning to take place in the control-oriented banking system.

---

[107] G. Pohl, *et al.*, *supra* n. 33, pp. 22, 23.
[108] *Ibid.*, pp. 22–23.
[109] S. Strom, 'Bailing Out of the Bailout Game: Tokyo Does the Unthinkable and Lets a Big Bank Fail', *New York Times*, 18 November 1997, p. D1.
[110] *Ibid.*
[111] *Ibid.*
[112] S. Strom, 'Large Japanese Securities Firm Collapses', *New York Times*, 24 November 1997.

An alternative Western model is provided by the Anglo-American 'market-based' system.[113] Whereas in the United Kingdom there is a large degree of reliance on market discipline based on unwritten but well-understood rules of self-regulation, with minimal legislation in place, the United States' system is heavily legislated, regulated and litigated.[114] Moreover, a market-based system is heavily dependent on a fairly sophisticated and large securities industry, stock exchanges, retail brokerage houses, credit-rating agencies for bonds, and other related institutions and professionals. Additionally, in the United States, the securities market relies heavily on enforcement by individual creditors or investors. This means that the judiciary are required to have sufficient expertise in adjudicating these types of fairly sophisticated legal issues.

Furthermore, the Glass-Steagall Act[115] prohibits US banks from owning non-financial companies (such as telecommunications firms or heavy industries). The Glass-Steagall Act also prevents US banks from underwriting securities and offering brokerage services to the public to trade securities. Thus, US commercial and investment banks have separate functions, and are prohibited from owning industries or non-financial firms. Moreover, insurance companies and mutual funds are also limited in the amount of equity that they may purchase from private corporations, and are restricted in the voting rights they are entitled to.[116]

Although the conflict of interest issues described under a bank-based system are not strictly relevant in a market-based system, other problems are apparent. For example, the Anglo-American reliance on market discipline often means that institutional investors (e.g., insurance companies, mutual and pension funds) exercise limited corporate governance and 'tend to vote with their feet'. Thus, the displeasure of institutional investors is expressed by selling their shares in the offending corporation.

Yet market-based corrections are often difficult to make, and regaining investor confidence is a time-consuming task. Therefore, in certain instances, it may be argued that a bank-based system which allows private negotiations and work-outs is more conducive to rehabilitating floundering enterprises. Selling shares may be the harshest form of communication between investors and the corporate officers of a faltering firm.

Ideally, a developing country should utilize components of both bank-based and market-based financial systems in accordance with its priorities. The structure and liquidity of its existing capital market, and its prior institutional and legal history, should also be taken into account. With regard to the prudential regulation of financial markets, developing countries (particularly transitional economies emerging from command economy regimes) may find it easier, institutionally speaking, to begin with a bank-based system. Corporate and financial

---

[113] *Ibid.*, p. 6.
[114] *Ibid.*, p. 21.
[115] Glass-Steagall Act of 1933, Pub. L. 86-230, §23, 73 Stat. 466, 12 U.S.C. §378 (1997).
[116] See G. Pohl, *et al.*, *supra* n. 33, p. 6.

decisions can be made quickly on the basis of insider (rather than public) information. Moreover, it may be more practical for Eastern European countries to begin with the EU directives on securities market regulation in order to better integrate their capital markets with Western European practices.

While local enterprises are being restructured and made more profitable, the government of a developing country should consider adopting policies which encourage capital market growth. Once the capital market matures (especially with the participation of local institutional investors), the prudential regulation of local capital markets may change over time. In other words, once the capital market expands and becomes more liquid, the developing country can begin moving towards greater reliance on market discipline and self-regulation.

Reliance on market-based discipline means that government oversight can be minimized, and the private parties left to enforce their respective rights through civil litigation or other means. In the United States, the rights and protections accorded shareholders (including minority shareholders) are heavily legislated and litigated, whereas in the United Kingdom, more reliance is placed on the observance of informal rules.

4.2 Legal regulation of capital markets in perspective

Regardless of the degree of self-regulation adopted by the developing country, certain rules governing market behaviour need to be clearly understood by the market participants. Thus, initially, it may be wiser and safer to legislate a substantive securities statute along with a foreign investment code until the desired market behaviour is elicited. Once a certain comfort level is achieved, the government may consider permitting limited self-regulation without the fear of its overt abuse.

Substantive legal codes can be very important for developing countries since new legal norms may have to be created (or clearly articulated for the first time) in the process. Apart from substantive securities laws, the other area of law most directly affecting capital market growth is the foreign investment regime. Foreign investment laws are important not only for foreign investors, but for the developing country itself. A country's foreign investment regime defines (or redefines) the parameters of acceptable foreign intervention in the economy.

Market liberalization must be grounded on a transparent legal structure which clearly defines foreign ownership rights, and the means by which to enforce those rights. For example, dismantling trade barriers and permitting foreign competitors to enter emerging markets on commercially viable terms is a major challenge facing many developing countries. Foreign investment laws define the rules of the game, and may speed the integration of the emerging market economy into other market economies of the world.

The process of creating new legal norms in the securities industry can be quite difficult. Experience has shown that the underlying capitalist ethos may be understood very differently in different cultures.[117] It may be a pat assumption to believe that instituting legal principles, codes, standards and practices which conform to international standards is a relatively easy task where business law is concerned. If international business transactions are to be completed with any certainty, then creating a legal framework in support of these transactions seems to be a relatively culture-free task. This seems especially apparent when dealing with issues such as clearing and settlement of securities transactions, where the parties need to know that a transaction has reliably taken place. Computerizing the trade of the securities transaction is the first step in this direction.

Experience now reveals that the expectations underlying these international business transactions differ widely from culture to culture. For instance, a Western observer's expectation that Jordanians should prohibit insider trading in securities markets is grounded on the belief that this eliminates corrupt practices, price distortions and ensures market transparency. The Jordanians may not agree with this viewpoint. A Jordanian may be expected to provide insider information to his or her family and friends to help them enrich themselves, or pay for a son's tuition. To fail to do so may be regarded as a betrayal. Our expectation that Jordan should conform to Western legal norms may, in fact, render judgment on a different cultural norm, which may be for example, prevalent in Jordanian society.

---

[117] The impact of culture on law, even within a financial context, can be felt quite clearly. In a study completed by the IFC, the 'legal determinants of external finance' were explored in terms of the impact that certain legal regimes had on investor behavior. R. La Porta, *et al.*, 'Legal Determinants of External Finance', (1997) 52 *Journal of Finance* 1131. By using a sample of 49 countries, the quality and character of legal rules and regulations as applied to both equity and debt markets were explored. The results were quite remarkable. The authors concluded that the rules differ systematically by legal origin, to wit, English, French, German or Scandinavian. *Ibid.*

The empirical data collected by the authors reveal certain general trends, namely, that legal rules from different cultures differ significantly in content. Further, common law jurisdictions tended to protect shareholders and creditors the most, whereas French civil code countries gave the least protection. Germany and Scandinavian countries fell somewhere in the middle. *Ibid.*, p. 1132. The study also concluded that common law countries provided private companies with better access to equity than French civil law countries, and that adequate law enforcement of financial market-related issues has a 'large effect' on the depth and breadth of debt and equity markets. *Ibid.*, pp. 1137, 1146, respectively.

Thus, the authors conclude that good legal enforcement provides an incentive to invest one's capital, thus potentially increasing the size of capital markets. English common law countries offered the most legal protection and have the biggest capital markets. The French civil law countries, conversely, had the weakest investor protections and the least developed capital markets. The authors rather vaguely conclude that the absence of trust generally in French civil law jurisdictions accounted for the overall poor institutional development, including that of capital markets, but admit that this issue could not be adequately resolved based on their research. *Ibid.*, pp. 1149–1150.

Of course, the research parameters will change considerably when China enters global securities markets in earnest. The influx of equity and debt offerings will, no doubt, be overwhelming, and perhaps the same correlations regarding 'investor-friendly' laws will not be as apparent as they seem now.

The Jordanian example illustrates an important point: law is culture. By this, I do not simply mean that law is an expression of culture, but that law is a cultural norm in itself. Law may have certain immutable characteristics, perhaps most eloquently expressed in human rights law but, for the most part, law is an evolving cultural norm. Therefore, casting legal norms in an absolutist mould tends to further deter the development process. If clear and persuasive communication with actors in the developing world is to be established, then lawyers from more developed societies certainly need to be aware of the cultural component to law. This is often omitted or ignored.

For example, a developing country may wish to emulate the United Kingdom's example of a minimally-legislated, self-regulating securities industry. However, it is important to realize that the English securities industry is one of the oldest in the world. The absorption of British legal norms may not be impossible (as perhaps demonstrated by pre-1997 Hong Kong), but it takes time. Moreover, the appropriate incentives (including cultural incentives) must be present before substantive legal change will occur. The legal norms will change as the cultural context changes.

China has adopted a gradualist approach to capital market development with several well-coordinated components which have sustained fairly stable capital market conditions. The Chinese government set its own internal priorities, rather than attempting the wholesale adoption of external cultural norms. However, when the Chinese government realized that its practices were not conducive to integrating into global financial markets, it changed its policies.

For example, China's accounting and statistical system proved to be a serious hindrance to its integration with other market economies. China's original accounting system tended to confuse potential joint venture partners, discouraged FDI and FPI investment, and prevented Chinese companies from being listed in foreign stock exchanges.[118] Thus, there was a strong incentive for China to adapt its accounting practices to international standards, which it did in July 1993, passing an auditing law which went into effect in September 1994.[119]

Certainly, not all legal changes in terms of standardizing with or conforming to Western practices are necessarily bad or wrong. However, a developing country should give full consideration to the implications of such changes, and whether they really serve the country's broader development objectives. The 'modernization' of law is an intricate and complex domestic political process. By no means should legal modernization be resisted in an unthinking fashion but, on the other hand, conforming to Western standards and practices should not be viewed as a panacea for all development ills. Developing nations (in partnership with the industrialized world, where appropriate) need to reach an understanding about

---

[118] World Bank, *supra* n. 4, p. 101.
[119] *Ibid.*

which of their domestic laws need to be created, modernized or abolished, and why. Indeed, this is where a great deal of the work for the development lawyer lies.

In conclusion, emerging capital markets are assuming great importance both in terms of their size and success. With the decline in commercial lending and ODA assistance, the final development success of any developing country may hinge on its ability to join the new and growing cadre of emerging markets. For those left behind, the development picture is becoming increasingly bleak as we enter the new millennium.

Part III
A Human Right to Development

6.   Is There a Human Right to Development?

As this *fin de siècle* analysis has proceeded, it has become clear that profound shifts have occurred since the collapse of the former Soviet bloc in 1989. As the Second World (i.e., Eastern Europe and the former Soviet Union) merges with the First World through the adoption of radical legal, political, and macro-economic reforms, the three 'worlds' are becoming two. In significant ways, the division between the two reconfigured worlds of the 'haves' and the 'have-nots' continues to widen and deepen. As the millennium approaches, the fault lines between the developed and developing worlds are becoming more apparent.

The clash of ideals is nowhere more apparent than in the arena of human rights. This is the reason for including the public international law aspect of *Development Law*—it is in the area of human rights that the deep political divisions and the wide differences in perspective between the developed and the developing worlds are most clearly revealed. In some ways, this can be seen as a reflection of the different philosophical underpinnings of the two worlds.

The severe political and ideological division during the Cold War era heavily impeded the creation and enforcement of a workable human rights regime. The collapse of the Soviet Union now offers a new opportunity for a fresh dialogue concerning the human right to development, free from the polemical hostilities of the past. However, it has also been argued that the demise of the Second World may actually 'undermine important dimensions of the discourse of international human rights'.[1] In light of the vigour with which the former Soviet bloc is now pursuing integration with the industrialized nations of the West, it seems likely that its traditional support for social and economic rights may be wavering.[2]

As the countries of Eastern Europe and the former Soviet Union 'graduate' to First World status, so their traditional alliance (political and ideological) with the developing world, which previously supported the inclusion of social and economic values in the discourse on human rights, has diminished. The loss of the Second World's support regarding the human rights agenda may mean that important dimensions of the human rights dialogue have lost

---

[1] B. Cossman, 'Reform, Revolution or Retrenchment? International Human Rights in the Post-Cold War Era', (1991) 32 *Harv. Int'l L. J.* 339 at 339.
[2] *Ibid.*, p. 345.

a powerful advocate. This makes the role of the developing world in relation to such issues more difficult and problematic. The political will (and the political need) to attend to these issues also remains open to question.

The challenge of a new dialogue on human rights lies in a redefinition of the legal, economic, social and cultural values of developing countries, and the search for common ground with the developed world. The possible demise of the traditional emphasis on recognizing social and economic rights as 'human' rights by the former Soviet bloc may herald a new and different discourse on the human right to development. Before this potential challenge for the future is addressed, however, let us revisit what has transpired in the past.

1.   HISTORICAL ANTECEDENTS TO THE RIGHT TO DEVELOPMENT

The subject-matter of *Development Law and International Finance* emerged from the overwhelming historical, economic, political and legal changes which followed the conclusion of the Second World War. In the immediate post-war period, colonial regimes were gradually dismantled. It was in that climate that the idea of 'development' first emerged, and the 'development' potential of newly independent, non-Western states began to be examined seriously.

The first serious articulation of a worldwide concern with the subject of human rights, especially in relation to a human right to development, was set forth in the Universal Declaration of Human Rights (UDHR), adopted by the General Assembly of the United Nations on 10 December 1948.[3] The UDHR has now assumed the normative force of law, and is a universally accepted part of customary international law, even though at the time of its passage, in 1948, most of the developing world was still under colonial rule.[4]

Technically, the UDHR is a non-binding declaration concerning the individual's rights against the state. It gives international legal stature to the right to freedom from torture, slavery, and inhuman treatment. The UDHR also purports to give the individual the entitlement to, *inter alia*, equal protection under the law as well as the freedom of opinion, expression, and peaceful assembly.

The UDHR specifically addresses the right to development. Article 22 of the UDHR states that, 'Everyone, as a member of society ... is entitled to

---

[3] UN G.A. Res. 217 A (III), U.N. Doc. A/810, p. 71 (Dec. 10, 1948) (UDHR). Although the UDHR was adopted by a vote of 48 to 0, eight member countries abstained, namely, Byelorussia, Czechoslovakia, Poland, Soviet Union, Ukraine, Yugoslavia, Saudi Arabia and South Africa. See M. wa Mutua, 'The Ideology of Human Rights', (1996) 36 *Va. J. Int'l L.* 589 at 589, n. 1. See also A. Cassesse, 'The General Assembly: Historical Perspective 1945–1989', in P. Alston (ed.), *The United Nations and Human Rights: A Critical Appraisal* (1992), p. 31, n. 22.

[4] M. wa Mutua, *supra* n. 3, pp. 590, n. 1, 605.

realization ... of the economic, social and cultural rights indispensable for his dignity and the free development of his personality.' Further, Article 26(2) states that, 'Education shall be directed to the full development of the human personality and to the strengthening of respect for human rights and fundamental freedoms.'

In addition, Article 29(1) of the UDHR states that, 'Everyone has duties to the community in which alone the free and full development of his personality is possible.' Moreover, Article 28 states unequivocally that, 'Everyone is entitled to a social and international order in which the rights and freedoms set forth in this Declaration can be fully realized.'[5]

A precise definition will probably never be completely agreed to by the various state and non-state actors in the international development scene, but the UDHR makes it clear that 'development' was meant to include more than simply the economics of development. The UDHR, by including the 'development of the human personality' within its provisions, gives the right to development a place under the rubric of human rights law. The terms of the UDHR clearly recognize that man does not live by bread alone.

Not surprisingly, the UDHR reflects the Western bias of the states which formulated its tenets, especially since the majority of the developing world did not participate in the deliberations and debate surrounding the creation of the UDHR in 1948. Moreover, even a cursory review of its provisions reveals that it tends to mirror, in substance as well as in style, the Bill of Rights to the US Constitution.[6] The Western liberal democratic tradition is clearly expressed in the UDHR in the balance between an individual's liberties and rights, and the limited power of the state to deprive an individual of these rights. John Locke's philosophy[7] of ensuring certain freedoms for the individual against the interference and tyranny of the state is clearly articulated in the text and philosophy of the UDHR.

Thomas Hobbes' stark philosophy in which the state ('the Leviathan') is imposed on the individual to create order and prevent anarchy, has been tempered over time. His philosophy (bordering on a kind of panicked hysteria) has evolved into a Western liberal tradition where the individual is still an atomized unit, both alienated from and pitted against the tyrannical and overwhelming force of the state. Hobbes thus viewed the state as a 'necessary evil'.

Locke refined the relationship of the individual to the state. Certain liberties and rights cannot be denied to the individual by the state. In other words, the state is prohibited from interfering with or infringing upon liberties granted to the individual (generally understood, at least by Locke, to be a European, property-owning male). Those liberties ensured the integrity of a person and his property. These basic tenets which are derived

---

[5] See also V. Nanda, 'The Right to Development Under International Law—Challenges Ahead', (1985) 15 *Cal. W. Int'l .L. J.* 431 at 436.

[6] See P. Alston, 'U.S .Ratification of the Covenant on Economic, Social and Cultural Rights: The Need for an Entirely New Strategy', (1990) 84 *Am. J. Int'l L.* 365 at 381.

[7] See generally J. Locke, *Two Treatises of Government* (P. Laslett (ed.), 1988).

from and attributable to the Western liberal tradition, are clearly reflected in the UDHR.[8]

The UDHR is now recognized as the foundation for worldwide consensus on a 'universal' jurisprudence of human rights.'[9] The UDHR has been combined with two other UN Covenants to form the International Bill of Rights.[10] The two subsequent Covenants, both promulgated by the UN General Assembly in 1966, are the International Covenant on Civil and Political Rights (ICCPR)[11] and the International Covenant on Economic, Social and Cultural Rights (ICESCR).[12]

The ICCPR reflects the values and tenets of the Western liberal tradition by restating important prohibitions against government interference with the individual's right to self-expression and the accumulation of private property.[13] The ICESCR, on the other hand, reflects the values and priorities of the so-called Second World, stressing social and economic rights which the state has a positive duty to provide to the individual.

Whereas the ICCPR sets forth the rights and liberties of the individual against the state, the ICESCR delineates the positive duties of the state towards the individual. This difference in approach to human rights was considered to be irreconcilable. In recognition of this, the two Covenants were drafted as separate documents in 1966 in order to permit the ratification of one but not the other by participating states.[14] The two International Covenants thus reflected the ideological rift between the *laissez-faire* economies of the West, and the socialist economies of the former Soviet bloc.[15]

The United States has characterized social and economic rights as 'aspirations' rather than 'rights' and has questioned the legal validity and separate existence of such rights.[16] Even though there is no legal impediment to the

---

[8] See J. Donnelly, 'Human Rights and Western Liberalism', in *Human Rights in Africa: Cross-Cultural Perspectives* (A. An Na'im and F. Deng (eds.), 1990), p. 31.

[9] M. wa Mutua, *supra* n. 3, p. 589, n. 1. See also I. Brownlie, *Basic Documents on Human Rights* (3rd edn., 1992); Sir H. Lauterpacht, *International Law and Human Rights* (1950); Lillich and Newman, *International Human Rights* (1979).

[10] B. Cossman, *supra* n. 1, n. 7; M. wa Mutua, *supra* n. 3, p. 593, n. 10. See also Optional Protocol to the International Covenant on Civil and Political Rights, reprinted in *The International Bill of Rights*, p. 31 (Paul Williams (ed.), 1981), cited in B. Rajagopal, 'Crossing the Rubicon: Synthesizing the Soft International Law of the IMF and Human Rights', (1993) 11 *Boston U. Int'l L. J.* 81 at 95, n. 73.

[11] G.A. Res. 2200 A, (XXI) UN GAOR, 21st Sess., Supp. No. 16, at 52, U.N. Doc. A/6316 (1966) (entered into force on 23 March 1976) (ICCPR). See also Optional Protocol to the International Covenant on Civil and Political Rights, G.A. Res. 2200 (XXI), U.N. GAOR, 21st Sess., Supp. No. 16 at 59, U.N. Doc. A/6316 (1966) (entered into force on 23 March 1976).

[12] G.A. Res. 2200 (XXI), U.N. GAOR, 21st Sess., Supp. No. 16 at 49, U.N. Doc. A/6316 (1966)(entered into force on 3 January 1976) (ICESCR).

[13] See M. wa Mutua, *supra* n. 3, pp. 592–593.

[14] B. Cossman, *supra* n. 1, pp. 344, 352, n. 19.

[15] See *ibid.*, p. 352, n. 19. See also Humphrey, 'The International Law of Human Rights in the Middle of the Twentieth Century', in M. Box (ed.), *The Present State of International Law* (1973); O. Schachter, *International Law In Theory and Practice: General Course in Public International Law* (1985).

[16] B. Cossman, *supra* n. 1, p. 352, n. 19. See also E.W. Vierdag, 'The Legal Nature of Rights Granted by the International Covenant on Economic, Social and Cultural Rights', (1978) 9 *Neth. Y.B. Int'l L.* 69.

United States becoming a party to the Convention, ratification of the ICESCR since its submission in 1978 to the US Senate for its advice and consent by the Carter Administration, remains elusive.[17] In part, the reluctance to ratify the ICESCR stemmed from Congressional concern that its provisions setting forth the human right to food, clothing, housing, education, and access to physical and mental health care, might actually require the US government to take some action to guarantee these 'rights'.[18]

Philosophically, however, former Secretary of State Elliott Abrams made the distinction between the category of rights which no government is entitled to violate, and the social and economic rights which governments should do their best to secure.[19] This reflects the unease that the US government felt, and still feels, towards the obligations of a government towards its citizenry. Certainly, there is no doubt that there is a diverse, complex and well-entrenched legal framework for providing social, welfare, medical and other human services and benefits by the US federal and state governments. However, raising this polyglot of legal entitlements (which are constantly shifting in accordance with the priorities of the US Congress and individual state legislatures) to the level of an internationally guaranteed 'human right' requires a leap of faith which most US government officials would be unwilling to take.

Perhaps more importantly, an 'entitlement' to social and economic rights goes against the grain of Lockean-inspired legal jurisprudence. Although prohibited from interfering with an individual's self-expression, the state does not have a positive duty to support an individual's 'right' to benefit from social and economic entitlements. If, indeed, these economic and social benefits are to be treated as international 'human rights', this puts an inordinate strain on a domestic legal system that is already near breaking point. On a practical level, does it truly move the human rights agenda forward by assigning such social benefits the international legal status of 'human rights?'

Philip Alston provocatively points out that the division between civil and political liberties and the 'Soviet–Third World' concept of social and

---

[17] P. Alston, 'U.S. Ratification of the Covenant on Economic, Social and Cultural Rights: The Need for an Entirely New Strategy', (1990) 84 *Am. J. Int'l L.* at 365–366 and 366, n. 10.

[18] Paul Brietzke perceptively states that: 'Advocates of the right to development can properly gore the oxen of both sides evenhandedly. For example, it costs the United States Government little to permit meaningful freedom of speech, while guaranteeing the right to a job would be extremely expensive; job guarantees cost the Soviet Government little—a bit of additional inefficiency from overmanning—but true free speech might cause the regime to collapse'. 'Consorting with the Chameleon, or Realizing the Right to Development', (1985) 15 *Cal. W. Int'l L. J.* 560 at 586. Quoted with the kind permission of the *California Western International Law Journal*. Further, as Brietzke noted, the Soviet system, while guaranteeing 'work', could not guarantee a living wage or a participatory method of governance, and simply collapsed from within.

On the other hand, in the United States, and other industrialized Western European nations, expected guarantees of a certain standard of living and opportunities for full employment are more problematic. Changing demographics through the influx of immigrants and changes in international trade patterns often threaten job security or actually result in increased unemployment in many of these nations.

[19] P. Alston, *supra* n. 17, p. 373.

economic rights is a false dichotomy.[20] Alston argues that, in fact, President Roosevelt first legitimized certain social and economic 'rights.' [21] (It may also be argued that President Johnson's 'Great Society' initiative increased the reach of such economic and social rights.) Therefore, Alston feels that the US reluctance to ratify the ICESCR cannot be supported. He concludes that the persistent philosophical divide on this issue is misleading, and should be abandoned.

Although the future of the ratification of the ICESCR is uncertain, it is clear that the status of social and economic rights as legal or human 'rights' has not been fully accepted by certain Western democracies, most notably the United States.[22] With the dissolution of the Soviet bloc (and the realignment of their political and economic priorities accordingly), it is unclear whether there will be any real political pressure from any source to achieve full ratification and implementation of the ICESCR as an international treaty.[23] The burden tends to fall to the developing world. Therefore, it is imperative to understand what perspectives on, and philosophical approaches to, the human right to development are offered by the developing world.

1.1   A New International Economic Order

At the Sixth Special Session of the UN General Assembly on 1 May 1974, two important resolutions were adopted. The first General Assembly resolution was entitled, 'Declaration on the Establishment of a New International Economic Order', (NIEO)[24] and the second was entitled, 'Programme of

---

[20] Philip Alston points out that this type of philosophical resistance to the idea of social and economic rights does not reflect the current welfare commitments of other Western democracies such as France, Germany, Great Britain and others who have made significant commitments to their citizenry to provide for their economic security, physical and mental health needs as well as recreational interests. See P. Alston, *supra* n. 17, pp. 375–376.

[21] *Ibid.*, p. 387. Moreover, Louis Sohn argues forcefully that FDR's Four Freedoms—the freedom of speech and expression, the freedom of worship, the freedom from want, and the freedom from fear—also provide the foundation for economic rights. See L. Sohn, 'The Human Rights Movement: From Roosevelt's Four Freedoms to the Interdependence of Peace, Development and Human Rights', 8 March 1995 lecture delivered at Harvard Law School, (published by the Harvard Law School Human Rights Programme, 1995), pp. 8–13. (Publication is on file with author.)

    Charles Merriam, then Vice-Chair of the National Resources Planing Board expanded the Four Freedoms into a revised 'Economic Bill of Rights', including, *inter alia*, the right to work, the right to adequate food, clothing, shelter and medical care, the right to education, the right to personal growth and happiness, and the opportunity to enjoy life and take part in an advancing civilization. *Ibid.* The resemblance of these rights and those articulated in the ICESCR is unmistakable.

[22] It may also be argued that in light of the social and economic rights set forth in the UDHR, as ratified under the Truman Administration in 1948, which now has the force of customary international law, the US failure to ratify the ICESCR is immaterial. (Conversation between Professor Louis Sohn and author, 9 June 1997.)

[23] Philip Alston himself recognizes this by stating that, 'there is little reason to expect that [the] challenge will be taken up by many of the scholars, or activist groups, currently working in the human rights field'. P. Alston, *supra* n. 17, p. 392.

[24] UN General Assembly Res. 3201 (S-VI), 29 U. N. GAOR Supp (No. 1), p. 3, U.N. Doc. A/9559 (1974) (NIEO Declaration).

Action on the Establishment of a New International Economic Order'.[25] The NIEO was adopted by the UN General Assembly without a vote.

The underlying principles set forth in the NIEO Declaration and the NIEO Programme of Action were later rearticulated and supplemented by a subsequent UN General Assembly Resolution entitled, 'Charter of Economic Rights and Duties of States' (CERDS), which was adopted on 12 December 1974[26] by a vote of 120 for and six against (namely, Belgium, Denmark, the German Federal Republic, Luxembourg, United Kingdom and the United States), with 10 abstentions.

The significance of these UN resolutions in a discussion of a human right to development is twofold: first, these resolutions are cited in the preamble of the UN Declaration of the Right to Development (see below) and, therefore, are important antecedents to the principles set forth in that Declaration. Secondly, NIEO principles form the foundation of the ACP-EEC Convention of Lomé II, and its predecessor treaties, creating the backdrop to a new formulation of an African human rights regime. The African perspective on the right to development is important insofar as it sheds light on how that right is viewed within a developing country perspective. The dialogue between the developed and the developing worlds took a very significant turn with NIEO discussions, the implications of which will be explored below.

The concepts and principles underlying the NIEO and CERDS are controversial in terms of both the substance and in the manner of their adoption. In a post-colonial era, developing countries soon discovered that their hard-won political independence did not guarantee their economic independence. Developing countries were left struggling to establish their economic self-sufficiency.

In recognition of the continuing disparities between the developed and the developing worlds, the NIEO Declaration states:

The developing countries, which constitute 70 per cent of the world's population account for only 30 per cent of the world's income. The gap between the developed and the developing countries continues to widen in a system which was established at a time when most of the developing countries did not even exist as independent States and which perpetuates inequality.[27]

A serious concern of the developing world centred on the overwhelming economic power exercised by transnational corporations which controlled commodities markets for agricultural and other raw materials that many developing countries relied so heavily on.[28] The influence of such foreign

---

[25] UN General Assembly Res. 3202 (S-VI), 29 U.N. GAOR Supp. (No. 1), p. 5, U.N. Doc. A/9559 (1974) (NIEO Programme of Action).

[26] UN General Assembly Res. 3281, 29 U.N. GAOR Supp. (No. 30), p. 50, U.N. Doc. A/9631 (1974)[hereinafter CERDS].

[27] UN General Assembly Res. 3201 (S-VI), 29 U. N. GAOR Supp (No. 1), p. 3; U.N. Doc. A/9559 (1974); Preamble, para. 1.

[28] M. Ellis, 'The New International Economic Order and General Assembly Resolutions: The Debate over the Legal Effects of General Assembly Resolutions Revisited', (1985) 15 *Cal. W. Int'l L. J.* 647 at 652–653.

corporations over the natural resources, state sovereignty and national identities of developing countries caused great concern to the leadership of the developing world. Thus, there was a concerted effort to 'level the playing field' by creating the terms of a new international economic system.

To this end, Article 4 of the NIEO declared that developing countries enjoyed the right to: (1) the sovereign equality of all states, and the self-determination of all peoples (without discrimination based on economic or social systems adopted by developing countries); (2) the full and permanent sovereignty of every state over its natural resources and all its economic activities (including the right to nationalize such resources); (3) the preferential and non-reciprocal treatment of developing countries; (4) the extension of development assistance by the international community free of political or military conditions; (5) the promotion of the transfer of technology and the creation of indigenous technology for the benefit of developing countries; and (6) the strengthening of mutual economic, trade, financial and technical cooperation with developing countries on a preferential basis.

CERDS further articulated these principles by stating that: (1) all states are juridically equal and have the right to participate fully and effectively in international decision-making processes (Art. 10); (2) each state has the sovereign and inalienable right to choose its economic, political, social and cultural systems in accordance with the will of its people, and has the primary responsibility for promoting the economic, social and cultural development of its peoples (Art. 1); (3) each state has full permanent sovereignty over its wealth, natural resources and economic activities (Art. 2); (4) it is the individual and collective right of all states to eliminate colonialism, apartheid, racial discrimination, and neo-colonialism as a prerequisite for development (Art. 16); (5) developed countries should grant generalized, preferential, non-reciprocal and non-discriminatory treatment to developing countries in order to meet the trade and development needs of the developing world (Art. 18); and, (6) all states should promote the international transfer of technology and scientific and technical cooperation (Art. 13).

Apart from these revolutionary tenets, the developing world also began to use effectively General Assembly resolutions, namely the NIEO, to create customary international law. The NIEO was adopted, albeit without a formal vote, by the UN General Assembly. Professor Louis Sohn, for example, has argued that NIEO resolutions adopted by the General Assembly created new customary international law, and should be recognized as such.[29] After all, the earlier Universal Declaration on Human Rights had assumed the normative force of customary law without the participation of the developing states.

---

[29] L. Sohn, 'The Shaping of International Law', (1978) 8 *Ga. J. Int'l and Comp. L.* 1. Professor Sohn writes, 'there is wide consensus that these [NIEO] declarations actually established new rules of international law binding upon all States. This is not treaty making but a new method of creating customary international law.'*Ibid.*, p. 16.

Under the provisions of the UN Charter, however, the General Assembly has no formal legislative authority.[30] Although commentators may make distinctions between General Assembly resolutions and solemn declarations (the latter are generally accorded greater weight), neither create binding legal obligations on UN members.[31] Yet despite its lack of formal law-creating powers, General Assembly resolutions can, nevertheless, create customary international law.

Customary international law can be created if the following two elements can be adequately demonstrated: (1) state practice, and (2) *opinio juris*.[32] State practice, for example, would constitute a state's acts which rely on a UN declaration for the interpretation and resolution of disputes. This indicates the 'functional operation' of the declaration as a rule of customary international law. *Opinio juris* is the sense of legal obligation under international law compelling the state 'to act in a particular manner'.[33] However, state practice takes precedence over *opinio juris*, since actions speak louder (and more clearly) than intent.[34]

Moreover, state practice which establishes an international legal norm does not depend on the unanimous consent of all nations to be bound by such a rule in order for the rule to be operative.[35] Instead, all that is required is a 'general acceptance or consensus', even if the state to be bound by the rule comes into existence after the norm is established.[36] Since the international acceptance of such a rule is dependent on state practice, rather than the formal normative power of the public international body issuing such a rule, the lack of legislative or law-making powers of the UN General Assembly becomes irrelevant in this context.[37]

The UDHR, in fact, is a case in point illustrating this doctrine. The UDHR, adopted as a General Assembly resolution in 1948, is now customary international law along with other UN General Assembly declarations such as the Declaration of Granting of Independence and the Declaration of Elimination of Discrimination Against Women.[38] Indeed, there is even some scholarly

---

[30] M. Ellis, *supra* n. 28, p. 666.

[31] *Ibid.*, pp. 664, 665. See also O. Asamoah, *The Legal Significance of the Declarations of the General Assembly of the United Nations* (1966); Falk, 'On the Quasi-Legislative Competence of the General Assembly', (1966) 60 *Am. J. Int'l L.* 782; and Bleicher, 'The Legal Significance of Re-Citation of General Assembly Resolutions', (1969) 63 *Am. J. Int'l L.* 444 at 445.

[32] M. Ellis, *supra* n. 28, p. 688; see also Kunz, 'The Nature of Customary International Law', (1953) 47 *Am. J. Int'l L.* 662 at 665.

[33] M. Ellis, *supra* n. 28, p. 688; Kunz, *supra* n. 32, p. 667.

[34] B. Simma and P. Alston, 'The Sources of Human Rights Law: Custom, *Jus Cogens*, and General Principles', (1992) 12 *Australia Y.B. Int'l L.* 82 at 88.

[35] Sir H. Lauterpacht, *The Development of International Law by the International Court* (1958), p. 191.

[36] See M. Ellis, *supra* n. 28, pp. 670-671.

[37] See *ibid.*, p. 672. Mark Ellis correctly points out that the mere fact that the UN General Assembly is a highly political body (where many controversial views may be expressed) should not detract from its rule-making authority or from the legal effect of its resolutions. *Ibid.* In similar fashion, the legislatures (or parliaments) of other countries are highly political bodies that are designed to elicit and express a wide variety of political opinion within the legislative process.

[38] See *ibid.*, p. 667, and n. 126.

speculation that the UDHR has risen to the level of *jus cogens*.[39] *Jus cogens* is defined by Article 53 of the Vienna Convention on the Law of Treaties as a:

preemptory norm of general international law [which] is a norm accepted and recognized by the international community of States as a whole as a norm from which no derogation is permitted and which can be modified only by a subsequent norm of general international law having the same character.[40]

Under Article 38 of the Statute of the International Court of Justice, legitimate sources of law include international conventions, international custom, general principles of law, and judicial decision and teachings.[41] Thus, if the UDHR is considered an international legal custom, or even a general principle of law, under the doctrine of *jus cogens*, the legal standing of the UDHR can be raised to the level of an international legal norm.

In fact, the normative power of the UDHR has been expressed in US domestic law. For example, in a case brought by Paraguayan citizens concerning the killing of their son by torture, the US Second Circuit (Federal Court of Appeals in New York) in *Filartiga v. Pena-Irala*,[42] held that torture of an individual under the colour of official authority violates universally accepted norms of international human rights. The Court of Appeals held that, 'the right to be free from torture ... has become part of customary international law, as evidenced and defined by the Universal Declaration of Human Rights'.[43]

Further, the Court found that:

UN Declarations are significant because they specify with great precision the obligations of member nations under the [UN] Charter. Since their adoption, '[m]embers can no longer contend that they do not know what human rights they promised in the Charter to promote'. [Citation omitted.] ... Accordingly, it has been observed that the Universal Declaration of Human Rights 'no longer fits into the dichotomy of 'binding treaty' against 'non-binding pronouncement', but is rather an authoritative statement of the international community'. [Citation omitted.]... Indeed, several commentators have concluded that the Universal Declaration has become, *in toto*, a part of binding, customary, international law.[44]

---

[39] *Ibid.*, p. 699.

[40] Vienna Convention of the Law of Treaties, 1155 U.N.T.S. 331, reprinted in (1969) 63 *Am. J. Int'l L.* 875 at 891. It has been argued that Art. 53 of the Vienna Convention provides the basis to void the operation of treaties which conflict with peremptory international norms. See H. Charlesworth and C. Chinkin, 'The Gender of *Jus Cogens*', (February 1993) 15 *H. Rts. Q.*, 63 at 64–65. Further, developing country support of the inclusion of a *jus cogens* doctrine in the Convention stemmed from the desire to mitigate the effect of *pacta sunt servanda*, or the doctrine requiring that international obligations be observed by the signatories. *Ibid.* The *jus cogens* doctrine was adopted in the Vienna Convention despite reservations concerning the vagaries of state practice in defining peremptory international norms. *Ibid.*

[41] Statute of the I.C.J., Art. 38, 59 Stat. 1055, T.S. No. 993, 3 Bevans 1179.

[42] 630 F. 2d 876 (2d Cir. 1980).

[43] *Ibid.*, p. 882.

[44] *Ibid.*, p. 883. See also B. Simma and P. Alston, *supra* n. 34, p. 91 (noting that governments conferred the UDHR with the status of customary international law).

US courts have also been willing to consider NIEO provisions in resolving claims for compensation for the expropriation of private property. The US Court of Appeals in *Banco Nacional de Cuba v. Chase Manhattan Bank* stated that, 'actions taken by the General Assembly of the United Nations on this subject since 1962, while they do not have the force of law, *see* U.N. Charter, art. 10, are of considerable interest.'[45] The Court duly noted that the US delegate's request, *inter alia,* that the CERDS provision on expropriation be amended to include a provision providing for just compensation in the event of nationalization, was rejected. The United States voted against the CERDS (along with five others), and the Court concluded that:

This overview of the actions of members of the [UN] General Assembly presents at best a confused and confusing picture as to what the consensus may be as to the responsibilities of an expropriating nation to pay 'appropriate compensation', and just what that term may mean. The resolutions, the views of commentators, and the positions taken by individual states or blocs are varied, diverse, and not easily reconciled.[46]

Similarly, US federal courts have considered the substance of NIEO provisions in determining whether the acts of sovereign nations constitute commercial activities and therefore, are not entitled to sovereign immunity under the provisions of the Foreign Sovereign Immunities Act of 1976.[47] In *International Ass'n. of Machinists and Aerospace Workers v. Organization of Petroleum Exporting Countries*,[48] the plaintiff brought an action against OPEC, seeking monetary and injunctive relief for OPEC's alleged price-fixing of crude oil prices as a *per se* antitrust violation of the Sherman Act.[49] The US district court deciding this case construed the commercial activities of sovereign nations 'narrowly' and recognized that:

In determining whether the activities of the OPEC members are governmental or commercial in nature, the Court can and should examine the standards recognized under international law. The United Nations, with the concurrence of the United States, has repeatedly recognized the principle that a sovereign state has the sole power to control its natural resources. See e.g., Resolution 1803, G.A. Res., §I(1), 17 U.N. GAOR, 2d Comm. 327, U.N. Doc. A/C/2/5 R 850 (1962).... . Accord, Charter of Economic Rights and Duties of States, G.A. Res. 3281, Ch. II, Art. 2(1). U.N. Doc. A/RES/3281 (XXIX) (1974); Declaration on the Establishment of a New International Economic Order in 1974, G.A. Res. 3201 (S-VI) §4e, U.N. GAOR, 6th Spec. Sess., Supp. (No. 1) 3, U.N. Doc. A/9559; Resolution 3171, G.A. Res. 3171, 28 U.N. GAOR 30 (Vol. 1) at 52, U.N. Doc. A/9030 (1973); Resolution 3016, G.A.

---

[45] *Banco Nacional de Cuba v. Chase Manhattan Bank*, 658 F.2d 875, 889 (2d Cir. 1981); rev'd on other grounds, 462 U.S. 611, 103 S. Ct. 2591, 77 L.Ed. 2d 36 (1983); remanded 744 F.2d 237 (2d Cir. 1984).

[46] *Banco Nacional de Cuba v. Chase Manhattan Bank*, 505 F. Supp. 412 (S.D.N.Y. 1980), aff'd as modified, 658 F.2d 875, 891.

[47] 28 U.S.C. §1602, *et seq.*

[48] 477 F. Supp. 553 (C.D. Ca. 1979); *aff'd* 649 F.2d 1354 (9th Cir., 1981); *cert. den.* 454 U.S. 1163, 102 S. Ct. 1036, 71 L.Ed. 2d 319 (1982).

[49] 15 U.S.C. §1 *et seq.*

Res. 3016, Preamble and §1, 27 U.N. GAOR, Supp. (No. 30), U.N. Doc. A/8730; Resolution 2158, G.A. Res. 2158 §I(1), 21 U.N. GAOR, Supp. (No. 16) 29, U.N. Doc. A/6316 (1966). The United States' endorsement of this principle derives from its control, as a sovereign, of the development of its own land and resources. See e.g., US Constitution, Art. 4, Sec. 3, Cl. 2.[50]

Of course, the United States voted against CERDS, despite the fact that it may have agreed with a principle set forth in CERDS that a sovereign state has the sole authority to control the disposition of its own natural resources. Despite the legal stature that the NIEO and CERDS may have assumed in international law, the provisions of these declarations were never fully accepted or implemented by developed nations.[51] Even though the NIEO was adopted without a vote by the UN General Assembly, it has clearly not been accepted as an international customary norm by industrialized states.

It is true that unanimous acceptance of a General Assembly resolution is not required under international law, nor is a single negative vote sufficient to defeat consensus. Nevertheless, even if a resolution is adopted by an overwhelming majority, negative votes cast by even a few powerful states may ultimately defeat consensus.[52] Thus, in light of the six votes against CERDS cast by industrialized nations (including the United States), and the 10 abstentions by other nations, the requisite consensus for the adoption of CERDS (and even the NIEO) as normative legal instruments did not exist.[53]

Despite the failings of the NIEO-CERDS agenda, the NIEO precepts supported negotiations for the African-Caribbean-Pacific (ACP) and European Economic Community (EEC) pact for economic assistance known as the ACP-EEC Convention, or Lomé II Convention (Lomé II).[54] Lomé II was the fourth convention signed between EEC countries and newly

---

[50] See 477 F. Supp. 567–568. The Court determined that the activities of OPEC nations with regard to the taxation and the imposition of royalties for the extraction of crude oil from their respective territories did not constitute commercial activities, and that the defendants were entitled to sovereign immunity under 28 U.S.C. §1604. As a consequence, the court lacked subject-matter jurisdiction over the complaint. In reaching its decision, the court also found that: 'In view of our own State and Federal domestic crude oil activities, there can be little question that establishing the terms and conditions for removal of natural resources from its territory, when done by a sovereign state, individually and separately, is a governmental activity. (Footnote omitted.) Plaintiff, however, asserts that, while this may be true, the actions of the OPEC nations in coming together to conspire to fix prices is commercial and, thus, not immune. Plaintiff's position, however, is untenable. It is ridiculous to suggest that the essential nature of an activity changes merely by the act of two or more countries coming together to agree on how they will carry on that activity. The action of sovereign nations coming together to agree on how each will perform certain sovereign acts can only, itself, be a sovereign act'. 477 F. Supp. 568–569.

[51] See M. Ellis, *supra* n. 28, p. 660.

[52] *Ibid.*, pp. 693, 695.

[53] *Ibid.*, p. 695.

[54] ACP-EEC Convention of Lomé (II), Oct. 31, 1979, reprinted in *The Courier* (November 1979), cited in A. Young-Anawaty, 'Human Rights and the ACP-EEC Lomé II Convention: Business as Usual at the EEC', (1980) 13 *N.Y.U. J. Int'l L. and Pol.* 63 at 63, n. 1.

independent nations of Africa, the Caribbean and the Pacific. Part IV, Arts. 131–136 of the Treaty of Rome[55] (governing the EEC), established the Association system to govern economic relations with European colonies or dependent states with special relations with European countries for the purpose of furthering the development of such states. Under terms of the Association, free trade areas were established along with preferential trade treatment in exchange for EEC countries and nationals being permitted to establish themselves in ACP countries.[56]

With the independence of ACP states and territories in the 1960s, however, the Association was rendered obsolete, since these newly independent states now fell outside the jurisdiction of the Treaty of Rome. New negotiations between the EEC and these newly formed nations clarifying their new legal and economic status and relations were concluded with Yaoundé I and II, as well as Lomé I and II.[57] This discussion will only consider Lomé II, since human rights became a major stumbling block to its passage. At the time, European socialists lobbied to include a strong commitment to human rights within the framework of Lomé II, particularly in light of massive human rights abuses in Ethiopia, Uganda and the Central African Republic.[58]

Formal renegotiations for Lomé II began in July 1978, four years after the NIEO had been adopted. EEC members wanted to incorporate a reference to human rights by annexing the UN Charter and the UNDRD in the preamble of the Lomé II Convention.[59] The 58 ACP nations were opposed to this, however, based on the following grounds: first, that the Lomé II Convention was an economic instrument and that the UN (not the Convention) was the appropriate forum to discuss concerns about human rights; secondly, that conditioning trade agreements on human rights observances was unfair and inappropriate; thirdly, that this was a Cold War ploy; and, fourthly, whereas condemnations of apartheid in South Africa were acceptable, other types of human rights 'violations' in ACP countries were considered an internal affair that did not warrant international scrutiny or intrusion.[60] After many heated sessions, no mention of human rights was made in Lomé II.

---

[55] Treaty Establishing the European Economic Community, 25 March, 1957, Pt. IV, 298 U.N.T.S. 11, reprinted in *Office for Official Publications of the European Communities, Treaties Establishing the European Communities*, 163 (1973).

[56] A. Young-Anawaty, *supra* n. 54, at 54–74. (Note that Lomé trade preferences are not consistent with the General Arrangements on Trade preferences.)

[57] Convention of Association between the European Economic Community and the African and Malagasy States Associated with that Community (Yaoundé I), 6 January 1964, 7 J.O. Comm. Eur. 1431 (1964); Convention of Association between the European Economic Community and the African and Malagasy States Associated with that Community (Yaoundé II), 29 July 1969, 13 J.O. Comm. Eur. (No. L 282)ʾ1 (1970); ACP-EEC Convention of Lomé (I), 30 January 1976, 6 Collection of the Agreements Concluded by the European Communities 1003 (1976) (Official Publications of the European Communities) reprinted in 12 Comm. Mkt. L. Rev. 463 (1975), cited in A. Young-Anawaty, *supra* n. 54, p. 64, n. 4; 75, n. 47; 76, n. 50.

[58] See A. Young-Anawaty, *supra* n. 54, pp. 79, 95–96.

[59] *Ibid.*, p. 87.

[60] *Ibid.*, p. 80.

Despite the fact that the fiercely debated human rights issues did not appear in Lomé II, the Organization of African Unity (OAU) nevertheless carefully examined the political stance taken by the ACP countries in the Lomé II debate, and passed a resolution to draft an 'African Charter on Human and Peoples' Rights' during the OAU's July 1979 meeting in Monrovia.[61] This Charter will be the subject of later discussion.

What is the relevance of the objectives of the NIEO Declaration, NIEO Programme of Action, and CERDS in this context? Unlike the Universal Declaration of Human Rights which treats the individual's right to development, the NIEO and CERDS formulated the rights of developing states within the development process. The NIEO and CERDS declarations fundamentally changed the terms of 'development' to incorporate the interests, priorities and needs of the developing world.

Most importantly, the NIEO addressed the inherent inequality in the juridical stature and economic bargaining power of developing countries, and stressed their need for preferential, non-reciprocal treatment.[62] These considerations were not couched in human rights language as such, but highlight the fundamental concerns of developing nations regarding the ongoing development process which, in their view, both contributes to and perpetuates key inequalities and injustices.

CERDS set forth the parameters of a proposed new relationship with the developed world by requiring highly industrialized states to grant generalized, preferential, non-reciprocal and non-discriminatory treatment to developing countries in order to meet the trade and development needs of the developing world. This can be translated into practical terms by granting preferential treatment to developing nations in three areas: trade, capital, and technology transfers. In other words, granting MFN status to developing countries, and removing trade barriers erected by Western nations; granting debt relief in terms of preferential capital transfers from the West, as discussed earlier in the text; and agreeing to a new regime for intellectual property rights that adequately addresses the needs of developing countries, are all related concerns.

Negotiations surrounding the Lomé II Convention initiated an ongoing debate of whether trade relations or foreign assistance should be conditioned on human rights observances. The threat of imposing economic sanctions for human rights lapses continues to be a battleground between

---

[61] Decision on Human and Peoples' Rights in Africa, Organization of African Unity Assembly of Heads of State and Government, 16th Sess. (17–20 July 1979), reprinted in 34 U.N. GAOR, Annex (Agenda Item 23), U.N. Doc. A/34/552 (1979), p. 92.

[62] This type of preferential treatment has been termed a 'differential norm' insofar as such a legal norm 'on its face provides different, presumably more advantageous, standards for one set of States than for another set'. See Daniel Barstow Magraw, Legal Treatment of Developing Countries: Differential, Contextual, and Absolute Norms, (1990) 1 *Colo. J. Int'l Envtl. L and Pol'y* 69 at 73. In this case, the NIEO, and related UN resolutions, set forth differential norms which provide for different, and inherently unequal, legal treatment which has the effect of distinguishing developed countries from developing ones.

the Western industrialized countries and the rest of the world. This confrontation is often viewed in terms of the imposition of 'neo-colonialist' values or American hegemony on other countries.

The critical question posed by this debate is how 'fundamental' are certain basic human rights and dignities? Are certain human rights truly universal and inalienable? If so, should we expect less from developing countries because of their poverty? Does poverty legally deprive an individual of certain human rights? If so, then are certain human rights obtainable only by virtue of the relative wealth of an individual, or of a society? Should the development process be held captive until the offending country complies with international human rights norms?

On the one hand, one should be wary of hegemonic pretensions with regard to human rights, especially where such values are imposed through the threat of economic sanctions, trade embargoes and other punitive measures. Such judgments may reflect cultural values and priorities which are specific to a nation or culture. On the other hand, one should also be careful about establishing a lower tier of expectations for developing countries. If certain fundamental rights may be deemed 'inalienable' (and, clearly, an international consensus on this has not yet been formulated), then these rights should not be withheld from individuals merely because they live in the developing world. This is an opportunity for developing countries to shape the definition of, and the agenda for, human rights, rather than denying the entitlement of their citizens to these basic rights. Otherwise, 'development' becomes even more problematic and elusive. Basic human dignity should not be the exclusive prerogative of those living in economically prosperous nations.

Negotiating the more diverse and multicultural aspects of human rights does help to move the debate forward. Developing countries need to participate in the international dialogue concerning which rights are truly universal and transcend the vagaries of culture. Constructive participation in this discussion will help mould and shape the new legal outlines of these human rights, and make them truly universal (as opposed to Western) in character.

Using arguments of state sovereignty as a shield for failing or refusing to meet internationally recognized norms of basic human rights protection may be a self-serving strategy. Likewise, prioritizing economic 'development' over civic and political development takes a very narrow view of development which may also be self-defeating in the end. 'Development' is a very complex picture, and developing countries should strive to achieve more than just economic progress, particularly if we are to believe that 'man does not live by bread alone'.

Conditioning human rights on the relative wealth of a country, or dismissing the concept as Western-styled legal imperialism, may do a real injustice to the needs and aspirations of the peoples of a developing country. Assuring fair and equal treatment in the criminal justice system, minimal due process rights, and other basic human rights, for example, may be a vital component in the overall scheme for development. This is especially true if 'development' as a concept is to incorporate dimensions other than economic growth.

2.   THE HISTORY OF THE RIGHT TO DEVELOPMENT

At the 1972 inaugural lecture of the Third Session of Instruction of the International Institute for Human Rights in Strasbourg, Keba M'Baye, First President of the Senegal Supreme Court, gave an address entitled, 'The Right to Development as the Right of Man'.[63] In this presentation, he set forth a basic outline of the human right to development; the ultimate justification for that right being that man cannot exist without development.[64]

As Chairman of the Commission on Human Rights in 1977, Mr M'Baye further elaborated on the newly coined 'human right to development' in a paper delivered at the UNESCO Meeting of Experts on Human Rights, Human Needs and the Establishment of a New International Economic Order.[65] The Commission adopted Resolution 4 (XXX-III), recommending that a study of a right to development be undertaken.[66]

Also in 1977, the UN General Assembly linked human rights and development by stating that: 'Human rights questions should be examined globally, taking into account both the overall context of the various societies in which they present themselves as well as the need for the promotion of the full dignity of the human person and the development and well-being of the society'.[67]

Additionally, Karel Vasak, Director of the Human Rights and Peace Division of UNESCO in 1977, espoused the theory of three 'generations' of human rights.[68] The first generation of human rights are the political

---

[63] M'Baye, 'Le Droit au Developpement comme un droit de l'Homme', (1972) 5 *Revue Des Droits de L'Homme*, 503 at 505. See also H.G. Espiell, 'The Right of Development as a Human Right', (1981) 16 *Tex. Int'l L. J.*, 189 at 192; J. Donnelly, 'The 'Right to Development': How Not to Link Human Rights and Development', in C. Welch and R. Meltzer (eds.), *Human Rights and Development in Africa* (1984), pp. 261–262 ; J. Donnelly, 'In Search of the Unicorn: The Jurisprudence and Politics of the Right to Development', (1985) 15 *Cal. W. Int'l L. J.* 473 at 474; M. Bulajic, 'Principles of International Development Law: The Right to Development as an Inalienable Human Right', in P. de Waart, P. Peters, E. Denters (eds.), *International Law and Development* (Martinus Nijhoff Publishers, 1988), p. 359 ; and K. de Vey Mestdagh, *The Right to Development* (Sijthoff and Norordhoff International Publishers, 1981).

[64] M'Baye, *supra* n. 63, pp. 528, 530. See also M. Bulajić, *supra* n. 63, p. 359.

[65] The UNESCO meeting took place from June 19-23, 1978, and M'Baye's presentation was reprinted in UNESCO Doc. SS-78/CONF.630/8, p. 1. (See also J. Donnelly, *supra* n. 63, p. 474, n. 3.)

[66] Commission on Human Rights, Report on the Thirty-Third Session, 62 U.N. ESCOR Supp. (No. 6), U.N. Doc. E/5927 (1978). Jack Donnelly notes with disapproval that the 'right to development' moved through the UN system with unprecedented speed with practically no opposition. J. Donnelly, *supra* n. 63, pp. 474–475.) He also notes that despite the lack of precedent for the right and the lack of scholarly discussion, the right to development was proclaimed in the Declaration of the Preparation of Societies for Life in Peace, UN General Assembly Res. 33/73 (1978), and in the UNESCO Declaration on Race and Racial Prejudice, adopted by the General Conference of UNESCO on 27 November 1978. *Ibid.*

[67] UN General Assembly Res. 2626, para. 5, 25 U.N. GAOR Supp. (No. 28), p. 39, U.N. Doc. A/8028 (1970).

[68] K. Vasak, 'A 30-Year Struggle', *UNESCO Courier* (November 1977), p. 29. See also S. Marks, 'Emerging Human Rights: A New Generation for the 1980s?' (Winter 1981) 33 *Rutgers L. Rev.* 435 at 441.

and civil rights of the individual which the state is prohibited from interfering with or infringing upon. These liberties correlate to freedoms such
as the right to self-expression, the practice of religion, and other liberties
which John Locke thought may be unjustifiably abridged by the state.
These freedoms are eloquently expressed in the Bill of Rights to the US
Constitution and are set forth, in substance, in the ICCPR.[69]

The second generation of human rights are the social, economic,
and cultural rights whose implementation is the primary responsibility
of the state, and which roughly correspond to the ICESCR. These
rights include the right to work, the right to health, and the right to education. These 'rights' are more than simply liberties which the state cannot
arbitrarily deprive the individual from exercising. Rather, the state has
the affirmative duty to provide certain social and economic rights to the
individual.

The third generation of human rights are comprised of the so-called
'solidarity' rights, which include not only the right to development, but also
the right to peace, the right to a healthy environment, and the right to own
the common heritage of mankind.[70] Additional candidates for 'solidarity'
rights included the right to communicate, the right to be different and the
right to humanitarian assistance.[71]

Paul Brietzke points out that these three generations of human rights
correspond to the *liberté, egalité* and *fraternité* of the French revolution.[72] The
first generation of civil and political rights can be traced to the historical
antecedents of the American and French Revolutions. The second generation of social and economic rights can be traced back to the revolutionary
tradition beginning with the Russian Revolution. Finally, the third generation of so-called solidarity rights are still emerging from the decolonization
experience of the developing world.[73]

---

[69] Simma and Alston write that: 'there is a remarkable correlation between the norms
identified as customary rules, and the range of rights which has been incorporated
into the US Bill of Rights. This correlation may, of course, be considered to be
coincidental. Alternatively, it might be seen as a tribute to the foresight and
 perceptiveness of the drafters of the US documents or as a reflection of the dominant
influence of American values in the world. It is also possible, however, to view it as
an instance of what might be termed normative chauvinism, albeit of an unintentional
or sub-conscious variety'. See B. Simma and P. Alston, *supra* n. 34, p. 94. Reproduced with
the permission of the author. (See also ICCPR, Article 18.)

[70] K. de Vey Mestdagh, *supra* n. 63, pp. 33–34. See also H.G. Espiell, *supra* n. 63, p. 193, n. 17.
Note that the first three rights enumerated in the text have been recognized in Article 23
of the African Charter on Human and Peoples' Rights, discussed *infra*. (See e.g.,
P. Alston, 'Conjuring Up New Human Rights: A Proposal for Quality Control',
(1984) 78 *Am. J. Int'l L.* 607, p. 610–611.)

[71] P. Alston, *supra* n. 70, p. 610.

[72] P. Brietzke, 'Consorting with the Chameleon, or Realizing the Right to Development',
15 *Cal. W. Int'l L. J.* at 587. Qouted with the kind permission of the *California Western
International Law Journal*. See also J. Donnelly, 'The "Right to Development": How
Not to Link Human Rights and Development', in C. Welch (ed.), *Human Rights and
Development in Africa* (1984), p. 263.

[73] See P. Brietzke, *supra* n. 72, p. 582.

According to Brietzke, 'First generation rights emphasize form, while second and third generation rights look more to substance'.[74] Jack Donnelly goes a step further by stating that, 'There is not merely a difference in substance—in the object of the right—from the first two "generations" of rights, but a fundamental *qualitative* difference between solidarity rights and all (other) "human rights", based on radically different sources for the rights.'[75] (Emphasis in original.) Indeed, the notion of the individual is cast in three separate moulds. The first generation of human rights sees the individual as the independent entrepreneur; the second, as the revolutionary worker; and the third, as the oppressed, colonized individual.

A study of the right to development, requested in Resolution 4 passed by the Commission on Human Rights, was issued by the UN Secretary-General in January 1979 in preparation for the Strategy for the Third UN Development Decade.[76] Although Jack Donnelly has questioned the authority and authenticity of the legal antecedents to the right to development, the legal sources, as Donnelly himself admits, are varied and venerated.[77] The legal sources for the human right to development include, as discussed in the Secretary-General's Report, Articles 55 and 56 of, and the preamble to, the UN Charter, Articles 22, 26(2), 28 and 29(1) of the Universal Declaration of Human Rights, Article 1 of the ICCPR, and Articles 1(1), 2(1) and 11 of the ICESCR.[78]

The Secretary-General's Report defined the right to development as:

(i)   The realization of the potentialities of the human person in harmony with the community should be seen as the central purpose of development;

(ii)   The human person should be seen as the subject and not the object of the development process; ...

(iii)   Respect for human rights is fundamental to the development process;

---

[74] *Ibid*. Moreover, as the earlier discussion of Ms Cossman's analysis pointed out, the traditional support for the social and economic rights that came from the Soviet bloc is now jeopardized in light of the realignment of the First and Second Worlds. (See n. 1 and accompanying text.) The emphasis on the collective nature of the right to development where social and economic rights implicit therein are paramount is clear from the Soviet standpoint, whereas the individual nature of the right was clearly emphasized by the US delegate to the 15-member working group established by the UN Social and Economic Council in drafting a declaration of the right to development. See V. Nanda, 'The Right to Development Under International Law—Challenges Ahead', 15 *Cal. W. Int'l .L. J.* at 435-436.

[75] J. Donnelly, *supra* n. 72, p. 271. Reprinted by permission of the State University of New York Press, copyright (1984) State University of New York. All rights reserved.

[76] The International Dimensions of the Right to Development as a Human Right in relation with other Human Rights based on International Cooperation, including the Right to Peace, taking into account the Requirements of the New International Economic Order and the Fundamental Human Needs, Report of the Secretary-General, U.N. Doc. E/CN.4/1334 (1979). See also V. Nanda, *supra* n. 74 at 433; H.G. Espiell, *supra* n. 63, pp. 194–195.

[77] J. Donnelly, *supra* n. 72, p. 262.

[78] *Ibid*., p. 262.

(iv) The human person must be able to participate fully in shaping his own reality; ...

(v) [A] degree of individual and collective self-reliance must be an integral part of the process.[79]

The UN General Assembly recognized the right to development in U.N. GA Res. 34/46 adopted on 23 November 1979.[80] Since that time, the right has been reiterated by the UN General Assembly a number of times.[81]

However, in considering the declaration on the right to development at a UN meeting of the Third Committee convened on 28 November 1986, the comments of the participating UN delegates sheds some light on their reservations.[82] For example, the US delegate, in declining to join the consensus on the declaration on the right to development, expressed her concerns that the declaration as adopted by the Committee was 'imprecise and confusing', and tended to 'dilute and confuse the existing human rights agenda of the United Nations'.[83]

Additionally, the UK delegate did not accept the linkage between human rights violations and development, nor did she accept the linkage between protecting human rights and establishing the new international economic order.[84] Further, she expressed reservations regarding the right to development being the 'human right of peoples',[85] a sentiment echoed by the Japanese delegate who abstained from the consensus on the declaration, in part, because '[h]uman rights were rights of individuals'.[86]

Finally, on 4 December 1986, the UN General Assembly adopted the Declaration on the Right to Development (UNDRD) by a roll-call vote.[87] The United States was the sole nation to vote against the UNDRD. What impact does the sole dissenting vote of the United States in opposition to the UNDRD have?

In order for a UN General Assembly resolution to create customary international law upon its passage, the resolution must have been adopted

---

[79] The Secretary-General's Report, U.N. Doc. E/CN.4/1334 (1979). The Report also explains that the right to development arises from the duty of solidarity (§42); the moral duty of reparation for colonial and neo-colonial exploitation (§54); and world peace §§50-51). See J. Donnelly, *supra* n. 72, p. 262.

[80] See U.N. Doc. A/C.3/34/SR.24-30, 33-38, 41.

[81] See e.g., G.A. Res. 174, 35 U.N. GAOR (1980); G.A. Res. 133, 36 U.N. GAOR (1981); G.A. Res. 199, 37 U.N. GAOR (1982); G.A. Res. 124, 38 U.N. GAOR (1983), and the draft resolutions adopted by the Third Committee on Nov. 30, 1984, U.N. Doc. A/C3/39/L36.

[82] See Draft UN resolution A/C.3/41/L.4 adopting a declaration on the right to development by the Third Committee on Nov. 28, 1986, U.N. Doc. A/C.3/41/SR.61.

[83] *Ibid.*, p. 32.

[84] *Ibid.*, p. 33.

[85] *Ibid.*

[86] *Ibid.*, p. 31.

[87] U.N. GA Res. 41/128 (Dec. 4, 1986), adopted by 146 to 1 (United States voted against it), with eight abstentions (namely, Denmark, Finland, the Federal Republic of Germany, Iceland, Israel, Japan, Sweden and the United Kingdom).

by a 'consensus' of the members of the General Assembly.[88] Although unanimity in the passage of such resolutions is not required, 'near-unanimity with a few abstentions or dissents' is necessary.[89] Whereas a single negative vote may not be sufficient to destroy consensus in the matter, a few negative votes or a bloc of abstentions may be sufficient in this regard.[90]

Therefore, does the single negative vote cast by the United States have sufficient legal force to prevent there being a 'consensus', thereby preventing the UNDRD from achieving the force of customary international law?[91] Perhaps not in a technical legal sense, but nevertheless, the possibility of its universal recognition, and implementation, seems dim.[92] The prospect of fully accepting and implementing a 'right to development' seems remote.

2.1   Rights and duties under the UNDRD

The revolutionary character of the UNDRD is apparent at the outset. Article 1 of the UNDRD states:

The right to development is an inalienable human right by virtue of which every human person and all peoples are entitled to participate in, contribute to and enjoy economic, social, cultural and political development, in which all human rights and fundamental freedoms can be fully realized.

In the classical Western legal tradition, individual rights, as discussed earlier, were articulated in the form of 'negative freedoms'—that is to say, freedom from interference by the government in the exercise of such rights. Thus, the individual is accorded certain rights and freedoms, and the government is prescribed certain duties—chiefly, to respect the freedoms accorded to the individual, and to protect private property.

Since Western theorists, such as John Locke, view government as a 'fiduciary trust' that is delegated certain responsibilities and duties by the people,[93] there is no room to accord governments any 'rights' as such, other than the right to curb the criminal or anti-social behaviour of the

---

[88] See M. Ellis, *supra* n. 28, p. 694. In fact, consensus on an issue may be regarded as evidence of *opinio juris*, thus supporting the inference that the resolution is legally binding on General Assembly members. *Ibid.*

[89] *Ibid.*

[90] *Ibid.*, pp. 694–695. Ellis points out that CERDS was passed by the General Assembly by a vote of 120 for, six against, with ten abstentions. *Ibid.*, p. 694, n. 308. Ellis concludes that the 10 abstentions, even if the six votes against are not considered, were sufficient to defeat consensus on CERDS. *Ibid.*

[91] Perhaps it is to the United States' credit that it takes its international obligations so seriously, and will not regard the terms of the UNDRD as hortatory language only.

[92] L. Cao, Book Review, *Law and Economic Development: A New Beginning?* (1997) 32 *Tex. Int'l L. J.* 545 at 556.

[93] J. Locke, 'An Essay Concerning the True Original Extent and End of Civil Government', in R. Hutchins (ed.), *Great Books of the Western World*, Vol. 35 (Encyclopedia Britannica, 1952), pp. 61, 55–58.

people for the overall good of the polity. The state is delegated certain duties (and powers) by the individuals residing within.

Of course, Western societies did not come to a full halt at John Locke's doorstep. Since that time, the state has assumed a number of positive duties in addition to its original duty to refrain from interfering with the pursuit of happiness by the individual. The government in Western societies has assumed an important delegated role in providing for the social welfare of its citizenry. The redistribution of wealth through taxation, provision of social safety nets to provide unemployment, health, medical, and pension benefits, provision of educational opportunities and facilities, and support for the infrastructure needs of the population in terms of transportation, power and communications, are all duties which have been assumed by Western governments.

Over the course of the last century, there has been an explosion of positive duties assumed by Western states to provide for the welfare of their citizens. Yet, despite the serious and complex nature of these legal obligations, there is still a philosophical and legal reluctance to impose a legal 'duty' on the state to provide these entitlements to its citizens as part of an international human rights regime. Thus, there is a certain hesitation, on the part of certain Western states in any case, to elevate 'economic and social rights' to the same level as civil and political freedoms which are set forth as 'human rights' in the ICCPR.

For example, the UK delegate to the UN Third Committee stated that the United Kingdom, 'as one of the largest donors of development assistance, agreed that States should take steps to promote development, including that of developing countries, but could not agree that that should become an obligation under international law'.[94] This debate is not a new one: it requires that a clear distinction be drawn between a 'right' or an 'entitlement' and a mere aspiration. Although developed nations have shown their interest in and commitment to the development of other countries, there is a clear reluctance to transform the desire to facilitate the development of other countries into an actual legal obligation to do so.

In light of the above discussion, the legal problems associated with the UNDRD fall into several categories. First, the recognition of economic, social, cultural and political development as an 'inalienable human right' is highly problematic. The philosophical reorientation that is required to accept this proposition goes against the grain of centuries of Western political thought, ideology and practice. The pursuit of economic and social 'development' is traditionally viewed as the prerogative of the individual in Western society, and the state is expressly forbidden to interfere with an individual's choices, inclinations and desires.

Secondly, the right to development has both individual and collective aspects, creating further confusion and chaos in traditional Western legal

---

[94] See Draft UN resolution A/C.3/41/L.4 adopting a declaration on the right to development by the Third Committee on Nov. 28, 1986, U.N. Doc. A/C.3/41/SR.61, p. 33.

thinking.[95] Under the provisions of the UNDRD, the right to development is held not only by all individuals worldwide, but also by collective entities, such as 'peoples' and developing states. The UNDRD purports to give certain 'rights' to states (and 'human rights' at that), which is a *non sequitur* in the classical tradition of Western law. In Western human rights regimes, human rights can only be held by human beings, not by states. Moreover, since human rights violations are generally committed by, and actionable against, the state, giving developing countries a 'human right', some would argue, is a nonsensical proposition.

Thirdly, the duties imposed by the UNDRD are to be assumed by the developed nations, the international community, and world institutions which address development problems. These duties are imposed on advanced industrial nations in recognition, in part, that the past exploitation of developing countries did, in fact, contribute to their present state of 'underdevelopment'. These duties may also be regarded as a form of subtle restitution for the colonial histories of the past. Thus, the implicit confrontational, polemical overtones between the right-holders (developing countries) and the duty-bearers (developed nations) has resulted in an impasse between the two.

The intellectual divide between the proponents and opponents of the right to development is clearly expressed by Jack Donnelly, who writes:

All traditional human rights, both civil and political and economic, social and cultural, are rights primarily held *against* the state; whether the duties correlative to these rights require forbearance, protection or positive assistance, the state is the principal duty-bearer. Human rights are essentially instruments to protect the individual against the state or to assure that the state guarantees to each individual certain minimum goods, services and opportunities. Other legal, moral and social principles or practices aim to protect the legitimate interests of society in instances of conflict between the individual and the community. To confuse the two seriously risks undermining the protections provided by human rights. (Emphasis in original.)[96]

Jack Donnelly's Lockean view of human rights is very useful. He delineates the fault line between the industrialized Western states' view of and the developing world perspective on human rights. The right to development does not 'confuse' rights and duties, it reformulates them in unexpected and unprecedented ways that move far beyond the Lockean paradigm. The human right to development no longer preserves the static and hostile relationship between the individual and the state. It endows the states with rights (not just duties), and purports to establish a framework of human rights that includes nation-states as both right-holders and duty-bearers to one another as well as to all individuals.

To further confuse the picture, the international human rights scene has expanded well beyond the familiar confines of the lone individual locked into

---

[95] Lan Cao, *supra* n. 92, p. 556.
[96] J. Donnelly, *supra* n. 72, at 499. Reprinted by permission of the State University of New York Press, copyright (1984), State University of New York. All rights reserved.

an adverse relationship to the potentially tyrannical state. The Newtonian universe of human rights with predictable laws and relationships has been transformed into a Einsteinian universe where the actors, rights and duties are fluid, unpredictable and unstructured. Naturally, this is bound to meet with resistance and distrust, primarily from Western legal practitioners.

Jack Donnelly further writes:

Solidarity, which is often advanced as the single most important moral argument for a right to development, is merely a variant on this basic conceptual error of confusing rights and duties ... While solidarity may establish strong moral obligations to assist the underdeveloped, it does not establish a *right* to assistance, let alone a right to *development*. 'The innate responsibility to help one's fellow man' establishes at most a moral obligation to act to promote development, not a right to development. (Emphasis in original.)[97]

This illustrates what may be the fatal flaw in the way in which the right to development has been articulated: it lacks legal sufficiency, and can be seen as aspirational. It fails to impose a concrete duty/right that is enforceable by the respective parties to the right to development.

In addition, the human right to development has both individual and collective aspects. If seen as an individual right, then the right-holders are all individuals. If viewed in its collective aspect, then the right-holders are states (particularly developing states), and other collective entities such as municipalities, districts, communities, provinces.[98] The duty-bearers are developed nations, the international community, and world institutions addressing development problems. With regard to the individual aspect of this human right, the state owes individuals within its borders the positive duty to promote their development. In its collective aspect, developed nations and the international community also owe duties to developing countries.[99]

In light of this, Jack Donnelly argues that, 'If the right to development is a human right, then it is universal right, a right held by all. If it is equally a right of individuals, minorities, peoples, and states, it is a right of each and every individual, minority, people and state. This can only lead to countless and refractory conflicts of rights.'[100]

Indeed, it is unclear on how to implement the UNDRD since, as Donnelly correctly points out, the duties and rights are so 'refracted' as to be unenforceable in any coherent way. Thus, it is very doubtful whether the human right to development will give rise to 'human rights' which are enforceable in courts of law. But perhaps this is not what the drafters of the UNDRD had in mind.

---

[97] *Ibid.*, p. 491. See *supra* n. 96.

[98] H.G. Espiell, *supra* n. 63, p. 198.

[99] Perhaps these duties can also be regarded within a regional context such as Japan assisting other East Asian economies, and the United States helping out Mexico.

[100] J. Donnelly, *supra* n. 72, p. 266. See *supra* n. 96.

The notion of participation in development, an idea discussed earlier in this text, also has a place in the human rights discourse. The right to participation is no longer limited to states, but is now inclusive of individuals and non-state actors. For example, the Executive Directors of the World Bank and the IDA, respectively, have adopted parallel resolutions authorizing the creation of an independent, three-member Inspection Panel, which was formed in 1993.[101]

The Inspection Panel provides an independent forum to private citizens (or groups) who believe that they have been harmed by a project or undertaking financed by the World Bank. Private complaints may be filed with the Inspection Panel which may conduct investigations into the complaint lodged. Findings and recommendations are made to the World Bank's Executive Board, and the Board's final decision is made publicly available. This establishes an important legal nexus between the World Bank and the ultimate beneficiaries of its projects. The Inspection Panel is meant to encourage participatory development and ensure transparency in the development process.

Development is no longer a question reserved to the narrow confines of an individual's relationship with the state. Development involves the dynamic continuum of all nations and all individuals. The formation of the World Bank Inspection Panel is concrete evidence of the sea change in the international community's approach to development. No one is excluded from the equation. In fact, some have viewed the right to development as a 'synthesis' of all human rights.[102]

Donnelly further argues that states cannot have 'human' rights and that, if collective rights are to be included in the right to development, then a distinction should be made between human rights and peoples' rights (as found in the Banjul Charter, discussed below).[103] Donnelly summarily dismisses the peoples' rights aspect, and concludes that there can only be an 'individual' right to development (thereby preserving the Lockean relationship of the individual to the state), and finally states that:

we must carefully distinguish between a human right to *pursue* development, to strive for self-actualization in conditions of dignity, and a human right to *be* developed. The latter is extravagant and even dangerous; one does not have a right to be a fully developed person simply because one is a human being. A right to pursue personal development is on its face at least substantively plausible. But does it serve any real purpose? (Emphasis in original.)[104]

This question is certainly worth asking, and possible answers are discussed below.

---

[101] See IBRD No. 93-10, and IDA 93-6 (resolutions of the Executive Boards). See also *Annual Report*, The Inspection Panel (IBRD, IDA) dated August 1, 1994–July 31, 1996.

[102] *Ibid.*, p. 264; H.G. Espiell, *supra* n. 63, p. 205; Karel de Vey Mestdagh, *The Right to Development*, (Sijthoff and Norordhoff International Publishers, 1981), p. 49.

[103] J. Donnelly, *supra* n. 72, pp. 498–499. Reprinted by permission of the State University of New York Press, copyright (1984), State University of New York. All rights reserved.

[104] *Ibid.*, pp. 500–501.

3. AN AFRICAN PERSPECTIVE ON THE RIGHT TO DEVELOPMENT

The African Charter on Human and Peoples' Rights (also referred to as the Banjul Charter on Human and Peoples' Rights)[105] (hereinafter the 'African Charter', or the 'Banjul Charter')[106] was adopted by the 18th Assembly of Heads of State and Government of the Organization of African Unity (OAU) in Nairobi, Kenya in June 1981.[107] Five years later, on 21 October 1986, the African Charter entered into force upon the 26th ratification by a member state, as required by Article 63(3) thereof.[108] With ratifications by over 50 African states, the Banjul Charter is, to date, the largest regional human rights instrument in effect.[109]

The Banjul Charter is divided into three parts, the first of which consists of 29 articles. The first 12 articles delineate the expected norms of the individual's rights and freedoms (e.g., equal protection of the law, freedom of conscience and religion, freedom of assembly). Articles 13–18 set forth the individual's economic and social rights, which include the right to work, education, the best attainable physical and mental health, and the right to freely take part in the cultural life of the community. Articles 19–24 of the Banjul Charter apply to 'peoples', including Article 22 which sets forth the right to development. Part II of the Charter deals with the establishment of the African Commission on Human and Peoples' Rights, and Part III contains general provisions of a 'housekeeping' nature.

Article 18 of the Banjul Charter describes the state's special duty of care towards the family, women and children as well as the aged and disabled. In contrast, Part I, Chap. II, Arts. 27–29, sets forth the 'duties' of the individual towards his family, society and national community. This is a

---

[105] The term 'Banjul Charter' derives from Banjul, Gambia, the venue for the two Ministerial Conferences where discussions led to the final draft of the Charter. (This charter should not be confused with the Charter of the OAU.) See J. Swanson, 'The Emergence of New Rights in the African Charter', (1991) 12 *N.Y. L. Sch. J. Int'l and Comp. L.* 307, n. 1; R. Gittleman, 'The Banjul Charter on Human and Peoples' Rights: A Legal Analysis', in *Human Rights and Development in Africa*, p. 152.

[106] OAU Doc. CAB/LEG/67/3/Rev. 5 (1981), reprinted in 21 *I.L.M.* 59 (1982).

[107] R. Kiwanuka, 'The Meaning of "People" in the African Charter on Human and Peoples' Rights', (1988) 82 *Am. J. Int'l L.* 80 at 80.

[108] *Ibid.*, p. 81. The African Charter is not self-executing since ratifying members are required to adopt domestic legislative measures to give legal effect to the Charter. Article 62 provides that each ratifying member shall submit reports at two-year intervals from the date the Charter enters into force describing the legislative or other measures being taken to give legal effect to the provisions contained in the Charter. Ironically, the African Charter is considered to be self-executing by African francophone nations, but under a theory of reciprocity, will not be given legal effect until all anglophone nations have enacted it under their domestic law. Since this has not occurred, the Charter is not legally effective with either side. See C. Welch, Jr., 'The African Commission on Human and Peoples' Rights: A Five-Year Report and Assessment', (1992) 14 *Hum. Rts. Q.* 43 at 60.

[109] R. Kiwanuka, *supra* n. 107, p. 81. See also J. Swanson, *supra* n. 105, p. 327; A.P. Mutharika, 'The Role of International Law in the Twenty-First Century: An African Perspective', (1995) 18 *Fordham Int'l L. J.* 1706 at 1717.

marked departure from the Western view, where duties are incumbent upon the state, not on the individual.

Article 22 of the African Charter establishes the right to development and provides that:

(1)   All peoples shall have the right to their economic, social and cultural development with due regard to their freedom and identity and in the equal enjoyment of the common heritage of mankind.

(2)   States shall have the duty, individually or collectively, to ensure the exercise of the right to development.

The African Charter along with the European Convention for the Protection of Human Rights and Fundamental Freedoms,[110] and the American Convention on Human Rights,[111] are the three existing regional human rights instruments. The Banjul Charter is significant in a number of different respects. First, it establishes the right to development as a *legal*, not a *human* right. Further, the right to development is the right of 'all peoples', not of individuals solely. Most importantly, however, the multicultural (or at least, the non-Western) imprint of the African Charter, and its possible implications, is an important dimension in the dialogue on international human rights.

Unlike the UNDRD, which proclaims the right to development to be an 'inalienable human right', the African Charter sets forth the right to development as a *legal* right. In some ways, the articulation of the right to development as a simple legal right (rather than a 'human' right) simplifies matters, by eliminating the confusion caused by conferring 'human rights' on states and other non-human actors. As the previous discussion illustrates, much of the confusion in the minds of Western human rights scholars, commentators and sceptics is caused by the question of whether 'human' rights can be vested in the state. Certainly, certain individual freedoms, such as the freedom of assembly or association, are both individual and collective rights; but should this be extrapolated as a right of the state or of other collective entities?

Although logically, human rights can only be exercised by human beings, Professor Louis Sohn reminds us that:

It is not surprising, therefore, that international law not only recognizes inalienable rights of individuals, but also recognizes certain collective rights that are exercised jointly by individuals grouped into larger communities, including peoples and nations. These rights are still human rights; the effective exercise of collective rights is a precondition to the exercise of other rights, political, economic or both. If a community is not free, most of its members are also deprived of many important rights.[112]

---

[110] 213 U.N.T.S. 222 (entered in force, 3 September 1953).

[111] O.A.S.Treaty Series No. 36, p. 1, O.A.S. Off. Rec. Doc. OEA/ser.L/V/II.23, doc. rev. 2, reprinted in 9 I.L.M. 99 (1970).

[112] L. Sohn, 'The New International Law: Protection of the Rights of Individuals Rather than States', (1982) 32 *Am. U. L. Rev.* 1 at 48. Reproduced with the kind permission of the *American University Law Reveiw*.

Article 22 of the African Charter, articulating the right to development, is different from the UDHR in another important respect. The right to development under the Banjul Charter is a right of 'all peoples', rather than of all individuals. As discussed earlier, in 1979 Karel Vasak referred to collective rights, such as the right to development as the third generation of 'solidarity' rights.[113] Therefore, the Banjul Charter's definition of the right to development as a right of 'peoples' is in keeping with this characterization. The following section will explore the linkage between the right to development as a right of 'peoples'.

3.1 A peoples' right to self-determination

The legal concept of 'peoples' has its genesis in the right to self-determination.[114] The evolution of the legal concept of 'self-determination' is divided into two historical periods: the post-First World War period of redrawing the map of Europe, and the post-Second World War period of decolonization.[115]

The concept of 'peoples' owes a great deal to US President Woodrow Wilson. In introducing the concept to the League of Nations in Versailles in 1919 following the conclusion of the First World War, President Wilson described 'self-determination' as the 'right of every people to chose the sovereign under which they live, to be free of alien masters, and not to be handed about from sovereign to sovereign as if they were property'.[116]

Although Wilson proposed the inclusion of self-determination as a principle of the Covenant of the League of Nations, the risk it posed in terms of supporting secessionist movements in a polyglot Europe (not to mention applying the principle to European colonial possessions) was regarded as too great and, as a result, his proposal was rejected.[117] Nevertheless, Wilson's unflagging efforts ultimately brought international recognition to the right to self-determination of ethnic, religious or other minorities, and the doctrine became an established part of international law.[118]

The second most important context for self-determination was formulated in the aftermath of decolonization following the conclusion of the Second World War. The principle of self-determination formed the legal basis for the decolonization effort, and was incorporated into Articles 1(2) and 55 of the UN Charter.[119] Although the principle of self-determination constitutes a

---

[113] K. Vasak, 'A 30-Year Struggle', *UNESCO Courier* (November 1977) at 29.

[114] R. Kiwanuka, *supra* n. 107, p. 86.

[115] See M. Hill, 'What the Principle of Self-Determination Means Today' (1995) 1 *ILSA J. Int'l and Comp. L.* 119 at 121.

[116] D. Cass, 'Rethinking Self-Determination: A Critical Analysis of Current International Law Theories', (1992) 18 *Syracuse J. Int'l L. and Com.* 21 at 23–24.

[117] E. Cooper, 'Comment on "Transitional Constitutionalism": Politics and Law in Russia Since 1993', (1996) 14 *Wis. Int'l L. J.* 531 at 540, n. 28. See also L. Buchheit, *Secession: The Legitimacy of Self-Determination* (1978), p. 14.

[118] D. Cass, *supra* n. 116, pp. 24–25, 26. (The right to self-determination of religious and ethnic minorities is set forth in Article 27 of the ICCPR.)

[119] M. Hill, *supra* n. 115, p. 124.

founding principle of the UN Charter, it has no precise legal definition.[120] The principle of self-determination has been rearticulated in the UDHR, in Article 1 of the ICCPR and the ICESCR, respectively, and in the Definition of Aggression.[121]

More importantly, it is the subject of two important UN declarations: the Declaration on the Granting of Independence to Colonial Countries and Peoples (the 1960 Declaration),[122] and the Declaration on Principles of International Law Governing Friendly Relations and Co-operation Among States in Accordance with the Charter of the United Nations (the 1970 Declaration).[123]

The 1960 Declaration expressly stated that, 'All peoples have the right to self-determination; by virtue of that right they freely determine their political status and freely pursue their economic, social and cultural development.'[124] Article 1 of the Declaration states that, 'The subjection of peoples to alien subjugation, domination and exploitation constitutes a denial of fundamental human rights, is contrary to the Charter of the United Nations and is an impediment to the promotion of world peace and cooperation'. The 1960 Declaration along with the two International Covenants only conceived of self-determination in the context of colonial liberation, and did not extend the right to minorities wishing to secede from UN member states.[125]

Under the Banjul Charter, the right of 'all peoples' to pursue their economic and social development has its source in Article 22 (right to development) as well as in Article 20 (right to self-determination). Article 20 of the Banjul Charter recognizes the inalienable right of all peoples to self-determination. Specifically, Article 20(1) states that '[all peoples] shall freely determine their political status and shall pursue their economic and social development according to the policy they have freely chosen'. This, combined with the right to 'freely dispose of their wealth and natural resources' under Article 21, gives all African 'peoples' the right to political and economic self-determination.

---

[120] D. Cass, *supra* n. 116, p. 24.

[121] G.A. Res. 3314, 29 U.N. GAOR Supp. (No. 31), p. 142, U.N. Doc. A/9631 (1974).

[122] G.A. Res. 1514, U.N. GAOR Comm., Sess. Supp. No. 21, p. 166, U.N. Doc. A/4684 (1960).

[123] G.A. Res. 2625, Annex, 25 U.N. GAOR Supp. (No. 17), p. 66, U.N. Doc. A/5217 (1970).

[124] M. Hill, *supra* n. 115, p. 125, quoting the 1960 Declaration.

[125] G. Simpson, 'The Diffusion of Sovereignty: Self-Determination in the Postcolonial Age', (1996) 32 *Stan. J. Int'l L.* 255 at 256, 268–69. See also J. Wilson, 'Ethnic Groups and the Right to Self-Determination', (1996) 11 *Conn. J. Int'l L.* 433 at 460.
Paragraph seven of the 1970 Declaration, however, opened the door to legitimizing secessionist movements within an established nation-state. This idea goes back to Wilson's original conception that the legitimacy of government stems from its representation of all segments of the population. (See M. Hill, *supra* n. 115, p. 129. See also D. Cass *supra* n. 116, p. 36.) Therefore, the territorial integrity and the national unity of such a state will only be protected when the government governs 'with the consent of the governed'. (M. Hill, *supra* n. 115, p. 129.) Thus, an unrepresentative government may provide the necessary justification for an oppressed minority to claim its own self-determination, thus seceding on this basis. (See J. Wilson, *supra*, pp. 460–61. See also D. Cass, *supra* n. 116, pp. 36–37.)

However, the Banjul Charter does not expressly define 'peoples'. Moreover, Article 20(2) of the Banjul Charter, setting forth the right to self-determination, limits its application to 'colonized or oppressed' peoples. Thus, it has been argued that the rights of 'peoples' attach only to the ex-colonial population as a whole, and not to its constituent ethnic groups. Thus, some conclude that '"peoples' rights" serve the function of supporting decolonization without threatening the stability and unity of post-colonial states',[126] and that, accordingly, 'international law in its present form does not accommodate claims to self-determination by ethnic groups in the post-colonial context'.[127] If this interpretation is accepted, however, the application of the principle of self-determination is rendered meaningless in a post-colonial context.[128]

In contrast, Richard Kiwanuka argues that the definition of peoples in the Banjul Charter goes beyond its original context for the liberation from colonial rule. In his view, 'peoples' under the Banjul Charter may mean: (1) all persons in a geographically predefined area awaiting political liberation; (2) minorities; (3) the state (although the state is rarely a true representative of 'all peoples') or, (4) all persons within a state.[129] Moreover, in relation to the right to development set forth in Article 22 of the Banjul Charter, more than one of these definitions may apply.[130] Yet, he warns that, 'Peoples' rights cannot be a substitute for individual human rights.'[131]

If we accept this expansive definition, then the legal notion of 'peoples' contained in the Banjul Charter goes well beyond the post-war concept of political 'self-determination' for colonized or minority peoples. Indeed, commentators have argued that there is a growing international acceptance of a new, post-colonial right to self-determination which includes the right to limited secession,[132] as we have recently witnessed in Eritrea. Thus, by declaring the right to development as an intrinsic right of 'all peoples', the Banjul Charter gives this right yet another dimension of complexity. It moves the human rights focus off the individual and onto 'peoples', a notion that is both collective and subjective. After all, who decides which individuals constitute a 'people?'

3.2 The Africanization of human rights

Finally, with regard to the African cultural imprint of the Banjul Charter, the Charter has several noteworthy aspects. First, it moves towards reconciling

---

[126] J. Wilson, *supra* n. 125, p. 463.
[127] *Ibid.*, p 476.
[128] G. Simpson, *supra* n. 125, p. 275.
[129] R. Kiwanuka, *supra* n. 107, pp. 86–88. See also P. Kunig, 'The Protection of Human Rights by International law in Africa', (1982) 25 *German Y.B. Int'l L.*, pp. 138, 156–159.
[130] R. Kiwanuka, *supra* n. 107, pp. 100–101.
[131] *Ibid.*, p. 100.
[132] G. Simpson, *supra* n. 125, pp. 285–286. Simpson discusses four potential 'models' for self-determination, namely, national (the Basque separatist movement, the Aceh in Indonesia, and Tibet); democratic aspiration (South Africa, Portugal, Spain); devolutionary practice (Quebec, Scotland); and secession (Biafra, Bangladesh).

Western human rights traditions with the African experience. The Charter incorporates Western liberal thought, which pervades traditional human rights law, while changing the context to an African one. This is an important step, since Western liberal tradition provides the philosophical support underlying the UDHR, the two International Covenants (all three of which are collectively referred to as the International Bill of Rights), and the European and American regional human rights instruments.[133]

Secondly, the Charter redefines the role of the state in the context of shaping human rights. Thirdly, it delineates an enforcement mechanism that differs significantly from Western legal practice. And finally, while recognizing that individuals have rights, the Charter also imposes duties on the individuals claiming such rights.

3.3   An African view of human rights

The liberal tradition of political and legal thought, while a 'received' tradition in colonized Africa, was not part of the traditional African world view.[134] In the Hobbesian world view, for example, the individual was no longer a part of the whole of society, but an atomistic entity, constantly threatened by (yet in need of) the overreaching state. This desperate need for as well as deep distrust of the state is still an important underpinning of Western societies today.

The Lockean tradition of liberal political thought firmly moved the individual to centre stage, and restrained the potentially harmful interference of the state by setting aside certain spheres of life in which the state could not intrude. The sanctity of those civil rights and freedoms which may be exercised by the individual free of government intrusion is unquestioned even today. Over time, the feudalistic context for the individual as an inseparable member of society gradually eroded under the force of the new thinking of the European Enlightenment. The single revolutionary idea of positing the individual as the sole arbiter of his political and economic fate paved the way to capitalism and the formation of advanced industrial societies.[135]

The question is whether the Banjul Charter has successfully incorporated what is quintessentially Western philosophy. First, should these 'received' traditions of Western thought and political philosophy be accepted by African nations, and if so, has the Banjul Charter done so successfully?

---

[133] See J. Swanson, *supra* n. 105, pp. 324–326.

[134] See J. Cobbah, 'African Values and the Human Rights Debate: An African Perspective', (1987) 9 *Hum. Rts. Q.* 309 at 323, n. 41. See also M. wa Mutua, *supra* n. 3, p. 342. Mutua argues that since the modern African state was forcibly imposed by European colonizers without regard to existing African political and ethnic entities, that consequently the modern African state 'did not result from the natural progression or evolution of those societies'. *Ibid.* Thus, he concludes, 'the traditional liberal conception of the relationship between the state and the individual is of limited utility in imagining a viable regime of human rights'. *Ibid.*

[135] J. Swanson, *supra* n. 105, p. 325.

Secondly, are there African traditions which should change, ameliorate or reject certain Western traditions in a quest to formulate an African regime for human rights?

It has been argued that without the catalytic force of the Hobbesian-Lockean world view, a society tends to remain static, that is to say, in a pre-capitalist, feudalistic mode.[136] In this context, there is no differentiation between the rights of the individual that are separate and apart from the larger village, community, society, or ethnic, religious, or linguistic group. The traditional human rights regime which accords the individual certain important protections against an intrusive and dangerous state, and is deeply rooted in a Hobbesian world view.

In fact, unless a Hobbesian viewpoint is taken, and firmly imbedded as a cornerstone in an entrepreneurial, truly capitalistic state, 'human rights' as such cannot come into being. After all, traditional civil and political liberties are grounded in the individual's antagonistic relationship to the state. Thus, 'human rights', as understood in the West, are only possible in a post-feudal, capitalist, modern state. Thus, all other human rights regimes, concepts and practices which lie outside this context are ineffectual or, at least, met with deep scepticism by Western scholars.[137]

However, pre-capitalist, feudalistic societies characterize the vast majority of the developing world. In this context, the 'individual' tends to be both defined by and contained in his relationship to larger groups. Unlike the nuclear family which dominates Western tradition, the extended family and the collective, communitarian basis for most African (and, indeed, most developing world) societies tends to be predominate.[138] Thus, the stark individualism of Hobbes goes against the grain, and is not an easily digestible ideal for most African societies or, indeed, for most societies in the developing world. In fact, Hobbes did not address family, society or cultural parameters, and quite clearly saw the state as the Leviathan. This is a stark contrast to the African view of the individual's place in and relationship to society, which was not viewed as adversarial in nature, but as being mutually supportive.

Of course, the Enlightenment scholars also included Jean-Jacques Rousseau, whose formulation of the 'social contract' is a marked departure from the Hobbesian-Lockean view of society and the state, and may be somewhat closer to the African viewpoint. Rousseau writes:

The question, then, is to distinguish clearly between the respective rights of the citizen and of the sovereign, as well as between the duties which the former have to fulfil in their capacity as subjects and the natural rights which they ought to enjoy in their character as men.

---

[136] M. wa Mutua, *supra* n. 3, pp. 354–355. Mutua gives an excellent discussion of this issue concerning pre-colonial African societies.

[137] *Ibid.*, pp. 355, 357.

[138] *Ibid.*, 362-363.

It is admitted that whatever part of his power, property, and liberty each one alienates by the social compact is only that part of the whole of which the use is important to the community; but we must also admit that the sovereign alone is the judge of what is important.[139]

I would argue that even this world view differs substantially from the African standpoint, insofar as the relationship of the Rousseauan individual with society is by means of a social contract. This implies that the relationship is that of the individual solely with 'society', which is an abstraction, and that further, this is a negotiated relationship. Although this 'bargain' may include rights of, as well as duties to, the state by the individual, the contractual nature of this bargain differs from the African perspective. The relationship between an individual living in an African society can be seen as being more organic and familial, rather than contractual in nature.

The Banjul Charter has incorporated the traditional human rights regime of negative freedoms as well as the economic and social rights that are set forth, in principle, in the ICESCR. However, it is not simply an amalgamation of the two International Covenants for human rights. Articles 27–29 of the Banjul Charter define the specific duties of the individual, a concept that lies outside the traditional Western human rights regime.[140] The Charter recognizes the role and function of the individual in African society who both contributes to and is an integral part of that society. Thus, the rights of the individual against the state are balanced by the duties of that individual to society.

The Hobbesian view of the individual as a 'lone wolf' is mitigated under the Banjul Charter by imposing duties and legal responsibilities on that individual. Thus, the Banjul Charter begins to close the gap (perhaps not completely) between the Western, post-Hobbesian capitalist state and the human rights regime that evolved from it, and the neo-feudal, proto-capitalist, quasi-modern African society. It articulates a new human rights regime that incorporates multicultural elements of the particular history, sociology and modern dilemmas of the African individual.

Certainly, the Banjul Charter recognizes that the African man and woman on the street may be just as interested, if not more interested, in the right to work and the right to education as he or she is in political expression and religious freedom. Individual rights and entitlements as expressed in the Charter are, however, balanced by the duties owed by the individual to a much larger context and society of which the individual forms an integral part. The hostility, alienation, and antagonism of the Hobbesian individual in relation to the modern state is thus abated.

---

[139] J-J. Rousseau, *The Social Contract* (Henry J. Tozer (trans.), New York, Charles Scribner's Sons, 1898).

[140] U.O. Umozurike, 'The African Charter on Human and Peoples' Rights, (1983) 77 *Am. J. Int'l L.* 902 at 907; R. Gittleman, 'The Banjul Charter on Human and Peoples' Rights: A Legal Analysis', in *Human Rights and Development in Africa*, pp. 154, 155.

3.4　The Role of the state

The Banjul Charter also changes the role of the state. The state has many positive duties to perform in ensuring that the economic and social rights of its members are realized. Article 22(2) of the Banjul Charter specifies that 'States shall have the duty, individually and collectively, to ensure the exercise of the right to development.'

Whereas the state in Western society is admonished from interfering with the political and civic freedoms of an individual, the Banjul Charter views the state in very different terms. In particular, the Charter contains several 'clawback' clauses which permit the state to encroach upon certain individual rights and freedoms contained in Part I of the Charter, to the extent permitted under domestic law. Specifically, Article 6 states, in relevant part:

Every individual shall have the right to liberty and to the security of his person. No one may be deprived of his freedom except for reasons and conditions previously laid down by law.

A similar provision may be found in Article 5(1) of the European Convention and in Article 7(5) of the American Convention, as well as in Article 9 of the ICCPR.[141] However, these Conventions set forth the specific conditions under which such liberties may be denied to the individual, and establish comprehensive procedural safeguards (along the lines of 'due process') which provide clear restraints on arbitrary government action. The African Charter, in contrast, does not limit the conditions under which liberties may denied, 'except for reasons and conditions previously laid down by law'.[142] These reasons and conditions are not discussed or defined.

Secondly, unlike its other human rights instrument counterparts, the African Charter does not provide any procedural safeguards against government abuse. Richard Gittleman suggests that the provisions of the African Charter may be clarified to avoid possible confusion and misinterpretation, 'by enumerating a specific list of exceptions to the right to liberty and by setting forth appropriate procedures to be followed'.[143] Article 9 of the ICCPR, for example, may provide a model for establishing the types of procedural protections against the arbitrary deprivation of liberty, and unwarranted state intrusion onto personal freedoms.

Other examples of clawback clauses include Article 11 of the Banjul Charter, which provides that every individual shall have the right to assemble freely, but that the exercise of this right 'shall be subject only to necessary restrictions provided for by law in particular those enacted in the interests of national security, the safety, health, ethics, rights and freedoms of others'. The scope of this clawback clause and the vagueness of the term 'necessary restrictions' does not provide any real restraint on the state from

---

[141]　R. Gittleman, *supra* n. 140, pp. 158–159, 161–162.
[142]　Article 6, Banjul Charter.
[143]　R. Gittleman, *supra* n. 140, p. 159.

significantly curtailing the right to free assembly, or even legislating away certain freedoms associated with it.

Similarly, Article 14 of the African Charter guarantees the right to property which 'may only be encroached upon in the interest of public need or in the general interest of the community and in accordance with the provisions of appropriate laws'. There is no specified right to compensation or restitution for property seized or nationalized by the state. Once again, the breadth and the vagueness of this provision may give the state *carte blanche* authority to appropriate privately held property and, consequently, seriously compromise the free exercise of this right.

The African Charter contains no clause which would permit the state to derogate from its obligations under the Charter.[144] A derogation clause permits a right, granted under the Charter, to be temporarily suspended under certain circumstances. For example, Article 15(1) of the European Convention specifies that derogation may occur 'in time of war or other public emergency threatening the life of the nation'. A derogation clause is thus intended to define the circumstances during which individual rights and liberties may be curtailed (e.g., a national emergency). More importantly, a derogation clause also specifies which rights are 'non-derogable'. These rights may not be infringed upon even in times of national crisis when states are most apt to curtail personal freedoms.

The purpose of a derogation clause is quite different from that of a clawback clause. A derogation clause suspends previously granted rights, whereas a clawback clause restricts rights from the outset and therefore, is far more discretionary in nature. The inclusion of so many clawback clauses in the African Charter without putting adequate procedural safeguards in place, tends to weaken individual rights while strengthening the power of the state.[145] The absence of a derogation clause also means that 'non-derogable' rights are not specified, nor are the conditions under which such rights may be temporarily suspended. Insofar as adequate procedural protections are not established in the Charter, individual liberties may be subordinated to the powers of the state. Very little protection is offered to the individual against arbitrary state action. The patrimonial character of the state is apparent, and the 'state-centric' character of the Banjul Charter has been criticized for this reason.

3.5   Enforcing the Banjul Charter: The African Commission

Finally, the African Charter does not establish a human rights court. Unlike the European Court of Human Rights (established under the European Convention) or the Inter-American Court of Human Rights (established by the American Convention), there is no African court of human rights. This was

---

[144] U.O. Umozurike, *supra* n. 140, pp. 909–910.
[145] Clawback clauses in the African Charter include Art. 6 (right to liberty), Art. 8 (freedom of conscience and religion), Art. 9 (right to express opinions), Art. 10 (right to free association), Art 11. (right to free assembly), Art. 12 (right to freedom of movement), Art. 13 (right to participate in government), and Art. 14 (right to property). See R. Gittleman, *supra* n. 140, p. 162.

the specific intent of the Charter's framers, who wanted to establish the means for settling disputes or claims through amicable, diplomatic negotiations rather than adversarial court proceedings.[146]

This reflects the departure of the African Charter from its European and American counterparts, insofar as the violation of an individual right by the state does not give rise to a right of action against the state in an adversarial proceeding. Conciliation and bilateral negotiations are stressed as the traditional African means of dispute settlement.

The Charter establishes an 11-member Commission which may receive communications from member states who believe that a fellow member has violated the provisions of the Charter. The member state whose conduct has been questioned has three months in which to respond to the state, expressing such concerns. If bilateral negotiations between the parties fail, the matter is formally referred to the Commission.

Based on such a communication from the parties, the Commission may make reports and recommendations to the OAU Assembly of Heads of State and Government.[147] Whereas the Courts under the European and American Conventions can review matters considered by their respective Commissions, the OAU cannot take any independent action. It may merely request the African Commission to make reports, findings or recommendations.[148]

The roles of the individual and of the state in the African Charter are seen in remarkably different terms. The individual is far more integrated into society, and owes certain duties to society. Thus, the African Charter begins to reformulate the Hobbesian world view by moving the individual into a larger context with duties and responsibilities as well as rights and liberties. The adversarial nature of the individual's relationship to the state is ameliorated by making it more cooperative rather than confrontational. The state also has recognized duties towards the individual, family and community, and is accorded far more powers and duties than in traditional human rights regimes.

Additionally, the evolution of the right to development from an 'inalienable human right' to a legal right of peoples, not just individuals, is important. The notion of 'peoples' under the Banjul Charter has been expanded beyond the traditional confines of self-determination for oppressed minorities or ethnic groups. Further, the enforcement mechanisms, while flawed, also represent a clear departure from the traditional, adversarial posture of the individual asserting his rights against the state. Although the poor enforcement mechanisms and state-centric nature of the African Charter may jeopardize individual rights by not addressing the potential for state abuse, this need not be an irreparable problem.

Nevertheless, some have argued that Africa needs to aggressively move the human rights agenda to centre stage.[149] Kivutha Kibwana

---

[146] J. Swanson, *supra* n. 105, p. 330; U.O. Umozurike, *supra* n. 140, p. 909.
[147] See Arts. 47–53, Banjul Charter.
[148] U.O. Umozurike, *supra* n. 140, p. 909.
[149] See K. Kibwana, K. Acheampong and M. Mwagiru, 'Human Rights and Diplomacy in Africa: A Critical Perspective', available on internet at http://snipe.ukc.ac.uk/ international/papers.dir/kibwana.html (last visited on 13 August 1998).

and others, for example, urge: (1) all member states of the OAU to ratify the Banjul Charter; (2) that the Commission be given more independence, by giving it the power to investigate complaints, which is only possible now with the express permission of the OAU Assembly of Heads of States and Governments; (3) that African states begin to put their 'human rights houses in order';[150] (4) that the African 'preoccupation' with state sovereignty and non-interference with domestic affairs be toned down; and, (5) that a human rights 'watchdog' organization be set up to monitor human rights violations in Africa and in other regions.[151]

In sum, the African Charter represents a philosophical and institutional departure from the legal orthodoxy of other human rights Conventions. In fact, the value of the African Charter may lie in its distinctly different regional, philosophical and institutional approach, which may offer important lessons. The African Charter may be the first real evolution towards formulating a new human rights regime in a post-Cold War, more co-operative, global world. The fact that the fairly narrow confines of human rights concepts and practice as understood by Western nations are broadened in the African Charter to incorporate multicultural dimensions of the African perspective should be seen as a positive step forward.

Despite the positive intent to incorporate a distinctly African view of a human rights regime, the OAU is nevertheless now considering the merits of establishing an African Court on Human and Peoples' Rights. The draft protocol under consideration would establish an 11-judge court which would be empowered to consider cases submitted by: the Commission; an OAU state member; a state against which a complaint has been lodged; NGOs with observer status at the OAU; and individuals wishing to bring complaints before the Court.[152] The Court shall, if established, apply the provisions of the African Charter as well as other human rights instruments.[153] It is not clear that the African Charter's experiment with the amicable resolution of human rights abuses has been terminated, but a more formal, adversarial resolution of human rights abuses or violations is also now being considered. The final outcome has not yet been determined.

4.   PROSPECTS FOR THE RIGHT TO DEVELOPMENT

In light of the preceding discussion, is there a right to development? The sole dissenting vote of the United States in the UN vote for the UNDRD may not be legally sufficient to bar the necessary legal consensus to create a

---

[150] *Ibid.*, p. 13.
[151] See generally, *ibid.*, pp. 10–14.
[152] Arts. 5–6 of the Draft (Nouakchott) Protocol to the African Charter on Human and Peoples' Rights on the Establishment of an African Court on Human and Peoples' Rights (OAU/LEG/EXP/AFCHPR/PROT(2)), Second Government Legal Experts Meeting on the Establishment of an African Court on Human and Peoples' Rights, Nouakchott, Mauritania, on file with author.
[153] *Ibid.*, Art. 7.

legal norm. Perhaps we may conclude that, technically speaking, a 'human right to development' has been established. Under the African Charter, there is clearly a *legal* right to development; however, its enforceability is regional in nature, and even that is somewhat questionable. The dissenting vote of the United States, while not fatal, nevertheless reveals that there are strong reservations to the UNDRD. Thus, universal acceptance of its doctrines is not as yet a *fait accompli.*

Much of the dismay concerning the right to development centres on the lack of an appropriate legal pedigree. The right to development is often grouped with other 'new' human rights (including the right to rest, the right to leisure and even the right to tourism). Such rights are usually met with scepticism, since their proliferation diminishes the importance of the human rights regime, distances the possibility of enforcing these purported rights, and trivializes the human dimension in the international dialogue on these issues.

Some attention has been given to making the right to development more respectable, by rationalizing it after the fact. It has been suggested that 'new' human rights be subject to the following criteria: (1) that the new right be compatible with and not devalue existing rights; (2) that the desired new legal norm cannot be achieved through the progressive realization of existing rights; and (3) that the new right is recognized as being authoritative insofar as it creates an expectation that it will be complied with.[154]

Philip Alston examines potential legal criteria which may be applied in determining the legitimacy of a proposed new human right, yet concludes in his final analysis that, 'The application of a formal list of substantive requirements is ... an unworkable approach.'[155] He remarks that, 'the normative validity of rights recognized by the [UN] General Assembly cannot be made dependent upon their validity in terms of philosophical or any other supposedly "objective" criteria.'[156]

Further, he recognizes that there are no real safeguards against 'manipulation' or 'circumvention' of such legal criteria by a determined majority of the General Assembly.[157] Since there are no effective legal impediments to opening the floodgate to new, yet frivolous, human rights, the direction of a new dialogue on human rights is entirely dependent on the integrity, sincerity, and commitment of the individuals and international actors involved in it.

After this long digression, we finally return to Jack Donnelly's question of whether the right to development serves any real purpose. In my own view, the strength, utility and purpose of a new right to development lies not in its practical effectiveness in halting human rights abuses, but in the

---

[154] P. Alston, 'A Third Generation of Solidarity Rights: Progressive Development or Obfuscation of International Human Rights Law?' (1982) 29 *Neth. Int'l L. R.* 307 at 321; P. Alston, *supra* n. 70, p. 621.

[155] P. Alston, *supra* n. 70, p. 617.

[156] *Ibid.*

[157] *Ibid.*, p. 621.

new voice it gives to the concerns and philosophical orientation of non-Western human rights thinkers and activists.

The fact that the African Charter, in particular, offers a new perspective on the role of the individual and the state is important in this international discourse by serving to both broaden and deepen it. That is not to say that all the legal and philosophical contradictions of the past have been resolved, but the right to development is a significant evolution in this regard.

However, notwithstanding the potential contribution that a right to development may make in a new international discourse on human rights, this potential has not been achieved. Although adopting a multi-dimensional approach to international legal questions in a post-Cold War era is necessary to meet the needs of a less polarized, yet more confusing, world, the right to development falls short of its promise. My reservations about the right to development stem from both legal and practical concerns.

First, by adopting a diffuse approach in setting forth the terms and conditions of a right to development, the right ends up being something of a 'grab-bag' for individuals, peoples and developing states. By structuring the duties and responsibilities of the international actors in such a diffuse fashion, the right to development loses clarity, precision and legal discipline in the process. Thus, any attempt to implement the right to development naturally tends to be a confusing and contradictory exercise, especially since the developing state is both a right-holder and a duty-bearer. Defining the right to development as having both individual and collective aspects is certainly an acceptable starting point; however, further articulation of these different aspects, and the duties and entitlements that stem from them, may help clarify matters.

Secondly, the foundation of the right to development rests on certain 'self-evident' propositions. Accepting some of these concepts is quite problematic for some Western states, all of whom are important duty-bearers. In light of the confused antecedents of the right to development, its definition as an 'inalienable human right' as set forth in Article 1 of the UNDRD is one such example. In fact, the definition of the right to development as an 'inalienable human right' is problematic even for its supporters.[158] The international community, especially Western industrialized states, continues to be unwilling to accept this statement as a self-evident proposition.

These nations have not been convinced that the right to development is 'inalienable' in the same fashion as the right to the freedom of expression is considered to be. Notwithstanding the historical and philosophical explanations for this, the UNDRD (as it is currently worded) lacks the power to

---

[158] See Draft UN resolution A/C.3/41/L.4 adopting a declaration on the right to development by the Third Committee on Nov. 28, 1986, U.N. Doc. A/C.3/41/SR.61, pp. 31-32. The delegate from Ireland supported the adoption of the right to development, but found that the assertion of the right as an 'inalienable human right' to be 'unconvincing' in the text as adopted.

convince its sceptics. This may be due, in part, to the fact that the 'inalienable human right' to development may be invoked by peoples as well as by developing states.

Although one can appreciate that the proponents of the right to development are undertaking a revolutionary task by attempting to change the frame of reference for a human rights agenda. Shifting the exclusive human rights focus off the individual and onto broader, collective entities is a daunting task indeed. However, the task has not yet been accomplished, and many sceptics (including the author) remain unconvinced that such a shift has adequate legal support within the framework of the UNDRD.

Another example of the resistance faced by the right to development in achieving full acceptance by the international community is based on NIEO principles which are still highly problematic. As discussed above, the UNDRD cites the NIEO in its preamble, thereby invoking the NIEO agenda in a new human rights context. The NIEO is highly controversial, particularly with regard to its provisions requiring preferential and nonreciprocal treatment of developing states, promoting technology transfers to developing countries, and making development assistance available without conditioning such assistance on political or military reforms.

Again, it is highly unlikely that the nexus between an NIEO approach to development and a human right to development will be accepted as a self-evident proposition by Western, industrialized countries. This is not to say that the NIEO is irremediably flawed at the outset, or that it lacks relevancy in the context of development. However, what is clear is that developing countries have not made a compelling case for the acceptance of NIEO principles, nor has its relationship to the UNDRD been made in a convincing manner. In addition, the NIEO agenda applies differential legal norms to developed and developing states which is highly problematic, as the earlier discussion on substantive legal norms within development law indicated (see Chapter 2).

The twenty-first century ushers in a new millennium full of boundless possibilities, in light of which actors in the developing world should consider engaging in a new dialogue on the right to development. The opportunity for changing the conversation on the subject of human rights and development is daily becoming more manifest. Developing countries are becoming more politically powerful as they become more economically powerful, as China's example amply demonstrates. Rather than walking away from the right to development based on a fossilized and polemical stance, developing countries can now actively change the nature of the dialogue and, indeed, must change it if this new international legal right is to be given real meaning. And, indeed, perhaps the developing world has both time and history on its side in this regard.

A more practical concern, of course, is whether the right to development will have any impact in the real world, particularly in the world of intractable poverty where most individuals who may seek to exert that right actually live. The enforceability of the right to development, as discussed earlier, is unclear. Even if the Banjul Charter approach is adopted so that the right to development is enforced through consensual rather than litigious means, the method for doing so is problematic, as OAU states are beginning to realize. Failure to clarify the definition of, and the means for enforcing, the right to development has only added to the general confusion surrounding it. Indeed, it may be argued that the advocates for the right have lost an opportunity to win over new supporters.

Merely adopting a right to development, of course, does not mean that development will occur for that individual or that state. Indeed, achieving the promise of 'development' is far more than a legal or human 'right' can, in practical terms, confer. It is a means, however, of moving the discourse between the developed and the developing world forward. The pluralist approach and the non-Western orientation of the right to development is a noteworthy element in a legal evolution which has not ended. Insofar as the dialogue continues in a principled manner and within a legitimate legal framework, I believe that the right to development does have something new and important to offer.

Annex: Draft Protocol on Establishing a Capital Transfer Appellate Board

ARTICLE I: ESTABLISHMENT OF THE ORGANIZATION

1. The Capital Transfer Appellate Board (hereinafter referred to as the CTAB or the Board) is hereby established as an independent organ of the International Monetary Fund (IMF) and the World Bank Group.

ARTICLE II: MEMBERSHIP

1. All members of the IMF (the Members) automatically accede to this agreement (the Agreement).
2. Withdrawal by any Member from this Agreement shall be made by giving notice to the Chairman of the CTAB which shall take effect not less than thirty (30) days from the date of such notice.
3. No reservations may be made with respect to any provision of this Agreement.

ARTICLE III: FUNCTIONS

1. The CTAB shall be authorized to hear appeals (the Appeals) of the decisions issued by the Executive Board of Directors of the IMF or of the International Bank for Reconstruction and Development (the World Bank) brought by any Member of the IMF in good standing.
2. (a) The following bases for an Appeal must be satisfactorily demon strated by a Member bringing a matter for consideration or review by the CTAB:
    (1) that the IMF or the World Bank, in making or implementing the executive decision in question, failed to follow their respective policies or procedures with respect to an act or omission committed by either institution;
    (2) that an act or omission required of a Member by the IMF or the World Bank violates the Member's laws, rules, procedures, or public policy;

(3) that any act or omission required of the Member by the IMF or the World Bank violates the terms or conditions of a valid international agreement entered into, or other obligation incumbent upon, such a Member;

(4) that any act or omission required of the Member by the IMF or the World Bank, and duly agreed to by such Member, cannot be carried out due to unforeseeable, changed circumstances, other than a change in government or official policy made subsequent to such an agreement being entered into.

(b) The Member must certify in writing, and demonstrate to the satisfaction of the CTAB, that the following options have been exhausted or cannot be exercised:

(1) negotiation with the respective institution; and,

(2) cancellation of the underlying commitment, financing, loan or provision of assistance with the respective institution.

If the Member fails to do so, the appeal may be summarily dismissed by the CTAB.

(c) The Member must demonstrate that immediate, irreparable harm will result if injunctive relief is sought, or that direct or indirect injury to its interests will foreseeably result unless action is taken, or abated, as the case may be.

ARTICLE IV: POWERS

1. The CTAB shall be empowered to adjudicate Appeals, issue declaratory judgments and, on a limited basis, prescribe injunctive relief.

2. If, in the judgment of the CTAB, the information is presented during the course of an Appeal is insufficient or inadequate to reach a decision, it may stay the appellate proceedings until such time as such information is presented to the Board sufficient for it to render judgment. The CTAB shall also be authorized to direct the Inspection Panel of the World Bank to conduct an independent investigation of the Appeal under the direction of the CTAB while the stay is in effect. The stay shall be terminated within a reasonable time, as shall be determined by the CTAB.

3. The CTAB shall issue decisions on an expedited basis of not more than forty-five (45) days from when an Appeal is received, such a decision being final and binding on the parties with no further right of appeal. These decisions, along with filings and submissions made by the Member or other interested parties, shall be of public record, and made available to the public at a *de minimis* cost. Upon the request of a Member, the CTAB shall provide adequate protection of non-public, classified or other sensitive information contained in such documents, as appropriate.

4. The CTAB shall be authorized to issue declaratory judgments holding certain acts or omissions of the IMF or the World Bank; statements or provisions set forth in loan, or other, agreements by or between the parties; or undertakings expressly undertaken or agreed to by a member to be null and void. If a provision contained in a document is declared to be a nullity by the CTAB, such provision shall be stricken from said document. A declaratory judgment issued by the CTAB shall not affect the financing or other terms agreed to by the Member and the respective institution which may be the subject of the Appeal, unless so determined by the CTAB.
5. The CTAB shall be authorized to issue injunctive relief in exceptional circumstances where immediate and irreparable harm may result if such relief is not provided. The CTAB shall make provision for an oral hearing in such cases, as deemed necessary.

ARTICLE V: SCOPE OF POWERS

1. The CTAB shall be empowered to hear Appeals of any decision issued by the Executive Directors of the IMF or the World Bank, respectively, without limitation as to the nature of the decision, including, but not limited to, the nature of the underlying financing provided by structural adjustment credits or other means, the conditionality imposed whether on a macroeconomic, sectoral or sub-sectoral basis, or whether nonprojectized uses of such financing is permitted.

ARTICLE VI: STRUCTURE

1. The CTAB shall be composed of five (5) Board members who shall serve in staggered terms for not more than two terms of three (3) years each. The first Board shall be elected by the Executive Board of Directors of the IMF and the World Bank by joint decision, and thereafter shall be nominated and elected by the CTAB.
2. The CTAB shall be equally co-funded by the IMF and the World Bank Group, and shall make an annual budgetary submission for the joint approval by the Executive Board of Directors of each institution.

ARTICLE VII: LEGAL STATUS

1. The CTAB shall have legal, juridical personality, and shall be empowered by its Members with such legal capacity as may be necessary in order for it to perform its functions.
2. The CTAB shall be accorded by its Members such privileges and immunities as may be necessary for it to perform its functions.

3. CTAB officials and staff, as appropriate, shall be accorded by its Members such privileges and immunities as may be necessary for it to perform its functions.
4. The privileges and immunities which shall be accorded to the CTAB, its officials, and representatives by a Member shall be similar in nature to the privileges and immunities stipulated in the Convention on the Privileges and Immunities of the Specialized Agencies, approved by the General Assembly of the United Nations on 21 November 1947.
5. The CTAB may conclude a headquarters agreement.
6. The CTAB may issue internal regulations governing its conduct, and may issue rules and procedures concerning Appeals brought before it for adjudication.

ARTICLE VIII: MISCELLANEOUS PROVISIONS

1. This Agreement may be amended, from time to time, upon the unanimous, mutual written agreement of the CTAB Board. Proposals for amendments to this Agreement may be made by its Members, by the Executive Board of Directors of the IMF or the World Bank, respectively, or by any party acceding to this Agreement. Within ten (10) days upon receipt of such a proposal for amending provision(s) of the Agreement, the Board shall issue a public notice stating the text of the proposal, and opening up a public comment period not to exceed thirty (30) days, unless extended by the Board. The Board shall issue its final decision with regard to the proposal within ten (10) days after the close of the comment period.
2. This Memorandum of Agreement shall enter into full force and effect upon signature below by the Chairs of the Executive Boards of the IMF and the World Bank, respectively.

IN WITNESS WHEREOF, the Executive Board of the IMF, and of the World Bank, each acting through its duly authorized representative, have caused this Protocol to be signed in their name and delivered as of the date first written above.

INTERNATIONAL   INTERNATIONAL BANK FOR
MONETARY FUND   RECONSTRUCTION AND
                             DEVELOPMENT

By: _____   By: _____

Name: _____   Name: _____

Title: _____   Title: _____

Index

255

International Economic Development Law

1. J.J. Norton, T.L. Bloodworth and T.K. Pennington (eds), *NAFTA and Beyond*. A New Framework for Doing Business in the Americas. 1995
    ISBN 0-7923-3239-3

2. N. Kofele-Kale, *International Law of Responsibility for Economic Crimes*. Holdings Heads of State and Other High Ranking State Officials Individually Liable for Acts of Fraudulent Enrichment. 1995
    ISBN 0-7923-3358-6

3. Hani Sarie-Eldin, *Consortia Agreements in the International Construction Industry*. With Special Reference to Egypt. 1996   ISBN 90-411-0912-9

4. J.J. Norton and Mads Andenas (eds), *Emerging Financial Markets and the Role of International Financial Organisations*. 1996   ISBN 90-411-0909-9

5. B. Sodipo, *Piracy and Counterfeiting*. 1997   ISBN 90-411-0947-1

6. J.J. Norton and Mads Andenas (eds), *Emerging Financial Markets and Secured Transactions*. 1998   ISBN 90-411-0675-8

7. J.A. McMahon, *The Development Co-operation Policy of the EC*. 1998
    ISBN 90-411-0744-4

8. S. Arrowsmith and A. Davies, *Public Procurement: Global Revolution*. 1998
    ISBN 90-411-9662-5

9. Rosa M. Lastra and Henry N. Schiffman, *Bank Failures and Bank Insolvency Law in Economies in Transition*. 1999
    ISBN 90-411-9714-1

KLUWER LAW INTERNATIONAL – LONDON, THE HAGUE, BOSTON